EDWARD BOYKIN has devoted himself to the study and recording of American history. He was born in Petersburg, Virginia, and attended the United States Military Academy at West Point. After several years as a reporter and Assistant City Editor with the famous New York *Evening Journal,* he turned to public relations, with the Edison Company, and advertising, with the nation's leading agencies. During all these years, however, Mr. Boykin's interest in American history never waned. He wrote two historical plays, and six books. Among his works are *Congress and the Civil War, The Wisdom of Thomas Jefferson, Living Letters from American History.* His motion picture, *Thomas Jefferson and Monticello,* has been seen by about 5,000,000 school children, and his radio program, *Americana Quiz,* which he originated and conducted for ten years, earned him the title, "Radio Professor of American History." Mr. Boykin also acted as Master of Ceremonies for the coast-to-coast program, *National Radio Forum.* He headed the Thomas Jefferson Bicentennial Commission in Washington and was Director of the National Capital Sesquicentennial Celebration. Mr. Boykin now resides in Charlottesville, Virginia.

GHOST SHIP *of the Confederacy*

GHOST SHIP

THE STORY OF THE ALABAMA AND

by Edward Boykin

Carrington

FUNK & WAGNALLS COMPANY, *New York*

of the Confederacy,

HER CAPTAIN, RAPHAEL SEMMES

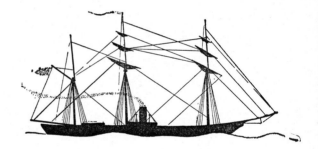

© 1957 by Funk & Wagnalls Company
Ghost Ship of the Confederacy
Library of Congress Catalog Card Number 57–6503
Printed in the United States of America
1

Designed by Betty Crumley

To my
friend and kinsman,
Frank W. Boykin,
of Mobile

Contents

Illustrations appear at page 180

⚓

⚓

Preface

The saga of Raphael Semmes and his raiding cruiser, the *Alabama*, has always seemed to me to comprise, by all odds, the best out-and-out adventure story of the Civil War. The quarry of the longest, biggest manhunt in United States naval history, Semmes left lasting lessons in how to get away by the skin of one's teeth. At the same time he left a record, still unbeaten, of destruction of merchant shipping on the high seas.

Like John Paul Jones and the *Bon Homme Richard*, Raphael Semmes and the *Alabama* are one and indivisible. Neither time nor history can ever separate them. So this book is as much the biography of the speedy *Alabama* as it is of her gallant captain.

As with many another warrior (Marc Mitscher, for example), Semmes' peculiar genius remained hidden until he found the war role especially fitted to his talents. Then, with the small, makeshift cruiser *Sumter*, he sank, burned, or captured eighteen Yankee merchantmen. It was on the *Sumter* that he discovered his genius for *guerre de course*. The first part of this book is devoted to his adventures with this little raider.

Applying the experience he gained on the *Sumter*, Semmes, with the *Alabama*, ran up a score of sixty-nine Northern merchant ships and one gunboat captured, burned, or sunk. By his torch and by the fear he generated, Semmes did more than any other single man to drive the American flag from the high seas. Besides all this, with his English-built and English-manned cruiser, he nearly brought about a third war between the United States and Great Britain.

Allied with Semmes, and indispensable to the Southern cause, was another officer, James Bulloch. Operating in England, Bulloch with one hand charmed English society while with the other he contracted secretly with shipbuilders for such as the *Alabama*, "the finest cruiser of her class in the world." His was a war waged partly in the drawing room against the Yankee diplomacy of Charles Francis Adams and partly in the world of lawlessness against turncoats and Federal agents.

Our prime sources about Semmes' adventures are his daily journal, which was saved after the *Alabama* succumbed to the gunfire of the U.S.S. *Kearsarge* in the English Channel, and his *Memoirs of Service Afloat During the War Between the States*. The first of these was published in 1894 by the Federal Government as part of the *Official Records of the Union and Confederate Navies*, the second by a private firm in 1869. The *Official Records* also contain Semmes' reports to his superiors and their instructions, few enough, to him. Most interesting are the orders to and reports from the many Union ships sent to hunt down the elusive Confederate commerce destroyer.

Semmes' journal reveals the heart and the mind of this fierce, keen-witted sailor-lawyer. Though verbose in spots, it is doubtful if any of the top-flight figures of the Confederacy published anything finer than Semmes' *Memoirs*. They are filled with drama, color, sentiment, adventure, lore of the sea, and here and there, bitterness. Semmes was a hard loser.

Though he wrote voluminously, there are no sizable collections of Semmes' letters and papers. And of those who served under him, only five wrote personal narratives of their experiences. One of these narratives is simply an enlarged pamphlet; another is readable but hardly trustworthy. United States diplomatic and consular reports have been helpful, as have contemporary newspapers and many old, faded clippings in the author's collection.

Idolized by the South, Semmes was hated, damned, and pilloried by the newspapers and politicians of the North, who branded him a pirate. Conveniently forgotten in the heat of a new war were the American depredations on British shipping in the Revolution and the War of 1812. Yet Semmes merely improved on and used against the North this form of warfare in which the American Navy had done so well. Indeed, when, to a large extent the result of Semmes' work, the United States expected a new war with England, the Navy Department prepared a number of especially-built swift cruisers to do to England's commerce what Semmes had

done to the North's! Citing as a parallel the cruise of the United
States sloop *Argus* in 1813, Professor James Russell Soley of the
Naval Academy summed up the case in 1883 in *The Blockade and
the Cruisers* when he said that a government would be fortunate,
if in time of war, it could rival the commerce raiding achievements
of Captain Raphael Semmes.

Semmes' postwar career has little place in this narrative, nor are
we concerned here with the diplomatic sequel, the *"Alabama*
Claims," whereby Great Britain settled in cash, rather than by war,
for the damage inflicted on America's merchant marine by the
Alabama and the other raiders built in English shipyards. Our
story comes to its end with the *Alabama* sliding beneath the
English Channel under the guns of a Federal cruiser.

To the Alderman Library at the University of Virginia, the
Library of Congress, the National Archives, and the Office of Naval
Records at Washington, and to the Confederate Museum at Richmond, I am most grateful for many favors during the writing of
this book.

Edward Boykin

Charlottesville, Virginia
January, 1957

GHOST SHIP *of the Confederacy*

Raphael Semmes, Captain of the Ghost Ship.

⚓

⚓

1 The First Blaze

"There's the flame! She's on fire!"

"She" was the *Golden Rocket*, a bark of Bangor, bound in ballast for Cuba and a cargo of sugar. Her Maine-pine decking, calked with old-fashioned oakum and paid with pitch, burned like tinder, lighting up the dark ocean for miles around. Standing several hundred yards from the burning vessel was the *Sumter*, first ship to carry the Stars and Bars to sea. Crowding the rail of the little Confederate cruiser was her crew, silent and solemn, watching the merchantman's fiery demise.

The night was dark. Invisible ten miles to the south lay the Isle of Pines; northwards, also unseen, was Cuba. This narrow stretch of water reeked with piratical memories. Hereabouts buccaneers once plied a profitable trade. A light breeze fanned the sea. Save for the roar and crackle of the soaring flames a vast quiet hung over the waters. Circling round and round above the burning ship were hundreds of seabirds drawn from afar by the glare. Their discordant cries gave a weird obligato to the scene. Soon the masts and hull of the *Sumter* were reflected on the mirror-like sea and the faces of the crew were lit up by the pyre of the *Golden Rocket*. The *Sumter's* crew gazed in awed fascination at their blazing handiwork. Not a sound came from the huddled deck. In their hearts beat a sense of triumph. The Confederate Navy had made its first "kill."

The *Golden Rocket* was the first prize captured in the Confederacy's hastily-launched attack on Northern seaborne commerce. In 1861 the United States possessed a commercial marine second only to that of Great Britain. Within three years the *Sumter*, the *Alabama*, and their sister Confederate raiders, racing about the seas, scuttling and burning, would all but sweep the American flag from the ocean, sinking a goodly tonnage and driving nearly half of America's remaining merchant fleet to the safety of foreign flags.

The bark from Maine was captured that afternoon—it was July 3, 1861—in the channel between the Isle of Pines and Cuba's southwestern coast, a well-beaten track for American craft trading in these waters. She was the try-out victim for the Confederacy's slashing campaign against Northern shipping. Much of the know-how of commerce-raiding would be learned from this first lesson.

It was the third day of the *Sumter's* roving. Outwitting the Federal blockaders at the mouth of the Mississippi the firefly Confederate craft, under both sail and steam, had steered a southeasterly course for the narrow channel that issues from the Gulf of Mexico between Yucatan and the westernmost tip of Cuba. This would bring her to ideal hunting grounds. Indenting the Isle of Pines were hideouts in which the little cruiser, if necessary, could conceal herself so well that the "devil himself would not find vessels unless he knew the locality." Well, indeed, did the captain of the *Sumter* know these waters. The Confederate government had given him freedom to select his own cruising grounds, and hereabouts he would find quarry enough for his crew to cut their raiding teeth. Then he would run down to Barbados to replenish his meager coal bunkers and strike for the Brazilian coast teeming with American trade. His sailing orders instructed him "to do the greatest injury to the enemy's commerce in the shortest time." He intended to do just that—to strike fast—and he set his eye on the waters off Cape St. Roque, Brazil, one of the great turning points of the commerce of the world.

At Washington this third of July the special session of the 37th Congress was assembling to hear President Lincoln's request for men, munitions, and money to crush the just-fledged Confederacy. The atmosphere was grim. At Richmond Southern officials were planning roadblocks of men, cannon, and bayonets to beat back the Northern onslaught. Along Bull Run in Virginia graybacks were mobilizing for a fast swoop on the Federal capital. Also at Bull Run Thomas Jonathan Jackson, little dreaming of fame soon to come, was fingering his new commission as Brigadier General just arrived from Richmond.

At 3 P.M. the lookout on the *Sumter's* masthead cried "Sail ho!"

Dead ahead, standing toward the *Sumter,* were two ships. The cruiser hoisted English colors. The nearer vessel, when intercepted and boarded, proved to be a Spanish brig bound for Vera Cruz. Inasmuch as Spain was neutral, she was sent on her way with good wishes. The *Sumter* now bore down on the second craft, which flew no flag. Her cut was unmistakably Yankee. "The American character was impressed upon every plank and spar of the ship." Coming within signal distance the *Sumter* fired a shot across the stranger's bow that made her heave to and brought her colors to the peak, the Stars and Stripes unfolding gracefully to the breeze. Now, hauling down the Cross of St. George, the *Sumter* raised the Stars and Bars of the Confederacy.

Off went the *Sumter's* boarding crew to fetch the skipper of the captured ship and his papers. Obediently, the taciturn but astonished Down-Easter obeyed the boarding officer's orders to accompany him back to the *Sumter* where he was ushered into the cabin of the captain of the Confederate cruiser, Raphael Semmes, who in this curtain-raiser off the Cuban coast made his debut as commerce-destroyer *sans pareil.*

Semmes rose and bowed as the Yankee captain entered the cabin. On the sleeves of his uniform gleamed the gold stripes of a Commander. The *Golden Rocket's* master indulged in no heroics though he confessed, "A clap of thunder in a cloudless sky could not have surprised me more than the appearance of the Confederate flag in these seas."

Semmes smiled and quietly asked for the ship's papers. Nervously twirling the ends of his pointed mustachios Semmes scrutinized the *Golden Rocket's* documents: her ownership, nationality, clearance. Clearly enough she was a United States merchantman, empty, worth about 40,000 dollars, bound for Cienfuegos, Cuba. There were no knotty points of fact or law to be unraveled; no intricate question of neutral ownership of freight. Semmes considered for a moment manning his capture with a prize crew and trying to run her through the blockade into a Southern port, but he discarded this idea. He could ill afford to spare a man at this early stage of the game.

Summing up the case, as Semmes was to do so often in future, he gave his verdict. It was irrevocable. He was the judge and jury, too. The ship was a Confederate prize of war; the skipper and his crew were prisoners; the *Golden Rocket* would be burned. The New Englander listened stoically though not without a show of quick emotion. He loved the *Golden Rocket*. He spoke out, "I have lost one ship and now to have this one destroyed will ruin me. I can never hope for another command."

Ventured Semmes as if to soften the blow, "My duty is a painful one, sir, to destroy so noble a ship as yours, but I must discharge it without vain regrets; and as for yourself, you will only have to do, as so many thousands have done before you, submit to the fortunes of war. Yourself and your crew will be well treated aboard my ship."

Semmes was setting a pattern for himself, too: no regrets. They had no place in the pitiless role in which he was now cast. Here at the start he ruled sentiment and penitence out of the undertaking. Sinking a ship must never trouble his sleep or his conscience.

Now back went the boarding party to gather up the ship's chronometer and flag, thus starting a collection that would grow rapidly. The *Golden Rocket's* flag was marked with the day, the latitude and longitude of the capture and consigned for safekeeping to the signal quartermaster. To Semmes it was the "old flag" though now only a trophy of the chase. In time Semmes would fill many bags with these "old flags," which to him were "mementoes that a nation once lived whose naval officers prized liberty more than the false memorial of it, under which they had once served, and who were capable when it became 'hate's polluted rag' of tearing it down."

Semmes gave the chronometers into the custody of a lieutenant whose duty it was to wind them every day though, as the collection grew, the task became unmanageable and the instruments were left to look after themselves. On the eve of the *Alabama's* duel with the *Kearsarge* off Cherbourg in 1864 the chronometers Semmes had taken on his sea-raidings were sent ashore to be sold in England. The proceeds of the sale were the only prize money ever received by the officers and men of the *Sumter* and the *Alabama*.

Throughout the afternoon of July 3 the *Sumter's* small boats ducked back and forth transferring to the cruiser provisions, cordages and paints that might be needed by the *Sumter*. Sacking the *Golden Rocket* took seven hours. Too long, thought Semmes, though he made no complaint to his officers. With practice the *Sumter's* crew would soon better this time. Night came down in all the calm, serene splendor of the tropic seas. A stillness settled over the water.

At 10 P.M. the *Golden Rocket* was fired. It was dark now, the proper time for this grim business. For burning his victims at night Northern newspapers and politicians would hurl at Semmes harsh words: "inhuman," "pirate," as well as threats of hanging. But it made for good hunting and, the fanfare of denunciation notwithstanding, it was legitimate sea warfare. A burning ship, seen afar at night, was bait for other enemy merchantmen who might hurry to the rescue and so into the *Sumter's* hot maw. Many Yankee skippers were to learn bitter lessons from their errands of mercy.

But Semmes must hurry. The Confederacy would soon be fighting for breath. The loose-jointed Lincoln blockade would tighten. Unless the wooden noose the North was looping around the South was sliced or loosened the Confederacy might be strangled in her crib. Fast cruisers like the *Sumter*, raiding Northern commerce, would compel the North to draw off her fastest and strongest fighting ships from the blockade to hunt these "highwaymen of the sea." Thus would the blockade be weakened and broached, Southern ports re-opened, and munitions begin to flow in from Europe and France. Or so it was hoped.

In launching its cruiser program in 1861 the Confederate government at Montgomery confidently believed the North would not permit its merchant marine—its beautiful, speedy sailing ships, its fast new steamers—one by one, to go up in flames or down to Davy Jones' locker. Mr. Lincoln would be forced by public demand if by nothing else to disband his blockade and send his warships wild-goose chasing after the Confederate marauders.

Standing on the *Sumter's* quarterdeck that night Semmes watched his boarding crew go through their incendiary routine. It was simple enough. The torch was applied simultaneously to the cabin, the main hold and the forecastle. It seemed as if Semmes was an old hand at the business, not just a beginner. His men were adept at their task.

Near him stood the skipper of the doomed ship. He was in tears. It was a sad sight for him to watch his fine ship committed to flames. The *Sumter's* officers, touched, made up a purse for him. Weeks later they would read in Northern newspapers how, after his release, he denounced them as pirates. It helped harden their hearts for the woeful work ahead.

The *Sumter's* deck now was packed with seamen gazing towards the doomed ship, staring through the darkness. Suddenly there was a faint glimmer of fire, then the flame leaped fullgrown into the air. Torrents of red rushed up from the main hold, from the cabin whose woodwork was seasoned bone-dry by many voyages to the tropics, from the forecastle reeking with paint and oil. Red brilliance suddenly glazed the sea, and by that light the *Sumter's* boarding crew could be seen shoving off from the sides of the inferno.

Of all the prizes captured and burned at sea by Semmes—there were fifty-nine of them—the *Golden Rocket*, his first, excited the finest of his literary powers. Few could have told the story with more feeling or more picturesquely than he:

"The forked tongues of the devouring element, leaping into the rigging, newly tarred, ran rapidly up the shrouds, first into the tops, then to the topmast-heads, thence to the topgallant, and royal mastheads, and in a moment more to the trucks; and whilst this rapid ascent of the main current of fire was going on, other currents had run out upon the yards, and ignited all the sails. A topgallant sail, all on fire, would now fly off from the yard, and sailing leisurely in the direction of the light breeze that was fanning, rather than blowing, break into bright and sparkling patches of flame, and settle, or rather silt into the sea. The yard would follow, and not being wholly submerged by its descent into the sea, would retain a portion of its flame, and continue to burn, as a floating brand for some minutes. At one time, the intricate network of the cordage of the burning ship was traced, as with a pencil of fire, upon the black sky beyond, the many threads of flame twisting and writhing, like so many serpents that had received their death wounds. The mizzen-mast now went by the board, then the fore-mast, and in a few minutes afterward the great main-mast tottered, reeled and fell over the ship's side into the sea, making a noise like that of the sturdy oak of the forests when it falls by the stroke of the axeman."

Semmes never forgot the *Golden Rocket*. Etched on his memory he often harked back to her. She became the trademark of the remorseless mission—"burn, sink and destroy"—on which the Southern Confederacy had sent him. But it was time to move on to other prey. The *Sumter's* propeller took up its monotonous refrain. Little did Raphael Semmes dream he had opened a Homeric odyssey. Whatever the future held he must not pause now so, "by the light of this flambeau, upon the lonely and silent sea, lighted by the passions of men who should have been our brothers, the *Sumter* having aroused herself from her dream of vengeance and run up her boats, moved forward on her course."

Tomorrow, now barely minutes away, was July 4, though, for Semmes, no longer the "Glorious Fourth." But there would be no celebration on the *Sumter*. The captain would not dine in the wardroom with his officers, as was the custom in the "old service." He would not tip a beaker to the time-honored day, nor would the crew be served an extra glass of grog. He was an officer of the Confederacy now. The "old flag" had become "a sham and a deceit" and the day itself reminded him too much of "the want of faith of a people with whom we had stood side by side in the great struggle of 1776 and with whom we were now at war. . . ."

To Confederate Secretary of the Navy Stephen R. Mallory, at Richmond, Semmes would report, "You can imagine that, as the flames which consumed that first holocaust laid upon the altar of our country upon the high seas leaped into the air and shed their lurid glare upon the waters around, we were much affected by so gratifying and at the same time so melancholy a spectacle."

Before turning wearily to his bunk Semmes knelt for long moments before the little shrine in a corner of his cabin. The Almighty had smiled "upon us and our cause, and may we show ourselves worthy servants of Him and it." He took a last look at the pyre he had lit. The red glow was fading in the distance. Soon the dark waters would take over the charred hulk of the *Golden*

Rocket of Bangor. He fell asleep wondering what they would say at Richmond when the news of his exploit reached the Confederate capital. They might even hang out a flag.

What would the Lincoln government say? More to the point what would they do?

⚓

⚓

2   Furore in Washington

The burning of the *Golden Rocket* touched off a blaze of Northern wrath. Federal officials raged at this act of Southern "piracy." Congress momentarily sidetracked President Lincoln's massive war program (calling for 400,000 men and 500 million dollars) while Northern statesmen hurled maledictions at the "barbarous rebel pirates" and pledged the nation's last ship and bottom dollar to exact vengeance.

Charging the Navy Department with dire negligence in letting the *Sumter* escape to sea Northern newspapers lashed themselves and their readers into frenzies. At Richmond salvos of cheers greeted the news Washington found so distasteful. The South had drawn first blood on the high seas!

The dispatch from Cuba imparting the *Golden Rocket's* fate reached Washington at a critical moment. The nation's capital was on edge. The big On-to-Richmond show was about to open the ball. General McDowell's army of 35,000 was poised to march out to Manassas and there demolish General Beauregard, his graybacks, and slavocracy itself at one fell blow.

Adding to the furore was the thunderclap intelligence that the *Sumter*, riding herd on six United States merchantmen she had captured after burning the *Golden Rocket,* was anchored at

Cienfuegos, Cuba, where, after a slight misunderstanding, the Confederate "pirate" was accorded the courtesies of the port. The *Sumter's* audacious captain was, indeed, sipping wine with the Spanish commandant, who had at first mistaken the little vessel's colors for the Jolly Roger. The two gentlemen had had a good laugh over the *Sumter's* blow to the "greedy Yankees." The very boldness of this man Semmes was galling. He had been afloat on the high seas barely ten days and there he was at Cienfuegos with six prizes.

It could not be denied that making a bonfire of the *Golden Rocket* and snatching six American freighters to boot was lusty, wholesale defiance of President Lincoln's manifesto of April 19, declaring a blockade of Southern ports and threatening the "punishment of piracy"—hanging—"for any person who shall molest a vessel of the United States, or the persons or cargo on board."

Caught off base old Gideon Welles, Lincoln's bewigged, bewhiskered Secretary of the Navy, shot blasts of venom at Raphael Semmes, "deserter from the service." Between puffs of his clay pipe the patriarchal Cabinet member likened Semmes to Captain Kidd, Henry Morgan, and sundry light-fingered gentry. The *Sumter* was a "pirate ship;" her captain and crew "robbers of the sea," and "Algerine corsairs." Welles little realized Semmes was to be a thorn in his flesh for months to come.

The alarm spread. As always Washington teemed with rumors. The *Sumter* might be anywhere, even poking up Chesapeake Bay. It was hard to believe one lone raider, which Semmes himself called a "tea-kettle," could have excited so much concern. Still, the news was frightening. Already rumor had it that the *Sumter* was invisible. The Confederates, so it was asserted, had coated her with something or other that enabled her to vanish from sight. Actually, Semmes had tried out crude camouflage on the *Sumter*, a mixture of whitewash and dark paint, but it failed to work, and was speedily painted over.

From the Navy Department building, just west of the White House, orders went flying out to the blockading squadrons off the leading Southern ports. The chase was to be relentless. One by one the *Keystone State, Shepherd Knapp, Iroquois,* and *Powhatan* were withdrawn from the cordons and ordered to beat about the

Caribbean and West Indies for the newly-spawned Southern commerce-killer.

Lieutenant David Dixon Porter, able and resourceful commanding officer of the *Powhatan*, vowed to wing the "Confederate hawk" in short order. Porter had reason to be avenged. In slipping through the Federal blockaders at the mouth of the Mississippi Semmes had hoodwinked the *Powhatan* and her sister watchdogs on duty there. Porter was to become Semmes' keenest pursuer. Able though he was, Porter was a boastful man with a tendency to traduce his superiors—or so Gideon Welles said in his diary. There would come a day when Porter would threaten President Lincoln, in person, with resigning from the service and getting the merchants of New York to give him a ship "so that I may show the Navy Department how to catch the *Alabama*."

Now, from the *Powhatan* off the Southwest Pass of the Mississippi, Porter offered to show how the *Sumter* could be caught. His scheme was tinged with braggadocio, but sound nevertheless.

I know as well as it is possible to surmise where the rendezvous of Semmes will be. His plan is to sink, burn and destroy all that is not very valuable, for he can do it with impunity. Let the Department fit out some fast steamers with rifle guns and send one to the bay of Samana at the east end of Haiti. He will be found there or I'll lose my head. There are hiding places there known to Semmes where a hundred prizes might lie concealed. There is also a place in the same island, Ocoa Bay, well known to Semmes (I was there with him) where a thousand vessels might lie concealed and no one know of it. There are places around the Isle of Pines where the devil himself would not find the vessels unless he knew the locality. I have been all through them and know them well; so does Semmes. If he gets hard pushed, he can find shelter among the reefs of the Mosquito Banks. No one would think of following him there.

Nor was it long before the *San Jacinto* joined the pack baying after the *Sumter*. This "old wagon of a ship," as Semmes was to dub her when he later slipped away under her very guns, lumbered about the Caribbean in futile chase. Later that year Captain Charles Wilkes, commanding the *San Jacinto*, overhauled the British mail steamer *Trent*, seized the Confederate commissioners

Mason and Slidell, and nearly involved the nation in war with Britain.

Presently into the Navy Department walked diffident Midshipman Alfred T. Mahan. Read what this promising youngster, with apologies for his "youthful presumption," suggested—through channels—to Assistant Secretary of the Navy Gustavus Fox.

The ravages of the pirate *Sumter* have reached a pitch that, if long continued, will cast an undeserved stigma upon the Navy. Her speed on the cruising ground she has chosen, will always enable her to obtain the twenty-four hours shelter granted by neutral powers, and thus a chance of escape by night, which can only be prevented by surrounding her with a chain of vessels more numerous than our small Navy and extended blockaded coast can at present allow us to devote to this object.

Can she not be decoyed under fire, or even boarded? . . . I have thought that a sailing vessel might be equipped with a heavy pivot gun and a light house built over it, such as are often seen on merchant ships, and which could not excite suspicion. Broadside guns requiring ports would be incompatible with the end in view.

Man the ship with a hundred men, more if necessary. Will there not be a probability of the steamer approaching confidently—if to leeward, within a distance to render boarding practicable; if to windward, so as possibly to be disabled or sunk with your heavy gun?

I am aware that my idea may appear rash or even harebrained. But suppose it fail, what is lost?

A useless ship, a midshipman, and a hundred men. If it succeed, apart from the importance of the capture, look at the prestige such an affair would give the service. If this is so fortunate as to meet your approval, and that of the honorable Secretary, and you should not wish to risk a better man, I beg to offer myself to lead the enterprise.

Nothing came from this proposal.

One suggestion for bagging the *Sumter* bore bitter fruit. From the Skipper of the old frigate *Macedonian* at Key West came the proposal that "a smart steamer like the *Iroquois*, with a smart captain, would stand a good chance for catching the *Sumter*, or for badgering her into port in a very short time," if he circumnavigated Cuba. It struck the higher-ups as a good idea. So the *Iro-*

quois, "a smart steamer" with a "smart Captain," James S. Palmer, made the five hundred mile circuit of Cuba, ran down the *Sumter* at St. Pierre, Martinique, only to have her slip away by grace of a stratagem so simple a child might not have taken the bait.

Excited shipmasters, merchant princes, and insurance company presidents implored President Lincoln to speed the entire United States Navy after the Confederate marauder playing havoc in the Cuban passages. Incidentally, when the war began "Uncle Sam's web-feet," as President Lincoln later called the Navy, consisted of exactly ninety ships—of which twenty-one were unserviceable.

Coastal cities flooded Washington with telegrams beseeching protection for their harbors just as they were to do nine months later when the ironclad turtle *Virginia** came out of her lair and waddled across Hampton Roads to crush the *Cumberland* and *Congress.* Governors, mayors, chambers of commerce joined in the outcries for help. Into the Executive Mansion strode California's stately Senator Latham demanding "in the name of the bankers of New York City and the State of California," armed convoys for the gold ships plying between Panama and New York. A treasure ship, indeed, the *Northern Light,* laden with "over 2,000,000 dollars in gold and near 1,000 passengers holding from 100,000 to 200,000 dollars more," was about to sail from Panama. She would skirt the very jaws of the *Sumter's* hideaway south of Cuba. What a fine haul she would make for the Confederate "pirate" with her strong-chest and passengers bulging with the precious metal.

President Lincoln listened to the cries of the countinghouse barons and politicians, then referred the gentlemen to irascible Gideon Welles. That old gentleman was adamant in his determination that come what might the blockade, gossamerlike though it was at the moment, should not be weakened. He believed heartily the doom of the Confederacy would follow the establishment of a strict, effective blockade. The search for Semmes would be carried on with whatever ships could be spared from that great effort.

On one thing the North was agreed: the moment he was caught

---

* The *Virginia* is better known by the name she bore under the United States flag, *Merrimack.*

Raphael Semmes was to be hanged from the yardarm. The official records are loaded with suggestions for catching this Confederate fox. All very well, but catching him posed an enormous "if." For Raphael Semmes, late Commander, United States Navy, was off on a destructive, adventurous cruise that is without parallel in naval history. Contemporary Northern historians and press handed Semmes down to posterity as a sadistic monster, who set his victims adrift on merciless seas as U-boats were to do in later wars. Even Gamaliel Bradford fell into this partizan error. Yet above the passions of the hour Raphael Semmes rises as the most romantic, glamorous, yet elusive, figure of the American Civil War.

Gray ghost of the Confederacy, he darted back and forth across the trade routes of the North and South Atlantic, the Caribbean, the Indian Ocean, the Arabian Sea, and the waters around the East Indies, baffling his pursuers for three years. Unhurt, undiscoverable save at his pleasure, he was the captain of a seemingly phantom ship that took enormous toll of American commerce. The search for Semmes and his successive ships, *Sumter* and *Alabama*, spread over vast waters. Tracked and trailed over immense wastes, he overhauled three hundred vessels of every flag, and burned almost seven million dollars worth of American shipping. His fierce swoops furrowed dread and fear into the hearts of American shipowners and ship masters. His depredations forced insurance rates sky-high and drove over a thousand American ships to the safety of foreign registry—a haven from which they never returned.

A deeply pious man, Semmes nevertheless had the sailor's belief in luck. "Luck is a lord" he was to say. When the luck of his first ship, *Sumter*, ran out he transferred to a second, the *Alabama*, whose luck was to hold for twenty-two torchbearing months. When the *Kearsarge's* gunfire sent the *Alabama* to the bottom of the English Channel Semmes knew his luck had played out. The curtain had fallen on his amazing drama, and, in fact, the sunset of the Confederacy was not far off.

A quiet, soft-spoken man whose previous career in the United States Navy held out no prophecy of his audacious role on the high seas Semmes ran up a legendary record, still unbeaten, of destruction of enemy commerce.

⚓

⚓

3 Like Trumpets Blowing

On the evening of January 11, 1861, Alabama seceded from the Union. At that hour Commander Raphael Semmes, United States Navy, was seated with his family at his home in Washington waiting for the "magnetic telegraph" to click off news that Alabama had cut the ties that bound her to the Union and joined the stampede into secession.

Semmes had already determined to shape his own course by that of his adopted State when and if she withdrew from the Union. Casting off his moorings was, he felt, the only decent, honorable course open to him. Abandoned in his heart was all hope of reconciliation between the two great sections of the nation. He was convinced the North and South could never resolve their forty-year cold war save by invoking the God of battles. For Semmes the die really had been cast when South Carolina, with bonfires, waving flags, ringing bells, and roaring cannon, sailed blithely out of the Union on December 20, 1860. In after years he admitted, "My intention of retiring from the Federal Navy and taking service with the South in the coming struggle was made known to the delegation in the Federal Congress from Alabama early in the session of 1860-1861."

On January 9 Mississippi severed her ties with the Union. Florida was making her exit, at the same moment. Georgia, too, had issued her secession call. Louisiana stood poised on the brink. Swept by the secession hurricane Texas was tugging at her anchors. The arc of secession was widening. The Southern States were lining up solidly behind their sovereign, King Cotton. All eyes now fastened on pivotal Virginia, still holding, though the ties were snapping, to the Union.

South Carolina batteries had already fired on the flag. Cannon had driven off a ship bringing food, munitions, and reinforcements to the Federal garrison beleagured at Fort Sumter in Charleston Harbor.

In his memoirs Semmes stated the case for secession candidly and soundly. Secession was an inherent right of the States. So deeply intrenched was this idea in his mind that he devoted the six introductory chapters of his *Memoirs of Service Afloat*, published in 1869, to an analysis and justification of the flight of the Southern States and their sons from the "old flag." It is doubtful that anyone ever expounded the secession theory more astutely than he.

Gazing back on his yesterdays, after the fall of the Confederacy, Raphael Semmes wrote his brother, Samuel:

"I approved the secession movement of the Southern States, although I had no agency in it. . . . Although I cared very little about the institution of slavery, I thought that the subordinate position of the inferior race was its proper position . . . I believed that the doctrine of State's Rights was the only doctrine which would save our Republic from the fate of other Republics that had gone before us in the history of the world."

In 1850 Semmes' devotion to the Union was profound. In that year abolition was riding the whirlwind and Henry Clay was seeking to weld the disintegrating nation together by his massive, six-pronged compromise legislation that threw sops both North and South. At this critical time Semmes forecast that the American flag "would soon encircle the globe as that of the greatest commercial nation on earth." He went even further to prophesy, "Our Pacific opens to us, and will enable us to monopolize, almost all the commerce of the East Indies, north and south. This will make us the carriers and factors of the world. Twenty years hence, and it will no longer be Britannia but America rules the waves." He believed it sincerely.

From that distance he saw no clouds in the sky. America's destiny was bright, serene. Nor was there in his own career up to this point any hint of the daring genius that was to flower in his world-startling cruises of the Civil War. Yet, observed from another angle, it would seem as if his whole experience in the United

States Navy was a slow build-up for the role he was to play under the Stars and Bars.

As the clash of arms drew nearer Raphael Semmes listened to the resounding virulence, keeping his sentiments and his intentions to himself. Most naval officers did so, as did their army opposites. Shelved among the graybeards of the Lighthouse Board at Washington Semmes pursued his peaceful, landlocked duties, revealing his inmost thinking only to his immediate family, and often not to them.

Even to his second son, Oliver J. Semmes, a cadet at West Point learning the rudiments of war, Semmes offered no advice. To this boy's letters seeking fatherly counsel in the dilemma that faced Southern youths at the Military Academy Semmes apparently avoided direct reply although his own mind was definitely made up.

Two nights after Alabama seceded Semmes called at the home of that State's Senator Clement C. Clay. When Semmes arrived another naval officer, likewise Southern, was chatting with the Senator and his gifted lady, Virginia, "one of Washington's brightest ornaments." Not knowing his brother officer's sentiments, nor venturing to reveal his own, Semmes decided to outsit him. The evening dragged on. With bright chatter Mrs. Clay sought to relieve the embarrassing dilemma. Hours passed in obvious restraint. Wearying at last, Semmes' rival bowed out. The Commander hastened to unbosom himself.

"As my Senator, Mr. Clay, I want to report to you my decision on an important matter. I have resolved to hand in my resignation to the United States government and tender my services to that of the Confederate States. I did not know what the intention of my brother officer was but I could take no risk with him."

In Washington many such scenes, as secret, as grave, as "treasonable," were taking place in these last weeks before the Confederate States became a reality.

Semmes was never talkative. Now he was less so than ever. Indeed, officers of the Army and Navy of Southern birth or leanings were reluctant to unfurl publicly the banners that were flying in their hearts. They spoke only guardedly, or tried to avoid the subject of secession. Choosing between State and country was a bitter, cruel decision. Semmes has described his own feelings succinctly:

> Civil war is a terrible crucible through which to pass character; the dross drops away from the pure metal at the first touch of the fire. It must be admitted, indeed, that there was some little nerve required, on the part of an officer of the regular Army or Navy, to elect to go with his State. His profession was his only fortune; he depended upon it, for the means of subsisting himself and his family. If he remained where he was, a competency for life, and promotion, and honors probably awaited him; if he went with the South, a dark, and uncertain future was before him; he could not possibly better his condition, and if the South failed, he would have thrown away the labor of a lifetime.
>
> All professions are clannish. Men naturally cling together, who have been bred to a common pursuit; and this remark is particularly applicable to the Army, and the Navy. West Point and Annapolis were powerful bonds to knit together the hearts of young men. Friendships were there formed, which it was difficult to sever, especially when strengthened by years of after-association, in common toils, common pleasures and common dangers. Naval officers, in particular, who had been rocked together in the same storm, and had escaped perhaps from the same shipwreck, found it very difficult to draw their swords against each other.
>
> The flag, too, had a charm which it was difficult to resist. Sentiment had almost as much to do with the matter, as principle, for there clustered around the "old flag" a great many hallowed memories, of sacrifices made and victories won. The Cadet at West Point had marched and countermarched under its folds, dreaming of future battlefields, and future honors to be gained in upholding and defending it; and the midshipman, as he gazed upon it, in some foreign ports, flying proudly from the gaff-end of his ship, had drunk in new inspiration to do and to dare, for his country.

The air of Washington was thick with talk of traitors and treason. Yet, on Capitol Hill, in the highest councils of the nation, there was no secrecy. Statesmen were winding up their verbal conflict with defiant blasts. Appeals to patriotism and the old ties went overboard. Southern senators and congressmen took the floor to

proclaim their dream of empire, a cotton kingdom that would en-
girdle the Gulf of Mexico and make it a Southern Sea. They
would even change the name to just that.

Across the upper chamber fire-eating Senator Wignall of Texas
sneered, "You cannot save this Union by making Fourth of July
speeches." Truculent Senator Iverson of Georgia envisioned Washington as capital of the Southern Confederacy-to-be and saw a
new flag floating over the unfinished dome of the Capitol. Government clerks bound by no oath of allegiance and fortified by innumerable whiskies, stood at Willard's bar and loudly vowed that
Abraham Lincoln would never take the oath as President. On the
street secessionists besported blue cockades, John Calhoun's old
talisman.

Crisis gripped the city founded by and named for the Father of
His Country. Beset by plot and counterplot, threats and alarms,
there was blood on the moon over Washington this January, 1861.
Officers of the Army and Navy from opposing sections of the nation gave scant courtesy to each other as they passed in the corridors of the department buildings. To the taunts of Southern
sympathizers aged, Virginia-born General-in-Chief Winfield Scott,
commanding the nation's meager army, announced his adherence
to the Union and melodramatically threatened to plant cannon
at both ends of Pennsylvania Avenue and "blow to hell" anyone
who dared raise a finger against the flag or the government.

On January 21 Raphael Semmes joined the throngs that
packed the Senate galleries and spilled over into the lobbies and
corridors of the new Senate wing of the Capitol. Even the walls
were lined with humanity. Today the South would walk out. Five
Senators whose States had seceded would make their formal
adieux. Around him in the gallery Semmes saw brother officers,
mostly Southerners, old companions in arms, come to watch the
curtain fall on the saddest scene in the Republic's legislative
drama. Their faces reflected the emotions that were tearing at their
hearts.

Conspicuous in the gallery were Southern women whose bright
faces and bonnets and flowered gowns masked the tragedy they
sensed in the scene they were about to witness. Near him sat
Varina Davis, gracious, sad-faced, beloved of the chief figure on

the Senate floor below. Yonder was the diplomatic corps, gold-braided, shining with pomp and splendor, holding its breath and prepared to watch a nation break into pieces.

One by one the Southern statesmen rose in their places to say farewell and warn of the consequences. With throbbing breast Semmes drank in the thunderous threat that issued from the throat of Florida's Senator Stephen Mallory, chairman of the Naval Affairs Committee and soon to occupy a similar post in the Confederate hierarchy. Little did Semmes reckon that he and this bold-talking lawmaker would soon be planning a strategy of annihilation of Northern seaborne commerce by fast-striking Confederate cruisers.

Lastly, amid tearful silence, rose slender, courtly Senator Jefferson Davis of Mississippi to offer his valedictory. Tears blurred Semmes' eyes as the pale, distinguished statesman submitted his apologia. Gaunt hollows shadowed his cheeks. Suffering, mental and physical, were inscribed on his face. A West Point graduate and veteran of the Mexican War, Davis was the symbol and spokesman of Southern ideals and aspirations. From him came no defiance, no threats, no bravado, yet his words were wreathed in determination that the South would stand and give battle, if the sword must be drawn:

> We will invoke the God of our fathers, who delivered them from the power of the Lion, to protect us from the ravages of the Bear; and, thus putting our trust in God and in our firm hearts and strong arms, we will vindicate the right as best we may.

For Semmes, deeply stirred, Davis' words were like trumpets blowing. Two days later he called at the spacious Davis home on F Street. He and the Davises were old friends. For half an hour the two men conversed quietly in the parlor behind closed doors. Neither of these two, who were to play outstanding roles in the clangorous drama of the Confederacy, left any record of what transpired at this meeting. Easily conceivable it is that Semmes offered his sword and that Davis accepted the offer.

In early February, 1861, Semmes confided to a friend, "I am still at my post at the Lighthouse Board, performing my routine duties, but listening with an aching ear and beating heart, for the first sounds of the great disruption which is at hand."

The "great disruption" was indeed at hand. On February 8, 1861, delegates from seven seceded "sovereign" States convened at Montgomery and hoisted the banner of the provisional Confederate government. Unanimously chosen to pilot their bid for independence was former United States Senator Jefferson Davis of Mississippi.

Of the ability of the new Southern Confederacy to sustain itself against assault Semmes had "no doubts of success . . . and no fear of the consequences." With secession launched he penned a letter to Georgia's Howell Cobb, one-time Speaker of the House at Washington, late Secretary of the Treasury, and powerful leader in creating the new Southern Commonwealth. Semmes suggested naming the newborn Southern alliance, "The Confederacy of the Cotton States." It was at the moment an exact description.

The long shadows of late afternoon were falling on Washington when a messenger brought a telegram to the Semmes home. The Commander was sitting quietly with his family. Tearing open the message, not a muscle of his face moved as he handed it to his wife. She read:

> Montgomery, Feb. 14, 1861
> Sir:—On behalf of the Committee on Naval Affairs, I beg leave to request that you will repair to this place, at your earliest convenience. Your obedient servant,
>
> C. M. Conrad, Chairman

The summons had come! The long suspense was over! "Here was the sound for which I had been so anxiously listening. Secession was now indeed a reality, and the time had come for me to arouse myself to action. The telegram threw my small family-circle into great commotion."

Within an hour Semmes' reply was clicked off to Montgomery:

> Despatch received; I will be with you immediately.

Yet, before leaving, he must arrange his family affairs, and he made it a point to observe the utmost punctilio in withdrawing from the Federal service. He prided himself that whatever steps he took must be aboveboard so that all might see. Veiled criticism had already stabbed at him. It behooved him to make his departure an open book for all to read.

Breaking up home and family, taking leave of friends of years' standing, tore at his heart, but this was the hour. Father of six children, three sons and three daughters, Semmes adored his fireside. "Hoping against hope" Mrs. Semmes had prayed that her husband would be spared the bitter ordeal though she had "nerved herself for the sacrifices and trials she knew were before her." To Semmes the swift rush of events had foretold only one outcome: war. A long war. Yet no more than were his fellow officers was he aware that his star was on the rise. He foresaw shore duty, perhaps at Mobile, Alabama, a port destined to assume vast scope in the rise and fall of the South's bid for her own place in the sun. Here, after a visit to her brother at Cumberland, Maryland, his wife would join him.

Next morning, February 15, Semmes walked into the Navy Department, composed his resignation from the service and delivered it himself to Isaac Toucey, Secretary of the Navy. In two hours he was a private citizen. Toucey formally accepted Semmes withdrawal, taking care to make the legal point of addressing him as "Raphael Semmes, Esq. late Commander U. S. Navy, Washington." To do the completely honorable thing Semmes next wrote to inform Commander Thornton A. Jenkins, Secretary of the Lighthouse Board, that having resigned from the service he could no longer retain his membership. In asking his release he clearly stated he was about to leave for the South, words that bore an obvious implication. To this communication Semmes received no reply.

All these steps were taken before Semmes ventured a foot from Washington. His resignation was accepted. Tradition says that Secretary of the Navy Toucey wished him well. Toucey's successor, however, testy Gideon Welles, charged Semmes with "treason to the flag" and castigated him as a "deserter from the service." Welles understandably smarted much under the Federal navy's inability to catch the elusive raider. To Welles' accusation of desertion, Semmes later replied, "The Federal government itself had formally released me from the contract of service I had entered into with it. . . . The Secretary of the Navy did not think of arresting me for telegraphing to the Congress of the Confederate States that I would be with it immediately; nor did he, though he knew my purpose of drawing my sword against the Federal government, if necessary, refuse to accept my resignation."

Taking his cue from Welles came Admiral David Dixon Porter, who nursed a grudge against Semmes to the end of his days. In his *Naval History of the Civil War*, published in 1886, Porter censured Semmes "as the most vindictive of all the officers of the Confederate Navy." This was absurd. Hating, vindictiveness, call it what you will, was, and still is, part of war's ghastly formula. North and South hated each other long before the shooting began. After the war opened the press, North and South, splattered their pages with stuff that chilled their readers' blood. *Harper's Weekly*, for example, drew terrifying, imaginary on-the-spot illustrations of "Southern barbarity," Confederate soldiers scalping and beheading Federal prisoners.

Porter was particularly indignant because Semmes, under the impact of war, was all at once transformed from a quiet, scholarly, courtly, mild-mannered naval officer into a daring, resourceful, energetic man of action, who single-handedly destroyed untold tons of shipping, baffled the Federal navy, and astonished the world.

Loudly did Porter proclaim that Semmes in the old navy had "little reputation as an officer . . . no particular taste for his profession. He was indolent and fond of his comfort. Although he had served many years in the United States Navy none of his associates ever supposed that in time of war he would exhibit so much efficiency. . . ."

Porter might have observed this same metamorphosis in a sober, self-effacing, staid professor, who in 1861 broke into the limelight as Stonewall Jackson. Surely Jackson's previous career promised no brilliance to come. And there was a man named Grant (whom Porter admired extravagantly), who had failed at everything, was cashiered out of the army and whose hopes by 1861 had reached the vanishing point.

Seadog Porter growled lustily because "from being the mildest-mannered man in the navy" Semmes had assumed a "character bordering on that of an ancient viking." Destruction of Federal shipping seems to have been an unpardonable crime in Porter's book of rules of war. He flared out, "Burning ships became a passion, and if ever a man had a bump of destructiveness on his cranium, that man was Raphael Semmes." Porter failed to mention William Tecumseh Sherman, who apparently had the same bump. Like Semmes, Sherman believed that destruction of an enemy's wealth—his resources, his factories, his supplies, his means of transportation—the loss of whatever would weaken an adversary—was a part of the routine of successful war. Sherman left a swath of ashes forty miles wide across Georgia in 1864. And lest we forget: General Philip Sheridan also took pride in his flame-throwing talents. With fire he swept the lovely "vale of the stars" so bare that "a crow flying over the Valley of Virginia would have to carry his own rations." *His own words!* His official report proclaimed he had burned "over two thousand barns filled with wheat and hay and farm implements; over seventy mills filled with flour and wheat" besides millions of dollars' worth of private property. Sheridan was burning his enemy's means of making war, the "granary of the Confederacy" that fed the gray armies. Raphael Semmes used the same technique, but his operations were against Northern property—and this was a fearful crime.

On February 16 Semmes took sorrowful leave of his family and boarded the ferry that connected with the evening train for Montgomery. His fortune and his fate were now staked on the new Confederate States. No one better than he realized the fearful odds confronting the South. Making war against the populous, industrial North, with its vast material and human preponderance, was a titanic undertaking that would have daunted less impulsive spirits. Yet the South, even the children, believed passionately in the justice of her cause—and, so believing, had no fear it could fail. Even so, Raphael Semmes, late Commander, United States Navy.

Semmes' impedimenta were scant. Strapped to his baggage was his sword. In his pocket was a small sheaf of papers on which he had jotted down ideas to submit to officials at Montgomery. Settled in his own mind months ago that the South would appeal to arms and knowing his own predilections, he had raced on ahead of hostilities.

Shortly before the war clouds had closed down Semmes had written "a distinguished member of the Federal Congress from the South," suggesting a naval policy "in case things came to a crisis." He had said, "If you are warred upon at all, it will be by a commercial people whose ability to do you harm will consist chiefly in ships and shipping. It is at ships and shipping, therefore, that you must strike." He first proposed employing private armed ships, or privateers, but he abandoned this idea. Now he envisioned swift cruisers, well armed, fast enough to outrun anything in the Federal navy. He recommended launching these raiders against the shipping of the second greatest commercial power on earth. It never once occurred to him that at fifty-two he could take a hand in such a mission.

Standing on the deck of the little steamer that bore him down the Potomac to Acquia Creek to board his train for the South Raphael Semmes watched the nation's capital receding in the distance. One by one the ties that bound him to the things the city had stood for were snapping. The ungainly, unfinished Washington Monument bulked against the twilight sky. No one dreamed, least of all Raphael Semmes, how soon it would be a military lookout. Beyond rose the weblike, unfinished dome of the Capitol, a huge ironwork filigree, surmounting the vast architectural pile where the nation's lawmakers, now minus their Southern confreres, sat wondering and waiting for the Man from Illinois.

The train rattled southwards. At every station and watertank anxious knots of citizens plied for news from Washington. Would there be war? Would the North fight? Semmes parried with queries of his own. Would Virginia fight? Would she join the Confederacy? What about North Carolina? As the train chugged deeper into the South he entered a land overlaid with the fresh, tender beauty of spring, yet aflame for war. Like a conservatory the deep South was sweet with young blossoms and pastel foliage. War could never, it seemed, lay its blighting hand on this vast garden abloom with so many things of such loveliness.

On the evening of February 18 Semmes' train skirted a blazing pine forest. Here his emotions beset him mightily. They give an insight into the stirrings of his soul as he stood on the threshold of the career that was to bring him fame. Long after the flags were furled and the last shot fired, he opened his heart to say, "This night ride, through the burning pine woods of Alabama, afterward stood as a great gulf in my memory, forming an impassable barrier, as it were, between my past, and my future life. It had cost me pain to cross the gulf, but once crossed, I never turned to look back. When I washed and dressed for breakfast, in Montgomery, the next morning, I had put off the old man, and put on the new. The labors, and associations of a lifetime had been inscribed in a volume, which had been closed, and a new book, whose pages were as yet all blank, had been opened."

⚓

⚓

4   Portrait of a Stormy Petrel

Strewn behind Raphael Semmes were the dead leaves of his long naval career that began in 1826 when President John Quincy Adams appointed him a midshipman. There was no Annapolis, no training school as such for naval officers in that day. They acquired nautical education afloat, and precious little out of books.

His first assignment was to the sloop of war *Lexington*, a small warship rigged with clouds of canvas, and his first distant cruise was to Trinidad on the southern shore of the Caribbean. It was from the deck of the *Lexington* that Semmes caught his earliest glimpse of far blue horizons and romantic seas.

His apprenticeship on that small, wind-driven vessel was hard and profitable. The ship and the sea were his college. Midshipmen, the raw stuff of future admirals and captains, were not coddled. They existed in cramped, smelly quarters below decks, slept in hammocks, fought legions of cockroaches and rats, ate poor, mildewed fare, learned the rigging and the sails, studied seamanship and navigation at first hand, played pranks on each other, and roamed faraway places. Out of such rudiments the naval officer of that day acquired the necessary know-how of his profession. In this lowly grade began not only Semmes, but also the two Davids, Farragut and Porter, and all the other naval leaders of the Civil War, including a youth named John Winslow with whom Semmes was one day to have a fateful rendezvous in the English Channel.

When Semmes first went to sea the transition from sail to steam was just beginning. It would take four decades to complete, and Semmes was to be a daring, conspicuous figure in the final obsequies of canvas-driven ships.

For two years on the *Lexington* he cruised the Caribbean, the Gulf of Mexico, the West Indies, the Mediterranean. Transferred to the sloop *Erie* and then to the *Brandywine*, frigate, he was off again over the same waters. In time he was to know almost by heart the glassy, gleaming mazes of these Southern seas—the reefs, shoals and bars, the river mouths and shallow, tortuous channels, the islets and white beaches, the winds and the currents. He poked into ports and harbors reeking with villainous smells and centuries of romance; intercepted slavers and scores of sail suspected of carrying black ivory; lay becalmed for days or rode out tropical hurricanes and mountainous seas. Long voyages to the tropics set singing the poetry of his soul.

It would seem as if this earliest training were shaping his destiny. On these very waters whose idiosyncrasies and intricacies he came to know so well he would one day find the chief theater of his prodigious exploits.

But, perhaps, before going further, we should pick up the Semmes story at its start. Raphael Semmes was born in the tobacco village of Piscataway, Maryland, on September 27, 1809. On that day Abraham Lincoln was seven months and two weeks old. Five generations back Benedict Joseph Semmes of Normandy, France, had crossed the sea in the *Ark and Dove* with Lord Baltimore to found at St. Mary's on the Potomac a refuge for Roman Catholics in the New World. Thus was Catholicism bred in Raphael's bones.

To him his father had passed on deep reverence for the ancient faith.

His mother was Catherine Middleton, of Protestant background, whose forebear, Arthur Middleton, is better known for his centuries-old azalea gardens than for his signature on the Declaration of Independence. Young Semmes grew up a Southerner. He was born almost in sight of the Potomac "in whose waters I used to swim and fish as a boy." Maryland was a Southern state, intimately bound to Virginia by sentiment, tradition, and trade. The Potomac was a Southern river. Its broad, shining waters were a bond, a unifying influence, rather than a dividing line. The people who lived along its shores shared a common culture and a common interest.

The First Congress had established the nation's capital on the Potomac because it was a Southern location. The river played a historic role in the Hamilton-Jefferson logrolling deal in 1790. For the honor of having the nation's seat of government located on a Southern river, the Potomac, the Southern bloc in Congress had voted for Hamilton's Assumption Bill. Thus, early in life, was Raphael Semmes accustomed to look to the South, not the North, and thus were woven the ties that drew him irresistibly when civil strife swept the nation.

Had Admiral Porter reasoned thus he might not have written, "Being a native of Maryland Semmes had not even the excuse of siding with his State, for if he had, he would have fought against the South." Porter chose to forget Semmes' background. Was he not aware that Maryland dangled perilously close to casting her lot with the Confederacy, that only bayonets and the dogged determination of Abraham Lincoln held her to the Union?

At ten years Raphael was an orphan and committed to the care of an uncle, also named Raphael Semmes, who resided in fashionable Georgetown, just across Rock Creek from the nation's new capital. It was a home where social grace and Southern sentiment prevailed, a mecca for Southern society of that day. In the drawing room of his uncle's home young Raphael first felt the clangor of the long-drawn-out cold war between North and South. The fierce debates on the Missouri Compromise were convulsing the nation as Semmes entered his teens. From heated exchanges on Capitol Hill Southern fire-eaters hurried to the Semmes home to breathe further defiance at their Northern brethren for daring to tamper with the ancient institution of slavery on which the Southern economy depended.

It was a setting pre-eminently Southern by culture and tradition. Across the river was classic, white-pillared Arlington, laden with relics of George Washington and presided over by his adopted son. Nearby was a fine, yellow-stuccoed mansion, Tudor Place, built with funds left by George Washington and designed by William Thornton, the man who planned the nation's Capitol. The Virginia Dynasty was in its third presidency, and the Magnificent Monroes occupied the White House. As a boy Raphael Semmes seems certain to have talked with men who had conversed with George Washington. To his uncle's home came distinguished lawyers, powerful debaters, who threshed out constitutional questions with keen, persuasive arguments. He listened to vehement discussions of state's rights, slavery, secession, and even war. Into the Georgetown house one day walked a lofty naval hero, Stephen Decatur, basking in the glory of having lately trounced the Barbary Pirates.

At sixteen Semmes was tossed between the choice of professions: The sea or the law. The call of the water was strong. The Potomac may have had something to do with it. However, he was equally fascinated by legal matters. Could one man be a sailor and be a lawyer too? Semmes felt he could try, at least. His fine intelligence easily took to law. In time he could argue the nicest, most intricate international questions with a skill that baffled his enemies and amazed his friends.

In 1832, six years after his appointment as midshipman, Semmes was warranted Passed Midshipman and ordered to the Norfolk Navy Yard for mathematical studies. He was then 23 years of age. Much of the next three years he spent in the vague capacity, "master of chronometers." Somehow these precise clocks, without which the navigator toiled in vain, fascinated him. The knowledge and care of these time-pieces became a hobby and was to manifest itself in his meticulous care in appropriating the chronometers of the prizes he took on the *Sumter* and the *Alabama*.

Given a long leave of absence he settled in Cumberland, Maryland, to read law in his brother's office. Admitted to the bar he considered resigning from the Navy and practicing law in Washington, but he was too much in love with the sea and the service. In 1835 he was appointed acting sailing master of the old frigate *Constellation*, victor over two French frigates in our quasi-war with that country. On her for two years he cruised back and forth between the hemispheres of the Western World. The Spanish Main again became a well-beaten track he could have charted almost in his dreams. In leisure hours, he buried himself in law books. Wherever duty and the winds carried his ship, Semmes always took with him his Blackstone, his Kent and his Coke. To the sounds of the sea he stowed away his cargo of legal lore.

In 1837, Semmes, then 28 years old and with eleven years of naval experience, was promoted to lieutenant, and on May 5 came marriage to Anne Elizabeth Spencer of Cincinnati, "a stately, handsome girl" whose Protestant affiliations and Northern forebears were no obstacle to a happy union that was to last to the end of his days. Anne became a devout Catholic. Her later attachment to the Confederacy was as deep as her husband's.

While stationed at the Pensacola, Florida, Navy Yard in 1841, Semmes established his legal residence in Alabama on land purchased on the west bank of the historic Perdido River, which separates the two states. It was a far-reaching political step. Without ado or formality he became a citizen of Alabama. Here he settled his family until 1849 when he gravitated to colorful, glamorous Mobile, a city that was to become the home of his heart and longings for the rest of his life.

The annexation of Texas in 1845 brought trouble with Mexico. Semmes heartily favored President Polk's policy of territorial expansion at the expense of the nation's neighbor to the south. Polk really rushed to meet hostilities. On its part Mexico had never relinquished her claim to Texas, now the 28th State and a prime *casus belli*. With Polk, Semmes believed it was America's manifest destiny to encompass the entire continent as far south as Panama.

Clash of arms between the two nations seemed inevitable, yet in April 1845, with war in the offing, Semmes, commanding the *Poinsett*, had sailed for Mexico with a presidential envoy to assure

the Mexican government that notwithstanding the proposed annexation of Texas the United States hoped for peaceful relations.
Semmes made the overland journey to Mexico City. It was a soul-
inspiring experience for so impressionable a man. Mexico's natural color and splendor dazzled and charmed him.

On the outbreak of war Semmes was placed in command of the
ten-gun brig *Somers*. He was ordered to blockade duty off Vera
Cruz. Misfortune and sinister fame had some years earlier come to
the *Somers*. In 1842 the hanging of the son of the Secretary of
War from her yardarm for conspiring to mutiny had aroused a
wave of protest across the nation. Since then officers had shunned
service on her. Not so, Raphael Semmes. As fate would have it the
Somers completed her circle of tragedy under him.

Caught in a violent tropical storm in August, 1846, off Vera
Cruz the *Somers* was overwhelmed by heavy seas and quickly sank
with heavy loss of life. Semmes did what he could to save his ship,
and after there was no hope, to save his men. Exonerated by a
court of inquiry he was immediately appointed flag lieutenant to
Commodore Connor, commanding the blockading fleet.

While General Scott's invading army was fighting its way along
the old Cortez trail towards Mexico City, Semmes was despatched
on a melodramatic military mission. His object was to protest the
treatment of Passed Midshipman R. C. Rogers captured in a naval
attack on a powder magazine near Vera Cruz. Accused of espionage
Rogers was held incommunicado. Presumably he was to be tried
for his life. Semmes reached the front and was parleying with the
Mexicans when Rogers escaped and returned to the American
lines, to the relief of all.

But Semmes' imagination had taken fire at the thought of going
to the Halls of Montezuma with the army. Offered temporary service as a "soldier" he joined General Worth's staff and participated
in the battles that brought the fall of Mexico City. Communication with Vera Cruz and the fleet had been cut off, and thus "I
had an excellent excuse for remaining with the Army."

In 1850, three years after the event, Semmes wrote his *Service
Afloat and Ashore During the Mexican War*. Rich, colorful, and
detailed, it was a best seller. For Semmes' artistic eye Mexico was
a kaleidoscope. The book gleams with pen-cameos of Mexico's

natural beauties, her wonders, her lovely women. It was a magnificent word-canvas dripping with breath-taking imagery. The valley of Mexico inspired him to ecstasies. Tucked between his rapturous outpourings were down-to-earth, accurate appraisals of the leaders of this first American expeditionary force. On an engineer officer whose abilities Semmes admired exceedingly he bestowed this accolade, "The services of Captain Lee were invaluable to his chief. Endowed with a mind which has no superior in his corps, and possessing great energy of character, he examined, counseled, and advised, with a judgment, tact, and discretion worthy of all praise. His talent for topography was peculiar, and he seemed to receive impressions intuitively, which it cost other men much labor to acquire."

In 1848 Semmes took command, first, of the *Electra*, and five months later the *Flirt*, for patrol duty on his old stamping grounds, the Southern seaboard and the Caribbean. The logs of these ships are replete with entries of lashes administered for infractions of discipline. The cat-o-nine-tails was still used to keep order on shipboard. Transgressions brought, often, not only lashes but irons as well. Semmes employed both freely. These logs disclose something, though not of the means, yet certainly of the iron will and hardboiled exterior, that were to enable him to master the motley, rough-and-tumble crew of the *Alabama* that was dredged up from the Liverpool waterfront.

Semmes, pushing forty-one, was ordered in 1849 to detached duty. Never again, as a United States naval officer, was he to see blue water service. On waiting orders he moved to Mobile where he practiced law. Six years later, and still awaiting orders, he was promoted to Commander. A year later he entered the lighthouse inspection service, and in 1858 he was summoned to Washington as secretary of the Lighthouse Board, where the outbreak of civil strife was to find him.

The nation was fast dividing. Henry Clay's stopgap compromise of 1850 was on the scrap heap. The drums were beating louder and closer. Two great sections were squaring off to settle their long dispute with blood and fire. Raphael Semmes was among those veering to the belief that only in secession could the South find its rightful destiny.

Washington blazed with talk of the "irrepressible conflict." Capitol Hill flashed with threats of secession and marching armies. Statesmen lunged at each other with verbal rapiers. Out in Illinois a small-town lawyer and powerful Senator were spotlighting the slavery issue in a debating duel that caught the nation's imagination.

In the drawing rooms of Washington fine folk of the North and South mingled with no thought of the morrow. Statesmen, who a few hours before had vilified each other on Capitol Hill, bowed and scraped and made merry. As at Lady Richmond's ball before Waterloo "There was a sound of revelry by night." The giddy whirl stepped up its tempo, as if the explosion, hurrying on inexorably, was only a bad political dream.

Semmes was no slave-owner. Since the Mexican War his views had slowly jelled in a different mould. Talk of a "Confederacy of the South" had set him dreaming. A Southern empire! Under her own flag, the empire would stand on its own, bulwarked by millions of bales of that cotton which dotted nearly every acre of the deep South. The merchant fleets of the world would come sailing into her spacious land-locked harbors and up her flower-fringed rivers to bear away the "white gold" piled on wharves and stored in thousands of warehouses. To Semmes it seemed as if God had lavished the cotton boll as a special blessing on the people of the romantic, smiling lands stretching from the Rio Grande to the Atlantic.

While the furies whipped up the fearful American fire-dance Semmes went quietly about his daily tasks. Clearly the day was not far off when he must make a fateful decision. The election of Abraham Lincoln in November, 1860, fixed his future: whatever the South would do he must do. So, in this mind, he waited "knowing the destined hour would find us men."

Anyone visiting Semmes would have met a reserved, lean, businesslike officer, who listened attentively and fixed the newcomer with "twinkling gray eyes" that turned bluish and piercing when his temper flared or when chasing after a prize. Semmes' foes were to make capital of this. "Pirate's eyes," they said, or "fanatic's eyes." It was an absurdity hatched at a time when the North was paying an enormous price for Semmes' depredations. John Paul

Jones and Semmes had eyes that matched. Jones, too, was cursed as "pirate" because he preyed on enemy commerce. He hit where it hurt.

This canard was enhanced by an exaggerated description furnished by Captain Hagar, master of the *Brilliant*, which Semmes burned in the North Atlantic in October, 1862. From the columns of the New York *Herald* came this account written by a reporter who interviewed the luckless skipper:

> Captain Hagar says that, however much Semmes may have had the appearance of a gentleman when an officer of the United States Navy, he has entirely changed now. He sports a huge mustache, the ends of which are waxed in a manner to throw that of Victor Emmanuel entirely into the shade, and it is evident that it occupies much of his attention. His steward waxes it every day carefully, and so prominent is it that the sailors of the *Alabama* call him "Old Beeswax." His whole appearance is that of a corsair, and the transformation appears to be complete from Commander Raphael Semmes, U.S.N., to a combination of Lafitte, Kidd, and Gibbs, the three most noted pirates the world has ever known.

But what sort of a man was Raphael Semmes? Look closer at this future "Confederate pirate." His thick, graying hair was upswept from his forehead. Though years of seawind, salt spray and sun had bronzed his skin, his cheeks were sallow. In repose he had a "preacher look." There was nothing in him at all to suggest a corsair. Never was he a strong, ruddy, eye-filling figure like, say, Jeb Stuart, rollicking, fighting cavalryman. But he would have made a splendid task force commander in modern war.

Semmes might have passed for a poet, or an artist, certainly not for a commerce raider. Fastidious in his personal appearance, he was scrupulously neat in uniform and out. There was a certain elegance about him. His hands were thin, his fingers, tapering. Like John Paul Jones Semmes took long, desperate chances, reveling in whirlwind, daring action. He enjoyed fine literature and music, beautiful manners, cultured salons, the company of lovely women, and dreams of domesticity. A dreamer, indeed, but a hard-hitting one, as Northern shipowners were to discover.

Gamaliel Bradford, a New Englander, claims to have found a

"coarse streak" in Semmes' nature. On the contrary, Semmes was courtly, a Southern gentleman. He could be sociable, and even jovial with friends. Sometimes, however, he became quite the opposite, silent and inscrutable. His orders were precise and to the point. He did not waste words when business was at hand. Neither did Ulysses Grant, who once despatched Sheridan on a prodigious operation with two words, "Go in." Sensitive, high-strung, and nervous, Semmes was given to drumming on his desk. A pious man, religion played a part in his daily life. He began his day kneeling at the little shrine in his cabin. He closed it in the same manner.

Semmes' facial embellishment, as Captain Hagar testified, was impressive. His sizable, carefully-groomed mustache grew outwards from his upper lip, curving downwards and ending in two sharp, upturned points like the mustachios of Kaiser Wilhelm II, villain of the piece in World War I. But Semmes had a feature the Kaiser lacked: a small beard on his lower lip. These magnificent adornments gave his countenance a slightly Mephistophelian cast. This was the "devilish look" reported by masters of the vessels he captured, and Semmes, perhaps consciously, furthered this impression by twirling the ends of his great mustache when he was thinking his way through a problem.

From the German warlord whose U-boats in 1914 carried to great heights the art of sea raiding came this tribute: "I reverence the name of Semmes. In my opinion he was the greatest admiral of the Nineteenth Century. At every conference with my admirals I counsel them to read and study closely Semmes' *Memoirs of Service Afloat*. I myself feel constant delight in reading and re-reading the mighty career of the Stormy Petrel."

5 Gaudeamus Igitur

Montgomery, capital of the brand-new Confederacy, was festive with flags and flowers. The roseate hues of the dawning hour of the Southern Republic still glowed. Garlands wreathed doorways in the Cradle of the Confederacy. Entwined over the entrance to the Exchange Hotel, headquarters of the "incubating government," was a huge "CSA" wrought in spring flowers. For the South, the millennium was at hand, or so it seemed. It was all so new, so wonderful, so exhilarating.

Crowning the green hill at the head of Dexter Avenue was the Greek-temple State Capitol where crowds had gathered yesterday to witness and applaud the inauguration of the Confederacy's provisional president, Jefferson Davis. Its white dome gleamed in the balmy February sunshine, a diadem as it were for the freshly-anointed King Cotton.

In his grave at Charleston John C. Calhoun, fiery apostle of a sovereign slavocracy, must have smiled in his sleep, "It has come at last: that for which I dreamed for half a century, the independence of the South." Tragedy it was to be, but flushed with dreams of empire, there were few who saw it.

The streets were still littered with yesterday's faded bouquets, tossed as the carriage of the President-elect passed on its way to the white-pillared Capitol where Davis took his simple oath of office. Truly, the Confederacy has been launched under cloudless, heaven-sent skies and christened with "smiles, plaudits and flowers."

Yet those there were aware that showers of petals and tumultuous acclaim could never enable a defenseless country, without army, without navy, without the sinews of war, to withstand the assault of Northern armies. However bold and brave and optimistic the Southern people, the grim realities were staggering. On one man, Jefferson Davis, had suddenly devolved the task of supplying the inspiration and guidance for the new nation. As another President, in another generation, was to proclaim, it was a "fearful thing to lead a great, peaceful people into war."

The lobby of the Exchange Hotel swarmed with "important" personages, small-time politicians, "taking dry smokes from unlit cigars"; hungry place-hunters, pretentious statesmen, uttering platitudes with magnificent gestures; congressmen in grave consultation; lawyers looking especially legal; planters in broad-brimmed hats; merchants seeking preferment for some thing or another; gentlemen in frock coats; a general or two in new Confederate gray; militiamen in variegated uniforms; women in expensive gowns and flashing jewels. And lobbyists! "No point in Montgomery was remote enough to escape the swoop of the lobby vulture, fierce for his fresh banquet," said Thomas C. De Leon, who was there.

The streets rang with a new, catchy tune, "Dixie." It caught Raphael Semmes' ear as he stepped out into the fresh morning. For him it was "the soul-stirring national anthem of the newborn government." Yesterday the crowds had gone wild when Herman Arnold's band, leading the inaugural procession up the sloping avenue to the State Capitol, broke into Dan Emmett's minstrel piece, specially orchestrated for the occasion. It would soon become the Marseillaise of the Southern legions. Could Semmes have listened into the future he might have heard a ship's band playing "Dixie" one bright August Sunday 1862, off the Azores, as he christened a new cruiser, *Alabama*, and embarked on his greatest adventure.

Yet, beneath the fervor and the flowers, the gladness and the glory, ran an ominous undertone, a sense of unreality, of doom impending. Could it be a dream? Fantastic, impossible, yet magnificent, it had, in its entire concept, ingredients out of which Richard Wagner might have fashioned another *Götterdämmerung*.

In the hotel lobby Semmes saw something that fascinated him: the first flag of the Confederacy—a banner with three broad stripes, one white between two red, and the union blue with a circle of seven white stars, one for each of the seven seceded States. The Stars and Bars, it was designed by two women of Alabama. Beside it stood an honor guard of two militiamen in the blue trousers and red jackets of the Columbus Guards. Semmes studied it closely. This was now *his* flag.

While optimism ran uncontrolled through most, others were thinking of the morrow and the obstacles ahead. Diarist Mary Boykin Chestnut had apprehensions, "This Confederacy must be supported now by calm determination and cool brains. Everywhere political intrigue is as rife as in Washington. We have risked all, and we must play our best, for the stake is life or death. We have to meet tremendous odds by pluck, activity, zeal, dash, endurance of the toughest, military instinct. Everybody who comes here wants an office, and many who, of course, are disappointed, raise a cry of corruption against the new who are successful. I thought we had left all that in Washington."

In his inaugural address Jefferson Davis had warned his compatriots of inevitable aggression "by the government from which we have separated . . . we must be prepared to meet the emergency and maintain, by the final arbitrament of the sword, the position which we have assumed among the nations of the earth . . ." Davis levelled the Southern lance directly at the North: Should the North attack it would bring on a conflict wherein "the sufferings of millions will bear testimony to the folly and wickedness of our aggressors."

In his heart, as in the hearts of the powerful coterie of politicians around him, Davis knew the North *would* make war. It was as certain as the God who looked down on this historic hour. Such, too, was the feeling in the heart of Raphael Semmes as he dutifully went to report to Charles M. Conrad, Chairman of the Naval Affairs Committee, whose telegram had summoned him to Montgomery.

A score of high officers of the Federal Navy were already on hand, including Lawrence Rousseau, the senior Captain and Victor M. Randolph, former commandant of the Pensacola Navy Yard. Other arrivals were appearing daily. The legislative mill was at the moment grinding out a Navy Department that would soon open for business with four Captains, four Commanders and about thirty Lieutenants,—but no ships. Semmes was the junior, but one, of the Commanders. Of the older naval officers who hurried to Montgomery some were of dubious fitness for service. They had come, as Semmes said, "bringing with them nothing but their patriotism and their gray hairs—their poverty and their swords." In this category Semmes had modestly classed himself.

At noon Semmes repaired to the State Capitol. He was escorted onto the floor of the provisional Confederate Congress, an honor he had not anticipated. In the chair was leonine, impassioned Howell Cobb of Georgia. Around the floor Semmes recognized men whose voices had shaped the Confederacy. To greet him cordially came brilliant Robert Toombs, soon to be Secretary of State of the new government. This "august assembly" was to Semmes "by far the best Congress ever assembled under the new government, full of the best talents of the South."

Yet how different the same spectacle appeared to commentator Thomas C. De Leon, who took a dim view of the "worn-out politicians." To him they "looked like the Washington Congress viewed through a reversed opera glass . . . men hot from Washington, reeking with the wiles of the old House and with their unblushing buncombe fresh upon them . . . and the rank old Washington leaven threatening to permeate every pore of the new government."

Bowing out of the legislative scene Semmes hurried to the Exchange Hotel where President Davis had set up the executive shop in "unpretending style," in a large parlor of the hostelry. Little was the ceremony that hedged in the Chief Executive. His desk was a round, polished table littered with papers. He lacked even a private secretary. Visitors entered and left almost as they pleased. Davis received each one courteously, extracted the pith of what they came to tell him and passed on to the next. At the moment he was the very idol of the people, the grand embodiment of their grand cause. Whatever he said, whatever he did, they accepted.

His welcome to Semmes was cordial and the doors were then closed. Calm and unmoved, he was apparently undaunted by the gigantic, dual task of launching a new government and arming it for war, though a tempering caution ran through his glowing optimism. He knew the odds were overwhelming. Unremitting tension and excitement had cut deep imprints on his thin features.

Arming the new nation was his immediate task, Davis realized. Peace overtures had died aborning. In a fortnight Abraham Lincoln would take office. Anything might happen at Charleston where the war of nerves over Fort Sumter threatened to explode hotly any moment. This grim, cannon-ringed tableau had reached the breaking point. South Carolina was stepping up her demands for the evacuation of Fort Sumter.

Of naval equipment the Confederate cupboard was bare, revealed Davis. Not a warship. Southern officers commanding Federal ships of war had sailed their vessels into Northern ports and delivered them to United States authorities before handing in their resignations. If the Confederacy was to have a navy, ships must be built, bought, or captured. The South had taken over the forts and arsenals within her borders, except Fort Sumter, and Fort Pickens at Pensacola. The Pensacola Navy Yard was in Confederate hands, but Federal forces at Fort Pickens prevented its use. The only other important naval station in the South was at Norfolk, Virginia—and Virginia had not yet chosen sides.

In a fighting speech to a Montgomery crowd Davis had thrown down the gauntlet to the North. "The South will make those who oppose her smell Southern powder and feel Southern steel." Brave, challenging words, but there was little or no powder to smell. Certainly not enough to fight battles with. Nor was there steel. Nor guns, nor heavy armament of any sort. No rolling mills or foundries, no heavy industries, no machine shops. Southern railroads were inefficient. Most of their rolling stock was long overdue at the scrapheap. Throughout the seceded States there was not an iron mill capable of casting cannon, though if Virginia seceded, the Confederacy could count on the small Tredegar Works at Richmond. There was not in the entire Confederacy a plant capable of turning out a steam engine. Because of this Semmes was later inspired to say, "many of her naval disasters are attributable to this deficiency."

The Confederacy needed everything: guns, rifles, caps, powder, ships, mechanics skilled in cannon and projectile production. The Navy Department, barely a name, was not yet organized. In the meantime the Confederacy could utilize Semmes' services in another direction. "I told the President that my services were at his command, in any capacity he thought fit to employ them," said Semmes.

Jefferson Davis then proceeded to draw up, with his own hand, a remarkable set of instructions commissioning Semmes to proceed North at once and purchase war materials for the South. Davis was amazingly precise. It was the first Confederate war order. To-day Semmes' assignment would be called secret service though there was apparently nothing clandestine about it. Davis identified by name a powder-manufacturer from whom Semmes could obtain "cannon and musket powder." Semmes was to propose to the proprietor building a plant within the confines of the Confederacy. Semmes was to hire mechanics skilled in the specialized trade of making rifles. He was even to pick up a "few fifteen-inch guns" along with others of various calibers.

Davis had an intimate knowledge of Northern war potential that amazed Semmes. An efficient Secretary of War in President Pierce's Cabinet, Davis had never relinquished his contacts with war-business. He knew the Federal War Department and its suppliers like a book.

On February 20 Semmes participated in a joint session of the Naval Affairs committees at which defense measures were discussed. Armed with Davis' instructions he started north next morning, pausing first at the Tredegar Works, which were to assume a leading role in casting cannon for Confederate armies. This plant was later to roll the armor for the ironclad *Virginia*, or *Merrimack*.

He spent a week in Washington where he visited the Arsenal, inspected a new percussion-cap machine and talked with gun mechanics, several of whom he induced to go South. Refusing to witness the "desecration of the capital" by the inauguration of Lincoln he shook off the city's dust just as "the glorious pageant was getting under way."

In New York he set up a Confederate purchasing agency. No effort was made to curb his activities. He toured New York and New England factories unmolested. Never once was he even threatened with arrest.

Doing business with Northern war merchants amused and astounded Semmes. The gross commercialism of some of these gentlemen was fantastic. For cash, it seemed, they would have sold their bodies and souls. With tension mounting, hotheads clamoring for war, sparks flying round the powder pile, they had few scruples against selling munitions that might be used to kill Northern boys. As agent for the Confederate government Semmes was wined and dined "at their comfortable residences near their factories, where the music of boring cannon, accompanied the clatter of dishes and popping of champagne corks." The Du Pont firm, which manufactured a third of the gunpowder produced in the United States, was a conspicuous exception to this experience.

Thanks to sales-hungry Northern contractors Semmes was able to ship South quantities of powder, rifles, and percussion caps. These shipments were disguised in the same manner as the rifles that New England abolitionists shipped to "Bleeding" Kansas—in boxes marked "Bibles." Semmes even arranged with a prominent Northern war-dealer a secret telegraphic code for use in reordering munitions after he had returned to Montgomery.

About the middle of March Semmes boarded the Hudson River dayboat *Queen of the Mohawk*, and went to West Point to see his son, Cadet Oliver J. Semmes, "A stocky, broad-breasted youth" of twenty, now in his third year at that already illustrious institution. It was a meeting the son had yearned for. Those young men at West Point faced hard, soul-searching decisions between state and country. Many had already doffed cadet gray, walked through the sallyport, and hurried South. Others had waited, dangling on the edge of perplexity. The majority of the Southern boys felt as did a cadet from Alabama, John Pelham, who "had hoped, fondly hoped, to graduate here. It would be exceedingly gratifying to me, and I know to the family also, for me to receive a diploma from this institution, but fate seems to have willed it otherwise. I don't see any honourable course other than that of tendering my resignation when Alabama leaves the Union and offering my service to her. In this I did not wish to act precipitately, but in a manner worthy of myself, of my family and of my section of the country."

Thus John Pelham, close friend of young Oliver Semmes. He was destined, after Fredericksburg, to receive from Lee the accolade "Gallant Pelham" and to fall "with the cry of battle on his lips" at Brandy Station, St. Patrick's Day, 1863.

Many cadets had held on, waiting for Virginia's decision. If Virginia stood fast for the Union, they might do likewise. West Point tradition says Raphael Semmes advised his son after the manner of Robert E. Lee, who, on resigning his colonelcy in the United States Army, sent this message for his perplexed son, "Tell Custis he must consult his own judgment, reason and conscience as to the course he may take. I do not wish him to be guided by my wishes or example. If I have done wrong, let him do better. The present is a momentous question which every man must settle for himself and upon principle."

Raphael Semmes might have known, though it is doubtful, that in the Ordnance Laboratory at West Point experts were then perfecting a rifling machine that would have been invaluable to the Confederacy. Just across the Hudson he might have seen smoke rising from the West Point Gun Foundry that would, in the next four years, cast over three thousand cannon and nearly two million projectiles for the Union armies.

It should be recorded that Oliver Semmes waited until April 22 before resigning his cadetship. By that time Fort Sumter had fallen, Virginia had slipped her moorings, and President Lincoln had summoned seventy-five thousand volunteers to invade the seceded States. On that day, a sorrowful one for West Point, young Semmes, John Pelham, and others laid aside their cadet uniforms and headed South for weal or woe.

Returning to New York Raphael Semmes found a message from the newly-appointed Confederate Secretary of the Navy, Stephen J. Mallory, directing him to purchase fast, light-draft vessels capable of mounting one eight- or ten-inch gun and of operating in the shallow coastal waters of the South. They were to deal with the smaller gunboats of the North should they approach too boldly the coast. "Their speed," wrote Mallory, "should be sufficient to give them, at all times, the ability to engage, or evade engagement."

Diligently, but futilely, Semmes combed the waters of New York Harbor and Long Island Sound. He refused to buy aged hulks that were offered him, though these same rotting bottoms were later foisted off on the Federal government at robbery prices.

Now, all at once, near the end of March "the warcloud was assuming darker and more portentous colors." Merchants who had received him with open arms four weeks ago shied away from him. It is possible his movements were shadowed, though the laxity of Federal intelligence agents was notorious. Happily, the New York-Savannah steamers were still running though under double colors, the Federal flag at the peak and the Confederate flag at the fore. Taking passage Semmes reached Montgomery on April 4 to find that charming little town had in his absence become an armed camp.

White tents of militia companies dotted the open fields around the city. Bugle calls and drumbeats aroused the citizenry at dawn. Clad in ill-fitting uniforms boys from plantations and the small places of the South stood on street corners gazing and gaping at the dome of the State Capitol where politicians were busily polishing the facets of the Southern revolution for which these youths would pour out their blood and their lives. Soldiery drilled in every open space in the city. Many of them shouldered muskets of War-of-1812 vintage. The streets were alive day and night.

If we are to believe the London *Times* correspondent, William "Bull Run" Russell, violence reigned in the streets of "the very capital" of the Confederacy. The Exchange Hotel, where he tarried for a few days, was "full of Confederate congressmen, politicians, colonels and place-men," many of whom were armed with "bowie knifes or a six-shooter or a Derringer." He might have added gamblers and camp followers to his list. He said "more murders were perpetrated in the very capital than known in the worst days of medieval Venice or Florence." There was, he reported "No security for life!" though "Property is quite safe."

New duties awaited Semmes at Montgomery. In his absence the Confederate Congress had established a Lighthouse Bureau, which he had recommended, and given him charge of it with the rank of Commander. His recent experience at Washington justified the appointment. Thus was he to while away the conflict. It was a logical assignment. He was nearly fifty-two. His age apparently precluded all idea of active fighting. Dutiful though he was Raphael Semmes had no idea of taking a back seat in a hot war. Sitting at a desk presiding over a few clerks and a set of books, with an occasional inspection tour of lighthouses, was not the way he intended to fight. He wanted action and though it seemed distant at the moment, he was to get it fast.

He had barely opened his books and hired a clerk or two before the shooting began. So keenly was his whole being attuned to the rising fervor that he could almost hear, even at Montgomery, five hundred miles away, the roar of Beauregard's guns opening fire on Sumter at dawn, April 12. The ball had started! News of the attack on Sumter was flashed to Montgomery before breakfast. All day while Confederate cannon battered the fort the South held its breath. On April 13, after a blazing twenty-four-hour duel, Fort Sumter capitulated, and joy swept the South.

In Montgomery business suspended. The Confederate Congress recessed hastily and joined the exulting mêlée in the streets. It seemed as if utopia was suddenly spread out in glorious colors before the very eyes of the South. *Gaudeamus igitur*. Champagne was "poured in libations wonderful to see" as patriotic citizens toasted *beau sabreur* Beauregard, President Davis, and everybody and everything remotely associated with the grand and glorious Confederacy. The glad tidings flickered across the city and the land. Men, women and children locked arms and snake-danced in the streets in a triumphal jamboree. Bands stood on street corners blaring out "Dixie" and "Bonnie Blue Flag," and a calliope, drawn by four mules, paraded through the town, with all stops out, screaming "Dixie" at the top of its steamy lungs.

In front of the "Government House," a large red brick pile originally built for a cotton warehouse and hastily converted into public offices, a battery of cannon roared salutes to the first Confederate victory. Speechmakers popped out of every window and balcony. Crowds flocked to the temporary White House of the Confederacy, at Lee and Bibb Streets, to serenade the First Lady of the Republic, Varina Howell Davis, who came out on the porch and graciously thanked the cheering visitors. "All the great, and many of the little men of the government, were serenaded."

It was the South's Great Day. There would never be another like it, and the South made the most of it.

For Semmes the hour had struck. His post at the Lighthouse Bureau was no longer tenable.

"It had become necessary," he said, "for every man, who could wield a sword, to draw it in defense of his country, thus threatened by the swarming hordes of the North, and to leave the things of peace to the future. I had already passed the prime of life, and was going gently down that declivity at whose base we all arrive, sooner or later, but I thanked God, that I still had a few years before me, and vigor enough of constitution left, to strike in defense of the right."

On April 15, 1861 while the impact of Sumter's fall still echoed Raphael Semmes called to see Secretary of the Navy Mallory and asked to go afloat.

⚓

⚓

6 *"Give Me That Ship, Mr. Secretary"*

Of the countless "if's" of the American Civil War one has been dismissed too lightly or played down as inconsequential. Measured at today's distance this "if" bulks formidably in the ultimate fate of the Confederacy.

Among the imperative, immediate needs of the new-born government was a battle fleet to contest the Northern blockade and keep open Southern ports and the sea-lanes leading to them. Had her statesmen seized the opportunity thrust upon them the Confederacy might easily have secured at one stroke such a fleet early in the war. This ready-made navy could have raised the then-nebulous blockade, wreaked havoc with American shipping, and given battle to anything the United States might send to drive it off.

In 1861 the East India Company (which had provided the tea for the Boston Tea Party) began selling off its assets and surrendering its vast powers to the British crown. Among its properties were ten first-class East Indiamen, offered for sale at half price.

Built in Britain, these steamships were of great size, power, and speed. They were capable of transporting troops, cargo, or treasure and were designed to be armed. Properly gunned they would be a menace hard to shake off, able to cope with almost any fighting ship this side of the Atlantic. In April, 1861, a leading British banking house obtained an option on this fleet which was transmitted at once to President Davis in Montgomery. The total cost of buying, arming, manning, and fitting out the ten ships and putting them on the Southern coast ready for action, was estimated at two million dollars, a sum that could easily have been covered by forty thousand bales of cotton. At the moment the Confederate government had amassed over three million bales in warehouses throughout the cotton States.

Negotiator of this deal was C. K. Prioleau, partner in the firm of John Frazer and Company, with offices at Liverpool and Charleston. "This fleet," said Mr. Prioleau, "would have appeared off Boston and swept the coast thence to the Gulf, an achievement which would have compelled prompt British recognition of the Confederacy."

General Beauregard, whose prestige, as captor of Fort Sumter, was at its height, promptly went to Montgomery to urge President Davis and his advisers to snap up this colossal bargain. These ships, he pointed out, would have an incalculable influence on the outcome of the war. But Beauregard's warm espousal of the idea was charged off as impractical Gallic impetuosity. What did he know about naval affairs, anyway? He was a soldier. Why burden the new government with this fleet? The war would be over in ninety days. Beauregard disagreed sharply. The war would be drawn out and bloody. The blockade had menacing aspects.

Never was it revealed who made the fateful decision not to buy these ships. The secret was buried in the debris of the Confederacy. Rejection rested most likely on two men, President Davis and his Secretary of the Navy, Stephen R. Mallory. There is no indication that Raphael Semmes was ever apprised of the offer of the Indiamen. It was probably too secret to be divulged outside the Cabinet.

"The Confederate government could never have entered into such a gigantic scheme," concluded John C. Schwab in his financial and industrial history of the Confederacy. Yet Raphael Semmes had already sought in vain to purchase ships in the North. Even while the government was bypassing this opportunity, President Davis was despatching a secret emissary to Britain to contract for building a fleet of armed vessels in British shipyards—both ironclads and swift cruisers. But these vessels, no matter how fine, could not be ready for months or years. The Indiamen were available immediately.

Failure to acquire this fleet was, said Beauregard's biographer, Alfred Roman, "the first of a long series of irremedial errors committed by the administration." Viewed from afar it looks as fatal and destructive in its ultimate effect on the destinies of the Confederacy as were the cotton embargo, the crop restrictions, and the burning of cotton stocks—all futile efforts to coerce Britain into intervention on behalf of the South.

Officered by such fighters as Semmes, Buchanan, Maffitt, Reid, Ruger, and others, armed with Britain's modern naval ordnance, these East Indiamen could have been battling off the Atlantic coast within six months. Lincoln's paper blockade would have crumbled and been written off as another expedient tried and found wanting. This fleet might even have posed the threat of a counterblockade of Northern ports and have immobilized the great city of New York itself.

The United States Navy was, in 1861, inadequate for its great task, the blockade of 3,000 miles of Southern coastline. Its ships, those that it had, were, as a rule, excellent. The new steam frigates and steam sloops were much admired in Europe. They were well armed with heavy guns of the latest pattern, for the American Navy, through the efforts of Captain John Dahlgren, was a world leader in the field of ordnance. All the ships, however, were built of wood. Indeed, when the Civil War broke, there were but two ironclads in the world, France's *Gloire* and England's *Warrior*. This war was to prove beyond doubt the decisive superiority of armored ships over wooden.

Excellent though the Navy's ships were, they were few in number and many were old. The greater proportion relied on sail alone. Of a fleet of about ninety ships, only twenty-four were steamers, and these twenty-four were scattered as far as Brazil, Africa, and China. It would be months before all these distant vessels could be called home and despatched to blockading stations off the Southern coasts. A good many ships, including some steamers, were "in ordinary" at the various navy yards, unfit for sea. They would have to be made ready and crews would have to be found for them. Most of the decommissioned ships were in Northern yards, but seven, one the fine steam frigate *Merrimack*, were at Norfolk. These ships were burned and then sunk in the Elizabeth River to prevent their capture when the Virginians seized the navy yard.

It is evident then that had the South possessed, within six months of the war's opening, a homogeneous squadron of ten powerful vessels, such as the Indiamen were, it might well have smashed the blockade, changed the course of the war, and, in consequence, the course of American history.

But in 1861 few Southerners recognized the importance of seapower. There was one member of the Confederate cabinet who did perceive the overwhelming influence of a navy on the future of the South. This man, Stephen Mallory, believed that the fate of the Confederacy would be settled even more by what happened at sea than by what occurred ashore.

Because of his intimate association with Raphael Semmes, we should draw a better focus on Mallory. A squat, undistinguished looking Irishman, his round jaw bordered by whiskers, Mallory enjoyed fine wines and good living. More important, he was industrious, full of spirit, and thoroughly conversant with naval affairs. This man—until recently neglected by biographers and overshadowed by less competent, better publicized figures in the Davis Cabinet—turned in the most efficient record of any member of the executive family, even when one takes into account his blunder over the Indiamen. He was born at Trinidad in 1813, son of a Yankee sea captain and an Irish mother. Most of his boyhood was spent at Key West, the southernmost outpost of the United States and a port for vessels from every corner of the earth. Mallory's entire life and training savored of the sea. His youth was framed against the colorful panorama of the Gulf of Mexico. He was reared in a world of shipwrecks, hurricanes, and salvage. The reefs of the Florida keys were dotted with sunken Spanish galleons and pirate ships. It was a romantic, adventurous background for a growing boy.

Maritime law intrigued young Mallory and he practiced it successfully. At twenty-five he married a beautiful Spanish girl, Angela Moreno, whose brother, incidentally, he later appointed to West Point.

Self-educated, he worked his way up the political ladder until 1851 when Florida elected him to the United States Senate. Recognition of Mallory's knowledge of the sea and ships brought him the chairmanship of the Senate Naval Affairs Committee, a post he discharged with vigor and ability until his State seceded. Never a warm secessionist, he was not just a party-horse cantering around Washington, as a disgruntled Southern editor once charged. When Florida cut loose from the Union Mallory dutifully resigned his seat only to be summoned to head the Confederate naval portfolio.

Mallory was a man with ideas. He disagreed sharply with the Davis policy of embargoing cotton. He pointed out that President Thomas Jefferson had tried peaceable coercion on Britain in 1807, but it had backfired and only the Americans suffered. Consequently he was not deluded by the notion that withholding cotton from England and France would bring them to the aid of the Confederacy. He wanted to rush cotton to Europe and build up much-needed credit before the Federal blockade became fully effective. He was thoroughly conversant with new developments in naval science and he was an enthusiast for ironclads. Convinced that the blockade held life or death for the Confederacy, he dedicated his remarkable energy and intelligence to destroying it.

Intelligent, imaginative, and open to ideas other than his own —which some say Jefferson Davis was not—Mallory was tailor-made for his post. Knowing Northern naval power at first hand he was the very man to direct the combat against it. President Davis could hardly have chosen a better-informed or better-equipped man to conduct Confederate naval affairs.

Mallory's problem was complex. Starting from nothing and conjuring a navy out of thin air was a task of staggering magnitude. Yet it was an essential task if the Confederacy were to succeed. The first duty of his as-yet-nonexistent navy was to defend the 3,000 mile coastline extending from the Potomac to the Rio Grande. The innumerable rivers, harbors, inlets, bays, and most important, the eight major ports, had to be made safe from capture by Federal forces.

Secondly, the Northern blockade had to be cracked open. Third, the North's valuable commerce with Europe, Asia, and South America, would have to be attacked. Not only would this destroy Yankee property and cause war weariness in the North, but it would, Mallory hoped, divert cruisers from the blockade in order to hunt down the raiders and protect the merchantmen.

Had the South possessed those Indiamen which her leaders had turned down, she might very well have achieved all these aims at one stroke, through bringing to battle the big steam warships of the Federal Navy. Success in battle, which might have been achieved early in the war when the Union ships were scattered and the squadrons weak, would have freed the Confederate coastline from the dangers of blockade and of assault from the sea. Furthermore it would have immediately opened Federal commerce to devastating attacks. Indeed, such a success might have made the ports of the North, rather than those of the South, the victims of a blockade. Lacking such a force Secretary Mallory (for President Davis was singularly uninterested in naval problems and left them all to Mallory) was forced to improvise.

Protection of the Confederacy's ports and coastline was a joint army-navy venture. The army would man and supply the huge fortresses at harbor entrances. The navy would provide gunboats, converted from locally-available commercial vessels, for protection of lesser places and to dispose of secondary thrusts. Ironclad steamers, mobile fortresses in effect, could, among their other duties, engage Union vessels beyond range of the forts. In shallow waters torpedoes (we call them "mines") could be laid to bar entrance to hostile ships. Occasionally floating batteries could be moored where it was neither possible to place a fort nor to maneuver a ship.

To smash the blockade thought was given at first to building a fleet of powerful wooden warships. The seven Federal ships scuttled at Norfolk were raised for a starter. But rebuilding had hardly begun when it became evident that the South could never match the Union in a race to create a wooden navy. So work was stopped on all save the lone steamer, the *Merrimack.* That vessel was transformed into something quite different, an ironclad coastal defence ram. Though not fit for ocean cruising, she and her successors, so long as they stayed in sheltered waters, were quite capable of dealing with the North's wooden ships. They never did succeed, however, in cracking the blockade of any Southern port.

For ocean raiders the Confederacy relied on both privateers and regular navy cruisers. The former were privately-owned and -armed, operating under licenses granted by the Confederate government authorizing them to capture enemy merchant ships and plunder them for profit. In past wars, privateering was a flourishing, profitable game. In the War of 1812 over five hundred such craft, some of them fine vessels, others nondescript nautical junk, prowled the Atlantic, exacting a terrific toll of British shipping. English shipping losses ran into millions of pounds and helped prepare the British government for a peace with the United States. Shares in the privateers were bought like shares of stock are now. Officers and crews signed on in return for a certain share of the proceeds from their prizes. A good many American fortunes were made in this manner, and a few were lost, too.

President Davis' announcement that he was ready to authorize privateering understandably set off a mad rush to get into the big money. Old slavers, tugs, fishing schooners, coasters, anything that might float, shipped a gun or two and scurried out to get rich quick at Yankee expense. Chief entrepôts of this devilish traffic were Charleston and New Orleans. Applications came even from New England whalers and ship-owners who had no scruples against putting profits ahead of country. But privateering was soon panting for breath under the stifling effect of the Federal blockade and in the event it was to figure little.

The Confederate cruisers, though, were something else again. Usually larger and more heavily armed than the privateers, they were manned by large complements of regular navy officers and men operating under naval discipline. Unlike the privateersmen, they did not hesitate to burn and sink their prizes. Nor, unlike the privateers, were these ships easy game for Federal warships either to catch or to destroy. It was, in consequence, the cruisers alone, *Sumter*, *Alabama*, and a few others, which cut such deep wounds into Northern commerce.

It is worthwhile to glance briefly at the Confederate ironclads even though this book is concerned with them only to the extent that they affected the destinies of the cruisers *Sumter* and *Alabama*.

Unlike the cruisers, the ironclads were almost totally unsuccessful. Nowhere did they succeed in breaking the blockade. In a few instances they did manage to deny certain limited bodies of water to Federal ships for a time, but all were overcome eventually either by superior force, by superior ingenuity, or by the advance of Federal armies.

Most important of all was the *Virginia*, *née Merrimack*, dredged up from the mud at Norfolk. Her armored casemate resembled the roof of a long, narrow house floating down the stream, with a smokestack at top center. The other ironclads did not much vary in this respect. The *Virginia* in one afternoon of March, 1862, sank two of the North's old wooden sailing ships, the *Congress* and the *Cumberland*. But the next day, when she went out to finish the job on the other wooden ships, she was frustrated by the little *Monitor*, just arrived from Brooklyn. Two months later she was blown up by her own crew when Federal troops took Norfolk from behind.

The Confederacy later built some ironclads, including a new *Virginia*, on the James River to protect Richmond from assault by the water route. These vessels were never really tested in battle and all were scuttled to prevent their capture when Richmond fell to General Grant's army in 1865.

In North Carolina the *Albemarle,* built in a cornfield, did deny the Roanoke River to the Federals for some months until finally she was destroyed by the daring Lieutenant William B. Cushing in a night "torpedo" raid into the lair of the iron monster. Despite her overwhelming strength and her invulnerability to Federal cannon fire, she never was able to prevent Northern ships from using the North Carolina sounds as they wished. Two ironclads built at Charleston, South Carolina, the *Chicora* and the *Palmetto State,* defeated a pair of Union gunboats outside Charleston on one occasion but the blockade was not broken and the episode never repeated. Near Savannah, the *Atlanta,* converted from a swift blockade runner, was easily taken by the monitor *Weehawken* after the latter had fired only five shots.

On the Mississippi River the *Manassas,* a made-over tugboat, once managed to chase some wooden blockaders out of the river itself, but the Union ships merely took station just off the entrances to the stream and the blockade remained intact. The *Manassas* went to her doom in action with Farragut's wooden ships when he attacked the forts guarding New Orleans in April, 1862. Farragut's success over the *Manassas* and the forts meant that that city was forcibly returned to the Stars and Stripes. It also meant that the incomplete ironclads *Louisiana* and *Mississippi* had to be blown up by their own people to prevent the Federals from getting them.

A few months after the fall of New Orleans the *Arkansas,* built on the Yazoo River, provided flag officers Farragut and Charles Davis with a humiliating morning when she ran through their combined squadrons a few miles above Vicksburg. But no great harm was done the Federals and the *Arkansas* shortly became the victim of her own mechanical ailments, for her steering gear failed, she ran into the river bank, and all was lost as the Northern ironclad *Essex* poured broadsides into the helpless vessel.

Most powerful of all the Southern armored ships was the *Tennessee,* built at Selma, Alabama, and floated downriver to Mobile, on the Gulf. She never disturbed Farragut's wooden blockading squadron, lying watchfully just beyond reach of the guns of Fort Morgan. When, on an August morning of 1864, Farragut and his fleet went into battle for possession of Mobile

Bay, neither Fort Morgan nor the torpedoes in the channel held them back. The *Tennessee* steamed out to bar the way. Against the Admiral's wooden steam sloops she gave better than she got. But the monitor *Chickasaw* moved into the fight, and it was soon over, with the *Tennessee* a prize of war.

Mallory did not rely entirely on the home resources of the South to produce ironclads. From English builders he ordered a couple of powerful ocean-going armored rams (as distinguished from the locally-built ironclads, which dared not get far from shore), but the government of Mr. Lincoln managed to force the sale of those sea monsters to European buyers. From France Mallory tried to obtain the *Gloire*. He was rebuffed, but then ordered a new ship, the *Stonewall,* from a French shipyard. The *Stonewall* would have had an easy time against any but the most powerful of the Northern ironclads. She was not ready for sea, however, until too late to be of service to the Confederacy, and she ended up in the Japanese navy.

Events were moving in swift succession. On April 15, two days after Beauregard's guns battered Fort Sumter into submission President Lincoln called for seventy-five thousand volunteers to put down "combinations too powerful to be suppressed by the ordinary course of judicial proceedings . . ." On April 17 Virginia crossed over into Secession. That same day, while booming cannon in Montgomery's streets welcomed the Old Dominion to the Southern fold, President Davis proclaimed the Confederacy's determination to resist to the last ditch President Lincoln's "intention of invading this Confederacy with an armed force for the purpose of capturing its fortresses, and thereby subverting its independence and subjecting the free people thereof to the dominion of a foreign power."

To implement the Confederacy's determination of meeting force with force Davis, as we have seen, authorized privateering by Southern merchant mariners. This form of war had been tabooed by the Declaration of Paris in 1856, a pact which, ironically enough, the United States had refused to sign.

President Davis' manifesto invited "all those who may desire, by service in private-armed vessels on the high seas, to aid this Government in resisting so wanton and wicked an aggression, to make application for commissions or letters of marque and reprisal under the seal of these Confederate States." It should be stressed that President Lincoln, ill-advised by Secretary of State Seward, on April 19 retaliated against the Davis proclamation by ordering a blockade of Southern ports and threatening "that if any person under the pretended authority of the said States, or under any other pretense, shall molest a vessel of the United States, or the persons or cargo on board of her, such person will be held amenable to the laws of the United States for the prevention and punishment of piracy."

In short, Confederate privateersmen, and sailors on any warship flying the Confederate flag, would be treated not as prisoners of war, if caught, but hanged as pirates. Seward, who had phrased the Lincoln proclamation, had palpably sought to invest both Confederate privateersmen and fighting ships with the legal character of buccaneers. The Lincoln government was apparently alarmed by visions of privateers swarming out of Southern ports to feast on the fatback of American shipping. These vultures must be frightened off. In a quick maneuver the Federal government offered to subscribe to the no-privateering convention, only to be snubbed by the signatory powers.

At the same time England pointed out the inconsistency of Lincoln's declared blockade of the South. The Declaration of Paris had defined blockade as a weapon to be used by two independent nations at war. The North contended the South was not an independent nation to which Britain, speaking through her Minister at Washington, Lord Lyons, replied that if the seceded states were not an independent nation, but simply rebels and insurrectionists, then the President's blockade was not binding on other nations. Interpreted by international law Lincoln's blockade proclamation was tantamount to legal recognition of the Confederacy as a belligerent nation. If Lincoln had by his own words recognized the South as a nation, the North could hardly blame Britain for doing the same thing. On May 14, 1861, England declared her neutrality and accorded belligerent rights to the Confederacy.

April 17 was a day long to be remembered by Raphael Semmes. His whole sea-raider career hinged on it. That morning he hurried to the temporary government building at Montgomery and entered the sparsely-furnished rooms that housed the nascent Confederate Navy Department. The gold-braid stripes of a commander gleamed on his still-blue uniform. He was ushered at once into the Secretary's office. His words came fast.

"Mr. Secretary, the war has begun and I've come to ask active service."

"You shall have it, Commander," replied the robust Mallory. "When will you be ready?"

"I am ready now." Semmes' gray eyes must have emphasized his words.

Semmes made it clear to Mallory that privateering did not comport with his ideas of how a Commander in the Confederate Navy should serve his country. He had advocated it but wanted no part of it for himself. Now he went directly to the real purpose of his visit. He dug out of his pocket a paper he had kept there ever since he hurried to Montgomery. On it he had sketched out a plan for attacking Northern commerce by fast cruisers. He would like, he said, to command a ship engaged in operations of this character. Semmes knew that a board of Confederate naval experts was rummaging through Southern ports for merchant steamers that could be purchased or seized, armed, and commissioned in the Confederate Navy for just those tasks he had in mind.

A tradition, once hinted at in the British House of Commons, avers that Semmes at the same time handed Mallory a crude sketch he had drawn of the ideal sort of craft for attacking Northern merchant marine. It was, so the tradition ran, the inception of the *Alabama*, even to the guns she would carry.

While Semmes expounded his theory of commerce destruction Mallory listened blandly. Whatever he thought he must have realized that Semmes was a man after his own heart. They were to have much in common for three turbulent years. Mallory revealed that the reports on vessels examined by his naval board were discouraging. Virtually every vessel inspected had been rejected as unsuitable, but he added, "Here is a report from New Orleans that came in this morning. Read it and see what you think."

Pondering each word Semmes perused the description of a small propeller steamer of five hundred tons, seaworthy, with a low-pressure engine and space for five days' fuel. She could be fitted to mount a battery of four or five guns. Under steam she could make nine or ten knots. There were no accommodations for the crew of a man-of-war. She was the packet *Habana*, plying between Cuba and New Orleans, but now tied up at the latter, impounded by the Federal blockaders at the mouth of the Mississippi. Loaded with defects, the examining board had condemned the vessel. Not so, Raphael Semmes. Something told him this was the "Moving Finger" writing.

In spirited, decisive fashion he made the choice that would make him a "pirate" to the North and a hero, the "Stonewall Jackson of the seas," to the South. Without fanfare or bluster he said quietly, firmly, "Mr. Secretary, give me that ship. I think I can make her answer the purpose."

"You shall have her," assured Mallory. "She's probably only a teakettle, but I'll issue the order at once."

The decision was made as quickly as that. Fast, prompt action, to be sure, but such was the new motif of Raphael Semmes' life. Aged fifty-two he had not heard gunfire since 1847, when he was under the walls of Chapultepec. He was now twenty years older than John Paul Jones had been when he overcame the *Serapis* with the dismal *Bon Homme Richard*; ten years older than Oliver Hazard Perry when he vanquished the British squadron on Lake Erie. He was three years the junior of Robert E. Lee when, in 1862, Lee took command of the Army of Northern Virginia. For Semmes the duel with the *Kearsarge* was thirty-eight months distant.

With his new appointment, the years dropped suddenly from Semmes' shoulders. Whatever inertness he had displayed in the old navy, whatever indolence his former companions may have noted, were submerged in a resurgence of vigor and determination. Now he was all movement and dash, yearning to be off.

Mallory continued: "On reaching the high seas you are to do the enemy's commerce the greatest injury in the shortest time. Choose your own cruising grounds. Burn, sink and destroy and be guided always by the laws of the nations and of humanity. Those are my orders."

"I shall obey them—implicitly, sir." Semmes paused, then, "What name shall we give our teakettle? 'Habana' will hardly do."

Mallory's eyes brightened. "What better name than 'Sumter'? Wherever she goes she will commemorate our great victory at Charleston."

" 'Sumter' she shall be," agreed Semmes.

Thus was born the Confederate cruiser *Sumter*, first ship of war to show the new Confederate flag on the high seas.

Semmes was to write in after years, "I had accepted a stone which had been rejected of the builders, and which, though it did not afterward become the chief cornerstone of the temple, I endeavored to work into the building which the Confederates were then rearing, to remind their posterity that they had struggled, as Patrick Henry and his contemporaries had struggled before them, in defense of their liberties."

There was no waiting. Next morning, April 18, Semmes was handed his orders:

Sir: You are hereby detached from duty as Chief of the Lighthouse Bureau, and will proceed to New Orleans and take command of the steamer *Sumter* (named in honor of our recent victory over Fort Sumter). The following officers have been ordered to report to you, for duty: Lieutenants John M. Kell, R. T. Chapman, John M. Stribling, and Wm. E. Evans; Paymaster Henry Myers; Surgeon Francis L. Galt; Midshipmen, Wm. A. Hicks, Richard F. Armstrong, Albert G. Hudgins, John F. Holden, and Jos. D. Wilson.

S. R. Mallory, Secretary of the Navy

Orders were immediately written for the officer complement to report to Semmes at New Orleans. Of the *Sumter's* officer personnel only one was appointed at Semmes' special request, Lieutenant John McIntosh Kell. Semmes later paid this tribute to this man, his executive officer on the *Sumter* and then on the *Alabama*, who stood with him when the latter dived to her watery grave in the English Channel: "When it was decided, at Montgomery, that I was to have the *Sumter*, I at once thought of Kell, and, at my request, he was ordered to the ship."

That afternoon Semmes boarded the river steamer *Southern Republic*, for Mobile. Trimmed with red and gold, with an improvised Confederate flag at her peak, the boat moved off down the tortuous Alabama River like a floating carnival. Crowds stood on the bluff above the landing and waved bon voyage while a calliope screamed out "Dixie" wildly. The long deck was packed. The gorgeous main saloon buzzed with excitement, but hardly a soul recognized "a slight, wiry man of about fifty, with twinkling gray eyes, prominent features and fierce gray mustache." Nor would anyone have dreamed that this quiet-mannered fellow passenger would so soon be headlined around the world for his bold deeds and blazing track across the seas.

Mobile was swept by war fervor. "One of the truest of Southern cities," it boiled with martial ardor. The lobby of the Battle House, Mobile's smartest hotel, was thronged with young men in military costume and to Semmes "all seemed going as merrily as a marriage ball." Another observer, also a passenger on the *Southern Republic*, remarked that, "The echo of the first gun at Charleston had roused her people and with wonderful accord they had sprung to arms." Far, far off, beyond even the worst of dreams, was the "dreadful revelry" of Farragut's guns in 1864.

Semmes tarried at his old home only a few hours before pressing on to New Orleans. At Mobile he fell in with Lieutenant Chapman, one of the officers detailed to report to the *Sumter,* "and he, being a minute-man like myself, took a hasty leave of his young wife, and we continued our journey together." The deep South was on fire, and war fever gripped the Crescent City. Jackson Square flared with the resplendent uniforms of volunteer companies marching and drilling. Long lines of bayonets bobbed up and down the narrow streets of Vieux Carré. On lampposts and front doors placards flaunted the watchwords, "*Aux armes, citoyens!*" Like animated rainbows—blue-jacketed, white legginged, red breeched—zouaves, hussars, chasseurs, went weaving through the crowds. The Crescent Rifles, panoplied in red and blue, with high Napoleonic shakos, drilled on the levee. Lovely Creole women in gay attire crowded the balconies and blew kisses to the Louisiana Tigers marching by. Scraped up from the waterfront, these thugs and plugs wore bowie knives at their belts.

New Orleans was immersed in the deceptive glamour of the first blush of war. Her youth was rushing to battle in the grand manner, songs on their lips, swords and roses in their hands. The agony and blood would follow. Shiloh would come soon enough, but now, as Semmes saw it, "the Confederate flag in miniature was pinned on almost every bosom. The enthusiasm of the Frenchman had been most easily and gracefully blended with the stern determination of the Southern man of English descent. . . . Nor was this patriotism demonstrative only, it was deep and real, and was afterward sealed with some of the best Creole blood of the land, poured out, freely, on many a desperate battlefield."

But Semmes could see that the city had changed for the worse. Paralysis had already set in, and it seemed to him as if a pestilence brooded over the city. "The levee was no longer a great mart of commerce, piled with cotton bales, and supplies going to the planter; densely packed with steamers, and thronged with a busy multitude. The long lines of shipping above the city had been greatly thinned, and a general air of desolation hung over the river front."

Standing on the deserted levee Semmes caught his first glimpse of the tiny *Sumter* (*née Habana*) docked at an Algiers shipyard on the west bank of the yellow Mississippi. There she was weatherstained, dingy, idle. Her stack was rusty, her rigging slack. Yet a surge of pride ran through him. For him she was "my new ship." Crossing the river with Lieutenant Chapman he took possession of her to find "only a dismantled packet-ship, full of upper cabins, and other tophamper, furniture and crockery, but as unlike a ship of war as possible. Still I was pleased with her general appearance. Her lines were easy and graceful and she had a saucy air about her that seemed to say that she was not averse to the service on which she was about to be employed."

But this was no time for sentimental reflection. On the bridge of the deserted *Habana*, gazing up and down the river, his words to Secretary Mallory came echoing back to him, "Give me that ship, Mr. Secretary. I think I can make her answer the purpose."

Time was essential, and there was little enough of that. All Semmes' patience and skill would be needed to convert this peaceful passenger steamer into a tool of war which he could launch against a commercial marine that was second only to that of Great Britain in magnitude and importance. In the old navy he "could go into a navy yard, with well-provided workshops, and skilled workmen ready with all the requisite materials at hand to execute my orders," but now "everything had to be improvised, from the manufacture of a water-tank, to the 'kids and cans' of the berthdeck messes, and from a gun carriage to a friction-primer."

That night, on his knees, Semmes besought blessing for his ship from the God of Battles and guidance for himself as her captain.

⚓

⚓

7 Running the Gauntlet

Of the numerous gallery gods who came to marvel at the conversion of the packet *Habana* into the cruiser *Sumter*, none was more fascinated than a New Orleans youth with a literary bent, George Washington Cable, whose "favorite of all the sea-steamers, the little *Habana*, that had been wont to arrive twice a month from Cuba, disgorge her Spanish-American cargo, and bustle away again, and that I had watched the shipwrights, at their very elbows, razee and fit with three big, raking masts in place of her two small ones, had long ago slipped down the river and through the blockaders, and was no longer the *Habana*, but the far-famed and dreaded *Sumter*."

Nor was the future author of *Old Creole Days* the only visitor who chattered at the "very elbows" of the shipwrights and mechanics toiling over the *Sumter*. Eager-eyed Confederate small fry swarmed aboard with a thousand questions. To these young folk Semmes was a hero overnight, if for no other reason that, wrestling with nigh-insurmountable tasks, he welcomed their visits and let them watch the *Habana's* face-lifting.

The *Sumter's* change-over from peace to war was a tedious, man-killing, piecemeal job that wore Semmes' patience thin. "I had not only to devise all the alterations, but to make plans and drawings for them." The superstructure of passenger cabins and saloons was scrapped; the main deck strengthened to support guns and carriage; a berth deck for the crew installed; quarters arranged for Semmes and his officers; engines protected with makeshift armor of "woodwork and iron bars;" the ship's rigging altered to convert her into a bark, with square sails on her fore and main masts; new suits of sails cut out and stitched; magazines fabricated; and fuel bunkers enlarged to carry coal for eight days instead of five. Raphael Semmes had to plan and direct all these things. He even had to show a nearby foundry how to cast shot and shell.

On a drawing board he devised a deck-carriage for an 8-inch pivot gun mounted between the fore and main masts. Luckily he found a mechanic, an inventive genius, who set up a workshop in the New Orleans customhouse where he "contrived most ingeniously and constructed out of railroad iron one of the best carriages (of the slide and circle variety) for a pivot gun which I have ever seen." The *Sumter's* guns were shipped from supplies recently captured at the Norfolk Navy Yard though Semmes had to despatch a lieutenant in search of the pieces, which were side-tracked somewhere east of New Orleans to make way for army supplies and troops.

Improvising where necessary, picking up materials where he could find them, Semmes never flagged. To every detail he gave personal attention, even to procuring a set of flags of all nations. He would need those. Disguising one's nationality was very much a feature of naval warfare.

He had hoped changing the ship's rig would increase her speed under canvas, though her propeller, having no hoist, would prove a drag on her when she was under sail alone. On her trial runs on the Mississippi she made nine knots under steam. As a crowning touch Semmes smeared the *Sumter* with black paint and whitewash, putting it on in streaks much as ships are camouflaged in this modern day. So outlandish did this make the *Sumter* look, and so unsatisfactory was the result that Semmes abandoned the idea, washed off the whitewash and painted the whole ship black.

Slowly, while Semmes fumed at the manifold, mounting delays and frustrations, the *Sumter* assumed the character of a fighting ship. Frail, vulnerable, nothing to marvel at, she was still the child of his sweat, his ingenuity, and his industry. His pride in her began to grow. An impromptu man-of-war at best she was, nevertheless, a *fighting* ship. Once he got her to sea he believed he could send shivers up the back of Northern traders—and a good deal more than that.

He had hoped to get the *Sumter* to sea before the Mississippi was sealed for good. The blockade was thickening off the delta. Four Union vessels would soon be watchdogging the Mississippi Passes. In mid-May, with the beginning in sight, Semmes made a modest request for funds to fill his sea-chest. He expected the *Sumter* to pay her own expenses after that. Hopefully he requisitioned the Secretary of the Navy:

> Sir—I have the honor to inclose, herewith a requisition for the sum of $10,000, which I request may be remitted to the paymaster of the *Sumter*, in specie, for use during my contemplated cruise. I may find it necessary to coal several times, and to supply my crew with fresh provisions, &c., before I have the opportunity of replenishing my military chest from the enemy.

On May 24 Semmes confided to his diary, "A month has elapsed since I began the preparation of the *Sumter* for sea, and yet we are not ready. The river is not yet blockaded, but expected to be tomorrow." Then he appended a defiant note, "It must be a close blockade and by heavy vessels that will keep us in."

Another week dragged by. The *Brooklyn, Niagara, Minnesota,* and *Powhatan*, all powerful ships, had taken station off the Passes of the Mississippi. Semmes' diary reflected his feelings like a mirror, "My patience is sorely tried by the New Orleans mechanics. Saturday June 1st finds us not yet ready for sea! We are losing a great deal of precious time. The enemy's flag is being flaunted in our faces, at all our ports by his ships of war, and his vessels of commerce are passing, and repassing, on the ocean, in defiance, or in contempt of our power, and, as yet, we have not struck a blow."

The *Sumter's* officers were Southerners all and Semmes was proud of them. A loyal, able band they were, most of them old Navy men. Ten of them were to serve with him later on the *Alabama*. The First Lieutenant was John McIntosh Kell, a suave, affable, middle-aged officer who had resigned his commission in the United States Navy the moment Georgia seceded. Six-feet-two and well proportioned, he wore a magnificent beard that inclined to red. His career in the old Navy had been sound but undistinguished. On the *Susquehanna* he had sailed across the Pacific with Matthew Perry in 1853 to open up the Hermit Kingdom to world trade. Years before at a court martial at Pensacola Semmes had defended Kell, then a passed-midshipman, against a charge of mutiny for refusing to perform what he considered a menial duty. Kell's eyes beamed with kindness and gentleness, but, averred Semmes, "You will scarcely recognize him, as the same man, when you see him again on deck, arraigning some culprit, at the mast, for a breach of discipline."

The *Sumter's* Second Lieutenant was Robert T. Chapman of Alabama, a wardroom jester and "life of the mess table," a witty, anecdotal fellow whom Semmes called a "preux chevalier," as ready for a fight as for a dance. Bred in the old Navy he was of the "pure metal." John M. Stribling, Third Lieutenant, was "a native of the glorious little State of South Carolina," whose eyes "when excited at the thought of wrong, or oppression, have a peculiar stare of firmness, as much as to say, 'This rock shall fly, from its firm base as soon as I.'" Fourth and Junior Lieutenant, also a South Carolinian and barely twenty-four years old, was William E. Evans, a recent graduate of the Naval Academy who "like all new graduates feels the freshness of academic honors." Semmes appointed him navigating officer though he qualified it by saying, "I always navigated my ship, myself. I have every confidence in the ability of my young lieutenant, but I always found that I slept better, when surrounded by danger, after I had fixed the position of my ship, by my own observation."

From Virginia came the *Sumter's* surgeon, Francis L. Galt; another South Carolinian was Paymaster Henry Myers; Chief Engineer Miles J. Freeman had occupied the same post as a civilian when the *Sumter* was the *Habana*. Marine Lieutenant Beckett K. Howell was a brother-in-law of the Confederate President. He, like some of the others, was later to serve on the *Alabama*.

Of the crew of the *Sumter*—seventy-two seamen and twenty marines—not half a dozen were Southern-born. A miscellany of nationalities, stranded by the Northern blockade, they volunteered in batches for service on the *Sumter*. Though these merchant seamen were inexperienced in navy work they were willing to learn. "I have the advantage, therefore, of picking my crew," said Semmes. To Secretary Mallory he wrote, "I have an excellent set of men on board though they are nearly all green, and it will require some little practice and drilling at the guns to enable them to handle them creditably."

On June 3, 1861, the *Sumter* was commissioned into the Confederate States Navy. Semmes was as proud of his fledgling as if she were a fine new steam frigate. It was a beautiful afternoon. The ship was dressed for the occasion. The deck was gay with crinoline and bright talk. To the rousing strains of "Dixie," played by a volunteer three-piece band, the Confederate ensign, cut and sewed by the patriotic ladies of New Orleans, was raised over the first ship of war of the Southern Republic. A collation was spread on deck. Champagne sparkled in toasts to the ship, her captain, and a bon voyage filled with "blazing honors." With rare good courtesy Semmes welcomed his guests and then the *Sumter* put out into the river to demonstrate her speed and her gunpower.

The *Sumter's* speed was disappointing. Her nine knots under steam could be matched with margin to spare by most Federal cruisers. "It was with such disadvantages that I was to take the sea, alone, against a vindictive and relentless enemy, whose Navy already swarmed on our coasts and whose means of increasing it were inexhaustible."

Yet Semmes was undismayed, for he believed his luck was running. "The Sailor has a saying that 'Luck is a Lord' and we have trusted to luck." He little knew what a tenacious grip he had on the fickle lady or how suddenly she would one day desert him.

On June 18 the *Sumter* was ready for sea. His sailing orders had arrived from Richmond, the new capital of the Confederacy. This dispatch has long since vanished. Only through Semmes' reference to it do we know that Secretary Mallory reminded him of the rules that must guide him on his cruise. Semmes replied, "Should I be fortunate enough to reach the high seas you may rely upon my implicit obedience to your instructions, 'to do the enemy's commerce the greatest injury, in the shortest time.'"

Accompanying Semmes' sailing orders was a suggestion that he devise a cipher code to render his despatches to the Navy Department, if captured, unintelligible to the enemy. At a New Orleans bookstore Semmes bought two copies of *Reid's English Dictionary*. One he sent to Secretary Mallory; he retained the other for himself. Semmes then proposed a simple, cheap device that had been employed by American secret agents ever since the Revolution, and which may still be in use. A word was designated by the numbers of the page, of the column, and of the number of the word from the top of the column. Decoding was easy. The receiver of a code message needed only a copy of the same book. *Reid's Dictionary*, having two columns to the page, Semmes proposed designating the first column, A and the second, B. "Thus, if you wish to use the word 'Prisoner,' my reference to it would be as follows: 323, B. 15; the first number indicating the page; the letter, the column; and the second number the number of the word from the top of the column."

Taking aboard his powder, Semmes dropped seventy-five miles downstream to anchor between forts Jackson and St. Philip, the "impregnable" forts that were to prove not-so-impregnable when Farragut blasted his way past them to capture New Orleans the following April.

After three more days drilling his crew, Semmes steamed off again onto the broad, swift current of the Father of Waters and on down to Head of the Passes, twelve miles from the Gulf, where the Mississippi trisected into its principal outlets: Southwest Pass, South Pass, and Pass à L'Outre. Anchoring here he sweated it out for nine exasperating days, in excessive heat, tormented by clouds of mosquitoes and blistered by the glare of the sunswept river. One propitious, unguarded moment when he could crowd on steam and run the gauntlet into the Gulf, was all he prayed for.

No prisoner plotting escape from a dungeon was ever more wary or vigilant. Semmes would use any channel he found unwatched though he preferred Pass à L'Outre. Sealing this outlet was the United States cruiser *Brooklyn*, faster by four knots than the *Sumter*. The *Powhatan* watched the Southwest exit, and the *Minnesota* and *Niagara* barricaded the South Pass. Semmes was securely caged—and outgunned, to boot, by any one of these guardians of the Passes.

It would have been simple for the blockaders to have sent one of their number to the Head of the Passes, where Semmes was poised, and corked up the river like a bottle. Here they would have commanded all three outlets and the trapped Semmes would have been like a tiger biting at the bars of his cage. Semmes admitted to his diary he could feel the "anaconda drawing his folds around us." In his last letter to Mallory before breaking through the cordon he expressed amazement at the Federal inertia.

C. S. Steamer *Sumter*
June 30, 1861
Sir: I have the honor to inform the Department that I am still at my anchors at the Head of the Passes—the enemy investing both of the practical outlets. At Pass à L'Outre there are three ships, the *Brooklyn*, and another propeller, and a large side-wheel steamer; and at the Southwest Pass, there is the *Powhatan*, lying within half a mile of the bar, and not stirring an inch from her anchors, night or day. I am only surprised that the *Brooklyn* does not come up to this anchorage, which she might easily do—as there is water enough and no military precautions, whatever have been taken to hold the position—and thus effectually seal all the passes of the river by presence alone; which would enable the enemy to withdraw the remainder of his blockading force, for use elsewhere. . . . At present the worst feature of the blockade of Pass à L'Outre is, that the *Brooklyn* has the speed of me; so that even if I should run the bar, I could not hope to escape her, unless I surprised her, which with her close watch of the bar, at anchor nearby, both night and day, it will be exceed-

ingly difficult to do. I should be willing to try speed with the *Powhatan*, if I could hope to run the gantlet of her guns, without being crippled. . . . In the meantime I am drilling my green crew to a proper use of the great guns and small arms.

"Sunday, June 30. *Dies Memorabilis*." The Latin was Semmes'. Thus he began his journal the day the *Sumter* outmaneuvered the *Brooklyn* and fled free into the Gulf. Twice had he put on steam and glided down the pass at full speed on false starts only to see, beyond the Delta marshes, smoke curling from the *Brooklyn*, waiting to pounce on him. Fretting, he steamed back, banked his fires and resumed his vigil.

While he waited a fresh complication arose to plague him. The pilots stationed at the Head of the Passes balked at the idea of steering the *Sumter* through the narrow outlet and over the bar. It may well have been fear of Federal gunfire. Whatever it was Semmes was in no mood to temporize with suspected treachery to the Confederacy. He sent an armed patrol ashore to fetch the leaders of the conspiracy, for as such he viewed it. With threats of condign punishment Semmes lined up the stammering, recalcitrant pilots in his cabin and notified them pointblank that one of them, to be relieved at weekly intervals, would remain a prisoner in his cabin until he had a chance to run the blockade. There was bite and menace in his words. His suspicion of defection was to come true. In April, 1862, Farragut, thundering up the river, found the pilots "faithful auxiliaries."

This bright Sunday morning muster was in progress on the *Sumter* when a fisherman brought word that the *Brooklyn* had chased off after a sail and was no longer in sight at her station off Pass à L'Outre. Semmes' decision was instant. He would take the tide at its flood. Mounting the horseblock by the mainmast he gave his orders calmly and distinctly. Muster was cut short. In ten minutes the banked fires under the boilers were glowing and steam was hissing through the pipes. The anchor was hove in and the *Sumter* "bounded off like a thing of life on this new race" for the "glad waters of the dark blue sea." As if to lend a helping hand the Mississippi added her four-knot current to the ship's speed. As the *Sumter* sped along the pilot's courage suddenly melted. Pale and agitated, he protested to Semmes he was unfamiliar with the bar of Pass à L'Outre for which they were speeding.

"I am a Southwest Pass pilot. I know nothing of the other passes."

Semmes exploded. "What! Didn't you know I was lying at the Head of the Passes for the very purpose of taking any one of the outlets through which an opportunity of escape might present itself? Yet, you dare tell me you know but one of them. You've been deceiving me."

The pilot stammered, but Semmes broke in. "Take us out!" His eyes resembled gray steel. "If you run us ashore or put us in the hands of the enemy, I'll swing you to the yardarm as a traitor."

Then he ordered the jack hoisted for another pilot. Determined not to squander this chance to make his getaway Semmes had decided, if unable to pick up a new pilot to drop the recalcitrant at once—which he did—and to steer his ship across the bar himself, banking on the slight knowledge of the channel he had acquired as the lighthouse inspector. Meantime the *Brooklyn* had spied the *Sumter's* black smoke and was dashing back to the bar under full sail and steam. The two ships were equidistant from the bar, but the *Sumter* had the advantage of the river current.

Turning to a lieutenant who had served on the *Brooklyn*, Semmes asked, "What think you of our prospects?"

"Prospect, sir! Not the least in the world. There is no possible chance of our escaping that ship. Even if we get over the bar ahead of her she'll overhaul us in a very short time. The *Brooklyn* makes fourteen knots, sir."

Nothing daunted Semmes replied, "That was the report on her trial trip, but you know all such reports are exaggerated; ten to one she has no better speed, if so good, as the *Sumter*."

"You will see, sir. We made a passage in her, only a few months ago from Tampico to Pensacola, and averaged about thirteen knots the whole distance."

Presently a welcome sight greeted Semmes' eyes, a boat shoving off from the pilot's station and making for the *Sumter*. Four stout blacks pulled at the ashen oars. The pilot seated in the stern sheets was swaying his body to and fro as though to hasten her speed. More appealing still "was a beautiful woman, the pilot's wife, standing on the balcony of the pilot house waving him on to his duty with a handkerchief. I uncovered my head gallantly to my fair country-woman . . . a few moments more and the gallant young fellow stood on the horseblock beside me."

First Lieutenant Kell, who stood at the head of the gangway, gave this touch to the *Sumter's* nip-and-tuck race for liberty, "In less time than it can be told the boat was alongside of us and a line thrown out to pull it to our gangway, and the next moment a stalwart young fellow jumped over our side and took his position at our pilot stand, saying 'Give her all the steam she can carry!' "

On swept the *Sumter* past the lighthouse wharf where other petticoats fluttered in the breeze, "the owners of which were also waving handkerchiefs of encouragement to the *Sumter*. I could see my sailors' eyes brighten at this spectacle, for the sailor's heart is capacious enough to love the whole sex."

The bar was half a mile away. Aground on the bar was a German steamer whose crew had run out a kedge, with hawsers stretched directly across the channel to haul her off. Quickly they slackened the lines to let the *Sumter* pass and "in another bound the *Sumter* was outside the bar, and the Confederate flag was upon the high seas!"

Had power been the only factor in this drama hastening to its climax the *Brooklyn* must have won. Simple arithmetic would have given the *Brooklyn* victory. But there was something more—superior seamanship—that, with the odds heavily weighted for the *Brooklyn*, tipped the scales in Semmes' favor.

As the *Sumter* cleared the bar and dashed for the open Gulf the *Brooklyn* was three and a half miles distant, maybe four, out of gun range. Semmes knew he had to keep away from the big Northern cruiser's heavy broadside. It would have crushed the *Sumter* like an egg shell. The log showed the *Sumter* making nine and a half knots and the chief engineer reported that as soon as the "foaming" in his boilers subsided he could add another half knot to her speed.

Once across the bar the *Sumter* slackened her speed for an instant to drop the youthful pilot who grasped Semmes' hand warmly as he went down the companionway, "Now, Captain," he said, "you are all clear. Give her hell and let her go!"

Smoke was pouring from the *Brooklyn's* funnel as she ate up the distance between the two ships. Semmes ordered the money chest and ship's papers brought on deck. He would throw them overboard if he was forced to strike his colors. He could see the *Brooklyn's* quarterdeck crowded with officers, their telescopes focused on the *Sumter*. Any moment he expected to hear the whiz of a shot, but the enemy held her fire.

Now Semmes played his last card. The breeze had lightened. Knowing the *Sumter* could sail closer to the wind than her foe and believing the Federal captain incapable of executing this maneuver too skillfully, Semmes swung into the breeze, hugging the wind as close as his yards could brace.

A sudden rain squall blew in from the Gulf, hiding pursuer from the pursued, drenching Semmes and his crew. As the rain swept off to leeward the *Brooklyn* reappeared. She had gained on him. Now she loomed closer than before, with her heavy battery and tall spars. Semmes for a moment feared the forebodings of his lieutenant would come true. The *Brooklyn* was drawing dangerously near, and "I could not but admire the majesty of her appearance, with her broad, flaring bows, and clean, and beautiful run, and her masts, and yards, as taut and square, as those of an old-time sailing frigate."

All at once the breeze picked up; it started blowing strongly, and Semmes' tactics began paying off. The chief engineer reported the foaming in his boilers had ceased, and his engine was working beautifully, giving the propeller a few additional turns per minute. The *Sumter*, under both sail and steam, skimmed through the dark water, gaining perceptibly. She was "eating the *Brooklyn* out of wind" as he had hoped. "I knew, of course, that as soon as she fell into my wake she could be compelled to furl her sails." Already the *Brooklyn's* great sheets were beginning to flap.

Semmes breathed more freely. On went the chase, for forty miles, with the *Brooklyn* at the *Sumter's* heels, but falling behind continually. In a last effort of desperation the *Brooklyn* fired a single shell from her huge pivot gun. It fell far short, with a great splash. Baffled, the *Brooklyn* abandoned the chase, veered about, and retraced her steps to Pass à L'Outre. Then it was Semmes witnessed the most beautiful of "many beautiful sights at sea" when the *Brooklyn* "let fly all her sheets and halliards at once, and clewed up, and furled, in man-of-war style, all her sails, from courses to royals." The hands of his watch pointed to half past three.

The gauntlet was run. The caged eagle was free. Semmes uttered a silent prayer. Yet, "we fired no gun of triumph in the face of the enemy—my powder was too precious for that—but I sent the crew aloft to man the rigging, and three such cheers were given for the Confederate flag, 'that little bit of striped bunting,' that had waved from the *Sumter's* peak during the exciting chase, as could proceed only from the throats of American seamen in the act of defying a tyrant."

To crown the day's adventure all hands were ordered to "splice the main brace"—drink to the success of the Southern Confederacy. In the wardroom Semmes and his officers poured a libation of choice Madeira, "gift from finest cellar in New Orleans," and stowed away for a momentous occasion.

Captain Charles Poor of the *Brooklyn* was severely censured for letting the *Sumter* escape, but his government failed to reckon with the resourcefulness of his foeman. Imputations of treason in the engine room of the *Brooklyn* were freely bandied about. Poor's undoing was in permitting himself to be lured off his station by every sail that passed in the Gulf. He had been ordered to watch Pass à L'Outre. Had he not romped off vainly after a scrubby blockade runner and a few prize dollars he might have thwarted the destruction of millions of dollars in ships and cargo that Semmes, in the *Sumter* and later the *Alabama*, was to send flaming to the bottom. As it was he edged almost within broadside range of the *Sumter*, within an ace, as it were, of blotting out the entire Confederate Navy—for such the *Sumter* was at this juncture—at one blast.

In the log of the *Brooklyn* Captain Poor entered the sad, pregnant words, "Abandoned the chase and stood back to the

Pass." They utterly fail to convey even a whisper of their momentous import.

The *Sumter* sailed on, shaping her course across the Gulf for the south side of Cuba. Enemy ships of war were coming and going and the *Sumter* might stumble on one of them any moment. One menace succeeded another. It meant eternal vigilance. But Semmes was now "upon my mission, to strike for the right! to endeavor to sweep from the seas the commerce. . . . What an eventful career we have before us!"

Night came down rapidly over the unending heave of the dark sea. The wind died gently as the sun declined and disappeared. Like a "liberated prisoner" Semmes drank in the pure air, "fresh from the Gulf, untainted by malaria and untouched of mosquito's wing." In the dusk he leaned on the carriage of a howitzer, reflecting on the great day's events. "The sun had gone down behind a screen of purple and gold, and to add to the beauty of the scene, as night set in, a blazing comet, whose tail spanned nearly a quarter of the heavens, mirrored itself within a hundred feet of our little bark, as she ploughed her noiseless way through the waters."

How singular that a year later another comet, Swift's, luminous, mysterious, should have hung in the sky the night the *Alabama* sailed away on her stupendous odyssey!

⚓

⚓

8 *Enter James Bulloch*

On June 4, 1861, the day after the *Sumter* was commissioned at New Orleans, Captain James Dunwoody Bulloch disembarked from the steamer *North American* at Liverpool. His roundabout journey from the capital of the Confederacy had taken exactly twenty-five days.

On his person Bulloch bore no credentials, no written instructions, no letters of introduction, nothing to reveal his identity or the undercover nature of his mission. No one would suspect that he was the secret naval agent extraordinary of the Confederate States of America. Yet locked in Bulloch's mental strongbox was the South's top naval secret.

James Bulloch was distinguished-looking. His modish mufti suggested a banker or merchant prince. Whatever his profession, one thing was easily apparent: he was an aristocrat to his finger tips. The most casual observer would have agreed to this. A Southerner, scion of a Georgia family of wealth and culture he was, in addition, the uncle of a small lad of three named Theodore Roosevelt. Adorning Bulloch's face was a huge mustache that flared sidewards into muttonchop whiskers. His scant hair was meticulously parted, carefully combed and slicked down on his well-shaped head. Ladies considered him handsome and adored his pleasantries.

Bulloch brought drama with him. His arrival in Britain touched off a sharp diplomatic collision, reeking with espionage and intrigue, that pushed England and America to the verge of a shooting war. Bulloch himself was to wage a bitter, private war with the secret agents of the United States, seeking to scuttle his plans. This man was the biggest figure in the host of emissaries, propagandists, spies, *agents provocateurs*, and diplomatic commissioners sent to England and France by the Confederate government during its four years of existence.

Bulloch had come direct from Montgomery. President Davis and Secretary Mallory had despatched him secretly to Europe to negotiate the purchase or construction of ironclads, as well as the acquisition of six propeller-driven raiding cruisers to be launched against Northern commerce. A fervent Confederate, Bulloch shared with Mallory a dream of constructing ships powerful enough to smash their way into Chesapeake Bay and up the Potomac to lay waste Washington, the very citadel of Yankeedom.

His job boiled down to creating in foreign shipyards a navy for a would-be nation whose ports were blockaded or about to be, whose ships, if built, would have no home ports open to them, and whose credit was always shaky. That was little enough to work with.

Bulloch moved easily into British social circles. He knew how never to let his right hand know what his left was doing. Hardheaded, affable, intelligent, sound in business judgment, a good diplomat, he was the ideal man for the task of violating Britain's neutrality without stirring up too great a rumpus and of piloting the Confederacy's English-built ships through the mazes of Britain's Foreign Enlistment Act and onto the high seas.

Behind Bulloch lay a naval career that had carried him through the Mexican War and the grade of lieutenant in the United States Navy. When Congress subsidized the California mail steamers with the rider that the ships be commanded by naval officers Bulloch was detailed to the mail service. But the pay was poor and seeking better emolument he had resigned and engaged himself to a private mail line.

On April 13, the day Fort Sumter capitulated to Beauregard's cannon, Bulloch was at New Orleans, master of the mail steamer *Bienville*, plying between that city and New York. Northern-owned, the ship was to sail the next day. Bulloch had not concealed his Southern sympathies. But first, he must return his ship to her owners at New York. When Louisiana authorities boarded the *Bienville* to seize her or buy her at pistol's point, Bulloch balked, insisting he had no authority to sell the ship and rather than submit to seizure would steam her down the river and take his chances running the guns of Fort Jackson. It grieved him to desert his friends in order to save the property of those who were his enemies. But such was James Bulloch.

A telegram to Montgomery laid the matter squarely before President Davis, who, happily, replied at once, "Do not detain the *Bienville*. We do not wish to interfere with private property." On April 14 the *Bienville* steamed down the Mississippi for New York, with the United States ensign snapping at her peak. She slid safely past Fort Jackson where there still waved a star-spangled flag, though all the stars were obliterated save the seven representing the Confederate States.

On April 22 the *Bienville* docked at New York where Bulloch found the Federal government had chartered the liner. Had it not been for Bulloch's high sense of honor the *Bienville* might have proved invaluable to the Confederacy. She was soon armed and sent off to join the Federal squadron blockading the port of Savannah.

Awaiting Bulloch at New York was a sealed message inviting him to speed to Montgomery without delay. Destroying the compromising missive, Bulloch waited a week before starting his circuitous journey to the Confederate capital. Acting too precipitately might bring on arrest. On May 7 he entered the office of Secretary Mallory, who promptly informed him that, "Our present Navy consists of a little steamer of five hundred tons, called the *Sumter*, under the command of Raphael Semmes."

It was pure coincidence that Charles Francis Adams, America's watchdog of British neutrality, landed at Liverpool on the very day—May 14—that England accorded belligerent rights to the Confederate States. It was depressing news for the just-arrived Minister—the North's first diplomatic defeat on the British front. With Adams and his agents Bulloch was to tangle oft and late in this drama for which the cast was assembling.

President Lincoln had reached into one of the nation's best-qualified families for his minister to London. Adams' father, one-time incumbent of the same ministry, had laid the foundations of American foreign policy. His grandfather, John Adams, after helping negotiate peace with Great Britain at the end of the Revolution, had served as the nation's first minister to the Court of St. James. Diplomacy ran deep in the Adams blood, and Charles Francis was now in his family's traditional element. He had inherited a distaste for Britain's diplomatic policies. Cold as a New England winter, precise, austere, he was the right man for the job of protesting, with sharp diplomatic jabs, England's ill-disguised aid to the Confederacy.

James Bulloch wasted not a moment getting at the business that brought him to England. Clearly he was cast in the ticklish role of tightrope walker. The legal hurdles were delicate. Britain's Foreign Enlistment Act forbade British subjects to enlist within the realm on vessels of either belligerent. What was done beyond British jurisdiction was something else again. Warships of the North and South were forbidden to bring prizes into British ports. The act made it a misdemeanor to fit out armed ships for either belligerent under penalty of fine, imprisonment and seizure. But it was silent on merchantmen built in Britain and armed on the high seas. The best legal advice added up to, "The mere building of a ship within her Majesty's dominion by any person, subject or no subject, is no offense, whatever may be the intention of the parties, because the offense is not in the building but in the equipping."

This was the loophole through which Bulloch drove his cruiser program. A discreet man, he realized that the construction of ironclads would arouse suspicions and endanger his whole plan. To build what were obviously ships of war would, here at the outset, resemble brazen defiance of Britain's neutrality, even if he could dig up a shipbuilder to take a chance. Concealing the purpose or destination of such vessels was out of the question—for the time being. Even the most gullible would never believe he was building ironclads for yachting in the Channel. He could not yet afford to drop his incognito and expose his hand.

Consequently Bulloch decided to give the cruisers precedence. He would speed construction of "merchant" ships that could weigh anchor from England unarmed, under British flag, British master, and British crew. The ships would be built for James Bulloch, private citizen. Fictitious indeed, but no apparent infringement of Britain's neutrality.

Proceeding to the yards of Miller & Sons, shipbuilders at Liverpool, he contracted for a merchant vessel, the *Oreto*. Interestingly, the ship followed the standard lines of an English gunboat. The Millers had a "tolerable notion" of her ultimate destination, but they kept their suspicions to themselves and Bulloch never confirmed them. His contract merely called for delivery at Liverpool of a screw steamer, fitted for sea. It was to be handed over to James Bulloch personally. Where he got the money to pay for his ship was no concern of the Millers, and they never asked. The name *Oreto* was bestowed upon the ship to foil inquisitive workers and curiosity seekers nosing through the yards. Ostensibly, she would fly the colors of a mercantile firm in Palermo, Italy. But the career of the *Florida, née Oreto*, is another story.

Enter now the Laird Brothers, the kingdom's biggest shipbuilding firm whose Birkenhead Iron Works stretched imposingly for a quarter-mile along the opposite bank of the Mersey above Liverpool. After arranging the deal for the *Oreto* Bulloch crossed the river one June day in 1861 and drove up to the Laird yard where he was soon closeted with the two sons of the founder. The Messrs. Laird listened eagerly to the suave Southerner. He wanted them to build a ship for him. Grapevine had brought whispers of this charming stranger from overseas, with ship orders in his pocket and credits piling up at the counting house of Fraser, Trenholm & Company, fiscal agents for the Confederate government. Never at any future time, however, were the Lairds to admit they had guilty knowledge of Bulloch's plan to utilize the ship they were to build for strikes at Northern trade.

Bulloch had pictured to himself a ship equal to any of Her Majesty's ships of corresponding class, but superior to any vessel in the world in ability to rove the seas at will, even though lacking both a home port and reliable sources of supply. Of course, Bulloch did not refer directly to any such revealing specifications. As with the Millers he sought an unarmed ship to be delivered to him "on the Mersey at the port of Liverpool." The Lairds' chief concern was financial security. Bulloch quickly reassured them in this respect. It is conceivable the Lairds were deceived as to the ultimate use of the ship. Tactfully, at least, they went through the motions of ignorance. Bulloch himself affirmed, "They did not know for what purpose the ship was intended when they agreed to build her." Never, he insisted, was the objective of the *Alabama*, for such she was to be, discussed or even alluded to until she was afloat as a Confederate cruiser. He disclosed nothing of her contemplated armament or where he procured it. Even today, mystery shrouds the source of the *Alabama's* weapons.

So much for that. Now to the building of the ship. John Laird, Senior, was proud of his firm's handiwork. Of the *Alabama* he later said, "She was the finest cruiser of her class in the world." Bulloch was minute in telling what he wanted from the builders. Speed was the first essential. She must be able to show her heels to anything on the ocean. He wanted fifteen knots. To this end she must combine the best of both sail and steam—canvas for cruising, steam for action, both when needed. Bulloch envisioned a self-sustaining vessel with resources within herself such as no other man-of-war could boast. She must be equipped to make ordinary repairs to her machinery, spars, and armament at sea or in ports where mechanical facilities were not available.

To insure speed he insisted on a contrivance whereby her two-bladed screw could be triced up into a propeller-well clear of the water and hence no drag on her when running under canvas alone. The hull of his ship was to be of wood, a requirement that retarded construction and hiked the cost, but necessary for the iron of which British merchantmen were now conventionally built was brittle and would crack and splinter dangerously when struck by the shot.

While Bulloch and the Lairds bargained and tinkered with rough projections—and it took over a fortnight—the North and South were drawing first blood at Bull Run three thousand miles away. England watched breathlessly. Her upper classes and high government officials read with undisguised delight the London *Times*, whose war correspondent, William H. Russell, would soon regale his readers with lurid, on-the-scene accounts of the Federal rout at Bull Run. The Prime Minister himself, Lord Palmerston, would add the unkindest cut of all by characterizing the battle as "Yankee Run."

On August 1, 1861, Bulloch signed a contract with the Lairds to build for his personal account a ship of the specifications agreed on. Now the shipbuilders went to their drawing boards. They were Scotch, and they built well. Pride of achievement was ingrained in them. Like Kipling's Anthony Gloster they had attained pre-eminence by keeping their light "shining a little in front o' the next." Critical, hard to please, they ransacked Britain for suitable timber for the stem, keelson, and sternpost. So meticulous were they that three sternposts were discarded after being partly bored to take the screwshaft because of ever-so-slight defects. Since they were accustomed to building iron ships, this one of wood would take longer. But soon things were humming in the dockyard slip assigned to her. The Confederate Navy Department had not yet picked a name for this embryo cruiser. Bulloch knew only that he was slated to command her or the *Oreto*. His ambition was sea duty, rather than building ships for others to command. Secretary Mallory had promised him command of the first British-built cruiser to reach his hands.

The Lairds gave the ship a serial number, 290. It meant simply she was the 290th vessel turned out by their yards. This numerical title was soon invested with fantastic implications. The fact is the cruiser bore three appellations in her passage from the drawing board to a commissioned ship of war. Nor was it long before the 290's comely frame, in the binding grip of her outside planking, began to emerge in the graceful curves of her counter and the delicate wave-lines of her bow. By contrast with the iron hulls people were accustomed to see in the Birkenhead slips and ways the graceful 290 stood out in bold relief at the south end of the yard. People began talking and wondering. Was this a warship? Whose? Suspicion fastened on her, only to be heightened by the Lairds' refusal to identify the ship's purchaser.

Bulloch watched over his creation like a fond father gazing on a growing child, though to avoid suspicion he visited the yard only when absolutely necessary to consult the Lairds on details of construction. He had, in fact, gone underground (in a sense) the moment he reached Britain. He was residing in a small cottage in a nearby Liverpool suburb, yet "I soon learned," he wrote, "that spies were lurking about, and tampering with the workmen at Messrs. Lairds', and that a private detective named Maguire was taking a deep and abiding interest in my personal movements." The furore was setting in. Soon ignorant Northern sympathizers were clamoring that the ship was labeled 290 because that many Southern partisans among Britain's rich aristocracy had raised a pool to finance her construction. New York newspapers, equally ignorant, seized on the innocent number and headlined it into an absurdly mysterious significance.

In his social contacts with John Laird, Senior, head of the firm, he maintained the pleasant fiction that the 290 was intended only for the inoffensive usages of commerce. Not even to his closest associates—not even to his colleague, Lieutenant James North, whom the Confederacy had despatched to England to implement Bulloch's ironclad procurement program—did the Confederacy's secret naval agent reveal more than was absolutely necessary.

Summer was passing. The indefatigable Bulloch had other fish to fry now—the ironclads Secretary Mallory had set his heart on. Mid-August brought more exciting news to England—particularly to Bulloch. Raphael Semmes and the *Sumter* had escaped into the Gulf and dashed into the Caribbean where he was having a grand time despoiling Federal shipping.

⚓

⚓

9 *Stars and Bars in Cuban Waters*

At daybreak on July 4, 1861, the dapper, pocket-sized *Sumter* was gliding leisurely along the south coast of Cuba, burning her meager coal supply far faster than her captain had calculated. Yet this contingency seemed not to daunt Raphael Semmes, who, after the excitement of the *Golden Rocket's* destruction the night before, was sleeping soundly when the officer of the deck reported two sail in sight.

Semmes was out of his berth and on deck in a moment. The trade wind was light. Rain squalls were occasionally spattering the cruiser. Through the misty dawn Semmes made out dead ahead two brigantines, both apparently American. There was no possibility of the ships eluding him, no need for ruse or stratagem. Running up the Confederate colors Semmes slowly closed quarters on his quarry. When a few hundred yards from her prey the *Sumter* lay to. The pattern of capture was repeated: shots across the bow to make the strangers heave to, boarding parties to fetch the ships' masters and papers. From the quarterdeck Semmes gazed on the scene like a hunter fascinated by two unsuspecting ducks he was about to bag.

His prizes were the *Cuba*, Captain Strout, and the *Machias*, both from Maine, and bound for England with Spanish-owned sugar. A sweet haul, to be sure, but therein lay the catch: neutral property. That alone kept Semmes from firing them as he had the *Golden Rocket*. It gave him, however, an opportunity to sound out Spain's disposition toward harboring prizes in her colonial ports. Here at the outset of his cruise he would, if he could, write the rules of the game he was playing, or, at least, seek to bend the laws of nations to his own purposes. Versed in the intricacies of marine statutes, he knew the history of prizes taken at sea probably better than any officer in the United States Navy. He saw a parallel between the *Sumter* in 1861 and the American raider *Argus* in 1813. In the War of 1812 the Navy Department had ordered commanding officers to "destroy all you capture, unless in some extraordinary cases that clearly warrant an exception." Semmes really had no desire to destroy his prizes, at least, not yet. The Confederacy needed ships. Perhaps, he could find a way out of using the torch though he was mindful of his instructions to "burn, sink and destroy." If not, so be it. He would light up the ocean.

England and France had warned both North and South against sending prizes into their ports. Spain had not yet spoken. Having no home port open in which to shepherd his captures, Semmes thought perhaps Madrid might be induced to pursue a more lenient course and give his trophies haven until a Confederate Admiralty Court could adjudicate them. Spain wasted little love on the United States. For years the Americans had dallied with the idea of snatching away Cuba, the Pearl of the Antilles, nearly the last of Spain's far-flung colonial empire in the Western World. Spain might welcome the warships of a new power that was about to knock the cockiness out of the despised Yankees.

Placing prize crews on the two ships Semmes took them in tow and headed for Cienfuegos sixty miles away. The determined skipper of the *Cuba* protested so violently against the seizure of his ship that Semmes curtly reminded him he was a prisoner of the Confederate States and would better hold his tongue. Five knots was the best the *Sumter* could make, impeded by the two heavily-laden prizes. The *Cuba's* towline parted twice. Towards nightfall he cast her off with instructions to the prize crew, Midshipman A. G. Hudgins and four seamen, to make sail and rendezvous off Cienfuegos.

The next morning, July 5, the *Sumter* was approaching Cienfuegos Light when the lookout sighted two more sail. By now the cruiser's crew were becoming enamored of this business "pretty much as the veteran foxhunter does in view of the chase. They moved with great alacrity in obedience to orders; the seamen springing aloft to furl the sails like so many squirrels." Down in the boiler room the firemen shoveled on more coal. The *Sumter* herself, trailing plumes of black smoke, seemed to spring forward in pursuit of the doomed craft as if she too knew what was going on.

The hunting could hardly be better. By dusk Semmes had grabbed off two more prizes, the *Ben Dunning* of Maine and the *Albert Adams* of Massachusetts. More Cuban-owned sugar, and documented correctly. There was just enough daylight left for Semmes to make this haul; an hour or two later and at least one of the vessels would have escaped. Manning them with prize crews Semmes ordered the ships to stand in toward Cienfuegos Light, distant about twelve miles. When the master of the *Ben Dunning* appealed to Semmes to release his vessel because two ladies, his wife and her companion, were on board, both convalescing from yellow fever, Semmes declined the petition but assured the ladies every tenderness and courtesy, including the services of the *Sumter's* surgeon.

July 6 dawned bright and beautiful, a perfect tropic morning. The Cuban shore, vivid with luxuriant, green vegetation and flowers of every hue, ran down to the water's edge like a many-colored carpet. Nature has never painted a more seductive landscape. From the shore a breeze, "blowing so gently as scarce to disturb a tress on the brow of beauty, came laden with the most delicious perfume of shrub and flower."

Three of his four prizes were circling gracefully to hold their positions off the light. The *Cuba* had not shown up. Semmes could not understand what was keeping her, nor was he to learn her fate for months to come. As the *Sumter* neared the harbor good fortune leaned over and literally slapped Semmes in the face. Coming on deck he noticed a smudge on the sky up the river that led to Cienfuegos.

"Is that smoke coming down the river?" asked Semmes of the young watch officer.

"I'll see in a moment, sir," replied the youngster. Springing up the ratlines he took a look and reported, "There's a small steam tug coming down, with three vessels in tow, two barks and a brig."

"What nationality?" asked Semmes.

"American colors, sir. All of them."

Luck had indeed—or so it seemed—thrown the fledgling sea-raider an unlooked-for bonanza. This one had a perplexing string tied to it, for all the vessels were still in neutral waters. If Semmes molested them within a marine league, three geographical miles, of shore, he would violate international law. Secretary Mallory had cautioned him to adhere to the laws of nations. Semmes himself was a stickler for obeying the rules, though at times he would interpret them to suit his needs. The setting called for finesse. Quickly Semmes ran up Spanish colors. At the same time he hoisted a Spanish jack at the fore to signal for a pilot. With a wink of his eye he ordered the deck officer to disarrange the *Sumter's* yards a little, cock-billing this one slightly in one direction, and that one in another, to give the appearance of a care-lessly-handled merchant ship. To complete the ruse he hustled most of his crew below. It left the possibility his unsuspecting victims would recognize two of his prizes as their companions at Cienfuegos the day before. Luckily, however, his prize masters took the hint and ran up American flags. This mystified the newcomers who, nevertheless, came on unsuspectingly until clear of the mouth of the harbor. Here the tug cast them off, where-upon all three raised clouds of canvas and pressed seaward.

The little steam tug, now ready for an upriver customer, chugged alongside the *Sumter*. The pilot leaped aboard. Semmes was waiting.

"Are you going to Cienfuegos?" asked the pilot in Spanish.

Semmes replied pleasantly in kind, "Yes, but I'm waiting a little to take back those ships you have just towed down."

"*Diabolo!*" exclaimed the pilot. "How can that be? They are *Americanos del Norte,* bound to Boston and New York."

"That's just what I want," said Semmes. "We are *Confederados,* and we have *la guerra* with the *Americanos del Norte.*"

"*Caramba!*" exclaimed the excited pilot. "That's good. Give her the steam quick, captain."

"No, no," replied Semmes. "Wait awhile. I must respect your Queen and the Captain General. They command in these waters, within the league. I'll wait until the ships have passed beyond that."

Semmes held off until the three ships had crossed the imaginary marine league, or rather until he, the pilot, and an English sailor on the tug estimated they had winged out of Spanish territorial waters. Then he unleashed the *Sumter* and pounced on the astonished prey. A gun boomed; the raider's Spanish flag descended, and the Confederate colors rose to the peak. Obediently, the merchantmen hove to as ordered: *West Wind* of Rhode Island, *Louise Kilham* of Massachusetts, and *Naiad* of New York. Another harvest of sugar, but again, neutral-owned. Semmes herded the captives back to join his growing prize flotilla. He had struck it rich. Eight prizes in all, counting the *Cuba* and the *Golden Rocket,* the greatest single-handed forty-eight hour haul in the history of American naval operations.

Proudly the *Sumter* led the triumphal procession into Cienfuegos harbor. At her peak fluttered the Stars and Bars; at her heels plodded six trophies. A startling spectacle to be sure. As she came abreast of the white fort a mile up the river a flurry of musket balls suddenly whistled through the rigging. On the parapet of the fort sentinels were gesticulating furiously to indicate the *Sumter* must come to anchor—or else. An antiquated cannon poked its nose through an embrasure as if it meant business. It was laughable but Semmes complied immediately though his prizes, all flying American colors, were permitted to proceed up to the city. Despatching Lieutenant Evans to the fort Semmes demanded an explanation of his gunpowder welcome. The answer he came back with was simple enough. The *Commandante* was not acquainted with the flag of the new Southern Republic. It belonged to no nation on earth he had ever heard of. For all he knew Semmes might be a pirate.

Appeal to vanity was not the least of Semmes' arts. The commandants of small Latin American forts were susceptible to the broadest flattery. So he hurried Lieutenant Evans back to the fort to invite the *Commandante* to split a bottle of wine with the captain of the *Sumter.* Presently that dignitary jangled up the companionway, arrayed in glittering splendor. A huge sword clanked at his belt. Semmes and his officers were drawn up smartly on deck. Snappy salutes and a flourish by the *Sumter's* three-piece band puffed up the visitor like a pigeon while Semmes captivated him with attention. He was an old hand at the charm business. In his cabin Semmes broke out a bottle of champagne and soon he and his guest were hobnobbing like long-lost friends. The *Commandante* was profuse in his apologies for the fusillade of musketry. With each glass he waxed mellower, more obliging. Semmes assured him he had no thought of storming the fort (an easy operation, confided Semmes later, as there was but a corporal's guard to defend the place). Nor did he intend "to sack the town of Cienfuegos, after the fashion of the Drakes and other English sea-robbers," who had left so vivid an impression upon Spanish memory as to make this remote, tiny outpost wary of all strange craft three hundred years after Drake's passing.

They laughed merrily over the *Commandante's* fears, just so much ado over nothing. Of course, the *Sumter* could proceed up to Cienfuegos. Semmes would find the governor of the city most hospitable. Came a last glass and Semmes' guest proposed a toast, *"Viva la Confederación del Sud!"*

So far so fine. The *Sumter* edged up the river. Hardly had her anchor splashed to the bottom of the city's embarcadero before the whole community began flocking to the landing, as if to welcome a hero home. Small boats swarmed around the little cruiser, whose crew was promptly lionized. Magically, baskets of wine, fruit, flowers and even "squalling chickens" were showered on the ship.

That night homes of the sugar-rich planters resounded to the strumming of guitars and popping of champagne corks while the *Sumter's* young officers danced with dark-haired, dark-eyed donas, who found irresistible fascination in the soft-voiced, courtly-mannered Southerners. Many were the shiny brass buttons that vanished from uniforms that evening, begged off by imploring black eyes, or bartered for a kiss, by ladies who would not be denied.

But festivities were not for Raphael Semmes. He was worried. His dash across the Gulf and the successive strikes at Northern shipping had burned coal extravagantly. Only a week had elapsed since the *Sumter* squeezed through the blockade. But already she was running out of fuel. Her bunkers had barely enough left for twenty-four hours' steaming. Coal was costly and his 10,000 dollar sea-chest would run out just as rapidly as his coal if he dug into it too often. Taking stock he realized that hopping from port to port, coaling once a week, would be a dead giveaway. Federal warships could pick up his trail and simply hang on until they caught up with him. Then, a broadside or two and the *Sumter* would rest at the bottom of the tropic sea.

He must cruise under sail to a position where he could lie in wait for his prey. Then he need put on steam only when stalking or waylaying such prizes as he was unable to lure within range of his guns. Cienfuegos was a trap, tighter even than the Mississippi, blockaded at all three Passes. One Federal warship off the Cienfuegos light would snuff out the *Sumter* after but a moment's fire. He decided, on leaving Cienfuegos, to steer for the great ocean passage off Cape St. Roque, where Brazil's great hump bulges eastward, out across the South Atlantic. It was the well-beaten track of vessels bound from the east coast to South America and California, not to mention the Far East. He had visions of reaping here "a rich harvest from the enemy's commerce." But coal he must have, and at once. It was abundant at Cienfuegos, but it took gold to get it—and the price was little short of extortion.

But, ahead of coal, came a match of wits with His Excellency Don José de la Pozuela, Governor of the City of Cienfuegos, an outwardly imposing old fellow whose diplomatic talent was slight and whose knowledge of international law was less. To this pompous old gentleman Semmes now addressed a masterpiece "written more for the eye of the Spanish Premier at Madrid than for the Governor of a small provincial town."

If Semmes could intrigue the Spanish governor into granting sanctuary to Southern prizes, it would virtually commit Spain to an alliance with the Confederacy. Cuba, lying athwart the Gulf of Mexico, was a strategic outpost of supreme importance. What a powerful bastion the South would have!

With these thoughts—and that of coal—running through his mind, Semmes took up his pen:

> Sir: I have the honor to inform you, of my arrival at the Port of Cienfuegos with seven prizes of war. These vessels are the brigantines *Cuba* (not yet arrived), *Machias*, *Ben Dunning*, *Albert Adams*, and *Naiad*; the barks *West Wind* and *Louisa Kilham*, property of citizens of the United States, which States, as your Excellency is aware, are waging an aggressive and unjust war upon the Confederate States, which I have the honor, with this ship under my command, to represent. I have sought a port of Cuba, with these prizes, with the expectation that Spain will extend to the cruisers of the Confederate States, the same friendly reception that, in similar circumstances, she would extend to the cruisers of the enemy; in other words, that she will permit me to leave the captured vessels within her jurisdiction until they can be adjudicated by a Court of Admiralty of the Confederate States.

From this take-off Semmes continued by apprising the Governor that the United States had seized all the naval forces of the old government and was thus "enabled to blockade all the important ports of the Confederate States." In granting belligerent rights to North and South leading nations had denied them the privilege of bringing prizes into their ports, but this restriction, Semmes felt, was unjust and—here he made a point he was often to make in future—"cannot be applied in the present war without operating with great injustice to the Confederate States" because their ports were "hermetically sealed" by the blockade and the policies of the great powers. The Confederate cruisers, with no ports open, could only destroy their prizes. It would be only fair to permit the Confederacy to use Cuban ports, say, Cienfuegos, for this purpose.

With soothing strokes of his pen Semmes expressed confidence he could rely on the friendly disposition of Spain, "who is our near neighbor," to receive the Confederacy with "equal and even-handed justice," that is, to let him park his prizes out of reach of recovery by United States warships. Actually, Semmes was asking a crossroads official three thousand miles from the source of government to commit Spain to prompt recognition of the Confederacy.

To Second Lieutenant Chapman, the *Sumter's* glamour boy, Semmes entrusted delivery of this impressive missive to Señor Don José de la Pozuela, who did exactly what Semmes hoped he would do: he telegraphed the entire letter to the Captain General at Havana, who, in turn, heaved the responsibility across the Atlantic to Madrid. Apparently awed by the masterly, almost unbelievable capture of seven prizes of war and the burning of the *Golden Rocket* right under his nose, the Governor immediately outdid himself extending the courtesies of the port to the *Sumter*. And Semmes could have all the coal he could pay for.

With the fetes and the flowers came forebodings. Ten minutes after the *Sumter* dropped anchor the United States Consul at Cienfuegos hustled a message over the telegraph line to Havana imploring his brother consul, Thomas Savage, to rush any Federal warship in sight to Cienfuegos to destroy the "piratical craft" that had broken in upon the quiet Cuban waters and the Yankee sugar and rum trade. Semmes heard of the message and he knew Federal ships on the Key West station were constantly browsing about after privateers. One was sure to stop at Havana and be alerted. If he loitered at Cienfuegos, he would be bottled up. Consulting his chart he calculated the steaming time from Havana to Cienfuegos and fixed the approximate hour a pursuer might arrive. Then he timed his departure a few hours ahead. This would give his pursuers "the satisfaction of finding that the bird, which they were in pursuit of, had flown."

At 8 A.M. July 7 sleepy-eyed Lieutenant Chapman reported to Semmes' cabin. He had had a night of it. On leaving the Governor's palace the evening before he was waylaid and carried off as an honored guest. Such partying! When the merriment ceased in the wee hours, "my tempest-tossed lieutenant was laid away in the sweetest and whitest of sheets, to dream of the eyes of the *houris* of the household that had beamed on him so kindly, that he was in danger of forgetting that he was a married man."

But Chapman brought news. The Captain General of Cuba had despatched the weighty question of prizes to Madrid. This was exactly what Semmes wanted—time. Anything could happen while the Cuban authorities went through the long distance process of consulting Madrid. The blockade might be broached and his prizes sail into a Southern port where an admiralty court could adjudicate them and restore the cargoes to their Cuban owners. It meant shelter for Semmes' prizes until the Queen's Ministers decided what policy to adopt in this ticklish business. If Semmes had violated Spanish territorial waters in his last three seizures, that is, captured them within a marine league of shore, Spanish courts would act thereon. A further knot must be unraveled. Semmes had darted out from neutral waters to make those last three captures. Illegal, outlawed, to say the least. This he was later to admit.

Semmes would be far away when Spain finally gave her answer. Legally, no cruiser of North or South had a right to bring prizes into Spanish ports. A neutral was compelled by law to restore to their owners prizes left in her ports, and this was precisely what Spain did weeks later. Yankee gold—so Semmes charged—had even seduced the pilot of the Cuban tug into reducing his estimate of the *Sumter's* distance from shore when snatching her last three prizes, from five miles to less than three.

At "so barefaced a proceeding" Semmes fulminated and promised himself to foment a "very pretty little quarrel between the Confederate States and Spain." If Spain refused to foot the bill for the robbery of these vessels, the Confederacy would foot it herself, at Spain's expense. Cuba would make a very respectable state, with her rich plantations of tobacco and sugar—or so he dreamed.

Meanwhile the coffee houses of Cienfuegos boiled with the exciting chatter of an insatiable populace. "The billiard players rested idly on their cues, to listen to Madam Rumor with her thousand tongues—how the fort had fired into the *Sumter*, and how the *Sumter* had fired back at the fort, and how the matter was finally settled by the *Pirata* and the *Commandante* over a bottle of champagne. Yankee captains, and consignees, super-cargoes and consuls passed in and out, like so many ants whose nests have been trodden upon, and nothing could be talked about but freights and insurance, with or without war risk to cover the cargoes."

But everyone asked, "Where are all the Federal gunboats?"

Appointing a prize agent, one Don Mariano Dias, to chaperon his prizes until Spain decided their fate, Semmes made ready to sail. Time was running out. Any moment a Federal warship might arrive off Cienfuegos. He took on one hundred tons of coal and five thousand gallons of water. Anxiously, Semmes trained his telescope down the river hoping to see the *Cuba* heave in sight. Abandoning hope of her arrival and not daring wait longer he left with Prize Agent Dias a letter of instructions for his missing prize master, Midshipman Hudgins:

> Midshipman A. G. Hudgins, Sir: Upon your arrival at this place you will put the master, mate and crew of the *Cuba* on parole, not to serve against the Confederate States, during the present war, unless ex-changed, and release them. You will then deliver the brigantine to the Governor for safe custody until the orders of the Captain-General can be known in regard to her. I regret much that you are not able to arrive in time to rejoin the ship, and you must exercise your judgment as to the mode in which you shall regain your country. You will, no doubt, be able to raise sufficient funds for transporting yourself and the four seamen who are with you, to some point in the Confederate States, upon a bill of exchange, which you are hereby authorized to draw upon the Secretary of the Navy. Upon your arrival within our territory, you will report yourself to that officer.

A hopeful letter that was never delivered. Why? Because Cap-tain Strout had turned the tables and re-captured the *Cuba* from Semmes' prize crew. Midshipman Hudgins had made the mis-take of falling asleep on deck without taking due precautions. Overpowered, clapped into irons only to inveigle his way out of them, Hudgins went off into anonymity after shooting it out with the doughty Yankee skipper, who delivered him a prisoner of war at New York on July 21 while the guns of Bull Run were booming down in Virginia. Semmes later charged that two of his prize crew were bribed into treachery. He was not to meet his midshipman again until the Confederacy had reached her dying gasps.

Near midnight on July 7 the *Sumter* weighed anchor and steamed down the harbor, passing under the Cienfuegos beacon whose lamp shed a bright glare on the deck of the little cruiser. Thus did Semmes bid farewell to the "Queen of the Islands." The next time he gazed on her scenic shores it would be December, 1862, and he would be walking the quarterdeck of a far finer ship, striking terror to Northern commerce. But now he shaped his course for happy hunting grounds far southwards on the Spanish Main.

In his cabin as the Cienfuegos beam faded in the distance Semmes posted eight entries on the credit side of a small ledger he kept for the purpose. He had rolled up a record that would resound through North and South. It could hardly be displeasing to the government that had entrusted this mission to him—eight enemy ships captured in four days!

⚓

⚓

10 *Gunpowder Diplomacy at Curaçao*

Bucking trade winds that blew half a gale the *Sumter* slammed east and a bit south. To Semmes' discomfiture her boilers ate coal ravenously, and he had to bend his course away from Barbados where he had planned to re-fuel and head for the nearer Dutch island of Curaçao.

The Caymans slid past in the night and Semmes noted in his journal that the chart-maker had erred in placing these islets fifteen or so miles too far to the eastward. An unwary navigator might easily strand his ship on these low-lying rocks and coral reefs, for even a sharp-eyed lookout could hardly see them on dark nights. Tall Jamaica soon came in sight. All day the *Sumter* skirted the island, "its blue mountains softened but not obliterated as the evening set in."

Letting the cruiser's fires die, Semmes ordered his men aloft to unfurl the sails. It was the *Sumter's* first tryout of canvas alone, and the "old sailors of the ship, who had not bestridden a yard in months, leaped aloft, with a will to obey the welcome orders." Semmes was in familiar waters and they invited reveries of the days he was taking his first lessons in seamanship, and inspired him to nostalgic musings: "The race of sailors has not entirely died out though the steamship is fast making sad havoc with it . . . the sailing ship has a romance, and a poetry about her, which is thoroughly killed by steam. The sailor of the former loves, for its own sake, the howling of the gale, and there is no music so sweet to his ear, as the shouting of orders through the trumpet of the officer of the deck, when he is poised upon the topsail-yard of the rolling and tumbling ship. . . . In future wars upon the ocean, all combatants will be on the dead level of impenetrable iron walls, with regard to dash and courage, and with regard to seamanship and evolutions, all the knowledge that will be required of them, will be to know how to steer a nondescript box toward the enemy."

Enemy, indeed! Not an enemy warship had he sighted since he baffled the *Brooklyn* off the Mississippi Passes. Now it was July 16 and, over the port bow loomed Curaçao, set on a sea of indigo blue. He ran along the coast until he stood off Willemstad, a picturesque little town reminiscent of Amsterdam. Here a colony of Dutch burghers had thrived for centuries. It was a free port, nuzzling close to Venezuela, and the land-locked harbor was engirdled by sterile, jagged peaks on which the Dutch had erected imposing battlements. Willemstad Palace, residence of the Dutch Governor, J. D. Crol by name, perched on the cliff looking placidly out to sea.

Semmes could now feel out Dutch neutrality. Holland's attitude towards the Confederacy was as vital as Spain's. Hoisting his jack he fired a gun for a pilot. That indispensable individual came aboard but said he was unable to negotiate the channel by night. He would return in the morning. Semmes scented trouble. Morning broke and with it came the pilot, bearing a dismaying message, "The Governor regrets, but he cannot permit you to enter, he having received recent orders from his home government to this effect."

Semmes' resentment rose, but he diagnosed the layout accurately. The cocky little Secretary of State, William H. Seward, had stolen a march on him. Seward had admonished American consular agents throughout the world to indoctrinate foreign officials with anti-Confederate propaganda. The so-called "Confederate government," the official line ran, was a mere rebellion that would be squelched in sixty to ninety days. Confederate ships must be regarded as corsairs and pirates, not entitled to belligerent rights.

It was a bitter foretaste of what Semmes was to suffer at the hands of Seward's minions, whom he labeled "political pests and panderers," "the smallest of men." If there was any one breed that Semmes detested, it was these State Department functionaries who assumed a pose and authority that enraged him. They were to frustrate him time and again. He understood precisely what had happened. When the *Sumter* appeared off the harbor Consul Jesurun donned his cocked hat and gold braid and marched to the palace to demand that the Confederate "pirate" be denied admittance. If the governor permitted this Southern buccaneer to enter the harbor, Mr. Seward at Washington would be so irate he might even send warships to blow the palace down around the governor's ears. Harried by this pronunciamento the Governor decided the *Sumter* must betake herself elsewhere.

A pretty kettle of fish this was. The cruiser had one day's fuel left in her bunkers. Something must be done. Semmes did not intend to have his cruise of destruction brought to a halt by a mere United States consul! He would fix this consul and his Dutch friend. Going to his cabin he composed a stiff note, loaded with legal ingenuity. Designed to confuse, compromise, and embarrass the recipient, it closed with a hint of gunfire.

Expressing surprise that "Your Excellency" should have refused admittance to the Confederate cruiser *Sumter* Semmes shot back: "I most respectfully suggest that there must be some mistake here . . . Your Excellency must be under some misapprehension as to the character of this vessel. She is a ship of war, duly commissioned by the government of the Confederate States, which States have been recognized as belligerents, in the present war, by all the leading powers of Europe. . . .

"Am I to understand from your Excellency that Holland has adopted a different rule, and that she not only excludes the prizes but the ships of war, themselves, of the Confederate States? And this, at the same time, that she admits the cruisers of the United States; thus departing from her neutrality in this war, ignoring the Confederate States as belligerents, and aiding and abetting their enemy? If this be the position which Holland has assumed in this contest, I pray your Excellency to be kind enough to say as much to me in writing."

Committing the explosive missive to Lieutenant Chapman, who had fared so well at Cienfuegos, Semmes waited. The letter had immediate effect. Through his spyglass he could plainly see the black-coated dignitaries of the island hurrying to the palace for a grand council of state. Semmes could even sense the agitation in the chamber, whose great windows opened to the sea. The apparent gravity of the council was an amusing reminder to him of the ponderous customs of New Amsterdam in colonial days as described by historian Diederick Knickerbocker. Meantime Lieutenant Chapman sat cooling his heels outside the chamber, chatting with an admiring circle of new-made friends and imbibing delightful mint juleps—"for these islands seemed to have robbed old Virginia of some of her famous mint patches." Inside, the burghers "smoked and talked and smoked again," pondering longwindedly the arguments pro and con.

On and on went the caucus. Hours passed. So, finally, did Semmes' patience. It was time for a bluff, time to use gunpowder diplomacy. If the Consul's threat of bombardment, still at a distance, had overawed the Governor, perhaps a whiff of smoke closer at hand would reverse his thinking. Semmes summoned First Lieutenant Kell.

"Mr. Kell," said Semmes with a twinkle of his eyes, "I think our men need a little target practice. Let's try out the pivot gun."

"Aye, aye, sir," answered Kell, who caught the idea and hurried to execute it.

The drum beat to quarters. Soon a target was in the water,

placed so that shells fired at it would pass across the windows of the council chamber. The big 8-inch pivot poked its black snout around and the charge was rammed home. Crash! Whiz! A shell went screaming by the chamber windows. The *Sumter* was hardly fifty yards from the mouth of the narrow entrance to the harbor and the explosion rocked the town like an earthquake, reverberating between the peaks. Like jacks-in-a-box sundry Dutch heads popped out of the chamber windows only to be hastily withdrawn as if their owners feared the *Sumter's* gunners might make a mistake in their aim. Or was Willemstad being bombarded?

Three more shells went spinning away to burst with beautiful precision around the target. It was a powerfully convincing demonstration for the burghers. They decided to take no chances with this fast-shooting newcomer who refused even to wait for their reply. He seemed to mean business. Unceremoniously they voted to recognize the Confederacy, *nemini contradicente*, and adjourned. Semmes could see their black-coated figures scurrying out of the palace like ants out of a tousled anthill. Lieutenant Chapman was hustled back to his captain with a cordial invitation to steam in and make himself at home. Semmes' bluff had worked like a charm. Turning to Kell he said he thought the "gunners had had enough exercise." The pivot gun was secured and the *Sumter's* crew enjoyed a good laugh.

Into the harbor steamed the cruiser to anchor and spread her awnings. Once more in port she soon resembled a carousel, ringed with bum-boats, laden with fragrant tropic fruit and chattering bum-boat women garbed in gaudy, parrotlike plumage. Amid a babel of voices "Jack," as Semmes dubbed his crew, pursued the joint business of spending his money, replenishing his tobacco pouch and indulging in a little flirtation.

Now for a week of painting, refitting, and overhauling. The *Sumter* was fitted with a new fore topmast, and replenished her coal and provisions. The cruiser's seachest seemed to have no bottom. Thanks to the washerwomen the *Sumter's* young officers appeared once again spic and span with glistening white shirt bosoms and collars.

To Semmes' cabin one morning came a visitor, "Don somebody or other," an emissary from the deposed President Castro of Venezuela, "one of those unfortunate South American chiefs," who had been beaten in a battle of ragamuffins and compelled to fly his country. Exiled at Curaçao this gentleman sought an alliance with Semmes. Together they could restore the outcast *presidente* to his chair. Had Semmes had piratical ambitions, as his detractors charged, here was his chance to become the Warwick of Venezuela and put the crown on another's head or even on his own, if he desired it. The prospect of an admiralcy in the Venezuelan navy and commanding a fleet of "piraguas and canoes" was flattering, but not alluring. Not being in the market for revolutionary junkets, Semmes politely declined.

At Curaçao one "John Smith of New York, Photographer," enjoyed a monopoly "taking the phizes of the staid old Dutchmen." One morning he bustled out in a small boat to take poses of the *Sumter*, her men, and her skipper. Naively, he told Semmes his pictures were intended for New York newspapers. They were, indeed, to show up long afterward in a copy of *Harper's Weekly* he found aboard one of his prizes. Semmes had no objection to his own or his ship's pictures adorning what he called a "rogues gallery." They could hardly endanger the *Sumter's* security because "we had the art of disguising the *Sumter* so that we could not know her ourselves at half a dozen miles distance."

The St. Thomas packet brought New York newspapers a month old from which Semmes got "nothing new except that the Northern beehive is all agog, with marching and countermarching of troops." Not a word had Semmes and his men yet received from home. They were on their own completely, working as it were in the dark, isolated, shut off from every means of communication with their government or their families. For aught they knew the Confederacy might be won or lost. This very day, July 21, Thomas Jonathan Jackson was standing like a stone wall at Bull Run and McDowell's demoralized army was fleeing back to Washington.

Yet the very solitariness of their life was already drawing Semmes and his men closer together. Aloof, uncommunicative, somewhat forbidding at times, Semmes was not an unsociable man so much as one who was not always sociable. Evenings he spent in the wardroom chatting with his officers and smoking good Havana cigars, boxes of which were showered on him by admirers at Cienfuegos. Yet, there was always that distance between him and his officers. So with Stonewall Jackson, and with most commanders at sea and ashore. Semmes was necessarily an opportunist. He was reckless and a taker of chances, but he had to be if he were to be a successful sea raider. Relying on his own decisions, he seldom consulted his officers for opinion or advice. He made mistakes but he never went back to correct them.

Utterly considerate of his men's welfare, nevertheless he brooked no insolence, no shade of disobedience. When angry, he could dress an offender down with a shriveling outburst of blasphemy. He knew his sailors' foibles and shortcomings. To give vent to his men's spirits pent up on long cruises he gave them a run on shore whenever he could. To see them getting drunk was distasteful to him, but he knew it was a good prescription for disciplinary ills. When on the beach they could settle their petty differences. If eyes were to be blacked, it would better be done away from the ship. Like Shakespeare's "fell sergeant" he was strict in his discipline afloat. Punishment fitted the crime and it came fast.

The men's belief in their captain's infallibility set in early. They saw he took chances with them, but equally, they saw his ability to get them out safely. They were astounded by the apparent dexterity with which they had captured eight prizes. His poise and coolness appealed to them. Still another factor influenced his crew's esteem for him—his reliance on divine guidance. They knew he knelt daily before the little shrine in his cabin.

Semmes faced a cold, hostile world. There was no Confederate Consul in any port on earth to whom he could appeal for help. On the contrary, wherever he sought haven he encountered an active, vigilant enemy in the American Consul, who, for all the pettiness of his character as painted by Semmes, fought a valiant, even crippling, running fight with him from port to port.

One crewman deserted at Curaçao, a simple lad named Orr, lured away by a Yankee pub-keeper and the busy-bee American Consul, who apparently tried to steal away Semmes entire crew. To his gratification only this one succumbed to blandishments. But the *Sumter* had work to do. On the eve of sailing Semmes "leaked" to his visitors "a great secret": he was heading back to Cuba. These busybodies would industriously spread the fiction. It would throw off the trail any Federal cruisers that came snooping into Curaçao. He never revealed his true movements ahead of time, keeping even his officers in the dark until the last moment.

Her bunkers full of good English coal, her engines overhauled, the *Sumter* sailed out of the harbor, with the populace lining the shore to wave goodbye. Contrary to the "great secret" he had disclosed, Semmes veered east along the Venezuelan coast to waylay vessels trading with Puerto Bello and La Guayra. Nor was he disappointed. Next day, July 25, the mountains of La Guayra loomed up, blue, mystic, and majestic. Dawn had hardly revealed the bold outline of the coast when Sail Ho! resounded from the masthead.

Away went the *Sumter* after a down-east schooner whose cut was as plain as the Puritans who built her. At 6:30 A.M. the *Abby Bradford* of New York, bound for Puerto Bello, was Semmes' Prize Number Nine. She was a good haul—a sturdy ship and a cargo of provisions, both American, with no neutral entanglements. Stowing her flag with eight others in his bag Semmes bore off for Puerto Bello just under his lee to fence with the *de facto* President of Venezuela, he who had just ousted Señor Castro. Semmes was confident he could entice one of these "beggarly South American Republics" to intern his prizes. He needed only one precedent, and if he could coax Venezuela into creating it, all would be well. His imagination ran on, but his gorge rose at the idea of kowtowing to these so-called republics "putting on airs and talking about acknowledging other people when they have lived a whole generation themselves without the acknowledgment of Spain."

Taking the *Abby Bradford* in tow, he squared away. Night came down and the *Sumter* stood off Puerto Bello harbor till morning when without ado she nosed in, her prize tugging after her. The sleepy town had a dusty, rundown, old-Moorish-seaport look. The harbor was empty. The only visible signs of life were a few turkey-buzzards drowsing on various rooftops. This place was panting for excitement, and that is what Raphael Semmes brought.

Having anchored, Semmes made a spyglass reconnaisance of the "castle," an old fort that brandished three or four rusty cannon on rickety carriages. The pieces were probably worthless, save for firing salutes. The *Sumter's* guns could quickly make rubble of them. But first to diplomacy. Tilting with "petty South American chieftains" was getting irksome to the raider. Nevertheless he penned a dignified appeal, urging the Venezuelan government to "permit both belligerents to bring their prizes into her waters." If Venezuela excluded his prizes, she would be favoring the United States, whose ports were open to their captures. The Confederacy, with her ports blockaded, had no recourse but to destroy hers. "A rule which would produce such unequal results as this is not a just rule . . . and as equality and justice are the essence of neutrality, I take it for granted Venezuela will not adopt it."

Lieutenant Chapman had hardly delivered the message to the Governor before barefooted orderlies began racing and chasing to summon a grand council as at Curaçao. "Mr. Big" in this town was the American Consul, who amalgamated his State Department functions with a country store where he dispensed Connecticut clocks, sarsaparilla, bacon, notions, and sundry odds and ends. The symbol of Yankee trade and gold, his nod was law in this forgotten little port. There was no waiting here as there was at Curaçao. Semmes got a brisk, snappy reply, about a foot square, put up in true South American style, sealed with a big daub of red wax and adorned with the words, *"Dios Y Libertad."* Breaking the seal he read a polite but blunt warning: Get out of the harbor and take your prize with you.

He might have bluffed it through as he had at Curaçao, or even fired a chastising broadside at the "castle," but he realized a single return shot might easily puncture the *Sumter's* boiler and make her a sitting duck for Federal cruisers. Meantime the American Consul was prodding the governor to crack down on the trespasser who refused to leave when ordered to do so. Going to the "castle" the governor gazed thoughtfully down on the *Sumter's* 8-inch gun and decided not to interfere with his uninvited, well-armed guest, who presently, at his leisure, moved out of the harbor with his prize tagging after him.

Semmes had resolved not to burn the *Abby Bradford* but to dispatch her to New Orleans hoping she might be able to elude the blockading squadron and run up one of the shoal passes west of the mouth of the Mississippi. Loath to spare an officer, he named a quartermaster, Eugene Ruhl, prize master, with instructions to crowd on sail and head for Barataria Bay, west of the Mississippi

Passes, the one-time stronghold of the romantic Lafitte brothers, who pitched in with Andrew Jackson to beat off the British in 1815. Urgently he cautioned his prize master: keep well away from the main passes.

To Ruhl he consigned his first report to the Secretary of the Navy. Using no cipher Semmes recounted his exploits *seriatim*. A dash of pride tinctured his closing sum-up, "We are all well, and doing a pretty fair business, in mercantile parlance, having made nine captures in twenty-six days."

After speeding the *Abby Bradford* off to New Orleans—or so they thought—the *Sumter* had hardly cleared away before her lookout sighted a Northern bark running down the coast, with all her studding sails set, "her taut and graceful spars, and her whitest of cotton sails, glistening in the morning's sun, revealed at once the secret of her nationality." She was the *Joseph Maxwell* of Philadelphia and she made a run for it, but shortly gave up the race and by the same token tossed a fresh dilemma into Semmes' lap. Half of her cargo belonged to a neutral business-house in Puerto Bello. Anchoring his prize outside the marine league Semmes steamed back to Puerto Cabello to ask haven for this prize, in which a Venezuelan citizen was interested. Back came his emissary—the paymaster this trip—with a peremptory demand from the Governor to bring the *Joseph Maxwell* into the harbor and deliver her to him until the Venezuelan courts could determine whether she had been captured within the marine league or not.

Semmes snorted. Such insolence was refreshing. He hardly knew whether to laugh or get mad, or both. Lying close under the fort he could see half-naked soldiers taking the tompions out of the guns. He suspected it was a ruse to intimidate him, though not until later did he learn the Federal Consul was stage-managing this little melodrama. Emboldened by the Consul's promise of Federal gunboats speeding south to send the impudent *Sumter* to the bottom the governor had ordered the *commandante* of the "castle" to go through the motions of preparing for action. Beating to quarters, casting loose his guns and with his crew standing at the ready, Semmes steamed out of the harbor and rejoined the *Joseph Maxwell*.

His conscience would not let him burn the prize on the spot.

Up to now he had snared ten enemy ships, and set fire to only one, the *Golden Rocket*. Under the law of nations he had no right to destroy neutral property and he was determined, if possible, to avoid complications with neutral governments but to find a legal way for the Confederacy to profit by his activities. Semmes' detractors have depicted him as a naval pyromaniac, who burned ships just to watch the flames crackling skyward. "I only resorted to this practice," he retorted, "when it became evident that there was nothing else to be done. Not that I had not the right to burn them, under the laws of war, when there was no dispute about the property."

So Semmes manned the *Joseph Maxwell* and sent her to join his prizes at Cienfuegos until adjudicated by a Confederate Prize Court. He clung to the hope that Spain, at least, "would dare to be just, even in the face of the truckling of England and France." He had no way of knowing that Spain had proclaimed her neutrality and had restored his prizes to their owners.

In the report to Secretary Mallory which he confided to the care of Prizemaster Ruhl, Semmes had said, "I do not deem it prudent here to speak of my future movements, lest my dispatch fall into enemy hands."

He hardly imagined his words would soon feast the eyes of his most relentless enemy, Commander David D. Porter, who on August 13, 1861 recaptured the *Abby Bradford* off the Louisiana coast as she was sneaking into Barataria Bay, running too close to the Passes against which Semmes had warned. Porter seized Semmes' report and the story of the first set-to at Puerto Cabello. Just why Ruhl did not destroy the papers the moment the *Powhatan* overhauled him was never revealed. Armed with this vital intelligence Porter dashed off to Pensacola where he induced Flag Officer Mervine to let him go *Sumter*-hunting. To Gideon Welles he addressed a too-confident prophecy, "Semmes is in a position now where he can't escape, if properly looked after. He is out of coal and out of credit."

It is possible Prizemaster Ruhl purposely told Porter Semmes had run out of money as well as coal. Whatever it was Porter swallowed it, though he, at least, had something definite to work on. His first suggestion for catching Semmes had been pigeonholed.

Now Semmes was on the Spanish Main. That pinned down his general whereabouts.

Up to now Semmes had roved at will. He had not seen a single Federal warship. Nor would he see one until well into November. Pursuit of the wily sea-raider was an unorganized merry-go-round. Admittedly, ferreting out Semmes over vast reaches of water, mousing into innumerable hideouts in the West Indies, was a difficult task, almost entirely dependent on luck. Where to find Semmes was anybody's guess—or where he'd show up. The Federal Navy knew nothing except he had visited Cienfuegos and parked six prizes. Rumor had the *Sumter* everywhere. Now he had broken cover at Puerto Cabello and Curaçao. Schemes and maneuvers for snaring him blossomed like summer flowers. But Federal cruisers that should have been sniffing him out were chasing after harum-scarum privateers whose aggregate damage to the Federal war effort was virtually nil. Engaged in such futility, the *Brooklyn* had let the *Sumter* escape.

Had Welles ordered his fastest cruisers to fan out across the Caribbean ten days after the *Sumter* escaped from the Mississippi the Confederate raider might easily have been captured or sunk within six weeks. So thought David Dixon Porter, most astute of the naval sleuths on Semmes' trail. Every passage to the sea should have been guarded as soon as it was known the *Sumter* had escaped, again quoting Porter. Such moves would have deprived the South of the one man who possessed a veritable genius for his fiery trade. Millions of dollars worth of shipping would be afloat instead of at the bottom of the sea. Thus discouraged, the Confederacy might have abandoned its cruiser raids. Welles' policy of virtually ignoring the raiders cost the United States a pretty penny.

Lincoln's Secretary of the Navy has been made by historians with Northern proclivities into a fabulous naval panjandrum, who decreed that the blockade, or what he called a blockade, was sacrosanct. Not a ship could he spare to whip after the Confederate wasp whom he dismissed as "pirate." In July, 1861, the blockade was an unjelled, ineffective patrol, hardly more than a rendezvous off a few major Southern outlets. Lord Russell, England's Foreign Minister, pointed this out to American Minister Adams. Look at your map of the Southeastern and Gulf coasts and imagine how much blockading you could do with only a hundred ships—especially when you have hardly any bases.

But the Old Man of the Sea (as Lincoln dubbed Welles) was sitting on the naval lid. Wreathed in pipe smoke, striking a posture like the Buddha of all wisdom, he went through the motions of launching a merciless search for the "pirate Semmes," yet actually doing precious little about it until pressured by the cries of Captains, Commanders, Lieutenants, and even Midshipmen, who saw opportunity slipping away and begged to be "allowed" to go manhunting.

The Official Records would seem to indicate a dearth of rhyme or reason in the pursuit of Semmes. Take, for instance, Welles' "sealed orders" to Lieutenant Eytinge, commanding the converted merchantman *Shepherd Knapp*. The "sealed orders" signed by Welles told him to run around the ocean a bit, "exercise your crew at the great guns and occasionally with shot and shell," and come on back to New York when his coal ran out. The *Sumter* was not even mentioned. However, Lieutenant Eytinge decided for himself that the *Sumter* was his logical quarry. He bubbled over with patriotic ardor at the very idea. "Place Semmes before me—I ask no more. I shall conquer or die at my guns." It sounded like Travis' last message from the Alamo, without the ring of deadly urgency. The *Shepherd Knapp* "pursued the traitor" Semmes all over the West Indian waters but found neither hide nor hair of him. Eytinge longed—or so he said in his report to Welles—to "sacrifice my life to sustain my country's honor." Be it said for Eytinge he shrewdly divined that after Semmes had played out his string on this side of the Atlantic and frightened American shipping into semi-stagnation, he would head for the Mediterranean. Apparently, nobody took Lieutenant Eytinge seriously—least of all, Gideon Welles.

⚓

⚓

11 Stars and Bars on the Spanish Main

Standing east along the Venezuelan coast Semmes shaped his course for Port of Spain, Trinidad. A lover of nature and her beauties he slowed his engines as he passed over the coral banks off Tortuga Island. For hours he and his men gazed rapturously down into the exquisite submarine landscape. In the coral gardens sea ferns waved like gorgeous fans. In and out darted fish, sparkling and gleaming in coats of silver and gold, green and scarlet. To Semmes' soul it was meat and drink, this scene of transcendent beauty and peace so far removed from the deadly drama in which he was cast.

Skirting the Frailes, or Friars, that thrust their many-shaped cones up from the sea not unlike hooded monks, Semmes entered the Gulf of Paria through the famed Dragon's Mouth. Here again memory harked him back thirty-five years to his "green midshipman" days when he first sailed this way on the *Lexington*. In his journal Semmes inscribed, "A generation has since passed away. So brief is thy life, O Man! But there stood the everlasting mountains, as I remembered them, unchanged."

By noon, August 4, the *Sumter* nosed into the roadstead of Port of Spain. A British merchant brig, passing out, dipped her flag in salute to the Confederate colors. To Semmes it was a good omen for this first and crucial visit to a British port—more to the point, a sign of hostility to the United States. The *Sumter* was again gasping for coal, and this meant sounding out the exact meaning of Britain's recognition of the Confederacy as a belligerent. The Queen's neutrality proclamation had arrived at Trinidad and Semmes was informed officially that he could expect the same hospitality a Federal warship might, and nothing more.

Semmes had a pressing problem in his prisoners, who were a sore burden, and a menace as well. He still held the crew of the *Joseph Maxwell*, and they were getting more refractory daily. To guard against a sudden insurrection he and his officers wore pistols

Cruise of the "Sumter"

at all times. These men were hostages, not prisoners of war. He told them frankly their fate—parole or hanging—depended on that of the crew of a Confederate privateer, the *Savannah*, a former pilot boat, captured off Charleston. The *Savannah's* crew was carried to New York in irons, tried and sentenced to be hanged as pirates. President Davis had retaliated with a promise to string up prisoner for prisoner.

To Semmes' relief a New York newspaper, given him at Trinidad, said the North had recanted. The *Savannah's* crew were accorded the status of prisoners of war, not freebooters. Hanging unoffending noncombatants at the yardarm was unpleasant business. Semmes had no heart for it though he made his position clear, "I would be stretching a point in undertaking retaliation of this serious character without instructions from my government, but the case was pressing and we of the *Sumter* vitally interested in the issue. The commission of the *Savannah*, although she was only a privateer, was as lawful as our own, and judging by the abuse that had already been heaped upon us by Northern newspapers, we had no reason to expect any better treatment at the hands of the well-paid New York District Attorneys and well-packed New York juries." He paroled his joyful prisoners at once.

As soon as the ship anchored Confederate sympathizers flocked to the *Sumter* to shake Semmes' hand until it ached. Every craft in the harbor ferried visitors out to see the raider. Lord Russell, Britain's Foreign Minister, had publicly tagged the Confederacy a "so-called government" though at the same time, behind the scenes, he was industriously moving every pawn he had to aid the South, and British officials overseas took their cue from his actions. In consequence courtesies must be of a *de facto*, rather than a *de jure* nature. No official salutes, no official visits. Everything must be unofficial. It avoided a lot of the mumbo-jumbo red tape for which the British were sticklers. To Semmes this was as ridiculous as saying to a man, "I should like, above all things, to have you come to dine with me, but as you know you haven't got the right sort of dining dress, you can't come, you know."

But nothing mattered much to the Confederate captain, as long as he got coal. The law officers of the crown searched every legal tome on the island for an answer to the question: was the *Sumter* entitled to be re-fueled in her Majesty's dominions? To their delight they discovered that the laws, pre-dating the birth of the steamship, said nothing about coal so they came up with the hairsplitting decision that fuel for the *Sumter* was not contraband. They knew it was, in fact, but the laws at hand were silent on the subject, and that was enough. Hence the *Sumter* could buy whatever she wanted except actual munitions. But, as David Porter pointed out, supplying coal to Semmes was a far greater injury to American commerce than all the munitions in the world could be without it.

While the crown conducted its bituminous quiz Semmes kept his composure. For this he had potent reasons which he freely admitted: "I had too much respect for the calibre of certain guns on shore to throw any shells across the windows of the council-chamber."

Lying in port, almost under the muzzles of the Confederate raider, was a Baltimore brig whose master decided to beard the gray lion in his den before venturing to sea. Rain was drumming on the *Sumter's* deck when a dinghy brought the Baltimore skipper alongside. To his question: would Semmes chase him if he put to sea? came Semmes' reassurance he had orders not to molest Maryland's commerce. He welcomed the skipper as a native of a sister State whose espousal of the Confederacy was just around the corner. The Marylander "went away rejoicing and sailed the next day."

Of a different mould was a visitor who came up the gangway on Sunday, August 4. The *Sumter* was getting up steam to put to sea. Church bells were chiming across the harbor when Her Majesty's stately frigate *Cadmus* swept into the bay. Countermanding his sailing orders Semmes hastened to exchange civilities with the first foreign warship he had encountered. The return salutes from the British warship were the signs of a diplomatic triumph for the Confederacy. With "honors of the side" Captain Hillyar of the *Cadmus* came aboard. Over a bottle of wine in Semmes' cabin the two sea officers dipped into the inescapable topic, war. Assuming a new role—Confederate missionary—Semmes proceeded to indoctrinate his visitor with the righteousness of the Southern cause. He drew an intriguing comparison between the North, an effete, tariff-rich burglar that had reduced the South almost to the status of a colony, and the Confederacy, a young giant, striking out on her own for the right and independence. A convincing talker was Semmes, a public relations expert far ahead of his times, a skilled, incisive delineator of Southern ambitions.

Captain Hillyar was impressed, as Semmes intended him to be. He would no doubt spread the tidings. Giving Hillyar a fast rundown of his exploits the cabin rang with hearty guffaws over how Semmes had caught the *Brooklyn* off base at the Mississippi passes. Like most officers the British captain measured the power of governments by the size of their navies and their armaments. He had seen little evidence of American naval prowess. Here was a lone, makeshift Confederate wolf running loose about the sea, invading America's marine fold and killing off ships at a prodigious rate. Northern commercial wealth was apparent, but where was its navy? The Captain was curious, "Why doesn't the United States send her navy, if she has one, to suppress this Confederate raider?" To a naval officer war vessels spoke louder than diplomacy and trading ships.

Meanwhile, the American Consul sat impotently on shore chewing his fingernails and railing at this fresh evidence of "British perfidy." The tete-a-tete on the *Sumter* was carrying things too far.

On August 5, the *Sumter* headed southeast, through the Serpent's Mouth, along the picturesque Guiana coast, for the hunting grounds of Semmes' dreams, off Cape St. Roque.

The *Sumter* was nearing the Equator. Behind her the north polar star was sinking fast. Nightly, new constellations glittered on the southern horizon. That starry wonder of all ages, the Southern Cross, appeared in the sky, a symbol to Semmes of the rise of the new Confederate Republic whose knight-errant he was, bearing her colors on the tip of his lance.

Anxious to reach Cape St. Roque, Semmes forebore chasing a tempting sail or two. Headwinds and the equatorial current drove him into Cayenne, French Guiana, for fuel, only to find none, or rather, that the Federal Consul—his irrepressible enemy in every port—enjoyed the coal monopoly. The cards were stacked against him here, so he back tracked to Surinam. As he sailed past the "Enfant Perdue" (Devil's Island) he could not resist displaying the Confederate flag to the convicts of this French penal settlement.

He entered the Dutch port of Paramaribo in Surinam where another of "Mr. Seward's small fry" sought to interpose between the *Sumter* and her very staff of life, coal. Here threats of Federal gunboats and the loss of Yankee trade were of no avail. Gold from the *Sumter's* seachest worked miracles, and soon black coals, most precious of all jewels to Semmes, were tumbling into his bunkers. Having more water tanks than he needed, Semmes ripped out two of them and enlarged his bunker capacity, thus increasing his steaming radius from eight days to twelve. "Still," he recorded, "the *Sumter* remains fundamentally defective, as a cruiser, in her inability to lift her screw" when she was under sail.

Glorious news greeted the *Sumter* and her crew at this port. General Beauregard had routed the Federal army at Manassas, hurling it back on Washington. Letters from home could have brought no greater joy. Jubilation broke out. Semmes ordered the drum beat "to grog" for the crew. Wine gurgled in the wardroom. Nor was it an exclusive Confederate *feu de joie*. It spread ashore. That night the citizens of Paramaribo joined in with a grand fandango, and the Confederacy was huzzahed to the skies. Champagne flowed. The beauties of the town, bedecked with diamonds and Parisian gowns, paired off with the *Sumter's* young officers in the mazes of the waltz to the strains of Latin guitars.

More ominous, though, was the note struck by a late paper from Barbados reporting that the *Keystone State*, an armed Yankee merchant cruiser, had touched that island searching for the *Sumter*. Fortunately, the captain of the *Keystone State* had swallowed the bait Semmes had tossed out "confidentially" at Curaçao —and relayed to Barbados—of his intention to cruise back to Cuba. Had the *Keystone State* taken the right track she should have pounced on her quarry by now. Semmes breathed easier. Two other cruisers, the *Niagara* and the *Crusader*, were panting at his heels, or so they thought, for they, too, had been summoned to Cienfuegos by the outcries of the American Consul.

Before leaving Paramaribo Semmes gave out he was speeding to Barbados to hunt for the *Keystone State!* But once clear of the harbor, he headed southeast for Maranham, Brazil. Displaying the Confederate colors at Cayenne, Paramaribo, and Trinidad had, he felt, had a stimulating effect on the fortunes of the brave Republic. On September 4 the *Sumter*, then opposite the Delta of the Amazon, crossed the Equator. *"Fortuna favet diligentibus,"* wrote Semmes in his journal. "We hoisted the Confederate flag, though there were no eyes to look upon it outside of our ship, to vindicate, symbolically, our right to enter this new domain of Neptune, in spite of Abraham Lincoln and the Federal gunboats."

Next day the *Sumter* had her first mishap. While negotiating the tricky entrance to Maranham harbor she grounded on a shoal and ripped off her false keel. For a moment it seemed as if catastrophe had overtaken the little cruiser. Backing off, she felt her way in. The concussion inflicted slight damage, but it opened a leak that never was healed.

To a Brazilian official who came aboard to inquire what strange flag the cruiser flew at her peak Semmes replied, "It is the emblem of a new empire of the South, the Confederate States of America!" Semmes could drip drama at times. He had arrived at a happy moment. It was the eve of Brazil's Independence Day, and the town was festive. In the harbor men-of-war and merchantmen tricked themselves out with flags from deck to truck. Yet the *Sumter's* officers were not invited to the grand ball and the merrymaking in the Government House that night near their anchorage. They could only listen yearningly to the sounds of revelry and imagine the muffled shuffling of feet. Neutral etiquette required the president of the province to rule out Confederate participation in the festivities.

Formalities done with, a legal duel over belligerent rights settled amicably, the Brazilians showered the *Sumter* with pleasantries. But coal, not cotillions, was Semmes' vital need, and the merchants of Maranham were exorbitant, demanding $17.50 per ton. Semmes' exchequer was all but exhausted. His ten captures had netted only 200 dollars in actual cash; his 10,000 dollars "military chest" was scraping the bottom. To his succor came a timely loan of 2,000 dollars, against a draft on the Confederate States by a patriotic Texan living in Maranham. Filling her bunkers, the cruiser ploughed seaward once more.

Could Semmes have read the report the American consul at Maranham, William H. McGrath, addressed to Secretary of State Seward, he might have taken considerable heart. That functionary, who augmented his State Department salary of twelve hundred dollars by practising dentistry on the side at Maranham, sensed the real danger in the depredations of the *Sumter:* "Your Excellency cannot imagine the effect which the presence of the *Sumter* on this coast has had on American trade. It is quite possible that it will be entirely suspended. Already several cargoes ordered a short time previous have been countermanded."

Now Semmes veered his strategy. The St. Roque cruising grounds still beckoned, but the tradewinds were blowing hard. Not until December would they moderate. On the wings of these winds, sweeping around St. Roque, the dullest ship could run away from the *Sumter* if the raider trusted to sail alone. Long distance chasing with steam was out of the question. So, postponing his favorite project, he made for the calm belt of the Equator where he could lie in wait for his prey, under sail, and if surprise or stratagem failed to pay off, he could get up steam and chase without using too much fuel. He went into ambush along the northwestern diagonal of an imaginary box covering seven degrees of latitude, between 2° 30′ N and 9° 30′ N, and the meridians 41° 30′ W and 47° 30′ W.

Somewhere hereabouts Raphael Semmes underwent a hardening of heart, or of policy, that was to set his course. Spain, Holland, Venezuela, England, and Brazil had denied his plea to send prizes into their ports. Despairing of finding neutral sanctuary for his prizes and unable to spare crews to sail his captures into Confederate ports, he turned to his last resort, fire. Henceforth he would "burn, sink and destroy" without mercy. Only when complicated by neutral property would he commute the verdict of flame, and not always then. Should a question arise he would give the benefit of the doubt to the Confederacy.

Just where David Porter got the information he transmitted to Secretary Welles after his stern chase of Semmes as far as Maranham, he never told, though he said, "It had been intimated to me by one of Captain Semmes' confidential friends that the *Sumter* intended to take no prizes, but would burn, sink and destroy all she might fall in with; more particularly, Boston and Eastern vessels, the performance of which feat he seemed to anticipate much pleasure in."

Hardly had the *Sumter* reached the calmer region just above the Equator when, on September 25, a welcome Sail Ho! rang from the masthead. Running up under steam and United States colors, Semmes overhauled the brigantine *Joseph Park* of Boston, six days out from Pernambuco in ballast. At hailing distance Semmes lowered his false colors and streamed out the Confederate ensign. He toyed with the idea of utilizing the *Joseph Park* as a scout-decoy ship to lure other victims, but this seemed unprofitable so the guns were run out and his crew fired away at a "live target." At nightfall he set her afire and a great blaze she made, lighting the ocean for miles around.

A columnist of the Confederate *Index*—the pro-Southern, well-edited weekly review published in London during the war—threw a still unexplained sidelight on the capture of the *Joseph Park*. When the *Sumter's* boarding officer asked the skipper of the prize what cargo he carried, his reply was, "None." "Have you any specie?"

"Not a dollar," was the answer.

"Then, captain, you must get in the boat and go with me on board the *Sumter*."

"What are you going to do with me when I get on board?"

He was told that would depend entirely on himself. If he behaved, was not unruly, concealed nothing, he would be kindly treated. His fate was in his hands. Obviously, he was frightened. He decided to make a clean breast of it.

"Well," he began, "I *have* got a thousand dollars down below, and I guess I had better give it to you."

Accompanied by the boarding officer he went to a cache below decks and took out a bag of gold which he handed over.

"Why did you hide this money?" asked the officer. "We were flying United States colors when you sighted us."

"I thought you were the *Sumter*," revealed the skipper. "I wanted to be on the safe side."

Neither Semmes nor any other biographer ever made reference to this alleged haul. It could be the answer to where Semmes got the wherewithal to buy coal at his next port. The one hundred tons he loaded at Maranham had taken most of the two thousand dollars he borrowed there.

Semmes cruised the calm belt for days only to find "the wary seabirds had evidently all taken alarm and winged their way home by other routes." Game was scarce or scattered. There was no percentage in running down neutrals. It wasted time, coal, and effort. He decided to make sail for the West Indies where he could touch at the French island of Martinique and obtain more coal.

September 27, 1861, was Raphael Semmes' fifty-second birthday. In a small volume, entitled *Cruise of the Alabama and the Sumter*, published at London in 1864, there is a quotation from Semmes' journal that peers deep into his heart on this, his natal day. Semmes denied authorship of this book. He vowed he "did not write a line of it," yet he admitted loaning his journal to the publishers. It is the feeling of this biographer that this entry was correctly quoted, even in the face of Semmes' denial and its omission from his journal printed thirty years later in the *Official Records*. Certainly it reveals the inner thoughts of the man who presumably wrote it. Just why he deleted it—if he did—is a free guess.

Friday, September 27th. This is my fifty-second birthday, and so the years roll on, one by one, and I am getting to be an old man! Thank God, that I am still able to render service to my country in her glorious struggle for the right of self-government, and in defense of her institutions, her property and everything a people hold sacred. We have thus far beaten the Vandal hordes that have invaded and desecrated our soil; and we shall continue to beat them to the end. The just God of Heaven, who looks down upon the quarrels of men, will avenge the right. May we prove ourselves in this struggle worthy of Him and of our great cause! My poor distressed family! How fondly my thoughts revert to them today. My dear wife and daughters, instead of preparing the accustomed "cake," to celebrate my birthday, are mourning my absence, and dreading to hear of disaster. May our Heavenly Father console, cherish and protect them.

Making northing slowly, the *Sumter* overhauled neutral after neutral until Sunday morning October 27, east of the Windward Islands, came a welcome Sail Ho! from the lookout. Jack was sprucing up for muster, donning his dress uniform, adjusting the ribbons on his Sunday hat. But sartorial considerations were forgotten the moment the *Sumter's* lookout raised the strange sail, dead ahead and barely visible miles off. The drum beat to stations. Engineers and firemen tumbled below to get up steam.

Semmes knew he had flushed enemy game. Soon his telescope revealed a New England-cut schooner, close-hauled, running fast under heavy sail. Breaking out Confederate colors, the *Sumter* raced after the newcomer, her smoke pipe gushing thick black smoke that trailed away behind her. For the crew of the *Sumter* it was an exhilarating and exciting chase over a choppy sea. The quarry was fast and the *Sumter* overtook her but slowly. Tense with excitement, all hands crowded the forward rail to watch the *Sumter* eat up the distance between her and her prey, much as if they were watching a race horse in the stretch suddenly come up from behind with a burst of speed to overtake the pace setter. For the first time since leaving New Orleans the mess-call pipe at six bells seemed to have no lure.

It took six hours to overhaul the New Englander, "which had probably been in an agony of apprehension, [and] for some hours past, saw that her fate was sealed." At 3 P.M. Semmes' twelfth prize hove to at the command of the *Sumter's* gun. The Stars and Stripes streamed out from her maintopmast head. Sweeping past the schooner, Semmes read the name lettered across her stern: *Daniel Trowbridge*, New Haven.

Semmes' prize was a fantastic windfall of provisions and Yankee goods in incredible profusion. It was his first proof of the feasibility of living on his prizes. The eyes of the *Sumter's* crew danced with joy. "Jack was in his glory," avowed Semmes. "He had suddenly passed from mouldy and worm-eaten bread, and the toughest and leanest of 'old horse' to the enjoyment of all these luxuries." Here was food enough to stock the *Sumter's* larders for six months, to regale the taste with beef, pork, hams, fancy crackers, preserved meats, lobsters, fruit, sardines, and wine. They had, indeed, seized a veritable gourmet's warehouse. For hours Semmes let his men revel and eat at will of this sumptuous banquet spread by a "kind Providence."

To reach the *Daniel Trowbridge's* cargo the raiders jettisoned thousands of "superincumbent articles," strewing the sea with a gayly-painted fleet of Connecticut wooden ware, buckets, foot-tubs, washtubs, and churns. For two bustling days the *Sumter's* crew ferried provisions over a smooth sea to the raider's yawning pantry. Semmes' Malayan steward, John, packed every locker in the captain's cabin with canned lobster, preserves, cookies, and delicacies galore, muttering as he did so, "Dem Connecticut mans, bery good mans—me wish we find him often."

Topping off the bounteous blessings of the *Daniel Trowbridge* were innumerable sacks of Irish potatoes and enough livestock— geese, sheep, and pigs—to give the ship's deck the look of a barn-yard. The *Sumter's* butcher slaughtered these innocents in quantities enough to supply all hands. This largess of fresh provisions came just in time. It would head off the symptoms of scurvy that had begun to appear among the crew.

On October 30, 1861, Semmes turned over the *Daniel Trow-bridge* to the torchbearers. She flared like tinder. Lining the rail, the *Sumter's* crew watched the flames break through and gave three rousing cheers for the dying *Daniel Trowbridge*, outstanding gastronomic prize of the *Sumter's* career.

The Captain's mood was toughening. For insolence to the *Sumter's* Sergeant of Marines, Semmes clapped irons on the master of the *Daniel Trowbridge*, though he relented next day when the skipper made a very humble apology.

But Semmes knew that pursuit was on in earnest. At his heels came the keenest sleuth ever to trail him, David Porter and the *Powhatan*. Pushing the old steam frigate's defective boilers as hard as he dared, Porter touched at Cienfuegos, Curaçao, Puerto Bello, Paramaribo, and Maranham, but always a lap or two behind his quarry. At that, he gained fifteen hundred miles on Semmes. At Surinam he was only three days behind his quarry. Nor was he deflected by Semmes' subterfuge of cruising back to the West Indies. With amazing foresight Porter divined that Semmes was heading towards Cape St. Roque and he figured he would have to touch at Maranham for coal. With a possible day's run fifty miles better than Semmes', Porter stood for the Brazilian port under forced draft. He missed contact, but deduced that the Confederate raider, instead of steering for Cape St. Roque, was heading for the Equator.

From newspapers given him by an overhauled British brigantine Semmes learned that the *Keystone State* which, when last heard from was at Barbados, had gone to Trinidad, had taken his bait, and turned back westward. These papers told him also that the *Powhatan*, with more sagacity, had pursued him to Maranham, arriving just one week after his departure. At a subsequent date Porter's official report fell into Semmes' hands. Plotting the *Powhatan's* track, Semmes found that, on one occasion, the *Sumter* and the *Powhatan* had been within forty miles of each other, near enough, on a still day, to see each other's smoke. Porter, on the other hand, calculated the distance as seventy-five miles.

Fatefully enough, at the very moment that pursued and pursuer came within striking distance of each other the smoke of the *Joseph Park* was rising skyward near the Equator. Porter's stern chase was to add up to nothing more than futility and regret.

In his cabin as the *Sumter* wore northwards toward Martinique Semmes took stock. He was grateful for the favors of Providence. To date he had eluded at least six Federal warships combing the waters behind him. With some pride he entered in his journal, "The enemy has thus done us the honor to send in pursuit of us the *Powhatan*, the *Niagara*, the *Iroquois*, the *Keystone State*, and the *San Jacinto*." He would soon boast he had lured a score of Federal vessels from blockade duty. He had burned three ships. This was the extent of this actual destruction. Nine others—so he thought—were cooped up in neutral ports. An impressive record, even to his foes, though it failed to tell the whole story. The *Sumter's* indirect damage to American shipping was mounting, if only in the first, frightened flight from the American flag. Semmes could say that his slow, makeshift cruiser was paying off handsomely for the Confederacy. Insurance rates had soared. Northern ports were crowded with ships whose owners feared to send them to sea. They must either rot or be sold to neutrals at bargain prices. Already ship masters were making long, circuitous, and costly voyages to avoid meeting the cruiser.

The Northern press flared with stories of Semmes' "atrocities." Every newspaper he picked up from neutral ships called him "hard names" and demanded he be strung up the moment he was caught. Porter, that tireless bloodhound, whose pursuit of Semmes was the brightest feature of the Federal Navy's attempt to run down the *Sumter*, compared the *Daniel Trowbridge* bonfire to something Captain Kidd might have done. "It does not seem to have occurred to him," commented Porter, "how much this resembled the achievements of the old buccaneering days when sea rovers overtook their victims and treated them in pretty much the same fashion, finally consigning their vessels to the flames. There is this to be said in Semmes' favor, that he did not make his prisoners walk the plank."

On November 8 the *Sumter* sighted the glittering shores of Martinique, with its waving palms and fields of sugar cane set against a backdrop of blue misty hills. Capping this ecstatic panorama rose the peaceful, purplish bulk of Mount Pelée which would, half a century later, erupt in volcanic wrath and wipe out an entire city of 30,000 people.

Fifty-five days out of Maranham, the little warship was tired. So were her crew and her captain. Her boilers "croaked." Coal was again down to the last shovelful. Semmes had fourteen prisoners, a burden of which he wished to be relieved. Her crew needed, above all things, a refresher, a run on shore. Since leaving Maranham she had overhauled seventeen sail, of which she had taken two prizes. She burned both of them.

As the *Sumter's* anchor rattled to the bottom of the harbor at Fort de France Semmes did not realize, of course, that at this very moment the over-zealous Captain Charles Wilkes of the *San Jacinto*, now in the Bahama Channel, was snatching Confederate Commissioners James Mason and John Slidell from the deck of the British mail packet *Trent*, a kidnapping operation that made England boil with warlike indignation and forced President Lincoln and his Cabinet to back down, albeit gracefully. Wilkes' act was disavowed and the prisoners sent on their way.

Nor had Semmes any way of knowing that Bulloch had reached England and was rushing construction of real warships for the Confederacy or that a far more efficient commerce-destroyer than the *Sumter* was taking shape under Bulloch's direction, a vessel he himself would one day command.

Even before reaching Martinique Semmes had made up his mind, after a sweep at shipping east of the Lesser Antilles, to cross the Atlantic and wipe out American shipping on the European sea lanes. The Northern net was tightening on this side of the Atlantic. Resourceful as he was, he knew that unless he moved his luck would inevitably run out.

⚓

⚓

12 "Semmes Was Too Clever for Palmer"

Commander Raphael Semmes certainly did not resemble the object of a prodigious manhunt as he stepped ashore at Fort de France and hurried off to pay his respects to his Excellency, Monsieur Maussion de Condé, Governor of Martinique.

As emissary of the Confederacy, and proud of it, Semmes was immaculate, clad in his naval finery, linen freshly laundered, uniform with hardly a wrinkle, sword flashing at his side. An extra twirl or two had sharpened the tips of his mustache like rapier points. A small throng of the curious escorted him from the quay to the very doors of the Governor's palace. They could hardly believe this was "le pirate," the sailor who was cheating the Yankee hangman. The newspapers on the island had heralded his exploits widely. Never did Sir Henry Morgan in his palmiest days create so much excitement as did the Confederate raider, who, it would seem, was affability itself.

But the frosty Governor informed Semmes that His Imperial Majesty, Napoleon III, had issued a proclamation of neutrality. With guarded politeness Condé offered Semmes the same courtesies a Federal cruiser might expect: he could buy coal, fill his watertanks, make needed repairs and land his prisoners—provided the United States Consul assumed responsibility for them.

The Governor pointedly advised Semmes to shift his anchorage to the island's commercial metropolis, St. Pierre, where coal could be obtained in the open market. Significantly, he said he wished to know nothing of the transaction. Veiled hostility lurked in his attitude.

Despatching Paymaster Myers to St. Pierre, Semmes was astonished to find the customs officials there openly hostile to his efforts to buy coal. Once again taking up his pen, Semmes expounded the fine points of neutrality for the Governor's edification.

> Am I to understand from the action of your officers at St. Pierre that you have withdrawn your implied assent given me and that France, through your agency, adopts a different and less friendly rule? Will France drive a vessel of war of the Confederate States from one of her islands to a British island to procure coal? And if she does this, on what principle will she do it?
>
> It is a well-settled rule of international law that a belligerent ship of war cannot increase her armament or crew in a neutral port, nor supply herself with ammunition; but with these exceptions she may procure whatever supply she needs.
>
> If, however, it be the determination of your Excellency to insist upon my departure without coal, I beg that you will have the goodness to say as much to me in writing. I should regret to be obliged to have to inform my government. . . .

The Governor caved in and ordered the customs officials to stand aside, but spat back at Semmes a note tinged with asperity: "I no more maintain that I have the right to control the market, to prevent coal being sold to you, than I believe I have the power to furnish you from the Government storehouse here." Monsieur Condé's attitude hardly reflected that of his Emperor, who already was conniving to embroil France and England in the American internecine war on the side of the South.

Meanwhile, in unofficial circles, Gallic friendship was manifest. The cruiser's decks were holystoned Saturday evening and fairly shone. By noon Sunday the ship was packed with admirers, entranced by the ceremony of muster. "The officers were all dressed in bright new uniforms of navy blue (we had not yet been put in gray along with the army) the gorgeous epaulettes of the lieutenants flashing in the sun, and the midshipmen rejoicing in their gold-embroidered anchors and stars. The men attracted no less attention than the officers, with their lithe, active forms and bronzed countenances, heavy, well-kept beards, and whitest of duck frocks and trousers. One of my visitors turned to me, after the muster was over and said, pleasantly, in allusion to the denunciation of us by the Yankee newspapers, which he had been reading, 'Ces hommes sont des pirates bien polis, Monsieur Capitaine.' "

On Monday Semmes sent his bluejackets ashore, one watch at a time. To each man he gave a gold sovereign. They "behaved tolerably well," avowed Semmes, though they waked up the echoes of the old town, drank all the grogshops dry and fagged out the fiddlers. To Semmes, liberty was troublesome but necessary—"Unless Jack has his periodical frolic he is very apt to become moody and discontented."

Down from St. Pierre hurried the American Consul to receive the *Sumter's* prisoners—except three who volunteered to serve on the cruiser. Before releasing them Semmes lined them up on deck and personally polled them for complaints. To a man the twelve sailors and two masters were unanimous in appreciation of Semmes' kindness. Even the skipper of the *Daniel Trowbridge* on whom Semmes had fastened irons for insolence uttered not a grumbling word.

Yet hardly were Semmes' captives free before they gushed stories of Semmes' cruelty. Wheedled by drink and greenbacks they found themselves heroes. Had Semmes' prisoners been harshly treated the American Consul would have blazed it out in his report to the Secretary of State. Atrocities were conspicuous by their absence.

Northern newspapers, however, enjoyed printing tales of inhumanity meted out by the "monster Semmes." They told how he chained his prisoners on deck in all weather, and thrust them into dark holes to be tormented by thirst, hunger, rats, and coal dust. True, Semmes had no cabins to house them in. Nor was the *Sumter*—or the *Alabama* to come—built as a floating jail. Prisoners of war, on land or sea, had hard going. At the same time they were a constant menace to their keepers.

On November 13, after filling his watertanks, Semmes hove anchor and sailed northwards a dozen miles along the picturesque shore to St. Pierre, whose beauties Lafcadio Hearn would one day paint with a pen dipped in rainbows. Northeast of the town by a few miles, Mount Pelée loomed like a sleeping sentinel, with a purplish cloud-cape over his shoulders.

The trumpet of fame had already proclaimed the cruiser's advent. "Le pirate" had come to town! Hardly had the *Sumter's* anchor tumbled down through the limpid waters before crowds flocked to the waterfront. Berthing close to the quay the *Sumter* began coaling at once. Those customs officials who had refused him coal and been overruled now came aboard with profuse civilities. Semmes, whose rule was never to be outdone in hospitality, broke out bottles of his best wine. The officials were deeply touched. At the same time the island's leading French newspapers made the marvelous "discovery" that Semmes was, after all, a Frenchman. The raider was exceedingly grateful for the compliment—"for a compliment indeed it was, to be claimed as a Frenchman, by a Frenchman—the little foible of Gallic vanity considered."

But this pleasant interlude was not to last. The next afternoon Semmes was speeding up preparations for his departure. The last casks of rum and sugar were stored away; coaling and refitting nearly done. In another twelve hours the *Sumter* would be off again for the boundless nowhere. At this moment fate intervened.

At two-thirty, siesta-time in town, onto the scene glided the villain. The interloper was the new United States sloop-of-war, *Iroquois*, twice as large as the *Sumter*, faster by three or four knots, more heavily armed, with 9- and 11-inch guns. Baying after cold trails, she had cruised these waters for weeks sighting neither hide nor hair of the "pirate Semmes." Sliding round the north tip of the island the *Iroquois* had cruised down the coast, keeping out of sight until suddenly she materialized in the St. Pierre roadstead. She came up slowly under Danish colors, unaware of the *Sumter*, which lay concealed in the shadow of the hills. The *Iroquois* was trying to disguise herself. Her yards were disarranged, her guns run in, ports closed. A past master at camouflage, Semmes was quick to detect flaws in her masquerade. The finely proportioned, taut, saucy-looking *Iroquois* "looked no more like a merchant ship for this disguise than a gay Lothario would look like a saint by donning a cassock."

Semmes sighted the *Iroquois* before she saw him. He knew he was caught up with at last. He had not expected it, but here it was. Being immobilized at St. Pierre for the duration of the war had no charms for him. Indeed, being blockaded was farthest from his imaginings. It would have ended the *Sumter's* career on the spot. Besides, for aught he knew, other Federal warships might be lurking outside until the *Iroquois* had flushed the *Sumter* out of her hiding place. He might be able to outwit one, but hardly two enemy ships.

The St. Pierre anchorage was a wide open bay, with an exit round half the points of the compass. The shore line curved in a semicircle with the town nestled at the centre. Through his glasses Semmes watched the *Iroquois'* quarterdeck packed with officers scanning the waterfront. Apparently, the captain of the *Iroquois* believed that if she were there, the moment the *Sumter* recognized his ship she would take to her heels and fly for life, or rather, for death, under his broadsides. This made necessary the precaution of disguising the *Iroquois* and creeping up like a tiger that has scented but not yet seen her prey.

A sudden commotion on the *Iroquois'* quarterdeck relayed to Semmes he was discovered. Water began curling from the Northerner's bow as she sprang forward under a full head of steam. Figures began running to and fro on the deck. Down came the Danish flag and up went the Federal ensign. From the *Sumter's* lookout the old quartermaster growled down, "There she comes with a bone in her teeth." Almost immediately the good citizens of St. Pierre began rushing for the beach and docks to watch the fiery climax.

For the diligent Captain James Palmer of the *Iroquois* this must have been an ecstatic moment. Yonder was the *Sumter*, flying the secession flag! For weeks he had gumshoed about the West Indies, running down many rumors of the *Sumter's* whereabouts. Here now before his very eyes was the object of his interminable search. The "American corsair" (as he called her) was at his mercy, or so it seemed. Palmer may have had fleeting visions of a Congressional resolution of thanks, a presidential handshake and, most desired of all, promotion, perhaps an admiralcy. The setting is reminiscent of Lord Cornwallis' hopeful prophecy the night he thought he had snared George Washington at Trenton, "We will bag the old fox in the morning."

Semmes and his crew watched the *Iroquois* edging toward them. The *Sumter* went on coaling as if unaware of the enemy's approach. Steaming slowly, the *Iroquois* came to within gunshot range. Her ports were opened; then her guns run out. At any moment she might let loose a broadside. Moving nearer, she pirouetted back and forth across the raider's bow, feinting at her, closing in and backing off. Semmes laid low. There was nothing else for him to do. He knew his slightest warlike move would precipitate a bloody brawl in which he must be the loser. Palmer's purpose was brazen: to tempt or taunt Semmes into firing the first shot. He may have hoped thus to avoid dragging his own country into a wrangle with a European power whose neutrality the United States very badly wanted at the moment.

With the same reasoning, Semmes' legal mind told him to do nothing. He realized he would probably lose a fight, no matter who started it. But if there was to be one, he wanted Palmer to start it. The Emperor Napoleon was anxious to wage war upon the Northern states and a brawl in a remote colony might be excuse enough for him. So, though doing nothing was risky, Semmes understood that it was less dangerous than any move he might make. His protection lay entirely in the neutrality of powerful France which Palmer was even at this moment violating seriously. Meanwhile, crowds jammed the waterfront. The market

square and the housetops, too, were packed with all those who
hoped to watch a good, bloody fight.

The *Iroquois* backed off—for the time being—only to repeat
her aggression of French neutrality that night. Three times in the
midwatch the *Iroquois* steamed slowly toward the *Sumter*, as if intending to board her, before sheering off. Semmes took no
chances. He and his crew made ready to repel boarders. Sidearms
were issued; cutlasses flashed out.

"On board the little *Sumter* there was a fiery spirit of resist-
ance," said First Lieutenant Kell. "These short Roman swords
had so nice an edge they might have been used to shave with."

So close did the *Iroquois* approach her foe in the night that
Semmes could hear her steam gong. Once she moved to within a
ship's length of the Confederate cruiser. Semmes' men slept at
their guns until daybreak.

The war of nerves was on. Next morning the *Iroquois* anchored about a mile from the *Sumter*. Promptly a French gunboat which had come over from Fort de France notified Captain
Palmer that violation of French neutrality, whether by maneuver
or by menace, must cease. If he wished to anchor, he could
do so; if he intended to blockade the *Sumter*, he must withdraw beyond the marine league. Should Palmer anchor he would
have to give Semmes a twenty-four hour start in case the Confederate put to sea first.

Palmer seems to have been whipped almost before he started.
He informed Governor Condé that there was a Southern pirate at
anchor in the port of St. Pierre and requested permission to come
in and destroy him. This, of course, was refused. Now read what
the already discouraged Palmer wrote to Welles in Washington, "I
feel more and more convinced that the *Sumter* will yet escape
me, in spite of all our vigilance and zeal, even admitting that I
can outsteam her. . . . I have done all I can, and if she escapes
me, we must submit to the distress and mortification."

Unusual words for a naval officer to write, and odd for a man
as industrious as Palmer but they are there in the *Official Records*.

Heaving in her anchor the *Iroquois* withdrew beyond the marine league. By day she cruised back and forth off the harbor,
just outside the three mile limit; by night, she drew in a mile or

two closer to her prey, well within the forbidden waters. Sentinel-like she lay off the center of the bay. To escape, the *Sumter* must run either north or south. Obviously, she would not attempt it by day. It was highly imperative for the *Iroquois* to get early warning of the little cruiser's course if she made a run for it by night. To this end Palmer arranged with the master of a Maine lumber schooner which was unloading planking a short distance from the *Sumter*, to watch the Confederate cruiser and signal her course if she headed to sea. A Northern sympathizer on shore volunteered to help in the eavesdropping. He set up on the schooner's deck a powerful night glass that was kept trained on the nearby *Sumter* from dusk until dawn night after night.

Semmes knew nothing positive about such an arrangement. But seeing an officer of the *Iroquois* visit the schooner he put two and two together and divined that a code of lights was being arranged between the *Iroquois* and the schooner to indicate the course the *Sumter* took when and if she ran. Said he, "I could not know what the precise signals were, but I knew what signal I should require to be made to me, if I were in Captain Palmer's place."

Nevertheless Semmes fretted not a moment over this espionage. His problem was to get out before a second enemy ship appeared and sealed him up effectually, and to get out without a fight and without being seen. It was a big order.

Days passed. Both Semmes and Palmer fired barrages of official protests at the harassed Condé. Palmer demanded that Semmes be driven out of the harbor where the *Iroquois'* guns could finish him off. As for the violation of French neutrality, the Federal officer told the Governor he would just have to swallow it.

Semmes complained he was receiving from France such protection "as a wolf might accord a lamb." He protested indignantly against Palmer sending an officer "into French waters to act as a spy upon my movement; and he has, no doubt, in his possession rockets or other signals with which to communicate my departure to his ship."

Meanwhile the town was agog. Eight days of tension, with the two ships glaring at each other, threatening to explode any moment, had the island on a keen edge.

Semmes went about his business as if no drama was in the making. He had weighed all the odds and waited patiently for a propitious night, preferably rainy. He knew the lookout schooner would signal the *Iroquois* the moment the *Sumter* got under way. He had no way of preventing it, if the Governor would not. He decided to turn these signals to his own advantage. Once he had given the *Iroquois* the slip, as he believed he could, he would race along the coast within the marine league until he had shaken off his pursuer.

November 23 dawned crystal clear. This was the ninth day. For Semmes it was time to get going or get caught. Fortune had favored him so far, but it would play out and he knew it. An uncanny presentiment told him that longer delay, even a few hours longer, might be fatal. At noon it clouded up, suggesting an overcast night, but by sunset the skies were smiling again.

Captain Palmer must have had a presentiment also, for that same day he addressed another apologetic epistle to the Secretary of the Navy: "It is now the ninth day that I have been blockading the *Sumter*. She lies off the wharf, surrounded by a crowd, all anxious for her successful escape . . ."

He then admitted transgressing French neutrality by setting up an espionage post near the *Sumter*. "I have some understanding with some loyal people on shore to notify me by signal of her departure," but he defiantly proclaimed, "The French will doubtless think it a great outrage upon their neutrality, but they will have to pocket this, as I have been as forbearing as they can expect . . ."

In effect he was being considerate to the French by not starting a war in the very streets of their colony. Then his fears burst through again, "Thus far we have had the moon, but it is now waning fast, and with the utmost watching and devotion I fear I may yet have to report her escape. Would that there were another fast steamer to watch the other point of the bay."

Semmes had this same moon to consider. Moonlight was undesirable at this critical juncture when the *Sumter's* fate and his entire service to the Confederacy were at stake. Indeed, as Palmer noted, the moon was waning, but not fast enough for Semmes' purposes. The stars, too, seemed to conspire against him, for "every star is a moon in these tropical climates." At sunset the planet Venus was three hours high, provokingly beautiful and brilliant, yet shedding as much light as a miniature moon.

Nevertheless Semmes at noon summoned First Lieutenant Kell and issued orders for every man to be at his post by sundown. The ship must be in sailing trim, steam up, guns loaded. Eight P.M. was the hour. The starting signal would be the firing of the garrison shore gun. It was the first intimation Semmes had given of his plans. Several of his officers had dinner appointments on shore, but they must break them.

The sun went down in a sky so clear "there was not a cloud to make a bank of violets, or a golden pyramid of." Night came on though it was barely more than a semi-transparent wrap. The bay was glassy smooth. Yet the townspeople were not to be denied their thrill. They had sensed drama impending and through the gathering twilight Semmes could hear the eager hum of the densely-packed waterfront.

Nearing eight o'clock the windlass was muffled and the anchor hove in. The chief engineer waited, his hand on the steam lever. Poised at the taffrail was a seaman with axe uplifted to cut the after mooring line. The *Sumter's* crew were at their posts, quiet, transfixed by tension. The *Iroquois* was dimly visible, lurking way out on the bay. Not a light showed on the *Sumter*. The binnacle was screened so that only the quartermaster at the wheel could see it. Even the lantern in Semmes' cabin wore a jacket.

Now a minute to go! Sixty seconds that strung out like hours. Then flash! and the boom of the eight o'clock gun. Down came the axe on the hawser. A turn of the steam lever and the *Sumter's* propeller began creaming the shiny waters. The cruiser was off on her race for liberty. So wrought up were the townspeople that the *Sumter* had barely moved twenty yards when prolonged cheers rent the quiet air, "Vive la *Sumter!* Vive la *Sumter!*"

Semmes stood on the horseblock, tense, alert. Noting as day closed that the *Iroquois* imperceptibly nosed towards the north point of the roadstead Semmes swung the *Sumter's* bow sharply south. It was precisely what the *Iroquois* and her informers ashore and on the schooner expected him to do. Silhouetted against the city lights the *Sumter* could easily be seen heading south.

She had run perhaps three hundred yards when a young officer dashed aft calling out, "I see them now, sir. Look! There are two blue lights, one above the other at the Yankee's masthead," which Semmes instantly decoded into, "Look out for the *Sumter!* She's under way, standing south!"

"Instantly," said Palmer, the *Iroquois* caught the signal and headed full speed for the south pass. It looked easy and might have been had not Semmes traded on the very signal that was flashing the message intended to destroy him. By now the *Sumter* was off the south end of the town where the mountains broke off abruptly down to the sea, throwing a shadow across the waters. Certain that Captain Palmer had taken his cue and was speeding at full steam for the south entrance to head him off Semmes suddenly and sharply shifted his helm and did what many a poor Reynard has done when hard pressed by the hounds: he doubled back and began scooting north under cover of the land shadows. He had seen two blue lights whose import was obvious: The *Sumter* was heading south. Had Semmes taken the north exit one light, or three, perhaps, would have been flashed.

At this moment, after Semmes doubled back, the two ships were steaming in opposite directions at top speed. He had tricked the *Iroquois* by a simple ruse. But it wasn't over yet. Twice he had to stop to cool hot engine bearings. Anxious moments! He knew the *Iroquois* would soon realize she had been tricked and would about-face fast. The *Sumter* was vomiting vast clouds of black smoke that might betray her, even though her hull was invisible. Suddenly a rain squall came pelting out of the skies, enveloping the *Sumter* in its impenetrable folds, muffling her dense smoke as if in a blanket. Sombre Mount Pelée threw out a welcome sable mantle. Hugging the shore as near as he dared, keeping well within French territorial waters, Semmes sped northwards while Palmer bustled south to find—nothing. So heavy was the rain that soon the *Sumter* was groping like a blind man, but safe.

Nerves were wracked that night on the cruiser. A quartermaster, hitherto famed for his keen sight, started seeing too many things. "If he saw one *Iroquois* that night he must have seen fifty," said Semmes. "I was obliged to degrade him in the first ten minutes

of the run . . . and break him from his high office." The crew
had expected a fight and Semmes was "not sure an old boatswain's mate and a hard-weather old quartermaster, who had
shaved their heads for a close fight, are not somewhat disappointed
that it did not come off."

Towards midnight the moon broke through the clouds, revealing the southern tip of Dominica and inspiring Semmes to effuse,
"the bold and picturesque outlines of this island, softened by her
[the moon's] rays and wreathed in fleecy clouds, presented a
beautiful night scene."

At 4:30 A.M. Semmes finally went below. The *Sumter* was free
again. He was infinitely grateful. On his knees before his shrine
his lips pronounced two words, *"Deo gratias,"* words that on the
morrow he would inscribe in his journal of that eventful day,
November 23, 1861.

Sunday dawn broke and the *Sumter* took a holiday. No muster,
no calling the roll, few duties. Jack had a day of rest and relaxa-
tion, with an extra tot of rum to celebrate the cruiser's good fortune. The wardroom rang with banter and the luckless Palmer
came in for many a jibe and jest. Sitting among his officers, puffing a choice havana, Raphael Semmes felt an upsurge of relief
that he expressed in the poet's couplet:

> *Far as the breeze can bear, the billow foam,*
> *Survey our empire, and behold our home!*

Two hundred miles south the *Iroquois* was licking the wounds
in her pride. That same Sunday morning one of her sisters, the
fast *Dacotah*, "with a bone in her teeth," growled into the St.
Pierre roadstead, looking for a fight, but in time only to console
her consort. In his cabin Captain Palmer was writing to Secretary Welles: "Sir, as I expected, I have to report the escape of
the *Sumter*, to the great dejection of us all, for never were officers
and crew more zealous for a capture. At 8 o'clock on the night of
the 23d. the signal was faithfully made us from the shore that
the *Sumter* had slipped southwards. Instantly we were off in pursuit, soon rushing at full speed to the southern part of the bay,
but nothing was visible. . . ."

Palmer's failure to snatch the *Sumter* could not be condoned. With a bigger, faster ship, and with an observation and signal system set up within the harbor, he had let the raider slip through his fingers. Newspapers howled for his scalp and Secretary Welles promptly obliged them by relieving Palmer of his command and demoting him. A rabid press, frothing over the escape of the "pirate," even charged the hoodwinked Palmer with treachery. Semmes himself came to the defense of his "late opponent," paying tribute to his vigilance and skill though not forgetting to score him for his "conscienceless" violation of French neutrality. Semmes ladled out his thanks generously: "I was duly grateful to the slab-sided lumberman, and to Governor Condé—the one for violating, and the other for permitting the violation of the neutral waters of France—the signals were of vast service to me."

Some historians have, even at this late day, sought to belittle Semmes' ingenuity in extricating himself from the snare at St. Pierre, citing that the unfortunate Captain Palmer was later exonerated and restored to rank. That still does not rob Semmes of the glory of his achievement. To play out the piece: Palmer was heartbroken despite his rehabilitation to rank. He fell an easy victim of yellow fever at St. Thomas, in 1867, near the scene of his humiliation.

Admiral Porter summed up the affair in six words: "Semmes was too clever for Palmer."

⚓

⚓

13 *Across the Atlantic in Forty Days*

Had Captain Charles Wilkes been more successful in his long hunt for Raphael Semmes the United States might have been spared some unpleasant crawling. Diligently, Captain Wilkes and his old war steamer, the *San Jacinto*, had combed the cracks and crannies between Cuba and the South American coast, but found not a trace of the Confederate raider. Wilkes wrote Secretary Welles from Cienfuegos on October 24 that "everything is quiet and no vessels have been molested in their peaceful commerce. I have obtained no information of the *Sumter* . . ."

But the pride of this high-strung, high-tempered man was at stake. He craved recognition and honors. Then, steaming around the coast to Havana, he found what he thought the greatest opportunity of his life: the British mail packet *Trent* had just cleared for England. On her passenger list were two Confederate diplomats, en route to Great Britain and France, under protection of the British flag, to press for recognition of the Southern Republic. Snaring these two would shower the captor and the navy with unending glory, or so thought Captain Wilkes. It would also appease a long-standing grudge, dating back to his Antarctic exploring days, that Wilkes held toward the English.

On November 8 the *Trent* was steaming though the colorful Bahama Channel north of Cuba when the Federal cruiser intercepted her. One shot, then another, passed in front of the mail steamer. The *San Jacinto* meant business. Her ship's company was at quarters, ports open, guns run out. Coming to a halt, the *Trent* lay to and ran up the Union Jack. Marines from the American ship boarded the *Trent* and, over the protest of her captain, bore off the Confederate commissioners in triumph. On the night of November 23, the very night Semmes escaped at Martinique, Wilkes triumphantly steamed into Boston Harbor and delivered his two prisoners at Fort Warren.

The cruiser skipper had actually committed a grave breach of international law, but most Americans did not view it that way. He was given a conqueror's welcome. City after city feasted him, as if he had saved the nation from dire calamity. On him New York bestowed the key to the city. Congress voted him the nation's thanks. Crowds gathered outside his H Street home in Washington and serenaded him as the "Hero of the *Trent*."

The news of Wilkes' highhandedness swept England into a rage. Such trampling on the British flag must be avenged. Queen Victoria's "two bad boys"—Lord Palmerston, prime minister, and

Lord John Russell, foreign minister—took speedy action. Despatching an ultimatum to Washington they demanded an apology and the release of Mason and Slidell. Already sympathetic with the South, Britain rushed preparations to plunge into the war againt the Union. Her North Atlantic fleet was ordered to prepare for war.

With war fever sweeping England, Secretary of State Seward went about Washington like a cockatoo looking for a fight, threatening to "wrap the whole world in flames." To add to the furore, the Old Sea Serpent (as *Punch* lampooned Secretary Welles) put down his clay pipe and took up his pen to congratulate Captain Wilkes on "the great public service you have rendered in the capture of the rebel emissaries." Public service, indeed! If the North wanted to win, what chance had she with England, the world's greatest naval power, allied with the Confederacy? The answer was obvious—at least to Abraham Lincoln, if not to the members of his cabinet. Perceiving he had two "white elephants" (as he called them) on his hands, he summed up the situation in five words, "One war at a time." He could hold on to the Commissioners and feel the full impact of British war power lined up with the hostile legions now massing south of the Potomac—or he could give up the two men whose mission was to prove fruitless anyway. He chose the second course.

With crowds threatening to burn the legation at London, American Minister Charles Francis Adams suddenly had his hands full keeping England from throwing her power onto the side of the South. The *Trent* crisis had sprouted like a mushroom, all at once, without forewarning. Forgotten, temporarily, at least, were the *Oreto* and the *290*.

Having ordered two cruisers, Bulloch then busied himself in other directions. On the Clyde, he purchased a fast steamer, the *Fingal*. Loading her with munitions, he took command and sailed her successfully through the blockade into Savannah. From there he hurried to Richmond to report to Secretary Mallory that the first British-built cruiser would soon be ready for sea. On November 30 he was given orders to take command of this ship, fit her out on the high seas, and start raiding Northern commerce *à la* Raphael Semmes and the *Sumter*.

Yet of these happenings Semmes knew little. Before making his getaway at Martinique news had filtered in that Wilkes had overhauled the *Trent*. It led Semmes to predict in his journal that "the English people will regard this as an insult to their flag and in this way it may do us good." It tickled him to know that "the *San Jacinto* was in search of us when she took Messrs. Mason and Slidell from on board the *Trent*."

Semmes had now been away from home almost four months. Dutifully, he had written his reports to Richmond and dispatched them by the best means available. Not a word had yet reached him in return from his government, his family, or his friends. For information of how the Confederacy was faring he depended on scraps of news picked up at ports of call or from newspapers on captured ships.

The *Sumter* was becoming weary. A frail ship at best, she was never intended for the racking pace her captain had set. For overnight runs between New Orleans and Havana she was ideal. But now her boilers were corroding and her decks rotting. Her propeller sleeve leaked. Still, she was not yet unseaworthy and Semmes was determined to sail her as far as she would go.

But fear of the *Sumter* had already done its work at sea. Northern sail had almost disappeared from the waters in which he was operating. So Semmes began pushing eastward to find better hunting in the European sea lanes. He nursed the hope of capturing a large merchant steamer and converting her—with the *Sumter's* guns—into *Sumter II*. Already he was dreaming of a bigger, better, wider-ranging ship. What he couldn't do with a vessel built especially for commerce raiding! He knew nothing yet of the 290, taking shape at Liverpool.

Two days after vanishing from Martinique and northeast of Antigua, Semmes seized a large handsome brig, the *Montmorenci* of Maine, carrying coal for the British steam packet service at St. Thomas. With the taking of this ship Semmes modified his technique. Sending prizes to break through the blockade, or leaving them in neutral ports in hope of peaceful internment, had not panned out. Unwilling to burn ships carrying neutral cargoes he resorted to bonding, a practice that gave the world something to talk about. His cabin and quarterdeck became courtrooms where masters of prizes might plead their cases. On the *Alabama* he later established the "Confederate States Admiralty Court at Sea." Semmes was prosecutor, judge and court of last resort. He scrutinized the manifests of captured vessels with a piercing eye. The faintest suspicion of false declaration, or improper execution, automatically consigned prize and cargo to the flames. Semmes handed down his decisions as soon as the boarding officer returned from the prize with her master and papers.

As to the ransom bond under which Semmes released a prize, it was really a bet on Confederate victory. It obligated the ship's owner to pay the captor the face amount of the bond six months or more after the ratification of a treaty of peace and independence between the North and South.

But Semmes had no idea of being hoodwinked by spurious claims of neutral cargoes. When Skipper Brown of the *Montmorenci* strode into Semmes' cabin fighting mad—as he later claimed—he found the raider calmly waiting for him, slowly twirling the ends of his piratical moustache. To Semmes' incisive questions about ownership of the *Montmorenci's* cargo, Master Brown fired back a volley of hot words. Brown charged Semmes with threatening to burn the ship and her neutral cargo of English coal and swore he accepted the ransom bond of 20,000 dollars with considerable reluctance.

"Semmes took all my firearms, powder, et cetera, including a sword," said Brown afterwards. "I told him I wanted my firearms. He said it was one of the most important things to disarm his enemies, but when I expostulated with him that I must have them, as I had ransomed my ship and must protect her against small pirates, he said I was right and gave them up to me after I got on board my own ship, sword and all."

Semmes gave a different version, and little of that. His memoirs dismissed the skipper briefly: "Captain Brown was civil enough to send me on board, with his compliments, some bottles of port wine and a box of excellent cigars. He and his crew were paroled not to serve against the Confederate States during the war, unless exchanged."

Had Brown displayed incivility or bad temper Semmes would have noted it, as he frequently did. The skipper sailed away home to be acclaimed as a hero, who had backtalked to "the pirate Semmes" and gotten away with it.

The next day Semmes struck again. He had hoped to fall in with an oldtime sailing frigate, confident the little *Sumter* "with her single long-range gun could have knocked her into pie, as the printers say, before the majestic old thing could turn around." Earlier that same day he had wasted coal chasing a Spanish sail that somewhat resembled one of those old-fashioned warships. Yet he was not to go unrewarded. Soon the lookout scented real game. After a two hour chase through an angry sea the *Sumter* forced her quarry to heave to. She was the *Arcade* of Portland, bound for Guadeloupe with a cargo of barrel staves to exchange for rum and sugar. There were no neutral questions to ponder. Before setting her on fire Semmes had her skipper's telescope and chronometer brought aboard the *Sumter* though he returned the telescope to the master on learning that the handsome spyglass had been presented to him in grateful recognition of his heroic rescue of lives from a sinking ship.

Semmes now had sixteen chronometers ticking away in a small cabin beside his own. One of his amusements was winding and comparing them daily. He made a practice of seizing the nautical instruments of every prize. When a ship's master protested that the chronometers, sextants, and telescopes were personal property Semmes countered by asking them whether their ships were owned by the government or by a private person. "They saw at once the drift of the question. I was making war upon the enemy's commerce . . . if her chronometers, sextants, telescopes, and charts were left in possession of the master, they would be transferred to, and used in the navigation of some other ship."

Fetching the *Arcade's* master and crew to the *Sumter* Semmes gave orders to fire her. "The staves being well seasoned, she made a beautiful bonfire, and lighted us over the seas some hours after dark."

Semmes now audited his problem. Once again, his bunkers were half empty. With his boilers leaking and hissing, he let the fires die and raised sail. What coal remained must be saved for quick dashes after prizes or for possible encounters with Federal warships. Out of fuel he had not half a chance in battle. So he must cross the Atlantic under sail alone. When cruising off South America he had reduced his fresh-water capacity in favor of more bunker space. Now his water supply—sixty days' worth—was barely enough to last him across, for the weather was becoming heavier. He had calculated it would take fifty days to make his easting, but the high seas could make it stretch out longer. He must forego the pleasure of the chase until well across the Atlantic. Furthermore, in the crew of the *Arcade* he had six more mouths to feed.

On December 3 another large prize slid into the *Sumter's* basket. She was Semmes' fifteenth. When sighted the stranger was bowling along toward the *Sumter*. The raider's boilers were cold, her hinged smokestack lying on the deck. It would have taken two hours to raise enough steam to chase. Semmes resorted to stratagem. Quickly throwing a spare sail over the prostrate stack to prevent betrayal, Semmes hoisted French colors and held his course, as if unaware of the approaching ship. Deceived by the Southerner's clumsy appearance and the tricolor at the peak the newcomer ran up the Federal colors and rushed straight into Semmes' clutch. Before she knew it she was "already under our guns."

A fine, new ship, she was the *Vigilant*, bound in ballast from Bath, Maine, for the guano island of Sombrero in the West Indies. Semmes valued her at 40,000 dollars. In the late afternoon he fired her, the flames swirling high towards the evening sky.

Ten of the *Vigilant's* crew were negroes, and Semmes arranged his prisoners into messes, "a white bean and a black bean placed, side by side, at the mess cloth, my first lieutenant naturally concluding that the white sailors of the Yankee ship would like to be near their colored brethren." Semmes set the negroes at the pumps, a task they welcomed inasmuch as "they are agreeably disappointed that they are not drawn, hung and quartered and have plenty of pork and beans without stint."

December 8 was the fifteenth anniversary of the sinking of the brig *Somers* in heavy weather off Vera Cruz with a loss of half her officers and crew. Now, amid the howling of another storm, Semmes was to write a different record. So violent was the storm that the raider's lookout did not sight the next ship until she was within five miles of the *Sumter*. Mistaking her for a warship Semmes drew up cautiously, but soon he bore down on her and snared his first whaler, the *Eben. Dodge*, twelve days out of New Bedford, bound for the South Pacific. Through a rough sea and under lowering skies, the *Sumter* harvested a quantity of much-needed peajackets, boots, and flannel overshirts.

Dusk was falling when Semmes gave the *Eben. Dodge* to the consuming element. The fire fairly leaped at the oilsoaked decking. Lining the rails the *Sumter's* crew gazed in fascination on their last pyre on this side of the Atlantic. "The flames burned red and lurid in the murky atmosphere, like some Jack-o-lantern; now appearing, and now disappearing, as the doomed ship rose upon the top, or descended into the abyss of the waves."

Now Semmes had forty-three prisoners, including twenty-two from the *Eben. Dodge*. Up to now the prisoners had enjoyed the run of the ship. But they were too many now, numbering half as many as there were in the raider's crew. To guard against "forty-three courageous men" rising and wresting control of his ship Semmes was obliged to put irons—handcuffs—on his prisoners though he ordered them manacled in relays, one half at a time. Every twenty-four hours he shifted the manacles to the other half. Northern newspapers and government officials were to crucify him for taking this necessary precaution.

Battling mountainous waves and raging winds the *Sumter* plowed eastward over a deserted sea. The crack at the propeller sleeve had widened and water was filling the bilge at the rate of ten inches an hour. Twice each watch the pumps had to be manned. The drinking water ran low and all hands went on reduced rations.

Christmas Day passed bleak and lonely, "bringing with it, away here in mid-ocean, all the kindly recollections of the season and home and church and friends. Alas! How great is the contrast between these things and our present condition! A leaky ship, filled with prisoners of war, striving to make a port through the almost constantly recurring gales of the North Atlantic in mid-winter."

But for all Semmes' doleful retrospections the crew spliced the main brace, with an extra glass of grog, and the wardroom rang with toasts to the Southern Confederacy and her valiant champion on the seas, the *Sumter.*

Semmes had intended touching at the Azores, but these islands were so guarded "by the furies of the storm" he was compelled to change course and strike for Cadiz or Gibraltar. From an English bark Semmes got news—sad news that all England was mourning the death of Prince Albert "the Good;" cheering news of the burning of a large Yankee merchantman, the *Harvey Birch,* in the English Channel by the Confederate *Nashville,* a ship whose existence was in itself news to Semmes; exciting news that England was rushing to war with the United States over the *Trent* Affair.

Porter claimed the sinking of the *Harvey Birch* put Semmes on his mettle for a fresh onslaught on American shipping once he had replenished his fuel. This was hardly true. Semmes needed no such stimulant. What he really needed was a new ship.

For a fortnight now the *Sumter* had been crossing a desert tract of ocean where a sail was seldom seen, but now she was approaching a heavily-beaten highway—the road leading from various ports of Europe to the Equator, the coast of Brazil, and thence east and west. Soon the cruiser fell in with a procession of merchant traffic streaming out of the Mediterranean. On a single day Semmes overhauled and boarded sixteen vessels. But not an American ship among them! How did this happen? Semmes explained it, "Commerce is a sensitive plant, and at the rude touch of war it had contracted its branches. The enemy was fast losing his Mediterranean trade, under the operation of high premiums for war risks."

He amused himself by polling the sympathies of the fleet through which he passed. To each ship he pretended to be a Federal cruiser, first showing United States colors; only, shortly afterwards, to haul them down and run up the Confederate flag. To his gratification only one, a Prussian, saluted the United States ensign while all the others, "with one or two exceptions" promptly saluted the colors of the Southern Republic the moment it unfurled to the breeze. Semmes interpreted this poll to suit himself. "We were then beating the enemy, and the nations of the earth were worshipping success."

On January 3, 1862, the *Sumter*, with barely three days fuel left, and her bilge pumps unable to cope with the propeller shaft leak, dropped anchor in the harbor of Byron's "Fair Cadiz."

It is probable that Semmes, having been reasonably well received at Cienfuegos, had anticipated a cordial reception at Cadiz. So he sailed in proudly, with Confederate colors whipping at the peak.

His crew gazed wide-eyed at the picturesque city. To her Semmes tossed a flowery memoir, "Thou art indeed lovely! with thy white Mooresque looking houses, and gayly curtained balconies, thy church-domes, and thy harbor thronged with shipping. Once the Gades of the Phoenician, now the Cadiz of the nineteenth century, thou art perhaps the only living city that can run thy record back so far into the past."

But this was no time for misty reveries. Glamorous, enticing though she was, the arms of "Fair Cadiz" gave him scant welcome. It was obvious the moment he dropped anchor that Spain intended to hector him into vacating her waters as fast as the *Sumter's* propeller could drive her. The Confederate raider was apparently too hot an object for Spain to handle at this critical moment. Spain was having an attack of diplomatic hysterics. England was pressuring her to join in presenting a united European front against the North in what looked like war over snatching the Confederate commissioners from the *Trent*. News of President Lincoln's decision to surrender the Southern envoys had not yet reached Europe. Britain's Mediterranean fleet, called to home waters for service on the American coast, had just touched at Gibraltar, throwing Spain into consternation.

In reply to Semmes' request for pratique, the courtesies of the port, and permission to land his forty-three prisoners, came a peremptory order to depart in twenty-four hours. Semmes was not to be brushed off so easily. He knew his belligerent rights by the book and shot back a protest that read Spain a lecture thereon. Telegrams flicked back and forth between Madrid and Cadiz. A Spanish frigate stationed herself a cable's length from the *Sumter*. Guardboats spied on her day and night.

Spain apparently regarded the Confederate government as a mere political convulsion. Like all absolute governments she had no sympathy for uprisers. "It was on this principle," said Semmes, "that the Czar of Russia had fraternized so warmly with the Federal President."

After much circumlocution Spain grudgingly consented to admit the *Sumter* to drydock, but only for utterly necessary repairs, just enough to get rid of her. She could have no provisions, no coal, no munitions. She could also deliver her prisoners to the American Consul. That gentleman in the meantime flashed telegrams to London, Paris, Rome, and Barcelona pleading for Federal warships to speed to Cadiz. This done, he and the American Chargé d'Affaires at Madrid, Horatio Perry, hatched a tidy scheme to foment desertions among Semmes' crew. From Madrid Perry wrote, "It would be a service of which you must well be proud and which the government would not fail to appreciate, if you could find the means to persuade the misguided men who form the crew of the corsair that their only chance of safety lies in a prompt and voluntary submission to the government of their country." Perry's wife even tried to help the good cause along. A Spanish lady of some pretensions, she sponsored a banquet, *in absentia*, to which she invited the prisoners Semmes released and as many, or all, of the crew of the *Sumter* who cared to join in the festivities.

There was a note of bitterness in Semmes' journal entry, "The very devil seems to have broken loose among my crew the moment we reached Cadiz." They had been confined to the ship ever since leaving Martinique and shore leave was necessary. So off they went for a rollicking binge, some to doff Confederate allegiance forever. Cadiz flowed with everything dear to a sailor's heart: luscious, friendly señoritas, amorous, tinkling guitars, sparkling wines, alluring sights and sounds, with bullfights at wondrous Seville nearby.

The *Sumter* had sailed out of a Southern port with a hand-picked company yet "I had not half a dozen Southern-born men among the rank and file of my crew. They were mostly foreigners, English and Irish predominating." So it was to be with the crew of the *Alabama* to come. "On one single night," said Semmes, "nine of my rascals deserted."

Semmes answered this challenge with stern measures and vigilance. Only threats to shoot staved off a stampede. On each shore boat stood an officer armed with a revolver, with orders to fire on any attempting to slip away. But time was running out for the *Sumter*, as were her funds. Semmes had wired the Confederate Commission at London an urgent appeal for money. With much demurring the dockyard officials gave the ailing *Sumter* a "once-over." Seeing no holes in her decrepit boilers, they refused to touch them. After patching the *Sumter's* false keel, scraped off on the bar at Maranham, Brazil, and caulking up the leak in her propeller sleeve, the Spanish officials ordered Semmes to clear out in six hours.

Rebuffed and exasperated Semmes boiled over at last. It was January 17. No money had arrived from London. He had asked credit at the dockyard only to be humiliated by a brusque refusal. For two hundred dollars' worth of repairs he had only seven dollars to pay. Now Spain could go to the devil for all he cared. Scraping the bottom of her bunkers the cruiser got up steam and weighed anchor unceremoniously. As she nosed seawards a government launch came chugging after her "with a man standing up in the bow shaking a letter at us with great vehemence." Her Gracious Majesty—so the letter said—had granted Semmes her "gracious permission" to remain another twenty-four hours.

With a sense of impending tragedy Semmes shook the dust, or rather the waters, of "Fair Cadiz" forever from his seaboots, and the *Sumter* sailed off again, round the corner towards Gibraltar. Perhaps he would find the British more hospitable. "This was the second Spanish experiment we had made in the *Sumter*," avowed Semmes. "I never afterward troubled Her Majesty, either in her home ports, or those of any of her colonies. There is no proposition of international law clearer, than that a disabled belligerent cruiser, and a steamer without coal is disabled, cannot be expelled from a neutral port, and yet the *Sumter* was expelled from Cadiz." Semmes neither forgot nor forgave.

Obviously, the doughty little cruiser's raiding days were numbered. Her decks were rotting and caving in, her boilers were leaking and tumbling down. Perhaps, she would go down—as Semmes would have wished—in a last slashing give-and-take with a Federal cruiser, her guns blazing and her decks a shambles, fighting off doom until the waters sucked her under. Semmes had envisioned such a scene. It was to come true, though not on the *Sumter*.

Bright and beautiful was the afternoon the *Sumter* emerged from the harbor of Cadiz and headed across the romantic waters where Nelson, Collingwood, and Jervis had written some of the finest traditions of the British Navy. Cape Trafalgar and Cape St. Vincent loomed just beyond his vision. Soon the *Sumter* was rising and falling once more with the welcome heave of the sea, and the sun went down on a scene of beauty and peace and tranquillity hard to reconcile with war.

Towards dawn the *Sumter* entered the Strait of Gibraltar. The high white cliffs rose majestically and abruptly on either hand, softened and beautified by the moonlight. Not a sail was visible on the quiet waters. The vessel was approaching her last port as a cruiser of the Confederate States Navy. Yet this first warship to raise the Southern flag on the high seas was not to pass from the vast stage on which she had played her sensational role without a last flaming scene.

Dawn was breaking when the lookout's telescope revealed two sail coming out of the Mediterranean. Giving chase, Semmes altered his course, "as so many barks, ancient and modern, heathen, Christian and Moor, had done before us in this famous Strait." Soon the telescope disclosed the nationality of the two ships, "they being, as plainly as symmetry and beauty of outline, the taper and grace of spars, and whiteness of canvas could speak—American."

The boiler fires, consuming the last black scrapings from the bunkers, seemed to burn with gleeful fierceness. The little ship surged ahead as if she knew this was her final fling and she must make it good and long remembered. No disguise, no ruse, this time. The *Sumter* would play it straight and fly the flag that rightly belonged at her peak. With eyes a little misty and a thrill in his heart Raphael Semmes watched the Confederate ensign fluttering in the gleaming rays of the morning. Two hours of pursuit and then Boom! a gunshot, the *Sumter's* last.

Running to within hailing distance Semmes gazed on a splendid, freshly-painted bark. Adorning her stern was a great gilded eagle spreading his broad wings under a coronet of stars. White and sweet were her decks after her morning's wash-down. She was a picture to look at, a treat for a sailor's eyes, and the *Sumter,* looked at her "as only a cat can look at a sleek mouse." But surprising it was that the "sly little mouse, looking so pretty and innocent, should have so much villainous material in his little pouch."

She was the *Neapolitan,* of Kingston, Massachusetts, bound from Messina, Sicily, with a cargo of volcanic brimstone—sulphur —for the gunpowder factories of New England. Contraband of war it was, but the *Neapolitan's* master sought to stave off destruction by claiming his cargo belonged to the powerful British bankers, Baring Brothers. Semmes' decision was prompt, inflexible. Cutting short all argument, he refused to investigate the "bona fides" of the claim of neutral ownership. Sulphur was the chief ingredient of gunpowder to feed the cannon that killed and maimed Southern boys. So he burned the *Neapolitan* in the broad, open daylight—"burned her in sight of Europe and Africa, with the turbaned Moor looking upon the conflagration on the one hand, and the garrison of Gibraltar and the Spaniard on the other" while the townspeople of Gibraltar rushed to Europa Point and the heights of the great rock to watch the fiery spectacle. As the flames soared to the skies with unearthly beauty artists, with book and pencil, began sketching the extraordinary scene, "extraordinary in any age, but still more extraordinary in this."

If ever Raphael Semmes rejoiced in the destruction of an enemy vessel it was in the monstrous torch of the *Neapolitan* and her cargo of the stuff of war. For him it was magnificent. With exultation in his heart he watched the sulphurous smoke and flame spewing skyward. He had come in the nick of time, like the avenging angel, to save the lives of thousands of lads in gray from the enemies of the Confederacy.

Leaving the *Neapolitan* aflame, the *Sumter* sped off in pursuit of the second sail, whose master had been warned by the fate of the *Neapolitan.* She was the bark *Investigator* of Searsport, Maine, with a neutral, properly-documented cargo of iron ore bound for Wales. Taking a ransom bond of 15,000 dollars less one-fourth (because the vessel was one-quarter owned in South Carolina) Semmes spared the *Investigator* to enjoy the dubious honor of having been the *Sumter's* eighteenth and last prize.

By now it was dark. Flames, still rising from the *Neapolitan*, threw a reddish glare for miles across the waters of the Strait, lighting up the shores of Spain and Africa, glazing the renowned Rock with crimson. Like a spent racer, winded and worn down by the grueling pace, the *Sumter* slowly limped into the shadow of the great fortress and nuzzled towards the man-of-war anchorage.

Thus did Raphael Semmes make his dramatic entrance on the European scene. Standing on the quarterdeck the *Neapolitan's* inferno played on him like a giant red spotlight. There was no need to tell the people of Gibraltar who the newcomer was. They knew it was Raphael Semmes, torch-bearer of the Confederacy, who had brought the American Civil War to their very doorway. They had witnessed his blazing handiwork with their own eyes.

That night Raphael Semmes slept soundly, "Neither dreaming of Moor or Christian, Yankee or Confederate."

⚓

⚓

14 Hail and Farewell!

Gibraltar! For the *Sumter* it was the end of the trail. For Raphael Semmes it was the threshold from which he would soar on to even more thrilling adventures under the Stars and Bars. His star was still in the ascendant.

Like a pinioned falcon he beat his wings against the frustration and inaction which now tormented him. Dreams of getting the little cruiser to sea again harried him day and night. Yonder, beckoning, were the English Channel, North Sea, Mediterranean, and

European coasts, swarming with enemy merchantmen awaiting his blazing ministrations.

To Commander James H. North, right bower to Captain James Bulloch at London, Semmes wrote despairingly, "I am now lying perfectly idle, waiting for funds. I cannot strike the first stroke toward repairing my ship until I am in funds, and even if my ship were in a condition to go to sea, I have not even the wherewithal to coal her! And you can imagine how galling this is to me, as I could sweep the whole Mediterranean in from fifteen to twenty days, if I had the means of locomotion."

Moreover, he could have done it without molestation. If he waited too long, the furies would catch up with him.

Climbing one day to the top of the Rock Semmes' gaze swept the waters of the Strait. From this eyrie he descried all kinds of ships coming and going through the legendary gateway. Of the signalman stationed at the apex of the Rock Semmes asked, "Are many Yankee ships passing nowadays?"

"No," replied the soldier. "Very few since the war commenced, but we had a fine view of your ship when you were chasing the Yankee the other day. We saw you set her afire."

Semmes' thoughts were ranging far afield. "Would it pay me to cruise in these seas?"

"No," replied the signalman. Semmes said nothing, but he thought otherwise.

From all eighteen of his prizes he had gleaned "the paltry sum of $1000 so close to the wind do these Yankee devils sail their ships." His last two had yielded pittances: the *Neapolitan*, eighty-six dollars; the *Investigator*, fifty-one dollars! His ten thousand dollar sea chest had gone with the winds of the Atlantic. To William H. Yancey, Confederate Commissioner at London, he wrote, "I was in hopes when I first took the sea, that I should be able to live entirely upon the enemy."

Gibraltar! "Where Christian, Moor and Turk, Jew and Gentile had assembled from all the four quarters of the earth." The magic of Semmes' name drew citizenry and military alike to the quayside to gaze on the man who had strewn the ocean with blackened hulls and to marvel at the diminutive cruiser with which he had done it. Naval prowess was very dear to British hearts, and

Semmes basked in glory. Not too long ago Nelson had walked Gibraltar's streets. Here, where the *Sumter* squatted on the water like a black, weather-beaten duck, his *Victory* had often moored.

For the harried captain of the Confederate cruiser stern-faced war had suddenly smiled. Courtesies flowed like the wine at the regimental messes where he and his officers were regaled and toasted while the *Sumter's* wardroom rang with good cheer and gay parties. The beauty and fashion of the town turned out to spread a carpet of welcome. For the cruiser's young officers life was suddenly transformed into a bright, colorful medley, "dinners and dances, girls and laughing glances." Semmes marvelled how his youthful entourage could hold up under long nights of revelry. Yet he was indulgent. They had stood by him well. It was fabulous, like a beautiful dream after an aching nightmare. Daily, visitors overran the ship whose three-piece band serenaded them with Southern airs and a liberal interspersing of "Dixie." So often did they play the South's national melody it was soon being whistled on the streets of Gibraltar. Even the band of the Coldstream Guards indulged in its rousing strains.

On the morning after his arrival—Sunday it was—Semmes betook himself to pay a formal call on Sir William C. Codrington, K.C.B., Governor of Britain's celebrated rocky outpost. Briefly, Semmes stated he wished to repair and re-fuel his fainting ship and asked extension of the same facilities a Federal cruiser in similar plight might expect.

Codrington, a soldier of some distinction, very "English and military" readily assented, but observed that Her Majesty was exceedingly anxious to maintain strict neutrality in America's "unhappy war."

"There is one thing, however," cautioned Codrington, "that I must exact of you during your stay. That is, you will not make Gibraltar a station from which to watch for the approach of your enemy and sally out in pursuit of him."

"Certainly not," agreed Semmes. "No belligerent has the right to make this use of the territory of a neutral."

The Governor's stickling amused Semmes, who had just walked through the shaded streets in an aura of glamour. Sentinels snapped to attention as he passed. Honors were falling like gentle, welcome rain. The Confederate raider was apparently something to marvel at and admire. His nation was a belligerent whose flag was neither recognized nor saluted, yet never was there such an outpouring of hospitality as he found at Gibraltar.

Promptly, next day, the Governor's aide, Colonel Freemantle, gorgeous in the regimentals of the Coldstream Guards, came up the *Sumter*'s gangway with the rest of the Governor's staff to return Semmes' call. (The Governor could not reciprocate personally without violating neutrality.) With ruffles, aboard the raider went the visitors, profuse in regimental colors and insignia, much resembling an animated spring garden. The *Sumter*'s salutes soared up the sides of the Rock to come booming back like distant thunder. From many a British naval and military tongue Semmes heard arraignments of the Palmerston-Russell policy that forbade them plunging into the fray to help the South.

From the naval commandant of the port Semmes got an anchor to replace the one he had lost though, first, it had to be approved by the "law officers of the Crown," who happily saw no violation of neutrality. A ship, after all, must have an anchor.

Escorted by Colonel Freemantle Semmes went ashore and clambered the battlements of the famous Rock. Burrowing into the heart of the huge bastion, he wandered through the maze of casemates and galleries that made the Rock an impregnable fortress. An ardent Confederate sympathizer, Colonel Freemantle was soon to cross the Atlantic, hobnob with the high command of the grayback armies and pen a delightful, colorful diary that still holds its fascination in the present upsurge of interest in the South's Lost Cause.

Into the harbor one morning swept the *Warrior*, proud showpiece of Britain's warfleet. This long, slender ironclad shared with the French *Gloire* the renown of being the most destructive weapon of those modern times. Semmes gazed on the monster with fascinated yearning. To his journal he prophesied, "She is a monstrous, floating impregnable fortress. Wooden ships as battleships must go out of use. With this single ship I could destroy the entire Yankee fleet blockading our coast."

Thus did he see eye to eye with the Confederate naval secretary, Stephen Mallory, whose brainchild, the ironclad *Merrimack*, re-christened *Virginia*, was soon to sally from her lair at Hampton Roads and sink two of the Yankees' wooden cruisers. Yet of the *Virginia*, Semmes at the moment knew nothing. Nor did he know anything of the *Monitor*, taking shape in Greenpoint, Brooklyn.

Semmes had wired the Confederate commission at London for 20,000 dollars. Came at last a draft on Fraser, Trenholm & Company at Liverpool for 16,000 dollars. Cash in hand, now to restock the *Sumter*'s bunkers! Shorewards he hustled efficient Paymaster Myers to trade with the coal sharpers and pay a dollar or two more than the prevailing price, if necessary. Back came Myers, baffled and blocked. Not a pound of coal would Gibraltar's dealers sell. The ever-alert Federal Consul, Horatio J. Sprague, had stepped into the picture. Semmes willingly admitted the resourcefulness of these "well-drilled officials of Mr. Seward." Nor can it be denied that Sprague indulged in a bit of intrigue and lightly-veiled threats to withhold coal from the famished *Sumter*.

The moment the *Sumter* appeared Sprague immediately canvassed the coal dealers. A good salesman, he appealed to the commercial instincts of these "barons," who were inclined to do business where they found it. Sprague reminded them that American ships had patronized their bins lavishly. The war had brought them many new customers flying the United States flag. This Southern would-be buyer was a lone swallow, skimming the seas without consorts, or hope of them. Surely, they did not want to lose American trade. If they supplied the *Sumter* with coal, he would advise his nation's ships to cross the bay and trade with the Spanish at Algeciras. The gentlemen were duly impressed. Thus did Consul Sprague embargo Gibraltar's coal for the cruiser's starving firebox.

Fertile in expedients Semmes now drew on his vast store of legal lore. If the dealers would not sell him coal, why not press the super-hospitable British officials, to accommodate him from the government piles he could see in the dockyard.

To the Port Commandant he addressed one of the shrewdest appeals of his career, basing it on Lord Russell's recent pronunciamento that it was "not inconsistent with neutrality, for a belligerent to supply himself with coal in a British port." Semmes argued keenly:

Coal has been pronounced, like provisions, innoxious, and this being the case it can make no difference whether it be supplied by the Government or an individual, and this even though the market was open to me; much more then may the Government supply me with an innocent article, the market not being open to me.

Suppose I had come into port destitute of provisions, and the same illegal combination had shut me out from the market, would the British government permit my crew to starve? Or suppose I had been a sail ship, and had come in dismasted and the dockyard was the only place where I could be refitted, would you have denied me a mast? And if you would not deny me a mast, on what principle will you deny me coal, both articles being declared by your Government to be innoxious?

The true criterion is not whether the Government or an individual may supply the article, but whether the article is noxious or innoxious. The Government may not supply me with powder; why? Not because I may have recourse to the market, but because the article is noxious. A case in point occurred when I was in Cadiz, recently. My ship was admitted into a Government dock and there repaired, firstly, because the repairs were innocent, and secondly, because there were no private docks in Cadiz. So here, the article is innocent, and there is none in the market (accessible to me); why may not the Government supply me?

Semmes' eloquent plea produced no coal. Re-fueling a Confederate warship from Government depots was stretching belligerent rights too far. The *Trent* warclouds had just blown over. England was edging away from deeper involvement in America's domestic brawl. Her reply to Semmes was a polite No.

Straws in the wind were flying from London that gave Semmes his first intimation of a new command—and something to think about other than the *Sumter*'s predicament. On February 2, 1862, he was secretly notified that a new ship, *Oreto*, Bulloch's first offspring, was in the finishing stages at Liverpool. The Confederate high command at London proposed sending this ship to Gibraltar to replace the *Sumter*. Semmes wired a hasty reply, "Do not send her. Can come for her."

Sealing the *Sumter*'s doom, however, was a factor more menacing and deadly than desertion, lack of coal, or woebegone, enfeebled boilers. Over the horizon suddenly materialized the Federal sloop of war *Tuscarora*. On her bridge stood truculent Commander T. Augustus Craven, panting as hard for the *Sumter's* blood as did Captain Palmer when he first sighted the cruiser at St. Pierre. Patterning her behavior after the *Iroquois'*, the *Tuscarora* came sniffing in to pirouette before the *Sumter*, as if preparing to demolish her under the frowning battlements of the Rock itself.

It was raining and Semmes was brooding gloomily in his cabin, but he was quick to complain to the British Governor, who promptly ordered Craven to cease his threatening pantomime and infringement of Britain's neutrality. Craven's reply was impudent. He sprinkled it with abuse of Semmes. Codrington's gorge rose. He sent Craven a reply that made his ears tingle:

> I have to express my regret that you should think it necessary to use such terms in your correspondence with me, as 'the captain of the pirate Sumter', 'notorious corsair' and 'a man regardless of truth or honorable sentiment.'
>
> The Government of England has recognized the United States and the socalled Confederate States of America to be belligerents, with belligerent rights. You are aware of this fact, and it renders your terms of 'pirate' and 'notorious corsair', applied to a Confederate vessel in this anchorage, incorrect and offensive to the authority. . . .

The *Tuscarora* promptly steamed three miles out in the bay. Yet it should be said that Craven would, at Mobile Bay, atone for whatever indiscretion he may have committed at Gibraltar. He will forever be remembered for his "After you, pilot," a heroic gesture that cost his life in his sinking ship. In any event, the wolf-pack was closing in for the kill. The *Kearsarge*, sister to the *Tuscarora*, pranced in, anchoring a cable's length from the *Sumter* until the British ordered her to withdraw. The *Ino*, a clipper converted to war uses, joined the cordon. Trebly-blockaded was Semmes.

Meanwhile desertion took its toll. Nineteen crewmen vanished, among them the coxswain of the captain's gig. Soon the ship's company was whittled down to forty-six. Semmes' journal gives flashes of this sad attrition, "Eleven of my vagabonds still on shore"—"Five men in confinement"—"The devil seems to get into my crew. I shall have to tighten the reins."

He appealed to British officials. Their reply was hands off. They had no treaty with the unrecognized Confederacy. Nor would they permit Semmes to recruit replacements. The *Sumter's* deserters roamed Gibraltar's streets at will.

Yet the drama fast closing must have its *opera-bouffe* touch. Anxious to be of service to the cruiser a Mr. T. T. Tunstall, "a citizen of the Confederacy," suddenly appeared on deck one day with news that fuel could be had at inhospitable Cadiz. Tunstall was once American Consul at that port but his questionable fidelity had cut short his diplomatic career. Accompanied by Tunstall, Paymaster Myers hurried off to board a little French steamer that plied between Gibraltar and Cadiz. Enroute the coaster crossed the Strait and touched at picturesque Tangier in Morocco, whose low white buildings, mosques, and minarets bespoke the setting of an Arabian Nights adventure. To while away the two-hour stopover Myers and Tunstall went ashore and sauntered through the polyglot streets of the romantic city.

As fate would have it they soon encountered the villain of the piece, one James De Long, the energetic, zealous American Consul, whose eagle eye, in a manner not yet revealed, discovered the presence of these Confederate tourists. Appealing to the Moorish Governor, Mohamid Sidi Bargash, "The Employed of the Throne Elevated by God," to lend him a hand with a squad of turbaned constabulary, De Long seized the two Southerners, imprisoned them in the consulate, put them in irons, shaved their heads like felons, and proclaimed loudly they were pirates for whom a large ransom would have to be paid, knowing that Moorish blood was strongly tainted with ransom ideas.

The alarming aspect of this from the Northern viewpoint was the possible spawning of an international situation similar to the seizure of Mason and Slidell in the *Trent* affair, only this time with France instead of England. French influence was strong in Morocco. The two men had been seized while passengers on a French ship *in itinerere*. It was political kidnapping, a hostile act, lamentable and unjust, committed in the city of a neutral power whose destinies were covered by the French tricolor. France barked a quick protest at Washington.

This ridiculous, bizarre imbroglio reeled off like oldtime melodrama. Its ingredients ran from high drama to low comedy: Moorish mob scenes—one "Christian dog" demanding the blood of other "Christian dogs"—flashing scimitars—enraged French nationals threatening to burn the American legation—escapes over Consulate walls—exchanges of hot notes by France, Italy, England, Spain, and Morocco—Semmes writing innumerable protests to everybody concerned and threatening to cross the Strait and blow the barbarians to bits—a beautiful lady trying to hide the two unfortunate objects of it all. To cap this farce, a squad of American marines, perhaps inspired by their predecessors who had dashed to the shores of Tripoli, crashed the Tangier gates and bore off the two luckless victims of this nightmarish sideshow that lacked only a sheik chasing an American out of his harem.

The two Southerners, Myers and Tunstall, were transported across the Atlantic and landed at Fort Warren, Boston, only to be promptly released by President Lincoln, with an apology and a "Sorry, if we've inconvenienced you."

Time ran out inexorably. The "last gleam of daylight" had faded. Poised outside the harbor were now three implacable avengers. There was no escape. Semmes knew it, though to the last he hoped to make a run for freedom. He had fought off the very idea of abandoning the *Sumter*, yet the die was cast of itself. His own board of officers had condemned the *Sumter*'s boilers as unfit and beyond repair. The leaks under only twelve pounds of steam doused the fires. From London on April 7, 1862, came authority to lay up the ship, pay off the rest of the crew and report for duty to the Confederate Commission at the British capital. Sadly, Semmes mused to his journal, "And so the poor old *Sumter* is to be laid up. I am *hors de combat*."

Neglected by writers, or passed by as too sentimental or inconsequential, was a scene in Semmes' cabin that evening. Towards sundown he summoned his officers. For this last heartbreaking conclave he was scrupulously garbed in a new gray uniform tailored for him at Gibraltar. Bright gold stripes adorned his sleeves. Never did he look finer. Every inch he was the Captain of a ship of war. Silently he greeted each officer as he entered with a sharp, brisk salute. In his gesture there was more than just courtesy. His affection and admiration was ill-concealed. These were strong, dependable men, who had never failed him. There was no aloofness today. He was one of them, and they knew it.

They had seen rough times together. Danger had stood at their right hand from the moment they slid through the Mississippi passes. Never a moment when a sword was not dangling, as it were, over their heads. The comradeship between them and their common faith in the Confederacy had bound them as by straps of steel. Yet, resourceful as Semmes was, he and they were now in the clutch of circumstances they could not break.

With a wrenching of his heart he spoke, "Today I received authority to abandon the *Sumter*. I had requested it, as you know."

An audible sigh ran through the little group.

"I've had a struggle to know what to do. There is nothing else." His gaze ranged from one bronzed face to another. "I need hardly tell you how grateful I am to each one of you for your courage and your loyalty to the Confederacy and to me personally. I shall always admire you. Perhaps, we shall serve together again. I sincerely hope so. You need not be ashamed of our record."

Tears ran down the beard of gruff, kindly, efficient First Lieutenant Kell. There was mistiness in Semmes' eyes and a tremor in his voice. At a nod from Semmes his Malayan steward, John, entered with tray, glasses and decanter. Fine Spanish sherry it was. Not a word as Semmes filled the glasses.

"Now, gentlemen!" He raised his glass. "To the *Sumter!*"

"To the *Sumter!*" they echoed.

Up came every glass, and the cruise of the *Sumter* was over!

Yet he could not cut the ties that bound him to the cruiser, her officers and crew without committing his feelings to a permanent record and recounting her exploits with unashamed pride. To the ship herself he paid high tribute—no less sincere than that he would one day lay on the memory of the *Alabama*:

> When I look back I am astonished to find what a struggle it cost me to get my own consent to lay up this old ship. As inexplicable as the feeling is, I had really become attached to her, and felt as if I would be parting forever with a valued friend. She had run me safely through two vigilant blockades, had weathered many storms, and

rolled me to sleep in many calms. Her cabin was my bedroom and
my study, both in one, her quarterdeck my promenade, and her
masts, spars and sails, my playthings. I had handled her in all kinds
of weather, watching her every motion in difficult situations . . .
She had fine qualities as a seaboat, being as buoyant, active and dry
as a duck, in the heaviest gales, and these are the qualities which a
seaman most admires.

To his men, he offered this sprig of verbal asphodel:

There are other chords of feeling touched in the sailor's heart, at
the end of a cruise, besides the parting with his ship. The commander of a ship is more or less in the position of a father of a family. . . . When men have been drenched, and wind-beaten in the
same storm, have stood on the deck of the same frail little ship, with
only a plank between them and eternity, and watched her battling
with the elements, which threaten every moment to overwhelm her,
there is a feeling of brotherhood that springs up between them that it
is difficult for a landsman to conceive.

There was another, and if possible, stronger chord, which bound
us together. . . . our faith. . . . We were battling for our honor,
our homes, and our property; in short, for everything that was dear
to the human heart.

The reader has been introduced to my Malayan steward, John,
whose black, lustrous eyes filled with ill-concealed tears, more than
once during the last days of the *Sumter,* as he smoothed the pillow
of my cot with a hand as tender as that of a woman, or handed me
the choicest dishes at meals.

I had governed my crew with a rigid hand, never overlooking an
offence, but I had, at the same time, always been mindful of justice,
and I was gratified to find, both on the part of officers and men,
an apparent forgetfulness of the little jars and discords which always grow out of the effort to enforce discipline.

Lastly, he hung up the *Sumter's* shield, emblazoned with her
record:

She captured seventeen [eighteen] ships. It is impossible to estimate the damage done to the enemy's commerce. The property actually destroyed formed a very small proportion of it. The fact alone
of the *Sumter* being upon the seas, during these six months, gave

such an alarm to neutral and belligerent shippers, that the enemy's carrying trade began to be paralyzed, and already his ships were being laid up or being sold under neutral flags. In addition to this, the enemy kept five or six of his best ships of war constantly in pursuit of her, which necessarily weakened his blockade, for which, at this time, he was much pressed for ships. The expense of my government of running the ship was next to nothing, being only $28,000.

On April 14, 1861, Semmes and his devoted First Lieutenant, Kell, embarked for Southampton. As the British packet swept out of the harbor through the gathering twilight Raphael Semmes cast a last, lingering look at the *Sumter* whose "once peopled decks were now almost deserted, only a disconsolate old sailor or two being seen moving about on them, and the little ship herself, with her black hull and black mastheads and yards, the latter of which had been stripped of their sails, looked as if she had clad herself in mourning for our departure."

But the epilogue of this staunch, romantic ship should be told: sold and re-named *Gibraltar*, she soon sailed off as a merchant ship to run the blockade into Charleston. Thus did she return, at least, this once, to the Confederacy whose flag she had flown so gallantly. Two years later, beating her way through watery storm and stress, she foundered in the North Sea, and—said Semmes— "Her bones lie interred not far from those of the *Alabama*."

⚓

⚓

15 *Escape of the* 290

London, April 20, 1862. Raphael Semmes now had no command. Nor did he entertain the prospect of one. He and Lieutenant Kell decided to run the gauntlet into the Confederacy, report to the Navy Department and seek commissions in the army massing to defend Richmond against the onslaught of McClellan's vast force driving up the peninsula to hammer at the very gates of the city.

It borders on the incredible that Semmes should have deluded himself so greatly. That he was ordained to command what Admiral Porter called "the most dangerous machine to be used against American commerce ever yet planned," was beyond even the vision of Semmes, who at other times seemed endowed with second sight.

Yet the lustre of the *Sumter's* audacious captain had outstripped him to London. English hearts warmed to him and English doors opened as by magic. To the lodgings he and Lieutenant Kell occupied on Euston Square came many passionate sympathizers with the South to greet him and shake his hand. Much-sought-after, he accepted only the quiet privacy offered by an Anglican cleric, The Reverend Francis W. Tremlett, who took Semmes and Kell "captive" and bore them off to the Parsonage in Belsize Park, near Hampstead, London. Out of this pleasant sojourn flowered a friendship between the quiet churchman and the hard-hitting man of the sea that was to survive war and after years.

The new ship, *Oreto*, hinted at as he lay at Gibraltar, had not materialized, or, rather, had vanished down the Mersey, foiling the schemings of those who tried to impound her, and sailed off to be armed and munitioned in Bahaman waters. Re-named *Florida*, she was entrusted to Captain James Maffitt, an old, valued friend whom Semmes esteemed as, "a perfect master of his professions . . . brave, cool and full of resource . . . equal to any and every emergency that could present itself in a sailor's life."

Semmes found London buzzing with excitement over the recent slugging match between the ironclads in Hampton Roads. These crude antagonists, *Virginia* and *Monitor*, had written a stern portent on the naval heavens. The world's greatest seapower had read its meaning aright and taken warning: the days of wooden navies were numbered. The steam-driven, armored battleship had arrived.

The man Semmes most desired to meet in London was the energetic and resourceful Captain James Bulloch. Behind closed doors at Morley's Hotel Bulloch and Semmes clasped hands for the first time. At the moment Bulloch was residing in Waterloo, a village near Liverpool, where he could keep a watchful eye on the "merchantmen" taking shape on the Mersey nearby. He had rushed to London the moment Semmes arrived. Now they were face to face. Bulloch's admiration for the sea raider was unbounded.

First, Bulloch briefed Semmes on the cruiser situation and the overall Confederate picture. The *Oreto* had sailed, gotten off as it were by the skin of her teeth. His hope of commanding her had faded before other duties more important to the top officials at Richmond. Keenly disappointed, he accepted without complaint. Dutiful and patriotic, whatever was best for the Confederacy was best for him. His ambition was now fixed on the 290, being readied for launching at the Laird yards at Birkenhead. Bulloch revealed in utter secrecy the ship was to be named *Alabama*.

Generously, Bullock offered to step aside for Semmes to command her. He would notify the Navy Department the ironclad project could not spare him and recommend that the ship be given to Semmes, who, he felt, had earned it through the spectacular cruise of the *Sumter*. Raphael Semmes shook his head. He was not one to steal another's glory. This was Bulloch's show and this was to be Bulloch's ship.

So far as we can pin it down, Semmes never saw the *Alabama* while he was in England. It is conjecturable, though, that he did. From their meeting at Morley's Hotel Semmes accompanied Bulloch to Liverpool to spend an agreeable week in the quiet retreat occupied by the Confederate secret agent and his attractive spouse at nearby Waterloo. There is no evidence that Semmes ever visited the Laird shipyards. It would hardly do for "daredevil Semmes" to be seen reconnoitering around the 290 yet it is conceivable that, some way or other, Bulloch gave Semmes a glimpse of the ship on which his pride and hope were fastened. Nor did Semmes or Bulloch ever divulge an inkling of such a move. It would pinpoint suspicion on the 290. If, somehow, Semmes took even a peep at the ship, the secret was well-kept.

Late in May Semmes took passage on the British *Melita*, a fast blockade runner, for Nassau. With him went Lieutenant Kell and Doctor Galt, former surgeon on the *Sumter*. The *Melita's* voyage was bona fide, that is, she was not running the blockade this trip. Semmes made doubly sure of this before embarking. Seizure by Federal cruisers held no allurement for him. There was a money prize on his head. The Federal government was exceedingly anxious "to get hold of me." Traveling under a British flag he was reasonably immune from capture unless another "zealous but indiscreet Captain Wilkes" should turn up and seize him, forgetting the diplomatic dirt Lincoln and his Cabinet had to masticate after the kidnapping of Messrs. Mason and Slidell.

From Nassau, he would make a run for it, take passage on one of the slippery daredevils that sliced through the Federal cordon into Wilmington, Charleston, and other sealed-up Southern ports with seeming impunity and as regularly as mail packets. Twenty days out of Liverpool the *Melita* entered the harbor of Nassau, famous Bahaman *entrepôt* of the American Civil War. The nerve centre of the fabulous business of blockade running, this Eldorado was all bustle and action. Here they were: Yankees and Southerners, working hand in glove, while their fathers and sons fought it out on the battlefield.

The Victoria Hotel where Semmes and his staff of two were quartered, was thronged with guests, Union and Confederate, rubbing elbows, both obeying the same greedy instinct of trading on the miseries of war. Scenting the feast afar they had come like vultures. The ill wind that brought such woe and wretchedness to South and North blew untold prosperity to Nassau whose harbor was matted with shipping and whose warehouses and quays bulged with merchandise of every conceivable character. From England, came argosies bearing guns and ammunition, drugs and luxuries, wines and liquors, silks and satins, anything and everything the South desired. Here this vast mass of material for war and for pleasure, for which so many sold their birthright, was transshipped to small, fast, light-draft vessels, for overnight runs to the waiting South. The traffic was tremendous; the runner fleet, an armada: 1,156 of these eel-like craft were captured by the Federal navy during four years of war.

Nassau was a turning point in Raphael Semmes' career. Here on June 15, 1862, he received from Secretary Mallory orders that turned his feet back to the sea and despatched him on a mission

such as he had dreamed of. He was to return at once to England
and assume command of the *Alabama*. It was the first identifica-
tion of the ship as *Alabama* in an official document. Incidentally,
on this day the 290 was making her trial run down the Mersey. In
this same despatch the Secretary notified Semmes of his promotion
to the rank of Captain. It was his reward "for gallant and meritori-
ous conduct." Thus, on the Confederate Navy List, he took the
place of Franklin Buchanan, who had been promoted to Rear
Admiral for his handling of the *Virginia* the day she sank the
Congress and the *Cumberland*.

Acknowledging the Secretary's letter, Semmes wrote:

> In obedience to your order, assigning me to the command of this
> ship, I will return by the first conveyance to England where the joint
> energies of Commander Bulloch and myself will be directed to the
> preparation of the ship for sea. I will take with me Lieutenant Kell,
> Surgeon Galt and First Lieutenant of Marines Howell.
>
> It will, doubtless, be a matter of some delicacy, and tact, to get
> the *Alabama* safely out of British waters, without suspicion, as Mr.
> Adams, the Northern envoy, and his numerous satellites in the
> shape of consuls and paid agents, are exceedingly vigilant in their
> espionage.
>
> We cannot, of course, think of arming her in a British port; this
> must be done at some concerted rendezvous, to which her battery
> and a large portion of her crew must be sent, in a neutral merchant-
> vessel. The *Alabama* will be a fine ship, quite equal to encounter any
> of the enemy's steam-sloops of the class of the *Iroquois*, *Tuscarora*
> and the *Dacotah*, and I shall feel much more independent in her,
> upon the high seas, than I did in the little *Sumter*.
>
> I think well of your suggestion of the East Indies, as a cruising
> ground, and I hope to be in the track of enemy's commerce, in those
> seas, as early as October or November next; when I shall, doubtless,
> be able to lay other rich "burnt offerings" upon the altar of our coun-
> try's liberties.

It should be recalled that, after contracting for his two ships at
Liverpool, Bulloch had purchased the *Fingal* and sailed a shipload
of munitions—arms very welcome to General Lee—through the
blockade into Savannah. Hurrying to Richmond Bulloch was
soon closeted with Secretary Mallory who unfolded the Confeder-

ate prize secret. The U.S.S. *Merrimack,* hurriedly scuttled at her berth when the South overran the Norfolk Navy Yard, had been raised out of the mud and was being converted into an impregnable, steam-propelled monster that would pose a threat to Northern coastal cities. She might even run up the Potomac and shell the Yankee capital. The Federal navy had nothing to match her.

Bulloch was instructed to speed back to Britain and give top priority to the construction of two double-turreted ironclad rams. At the same time he was to order two more cruisers from the Lairds. These ironclads—designed on Confederate Navy Department drawing boards—were to be armed with seven-foot metal beaks that could skewer Lincoln's wooden blockading ships like so many turkeys.

Bulloch next raised the question of naming the wooden cruisers then being rushed to completion in England. Officialdom had already selected their names, bestowing on the first, *Florida,* for the Secretary's own State; on the second, *Alabama,* for the natal state of the Confederacy.

When Bulloch pointed out that the *Florida* (still the *Oreto*) would probably be ready for sea before he reached England he was directed to get the ironclad project going and then take command of the second cruiser. He was, no doubt, gratified by this, knowing the *Alabama* would be by far the finer ship. Once again running the blockade he reached London in March to find the *Oreto* poised for flight. He engaged a British skipper to take her to a secret rendezvous in the Bahamas. There they would meet the freighter that carried her armament.

However, in Bulloch's absence complications had set in. The American Consul at Liverpool, Thomas Dudley, had been tipped off to examine two ships being built at shipyards on the Mersey for a Southern gentleman named James Bulloch. Off he hurried to survey the presumably innocent merchantmen. The *Oreto* was ready to depart. To the perceptive Dudley, she and the 290 resembled just what they were, embryonic warships. Fishing about, he grubbed up other bits of evidence and then hastened off to London to pour out his conjectures to the stern, unbending Adams. The ships being built were Confederate raiders—they would be armed on the high seas. Immediately, Adams began prodding the British Foreign Office with stiff, precise notes protesting the warlike character of the *Oreto*. In the meantime like phantoms, bearing tidbits of fact and fancy, informants were flitting in and out of the Legation on Upper Portland Place. The records are studded with these vague, undercover reports.

Presiding over the destinies of Britain's government at this juncture, was a trio of statesmen who should be better known to Americans. There was Lord Palmerston, "Old Pam," older even than the American government he appeared to despise, or, at least, seemed to regard as bad-mannered and bumptious. Over the Foreign Office reigned aristocratic, acid-tongued, haughty, Lord John Russell, who spoke unreservedly about "the late Union." Hoping the South would win, he shut at least one eye when viewing Confederate violations of the Foreign Enlistment Act. He intrigued against the North until it became dangerous, or, rather, until Minister Adams jabbed him with the famous dispatch, "It would be superfluous in me to point out to your Lordship that this is war!" Filling out this pro-Confederate triumvirate was William Gladstone, Chancellor of the Exchequer, ardent Southern sympathizer, who amused himself re-drawing the map of the United States, yet who, in later years, admitted he should have known better. The House of Commons was pro-Confederate five to one.

Thus, it would appear this distinguished threesome was not too concerned over the fate of the North in the no-quarter fight for the Union three thousand miles away. What difference did it make if the Confederates built a few ships in English yards—provided they were not outright vessels of war? Minister Adams' protest on the *Oreto* received scant scrutiny. Lord Russell demanded "credible evidence," not gossip purchased in waterfront pubs by a fertile-minded American Consul. As for munitions: both North and South were outbidding each other for all that British factories could turn out. England was profiting by the war. The *Sumter*'s toll of American shipping, the flight of Uncle Sam's ships to the British flag, made cheerful reading for her maritime interests. The "cotton famine" brought miseries to half a million English working men, but that would pass. (The Federal Government, pouring millions into England for war materials, was, in point of fact, a far better cash customer than the Confederacy whose financial underpinnings were wobbly at best.) Lord Russell did not hesitate to assert he would not immure ships so long as they were unarmed. His Lordship never once surmised that the sleek 290, rising gracefully at the Laird Yards, was destined to leave a crisscross trail of red-burning merchantmen from the Carribean to the Orient. Nor, for that matter, did any one else.

The Blue and the Gray were, by now, scratching and clawing at each other over England like two cats fighting in a strange alley. Bulloch waged a private, shotless, relentless war with United States espionage agents who swarmed about the shipyard. It was cloak and dagger work at its best. Bulloch later revealed that "spies lurking about tampered with the workmen at Messrs. Lairds . . . and a private detective named Maguire was taking a deep and abiding interest in my personal movements."

This was an understatement. He was shadowed night and day. His mail was rifled; his life threatened. Would-be detectives perceived his fine hand in every ship being built in England. But the chop-whiskered, high-powered bundle of energy, for so he was, went his way quite coolly, as if unperturbed by the violent lightning that flashed about his head.

Union officials began buying rumors wholesale. Scenting easy money, Liverpool waterfront loafers served up "hot tips" to order. Even trollops were not averse to this means of picking up a pound or two.

Bulloch's daily life brimmed with danger and thrills, obliging him to arrange a secret network of "Confederate friends" to keep him posted. Protection of his ready-to-hatch cruiser, 290, was imperative. Threats to blow up the graceful hull sprinkled his mail. One "friend of his," presumably a young official in the British Foreign Office, proved more valuable to him than the host of hired informers ever were to the Federal Legation.

Bulloch's letter to Secretary Mallory written shortly after the *Oreto* got to sea indicates his belief that the British Foreign Office, bedeviled by the insistent Adams, would eventually clamp down a stricter application of the Foreign Enlistment Act. Adams' pen was sharp. His pricking notes to Lord Russell were becoming more and more pointed. The American government would hold Britain responsible for every dollar of destruction inflicted by British-built cruisers. Yet, so well did Bulloch shield and conceal the "real character" of the 290, it was not until June 23, 1862, that Adams had evidence he himself considered worthwhile to bulwark his assertion that the ship was being constructed to prowl after American commerce. He assembled a mountain of affidavits. Proving that about an unarmed ship, even though her design suggested warlike pursuits, was not easy. But getting the 290 to sea through the interstices of the Foreign Enlistment Act and over the legal shoals of neutrality, was an enterprise involving far greater skill, tact and patience. James Bulloch possessed these necessary virtues in abundance. The Lairds were putting the finishing touches to the 290, without disguise. Repeatedly, they had refused to identify the mysterious customer. Bulloch himself admitted nothing. "I never told an employee more than was necessary for him to know, and never gave any reason for any order having reference to the outfit or movements of the ship. Everything was done quietly, without any excitement or appearance of haste. At the last moment she was hurried off with some precipitancy, but this will be explained in due course."

The 290, like the *Florida,* bore more than one name in passing from a mere entity in a dockyard to a commissioned warship. On May 15 the graceful hull was launched. Sticklers for tradition, the Lairds invested the baptism of their ship with ceremony, and wisely so. Departure from the time-honored custom would unsling fresh onslaughts of suspicion. Nor could the 290 slide into the mucky dockside waters of the Mersey anonymously, or with merely a number. A name she must have. To christen her *Alabama,* or anything remotely associated with the Confederacy, would of itself advertise her destination and purpose. This Bulloch knew well, though he did not discuss it with the Lairds. As the day neared he suggested that handing a ship into her natural element "would be more fittingly, though not so gracefully done, by one of the 'opposite sex.'" To an English lady whose hospitality and sympathy for the South had endeared her to Bulloch and his wife, he extended an invitation to christen the ship and bestow her own given name on the new ship. This lady graciously consented to perform the office and fulfilled it "in a comely manner, little knowing she was constructively taking part in a great Civil War and wholly unconscious that she was helping make work for five eminent statesmen at Geneva ten years after. I hope her conscience has never upbraided her since, and that she has not felt in any way responsible for the bill of three million pounds which her Most Gracious Majesty had to pay on account of the *Alabama* Claims."

So well did Bulloch mask the lady's identity that even today mystery veils it. Her name, we know, was Henrietta. To avoid embarrassment to the sponsor Bulloch resorted to Spanish, a language that provided "a flexible and mellifluous equivalent"—Enrica—for the given name of this lady, who splattered the *Enrica's* bow with a bottle of Rheims champagne. This mystifying Spanish touch sent Federal officials baying off on another scent. Gullibly swallowing rumors as if they were chunks of good Stilton cheese, they "took off" on the assumption that the *Enrica* was being built for the Spanish Government, or, at least, for a Spanish firm.

Hardly had the ship touched the water before derricks began swinging her first heavy pieces of machinery on board. The Lairds made quick work of installing her engines and completing her outfitting. James Laird declared her "the finest cruiser of her class in the world" and her trial run on June 15 gave promise of a vessel that could skim the seas like a bird. In six weeks Bulloch could take her away—unless in the meantime the British government yielded to Adams' prods and seized her.

Next on Bulloch's agenda was engaging a skipper for the *Enrica*. She must leave England under the British flag and a British master. This was a delicate business. His choice fell on an intelligent young English mariner, Captain Mathew J. Butcher, first officer of a Cunard liner. Bulloch sized his man up with keen insight. Butcher had the necessary qualities: absolute integrity, control of his tongue, and poise under pressure. He was employed merely to take a new ship to an appointed rendezvous, possibly off the West Indies, but certainly outside the British Isles, and deliver her to an officer authorized to receive her. He did not tell Butcher he expected to command her himself.

Obviously, the Southerner was obliged to take the skipper behind the smokescreen that had camouflaged the 290 or, as Bulloch put it, to confide to him "more than what appeared on the surface." It was a prodigious trust, putting the fate of the enterprise in the hands of this young man, a total stranger, who nevertheless proved the very soul of honor. Butcher had no faintest dream of what farflung exploits hinged on his integrity. A single careless, unguarded remark, would have spoiled Bulloch's months of well-laid planning; even a hint of gossip over a glass of ale, would have wrecked the entire naval program of the Confederacy in Britain.

Once on the high seas Butcher had absolute authority. By betraying his trust and sailing the ship straight to New York instead of to Bulloch's designated rendezvous, he would have received the plaudits of a nation as well as a handsome reward for double-dealing his employer. Closer at hand, he need only have walked into the American Consulate at Liverpool, revealed what he had been told and pocketed a tidy sum. Consul Dudley was bidding high for even shreds of gossip.

As master of the *Enrica* it was Butcher's duty to ship her crew. Bulloch was utterly explicit and legitimate in his instructions thereon. No man must be signed on under false pretenses. Nor must Butcher seek to induce any man to enter the Confederate service until the ship had passed beyond British jurisdiction (recruiting for the South was, in fact, not part of the bargain).

Next, Bulloch provided the *Enrica's* essential "furniture," the armament that would make her into a warship. He instructed a confidential ship agent to find a moderate-sized sailing vessel suitable for a West Indian voyage. He got just what he wanted, the *Agrippina*, an ungainly bark of about 450 tons that had crossed the seas for years. Staunch she was, though dirty and weatherbeaten. Certainly nothing to excite suspicion. Bulloch chartered her at once. Her skipper came with the deal, a dour, hard-bitten old Scotchman, Alexander McQueen, who brought the old freight carrier up to the London loading docks. McQueen was dependable and happy enough as long as there was a dram in the bottle. Bulloch saw that the *Agrippina* was well supplied with Scotland's "breath o' the heather."

Into the old ship's hold went the *Enrica's* battery, ammunition, small arms, clothing and hammocks for one hundred and fifty men, extra stores of all kinds, and 350 tons of Cardiff coal. McQueen knew nothing of the enterprise he was engaged in, nor did he ask. That the cargo was largely war materials made little difference. Scores of ships were shoving off for Nassau weekly loaded to the gunwales with everything from saltpeter to cutlasses. Bulloch told McQueen nothing. Apparently, Federal snoopers along the London waterfront failed to associate the bark taking on war stores with the suspect in the Laird Yards at Liverpool.

July 1, 1862. The *Enrica* was nearly ready for sea and Bulloch made preparations to depart. In two weeks, certainly three, the Lairds would deliver the ship. Lieutenant James R. Hamilton, C.S.N., had arrived for duty as First Lieutenant. Other officers were reporting daily. Bulloch had even mapped out his sphere of operations. He proposed to make a joint sweep with the *Florida,* Captain Maffitt, at the trade routes off the Atlantic Seaboard. He and Maffitt knew "our way into every harbor from Boston to the Mississippi."

Then, out of a clear sky, the blow fell: a despatch sped in from Secretary Mallory, crushing his hopes and plans. He was not to command the *Alabama*. The Navy Department deemed it advisable to hand the command to Captain Semmes. A bolt out of the blue, it hurt terribly. Grieved and chagrined, he read Mallory's despatch, "Your services in England are so important at this time, that I trust you will cheerfully support any disappointment you may experience in not getting to sea. The experience you have acquired renders your agency absolutely necessary. . . ."

Scant compensation were these words though Bulloch took the jolt in his stride, without a murmur other than the sad reflection in his memoirs, "This change coming so late, when the ship was, in fact, ready for sea, and had been delivered to me by the builders, was very embarrassing."

Yet, Richmond had issued the orders and Bulloch obeyed them. Sentiment must play no part in his war. Just why Bulloch was superseded was never made clear, officially. Mallory never explained. Nor did any other Confederate officer or official. Most probably the Southern naval hierarchy—President Davis, perhaps —felt it safer to entrust this first-class cruiser, designed and built for commerce raiding, to the man who had graduated in the art. Mallory, with his heart set on ironclads, must have urged that Bulloch was indispensable to the ironclad program he had just negotiated with the Lairds.

The tempo of the diplomatic duel was now stepped up fast. On June 23, almost eleven months after Bulloch ordered the 290 from the Lairds, American Minister Adams handed a package of official dynamite to Lord John Russell. He charged the building of the *Enrica* was a "manifest violation" of the Foreign Enlistment Act and demanded steps be taken to halt her impending departure. His Lordship immediately directed the Liverpool customs authorities to investigate. Hurrying to the Laird yard the customs men ransacked the *Enrica*. Not a gun, pistol, weapon of any kind, did they find. Not an ounce of powder. Not a shred of evidence of the ship's warlike intent. She could have been captured with a horse pistol and a bit of nerve. This official exploration whitewashed the whole affair.

On July 4, Lord Russell parried: Mr. Adams' suspicions were groundless. Notwithstanding, the American Minister was not to be shaken off so easily. Time was slipping by. The ship might sail any day. On July 21, 23, and 25 Adams submitted further depositions, supporting his charges of the suspicious character of the *Enrica*. One affidavit, by a seaman, declared that Butcher, the captain chosen by Bulloch, had revealed the ship was going out to fight for the Confederate States.

Lord Russell, alarmed perhaps, now submitted Adams' briefs to the Crown counsel, who, on July 29, recommended to the British Cabinet that the evidence, coupled with the character of the vessel, made it clear she was intended for depredations against the United States; and urged she be seized forthwith.

Yet the most powerful argument Adams offered was his hint that, if England did not step in and impound the ship, he would pack his baggage and go home—tantamount to breaking off diplomatic relations, the first step to war. Adams later accused Lord Russell with conniving in the *Enrica's* escape. This was never proved. It was, unquestionably, the jangling of Adams' diplomatic sword that moved Russell to action.

For James Bulloch, Saturday, July 26, 1862 was the payoff

day. On the day before, Adams had submitted his conclusive depositions to Lord Russell. About 8 A.M. that morning Bulloch received at his home a message written in as few words as could convey it. It was signed "A friend." There was no mark to identify its source though Bulloch at once knew whence it came. He revealed later, "On Saturday, July 26, 1862, I received information from a private but most reliable source, that it would not be safe to leave the ship in Liverpool for another forty-eight hours." Bulloch knew his man. The inference was obvious: seizure was imminent. Adams' importunities and threats had struck home. It is hard not to imagine that the whisper came straight from Downing Street.

John Bright, the great liberal and a staunch supporter of the Union in Parliament throughout the war, charged Lord Russell with being a party to the message to Bulloch. Who knows? One man's guess is as good as another's. Lord Russell never explained, though he did apologize for the escape of the *Enrica*.

Bulloch moved instantly. The *Enrica's* fate hung on a red-tape hair. Spic and span, she nuzzled proudly at the Laird docks. He was determined his bantling *Enrica* was not to be caught napping. Coaled, her stores stowed away—except for armament—she was ready to sail on short notice, though Captain Butcher had not yet shipped a full crew. The men might become restive and excite suspicion.

Posthaste, Bulloch hurried to see the Lairds, who were as proud of the ship as of a child they had raised and brought to polished manhood. Divulging not a hint of the tip-off he had received, Bulloch told them that though the initial trials had been satisfactory he wished to make an all-day run with the *Enrica*, reminding them that a second trial had been promised, if he desired it, *after* filling her bunkers and loading stores. He volunteered no more than that. Discreetly, the Lairds, who must have sensed something in the wind, asked no compromising questions.

Ordering Captain Butcher to ship a few more hands and keep the vessel ready to steam off on Monday's tide, Bulloch confided that the *Enrica* would not return from this second "trial" run. The crew must have no inkling of what was contemplated. That night Bulloch slept not at all. Nor the next. Early Monday, July

28, the *Enrica* sailed innocently out of the harbor, decked with flags, ostensibly off for another trial trip. Bulloch made a fête of it, inviting a number of friends to be his guests. Bright summer dresses enlivened this strange ruse. Bulloch was a genial host, adept at partying, bantering with the ladies, swapping wit with the gentlemen. Today he was at his level best. Buffet luncheon was served in the cabin. The day sparkled like the champagne that flowed in toasting the new ship. Over a sea as smooth as glass the *Enrica* went through her paces like a thoroughbred. Later Bulloch's wife poured tea. Only she, her husband, and Captain Butcher knew what lay ahead.

At 3 P.M. Bulloch informed his guests he intended to keep the vessel out overnight. Surprised, the company took it in good stead and returned to Liverpool on the tender *Hercules* in company with their host. Before leaving, however, Bulloch ordered Captain Butcher to steam down to Moelfra Bay on the Welsh coast and wait for him. On reaching Liverpool, Bulloch ordered the *Hercules* to meet him at the landing stage next morning at 7 A.M. That night, Bulloch again slept not a wink. He would not have returned to the ship, but the *Enrica* needed more men and he had arranged with a shipping master to round up about forty hands for a voyage to the Bahamas or possibly Havana.

At the quay, next morning, he found a ridiculous scene that gave a comic touch to the drama of the *Enrica's* escape. The *Hercules* was there. So was the crimp with two score seamen, and their ladies. It looked as if the bedizened demimonde of Liverpool had taken over the deck of the *Hercules*. They were "of that class who generally affect a tender solicitude for Jack when he is outward-bound, and is likely to be provided with an advance-note."

Bulloch was obdurate. The ladies must go ashore. He ordered the ship cleared. So heartrending were their outcries, the shipping master warned Bulloch that the women ruled the hour. Either they went along, or the men did not. If there were to be advance wages, the ladies must get their share.

Bulloch capitulated at once. This was no time to parley. Perhaps, he recalled Napoleon's advice, "Do not fail to give good dinners and to pay attention to the women."

At 4 P.M. the *Hercules* drew alongside the *Enrica* in Moelfra Bay. Rain was falling; the sailors and their fair friends were nearly starved, but they scrambled up the ship's sides like fancy-dressed monkeys. Jack was not yet in a suitable frame of mind to talk business so Bulloch proceeded to make him so. First, he ordered the *Enrica's* steward to serve up the best supper he could concoct, to serve it hot, plenty of it, and fast. To add "zest and cheerfulness to the meal, all hands were refreshed with a safe allowance of grog, the ladies participating. Well-fed, puffing his pipe, Jack began to mellow."

Now came the moment for business. Bulloch summoned the men aft, the ladies, too. He explained the *Enrica* had been cruising in the Channel for a last check on her engines and would proceed on her run to Havana without returning to Liverpool. Would they ship for the voyage? For each man one month's pay in advance would be laid down on the capstanhead. It was something to chuckle over afterwards, but at this moment a few dozen frowsy damsels held the fate of the *Alabama* in their hands. The people paired off for hurried whisperings. The ladies said yes. Jack could not gainsay them. One by one each man, with his lady, came to the cabin where Captain Butcher sat at a table spread with intriguing British cash. As he signed the Articles he was handed the stipulated month's advance, only to be promptly relieved of it by his lady, who clung even closer at this stage of their relationship.

It was midnight before the touching scene closed. Rain was blowing in spiteful squalls. Inhospitable as it seemed to turn a contingent of females out of doors on such a night, James Bulloch could do nothing else. Pressing considerations made it imperative daylight should not find the *Enrica* in Moelfra Bay. The last man was signed and paid, and the order given to "clear ship." So, over the side Bulloch eased the ladies with banter and a cheery goodnight and a last noggin of rum. Napoleon was right, thought Bulloch, as the *Hercules* chugged off for Liverpool: pay attention to the women.

Just before Bulloch had embarked from the landing stage that morning, July 29, a telegram was handed him from a "judicious friend," warning that the U.S.S. *Tuscarora* had hurriedly steamed out from Queenstown to head off the *Enrica*, when, and if, she took the southerly exit from the Irish Sea through St. George's channel. Taking a lesson from Raphael Semmes' technique at Martinique, Bulloch turned the *Enrica's* nose north about. The night was black and dirty. Prudence warned him this was no time to vacate a sheltered roadstead and venture into the Irish Sea, but he had no choice. The *Enrica* was on her own now, a fugitive, easy prey for anything with a gun.

Meantime, back at Liverpool, officers of the Crown, acting on instructions from Lord Russell, sped to the Laird Yards to intercept the *Enrica*. But the hawk had flown. A British gunboat dashed fruitlessly down the Mersey to catch her before passing beyond British waters. Nor did Bulloch know that the *Tuscarora* would shortly glide into Moelfra Bay to find nothing more exciting than blue water that told no tales.

On July 30, 1862, while the baffled Adams fumed about the Legation and called heaven to witness his promise of retaliation, the Surveyor of the Port of Liverpool was writing his official report of the near-seizure: "I have only to add that your directions to keep a strict watch on the said vessel have been carried out and I write in the fullest confidence that she left this port without any part of her armament. She had not as much as a signal gun or musket."

It was the old story. Semmes was too smart for Palmer at Martinique; Bulloch was too fast for the customs men at Liverpool.

It was 2 A.M. when the *Enrica* plowed into the Irish Sea, setting a course around the north of the Emerald Isle. Next morning she dipped past the Calf of Man. That evening towards dusk she stopped her engines off Giant's Causeway. In a pelting rain Bulloch hailed a fishing boat which landed him and the pilot on the rugged Antrim shore.

Ensconced in a little Antrim inn Bulloch heard the wind skirling and snifting about the gables while he and Pilot Bond ate dinner and sipped toddy of the best Coleraine malt. But "my heart was with the little ship buffetting her way around that rugged north coast of Ireland. I felt sure that Butcher would keep his weather-eye open, and once clear of Innistrahull, there would be plenty of sea-room; but I could not shake off an occasional sense of uneasiness."

Nevertheless Bulloch slept well that night—for the first time in ninety-six hours. He could well afford to rest.

To run out the *Tuscarora's* role to its bitter end: the cruiser had sped to England from Gibraltar at the request of Minister Charles Francis Adams to blockade the suspected departure of the "pirate steamer" *Enrica*. At Southampton, on July 29, the day of the *Enrica's* flight, Captain Craven received an urgent alarm from Adams: "The vessel is steaming out of the Mersey." Dashing into St. George's Channel, the *Tuscarora* touched at Queenstown, Ireland, where she picked up a second Adams' despatch: "The vessel is off Point Lynas," a jut of land overlooking Moelfra Bay, where Bulloch had anchored overnight. Adams' watchdogs were vigilant to be sure, but always half a step behind.

Rushing at forced draft to Point Lynas, the *Tuscarora* found nothing. The *Enrica*, well on her way to the Azores, had left no trail, leading Captain Craven to infer correctly that the "pirate went to sea by the North Channel." In a final desperate attempt to head off the fugitive ship the thwarted Adams ordered Craven to "follow the vessel across the Atlantic." Craven balked at this manifest absurdity. His official report explained the futility of Adams' closing-the-barn-door-after-the-horse-had-gotten-out instructions. Yet, Consul Dudley at Liverpool was unconvinced. On August 11 he notified the captain of the *Tuscarora* he would find the *Enrica* "in some creek or bay on the north coast of Ireland."

Outfoxed were all three—Adams, Dudley, and Craven.

Rounding the top of Ireland, the *Enrica* soon vanished into the mists of the North Atlantic. Bucking heavy swells and gales, she bent her course southwards for a rendezvous in the Azores, the quiet little bay of Porto Praya, off the island of Terceira. Bulloch had spotted this hideaway on his recent return voyage from the Confederacy. The open Atlantic was out of the question as a place for transferring guns and other awkward items from ship to ship. His choice of the Azores at which to complete the *Enrica's* outfitting was deliberate. It was Portuguese territory, and that nation was woefully weak. She might protest using her harbor for the business of arming a sea raider, but there was little she could do about it. Geographically, it was convenient, yet a bit off the beaten track. Here, reasonably safe from prowling Federal cruisers, the last pieces of the jigsaw puzzle could be tucked in.

To Captain Butcher, before a warm, goodbye handclasp, the efficient Bulloch gave last-minute, written instructions for transshipping the cargo of the *Agrippina* to the *Enrica* as soon as the freighter reached the rendezvous. In them you can read Bulloch's implicit trust in the young mariner:

> You are to consider yourself as my confidential agent, and I shall rely upon you as one gentleman may upon another. It is important that your movements should not be reported, and you will please avoid speaking or signalling any passing ship.

On Paymaster Clarence R. Yonge Bulloch invested the duty of indoctrinating the motley crew of the *Enrica* en route to the Azores:

> When the *Alabama* is fairly at sea you will mix freely with the warrant and petty officers, show interest in their comfort and welfare, and endeavor to excite their interest in the approaching cruise of the ship. Talk to them of the Southern States, and how they are fighting against great odds for only what every Englishman enjoys—liberty. Tell them at the port of destination a distinguished officer of the C. S. Navy will take command of the ship for a cruise in which they will have the most active service and be well taken care of. I do not mean that you are to make the men set speeches or be constantly talking to them, but in your position you may frequently throw out to leading men hints of the above tenor, which will be commented upon on the berth deck. Seamen are very impressionable, and can be easily influenced by a little tact and management.

Nor could Bulloch ring down the curtain without a sprig of laurel for Pilot Bond, who held the helm of the *Enrica* on her run for life. He was later to write of Bond:

> He was one of those men who perform every office of life with earnestness and zeal . . . His position was not elevated . . . but there was something in the heart and eye and manner of the man, which gave an importance and dignity above its seeming conse-

quence. He never asked an inquisitive question, and if it was necessary to give him any information, I never doubted that his lips would
hold it as a sealed envelope.

By rail and steamer, by way of Belfast, Bulloch dashed back to
Liverpool to arrange transportation for Captain Semmes and his
officers to the Azores. Now he took a long chance. By telegraph,
he notified the loading agents at London to despatch the *Agrippina* to sea. To Captain McQueen, he sent sealed orders that
were not to be opened until the freighter was clear of the English
Channel. Meticulous to the least contingency, Bulloch even devised signals by which the *Agrippina* could identify herself to her
consort on making the Azores.

On August 8, Captain Semmes reached Liverpool from Nassau
on the English steamer *Bahama,* which Bulloch promptly chartered for the run to Terceira. With customary precision and
promptness Semmes corralled as many of the *Sumter's* officers as
he could find. He had hoped to re-gather them all. Some had
vanished on other missions, notably Lieutenant Chapman, the
Sumter's jester and glamour-boy, whose banter Semmes would
miss on the long voyages ahead. Yet, he still had Lieutenant
John McIntosh Kell, his unfailing friend and dependable subordinate, and a host in himself.

Semmes' impedimenta was brief. Indispensable were his trophies: eighteen chronometers and eighteen flags taken from the
Sumter's prizes. And, completing his baggage, his law library.

Lastly, through the Confederacy's bankers, Fraser, Trenholm
and Company, Semmes arranged the finances of his cruise. He
never disclosed the size of his sea-chest though Lieutenant Arthur
Sinclair, in his authoritative *Two Years on the Alabama,* testified
there was a goodly sum of gold in the sea-raider's strongbox for
emergencies and that Semmes' "sterling bills on England, though
amounting generally to about 10,000 dollars at each coaling-port,"
were readily accepted by the merchants and tradesmen he dealt
with. "Indeed," said Sinclair, "the credit of the *Alabama* was, as
they have it in commercial parlance, A-1."

On August 13 the *Bahama* cleared the Mersey. Seven days
out of Liverpool Captain Semmes sighted, at an early hour, the
island of Terceira, hazy and indistinct. Gradually, Porto Praya

became visible, with its white houses dotting the mountainside. Nature's smile lay on the land. Eagerly, Semmes' glass scanned the bay. At 11:30 the *Bahama* steamed into the harbor and there, at her anchors, in all her rakish beauty, lay the ship that was to be, for Semmes, "not only my home, but my bride" for the next twenty-two months. There, too, alongside her, was the tender, *Agrippina*. The old Scot, McQueen, had not failed the rendez-vous. Already guns and stores and "things" were being trans-shipped.

Nor could Semmes refrain from revealing the emotions that smote him as his gaze first rested on the shapely *Alabama* around whom so much international lightning was to crackle. The surgings of his heart welled out in nine words, "She was, indeed, a beautiful thing to look upon." To him, at least, she appeared as impatient as a racehorse at the barrier, poised for fiery flight over the Seven Seas.

⚓

⚓

16 Rendezvous at the Azores

Then, sling the bowl! Drink every soul!
A Toast to the Alabama!
What 'er our lot, through storm and shot,
Here's success to the Alabama!
(1864)

It was ordained that the *Alabama* was never to behold the South-ern Confederacy whose flag she flew. She was the first steamship in the history of the world, excepting the defective little *Sumter*, "to be let loose against the commerce of a great commercial people." She became famous, though Semmes said, "It was the fame of steam."

The story of a busy, romantic ship like the *Alabama* is like a biography. The vessel assumes a personality that "walks the waters like a thing of life." She speaks. She becomes a part of those people who knew her. So with the *Alabama*. If ever a man and a ship were one, they were Raphael Semmes and the *Alabama*. He fell in love with her at first sight, said so unabashedly, and clung to her until her death.

Considerable swell was running the day, August 20, that Semmes reached the Azores on the *Bahama*. Transshipping guns weighing four tons each was a formidable task that called for fine seamanship even in calm waters. Semmes' first order sent the little flotilla—*Alabama, Agrippina,* and *Bahama*—steaming around to East Angra Bay on the opposite side of Terceira to find a lee.

That same afternoon about four o'clock Semmes set foot for the first time on the deck of his new ship. "I was as much pleased with her internal appearance and arrangements as I had been with her externally." To the eyes of a sailor who saw Semmes come aboard, he appeared, "middle-aged, about five feet nine inches in height, and had a fine presence, and, by reason of a pair of wonderfully pointed moustaches, looked more like a Frenchman than an American." Nor was this mariner-reporter, P. D. Haywood, whose accuracy has been questioned on other details, too far wide of the mark. "A presence." Semmes had it. Aweing, perhaps, at times austere, unsparing in discipline, he bore the stamp of action in every movement and feature.

At dusk, with fine courtesy, Semmes relieved Captain Butcher of his command and moved his baggage into the commodious, semi-circular stern-cabin where he was to spend "so many weary days and watchful nights." One of his first acts—duty, to him, indeed—was to restore the little makeshift shrine before which he had knelt so often on the *Sumter*.

He began at once fencing with the Portuguese functionaries, who feebly protested against the use their uninvited guests were already making of their beautiful waters. By now, of course, Semmes was an old hand at sparring with port officials. His practice on the *Sumter* had taught him many lessons. He went through the customhouse formalities demanded by the Portuguese merely because the *Alabama* was "still playing merchant ship," though he declared only his coal and not an item of the war materials that littered the cruiser's deck.

Yet Semmes was cautious. To finish off transferring the tender's cargo to the *Alabama* he steamed out beyond the marine league though the sea was ruffling and there was some little chafing between her and the *Agrippina*. The *Alabama* was perfectly defenseless. Any moment an enemy cruiser might look in upon her and nip her career in the bud. Yet three days of toil and anxiety brought order out of chaos and converted the *Alabama* into fighting trim, ready for her grim work.

By Saturday night the *Alabama* was shipshape; guns mounted, shot racks filled, shell and powder stowed, coal bunkers replenished from the *Agrippina*. That vessel was then despatched to Cardiff to take on a cargo of coal and keep a rendezvous with the *Alabama* at Martinique—Semmes' old stamping ground—in early November. Dust, grime and rubbish had vanished. Scrubbing and holystoning had worked wonders. Her decks were sweet and clean, awnings snugly spread, yards squared, rigging hauled taut. To Semmes she appeared "Like a bride with the orange wreath about her brows, ready to be led to the altar." To James Bulloch, who lent a hand in everything, the project seemed "benignly favored by Providence with mild, calm weather."

Now, look at the *Alabama*, yonder on the azure Azores waters, preening and pluming herself for her first dash at enemy commerce—a long, trim, debonair, black hull, elliptic stern, fiddle-head cutwater, long, raking, lower masts. The Lairds built ships as beautiful as they were staunch. "She sat upon the water with the lightness and grace of a swan," glowed Semmes with all the ardor of a lover. Less flowery was Lieutenant Sinclair's avowal, "She was the most perfect cruiser of any nation afloat."

Many have described the *Alabama*. Poetically, the finest pen-picture was drawn by Semmes himself; technically, Sinclair's ranks ahead of his captain's. A screw steamer, with full sail power, she measured 235 feet over all, with a beam of 32 feet. Using old-style measurement, she was just over a thousand tons. Two horizontal engines gave her a nominal 300 horsepower, though they

Raphael Semmes at Jamaica in 1863 after he sank the gunboat Hatteras.

John M. Kell, Semmes' executive officer.

The Sumter, Semmes' first raider, leaving New Orleans to dart down the river and out to sea.

A raider at work! A Yankee ship burns while the Confederate raider ghosts away.

James Bulloch, diplomat, secret agent, creator of the Alabama.

The Alabama, *Ghost Ship* of the Confederacy.

Raphael Semmes, foreground, and John M. Kell, on the Alabama at Cape Town, 1863.

The San Jacinto. Eluded by Semmes on the Sumter, outwitted by Semmes on the Alabama, this unlucky ship ended her service on a reef in the Bahamas.

The 11-inch pivot gun on the Kearsarge which ended the fiery careers of Raphael Semmes and the Alabama.

The Kearsarge. Victor over the Alabama in the English Channel in 1864.

The Vanderbilt. A former luxury liner, she chased Semmes thousands of miles without success.

The end of the raider Alabama under the guns of the Kearsarge.
At right background is the yacht Deerhound.

The victors. Officers of the Kearsarge pose for their picture after
the battle. The officer with three broad stripes on his sleeve is
Captain John Winslow.

all photographs, courtesy of the United States Navy,
except the last, courtesy the National Archives.

actually delivered 1,000. Fully coaled, she drew fifteen feet. Her bunker capacity was 375 tons, enough for eighteen days' steaming at moderate speed. What the *Sumter* lacked the *Alabama* had: a two-bladed screw that could be triced up into a propeller well, clear of the water and hence no drag on her speed under sail. Inability to do this made the *Sumter,* her fuel exhausted, "little better than a log on the water." In fifteen minutes the *Alabama's* propeller could be detached from the shaft and hoisted into its recess.

Bark-rigged, with long lower masts, her fore-and-aft sails had an immense "drop" or surface. Her "sticks" were of the best yellow pine and bent in a gale like a willow wand. Her standing rigging was of finest Swedish iron. Her two modes of locomotion were independent of each other, making her both a perfect steamer and a perfect sailing vessel. Her scantling was light, though no disadvantage because her mission was the scourging of commerce, not battle. Keeping her fires constantly banked, she could be shifted from sail to steam so fast that no enemy appearing on the horizon in clear weather could surprise the *Alabama* under sail, nor could a sailing vessel of superior speed escape before the raider got up her full steam-power.

Semmes freely admitted her speed was often overrated by her enemy. Under steam alone she was a ten-knot ship. On her trial trip she reputedly made eleven and a half knots. Under steam and sail she once logged thirteen and a quarter, or fifteen and three-quarters statute miles, a very good speed for sea-going ships of that era.

Her main deck was pierced for twelve guns though her actual armament only numbered eight: six 32-pounders, three on the broadside, and two pivot guns on the center line. On the forecastle was a 7-inch Blakeley pivot rifle, firing a 100-pound shot four thousand yards. This weapon was true to its mark and easily handled; the other, abaft the mainmast, was a smooth-bore eight inch. Semmes later claimed the Blakeley gun was of comparatively little use.

On the *Alabama's* double-wheeled helm, located a little forward of the mizzenmast, was inscribed the ship's significant motto: *Aide toi et Dieu t'aidera, (Help yourself and God will help you*), a motto that ran back to the American Revolution. She was nameless otherwise. Never was *Alabama* lettered anywhere on her hull.

She had other features not found on all the warships of her day, including an apparatus for condensing the vapor of sea-water into fresh water. A fine machine shop enabled her to repair spars, armament, and equipment while at sea, or in ports where mechanical facilities were unavailable or denied.

Built entirely for speed, her cabin accommodations were meagre. Her berthdeck provided hammock room for a crew of 120. She carried 24 commissioned and warrant officers, including a surgeon, paymaster, master, four engineers, two midshipmen, four masters mates, a captain's clerk, boatswain, gunner, sailmaker, and carpenter.

The bridge of the *Alabama* was a light structure spanning the deck, near amidships. In the twilight hours it was sort of a lounging place for the officers and for Semmes "to smoke my single cigar" and where he could "lay aside the 'captain' and gather my young officers around me, and listen to whatever might be going on." Semmes pointed out though that he always made sure "to tighten the reins, again, the next morning."

The quarterdeck, aft, was sacred to duty and etiquette. No one ever presumed to seat himself upon it, not even the Captain. Here the officer of the deck held sway, pacing to and fro, his speaking trumpet swinging idly when there was nothing to do.

As obedient to the touch of her wheel as a well-trained courser to the rein of his rider, was this formidable engine of destruction. To a sailor she was a dream-ship. From Lieutenant Sinclair came this effusion of sheer admiration of her sailing qualities:

> It will be fully appreciated by our sailor readers when we can say that the *Alabama* would go 'in stays,' and without fail, with a breeze giving her little more than steerage way; and in 'working ship,' later on, around prizes, the captains of these vessels would be struck with the remarkable quickness and sureness with which she was handled. Frequently has the writer heard them remark, upon hearing the orders given, 'Ready about!': 'Why, Lieutenant! You don't tell me this vessel will stay in this light wind?' and have been lost in admiration upon witnessing the manoeuvre successfully accomplished.

Indeed, she could be worked around a prize like a pilot-boat. There is nothing so excites Jack's pride and interest in his ship as to learn she can be depended upon in emergencies.

Sunday, August 24, 1862. A cloudless day and a gentle breeze faintly rippled the surface of the placid sea. On this day, a good omen in itself, the new cruiser was commissioned *Alabama*. At four bells—ten o'clock—she steamed out of the roadstead beyond the marine league, escorted by the *Bahama*. The *Alabama's* brasswork glittered like burnished gold in the August sun. Her rigging gleamed with newness. She was a shining, beautiful thing alive as she moved out for the ceremony that would ready her for sea. Nature herself seemed to have bedecked the picturesque island of Terceira as a backdrop for the historic scene. Entrancing was its checkered dress of lighter and darker green, waving fields, and orange groves. Off in the distance on a green-clad slope nestled the little town of Angra, an enchanting vision of red-tiled roofs, sharp gables and parti-colored verandahs, glistening in the Sabbath sun.

On reaching the offing the two ships hove to near each other. All hands were piped aft, including the men from the *Bahama*. Semmes and his staff were immaculate in new, full uniforms of snappy Confederate gray, neatly fitted and trimmed with handsome gold lacings. Dress swords shone like shafts of sunlight at their waists. Impressive, particularly to the sailors from the streets of Liverpool, were Semmes and his handful of officers. "Shockingly inappropriate to marine traditions" thought Lieutenant Sinclair of the gray that had replaced the regulation true blue of "the old navy," though he admitted it had a dressy eye-value that won instant favor with the stalwart fellows milling about the deck in every variety of merchant-ship toggery and had no small effect in winning the services of the pick of them.

Mounting a gun carriage, Semmes read aloud his commission as Captain from the President of the Confederacy and the orders of Secretary Mallory directing him to assume command of the ship. These orders, incidentally, were never found though it is safe to contemplate they endowed Semmes with absolute discretion in his operations. Officers and men ringed themselves about him, heads uncovered, deeply moved by the short, impressive ceremony that was, said Sinclair, "a grand subject for a painter."

Now Semmes had finished. A striking, inspiring figure was he, standing there on a "trinket of war" as if part of it. His gaze ranged from one bronzed, bearded face to another. Then, he spoke again, clear, distinct, in words charged with emotion, "I now christen this ship *Alabama!*"—words that stripped the hood from this falcon of the sea.

Slowly, two small balls might now be seen wriggling their way, one to the peak, the other to the main royal masthead—flag and pennant ready for breaking. Fingering the halliards of the Union Jack that still floated over the ship was Quartermaster Marmelstein, ready to strike the English colors. On the quarterdeck the ship's band stroked their poised instruments; by the weather bow gun stood a gunner, lockstring in hand.

Every eye was fixed on Semmes who suddenly waved his hand. It was the signal. Two sudden jerks on the halliards and the two small balls at the peak and masthead exploded, only to uncurl in the breeze into the starry bars and pennant of the newborn republic. From the gun came the roar of the *Alabama's* first salute, and with a right good will the band struck up the soul-stirring anthem of the young Confederacy, "Dixie." Three ringing cheers pealed out over the dancing waters. Slowly, the Union Jack descended.

"Thus," said Semmes, "amid this peaceful scene of beauty, with all nature smiling upon the ceremony, was the *Alabama* christened. Who could look into the horoscope of this ship? Who anticipate her career? From the cradle to the grave there is but a step. . . ."

At the moment the *Alabama* was still minus a crew. Now a Confederate vessel of war, she had not a single sailor. Of what use was the finest cruiser without men? Dramatically, Semmes embarked on the last scene of getting the *Alabama* to work on the high seas: recruiting the necessary crew. Spiritedly, enticingly, he addressed the grouped crews, some ninety odd, who had shipped out on the *Alabama* and *Bahama*. He told them frankly they were released from the contracts under which they had sailed to the Azores. Free passage home and pay until discharged at Liverpool, awaited them. The men drew closer. They were a conglomeration of Dutch, English, Welsh, Irish, French, Italian, Spanish, and even a Russian.

Semmes was no mean showman, he could play on men's feelings with considerable skill. For them he painted the glory and the gloom, the dark and the bright sides of the venture ahead. Under him, on the *Alabama*, they would fight the battle of the "oppressed against the oppressor." He promised them excitement, adventure. The *Alabama* was a fine ship, one they might fall in love with. Her object was to demoralize and cripple the commerce of the North. She would not fight unless she fell in with an enemy cruiser of about equal weight of metal. Prudence was essential. "Let me once see you proficient in the use of your weapons and trust me for very soon giving you an opportunity to show the world of what metal you are made." There was fire and force in his words, and a short-lived burst of cheers greeted them.

On went Semmes. It was now or never. The *Alabama* was no privateer, no irresponsible nondescript roving the ocean without discipline or order, to plunder like a pirate, but a Confederate man-of-war, duly commissioned, flying the flag of the South, ruled by the code of the Confederate Navy. He did not expatiate how rigorous was that code, bristling with death penalties. Yet, he minced no words. There would be hardships, cruising in all climes, boarding in all weather, night and day, and a possibility, if captured, of a halter about their necks. He would give them shore liberty to enjoy the delights of far-off lands and romantic ports. As in the British Navy there would be grog twice a day, and no finer rations on any ship afloat. Again, cheers, heartier than before.

Finally, Semmes touched their hearts in the softest spot, with lures of gold and prize money. He would double the wages paid by the English and pay it in gold in advance. Cries of "Hear! Hear!" hailed the magic word. "I put the budget to them, in its very best aspect." The *Alabama* would take prizes all over the wide oceans. For the risks they ran the Confederate Congress would vote them "lots of prize money," one half the value of the ships they burned or bonded. To these undisciplined minds Semmes' words conveyed unconsciously a hint of freebooting that was to break out later and be squelched aborning.

Semmes closed abruptly. He had made his pitch. Now to strike while the iron was hot. As he dismounted from the gun-carriage the men were "piped down" to disperse in groups about the spardeck. The paymaster brought the shipping list to the capstan. The officers passed through the men and gave out word for those who desired to sign to make it known now. One by one, hat in hand, Jack presented himself to the paymaster in the saloon, signed the articles of enlistment in the Confederate Navy and received his advance wages in jingling gold. Semmes said he got eighty of the ninety men. Sinclair upped this figure to eighty-five. The ship's complement would later be filled by volunteers from the prizes she took. Yet these men drove hard bargains. Stokers wangled out an unheard of £7 per month; ordinary seamen £4 10s.

There was a bit of irony in it all, as Semmes was to admit. This "public meeting," the first and only ever held on the *Alabama,* closed the "democratic part of the proceedings." Said Semmes, "When I wanted a man to do anything after this, I did not talk to him about 'nationalities,' or 'liberties' or 'double wages,' but I gave him a rather sharp order, and if the order was not obeyed in double-quick, the delinquent found himself in limbo. Democracies may do very well for the land, but monarchies and pretty absolute monarchies, at that, are the only successful governments for the sea."

Yet, these rough and tumble "waifs of the sea" grew to respect and love this hard-driving man. Most of his crew were British, with a goodly sprinkling of Irish and Welsh. Not one of them could call the Confederacy home. The very act of enlisting in the Confederate Navy had forfeited protection of the British flag. Above them floated a "banner with a strange device" they had never seen before. They were to buckle under discipline yet their exploits were to excite wonder, dread and admiration. At the last, as the shattered *Alabama* sank beneath their feet, they were to crowd around Semmes imploring him not to yield.

It was far into the night before the paymaster's task was finished, the last man signed and, for those who wished it, half-pay allotments made out for mothers, wives, and sweethearts in England. Eight bells. Time for Captain James Bulloch to say farewell and step out of the *Alabama* story forever. Gracefully, he did so. As unselfish as he was energetic, he had accepted disappointment and chagrin for the good of a cause destined to be lost. To him belonged the glory of creating the *Alabama* so perfectly in every detail that "not even the most trifling article necessary to the efficiency of the vessel," was ever found wanting. He was to leave his heart and his mark on the historic ship. Never again did he see her.

At midnight—so ran Bulloch's report to Secretary Mallory— "bidding Captain Semmes a cordial adieu, with heartfelt prayers for his success, I stepped over the *Alabama's* side with feelings very much akin to those which oppress a man when he leaves his home behind him. The heavens were brilliant with stars, a blazing comet illuminated the sky to the northeast, the lanterns of the *Alabama* gleamed brightly as she rose and fell to the sea, the signs were all favorably ominous, and banishing every sentiment but hope, I predicted a glorious cruise for the dashing craft and her gallant commander."

It was Swift's Comet Bulloch saw, luminous and mysterious, flaring across twenty-five degrees of the dark, starry heavens. Not since the War of Jenkin's Ear in 1739 had this bright portent appeared. That, too, was a conflict destructive to commercial shipping, and fought in the very waters where the *Alabama* was soon to ply her deadly trade.

In silence Semmes watched Bulloch down the gangway to board the *Bahama* for Liverpool. With a last three-cheers for the *Alabama*, the *Bahama* vanished across the dark waters. Out of Semmes' heart welled gratitude to this able man, James Bulloch, who had assisted him so greatly, "by his counsel and advice, given with that modesty and reserve which always mark true ability." Turning the *Alabama's* head to the northeast Semmes ordered his fore-and-aft sails set and his fires banked. The *Alabama* was alone upon the ocean, off to adventurous destiny.

⚓

⚓

17 "Cutter Away!"

Whaling was still big business in America in 1862. A single ship,
if lucky, could bring home 50,000 dollars worth of whale oil, and
war had driven even that price skyward. The enormous, sea-going
mammals were—according to James Bulloch—"a source of abundant wealth to our enemies and a nursery for their seamen."

America's whaling fleet had fished in the peaceful Azores latitudes for generations, usually until early October when the winter
gales set in and the whales moved off to other feeding grounds.
By dint of superior skill, courage, and perseverance the Yankee
whaler—who, Semmes said, was perhaps "the best specimen of a
sailor the world over"—had monopolized the industry. A lonely,
lusty calling it was, but profitable. At this season these happy
whaling grounds were speckled with "spouters," mostly Down-
Easters. Thus, close at hand, lay Semmes' target for his opening
strike at Northern commerce.

Leisurely, Semmes swung the *Alabama* southeast from Terceira,
beginning a circle about the Azores. Somewhere on the circuit he
would flush game. Bending southwards he rounded Santa Maria
through a tumbling sea and freshening breeze. This was her
shakedown cruise, and the *Alabama* paced over the waves like a
thoroughbred. "A fine sailor under canvas," she proved, a quality
that was to give Semmes a priceless advantage. Had he been
obliged to chase everything under steam, as he had in the *Sumter*,
he would have spent half his time darting into ports for fuel, dis-
closing his whereabouts, "whereas I could now stretch into the
most distant seas, and chase, capture and destroy, perfectly
independent of steam." With only half a dozen exceptions, the

Alabama made all her sixty-nine captures under sail, propeller out of water.

There was a further advantage. Keeping at sea three or four months at a stretch enabled Semmes to maintain better discipline. "Nothing demoralizes a crew so much as frequent visits to port."

Meanwhile, the *Alabama* prepared herself for her long cruise. Her deck was a beehive of industry. The crew was berthed, messed, quartered, and assigned to stations. Semmes was patient. Time and discipline would whip these men into shape. There were drills at big guns, at cutlass and pistol. Armed with pikes, the men were also taught how to repel boarders. They might need it later. Caulked in the damp chill of an English winter the *Alabama's* seams began to gape under the ardent heat of the semitropics. Two days it took to re-caulk her upper works against the heavy rollers that deluged the deck despite the cruiser's high freeboard.

On the twelfth day, September 5, 1862, the *Alabama* opened the ball. She was plowing along near the thirty-eighth parallel. The mountains of Pico and Fayal raised to the eastward. Semmes knew it couldn't be long now. At dawn the *Alabama* gave chase to a brig that showed her a clean pair of heels. "Outsailed us," conceded Semmes though the fugitive led him straight to his first prize, a whaler lying to about two miles to leeward. All hands rushed on deck with the lookout cry, "Sail ho!," to watch the *Alabama's* first crack-down on a prize.

Off romped the cruiser, running up United States colors. Semmes' memoirs take issue with his journal, which says, "we hoisted English colors." Whatever they were his quarry failed to flee though she broke out Federal streamers. Eagerly, the *Alabama* closed to boarding distance. Squatting on the water like a winged duck was a fine, large schooner, the *Ocmulgee*, of Edgartown, Massachusetts. Her sails were half-furled. Moored fast alongside her was a huge, dead sperm whale, "a big strike." Her crew were stripping blubber by the yard, four inches thick.

Suddenly, from the *Alabama's* quarterdeck, the trumpet spoke across the waters, "I'm sending a boat on board of you!" Next, closer at hand, "Cutter away!" With a creaking of tackles, down from the davits the cutter splashed into the water. With powerful sweeps the boarding party approached the *Alabama's* Prize Number One. It was less than one hundred miles from where she was commissioned. Up the whaler's sides the sailors scrambled like cats to face the *Ocmulgee's* wrathful skipper, demanding "Who are you? What do you want?"

Without a flicker Prize Master Fullam replied with the grim, historic and oft-to-be-repeated formula, "You are a prize of the Confederate States Steamer *Alabama*, Captain Semmes commanding. Fetch your papers and come with us."

Skipper Abraham Osborne was speechless. He obeyed like a man in a dream. Brandishing their long flensing knives, his crew dashed to his rescue, but he put out a restraining hand. Not until the cutter drew alongside the *Alabama* did Semmes lower the Stars and Stripes and hoist the Confederate colors. The skipper's face was a picture of unbelief. It is probable he had never seen a Confederate flag before. Into Semmes' cabin he strode, long, lean and as elastic, apparently, as the whalebone he dealt in. "A genuine specimen of the Yankee whaling skipper," commented Semmes, who greeted the weatherbeaten mariner with marked courtesy.

Quickly, Captain Osborne unbosomed himself, "When I saw the United States colors at your peak, I, naturally, concluded you were a gunboat sent out to protect us whalers. What will you do with my ship?"

Semmes broke it as gently as he could. Osborne's face went ashen and drawn as Semmes examined his papers and pointed out there was no question of Northern ownership, no neutral cargo. The *Ocmulgee* brimmed with whale oil. The ship had written her own death-warrant. She was to enjoy the distinction of being the first victim of the *Alabama*, though Semmes did not so express himself.

"I am under orders from my government," said Semmes in judicial tones. "There is only one thing I can do: take you and your men prisoners and destroy your ship. Pack your whaleboats with provisions and whatever else you may need, except your chronometer and your flag. Bring these to my cabin at once."

By nine that night the *Ocmulgee* was ready for her suttee, but Semmes chose not to burn her after dark. The flames would stampede the rest of the whaling flotilla nearby. Admiral Porter charged Semmes with disappointing his crew in not giving them a brilliant first-night spectacle to gloat over as he had the crew of the *Sumter* with her first prize, the *Golden Rocket*. Semmes was obliged, claimed Porter, to keep these "descendants of the Norsemen" amused lest they take the bit in their teeth, commandeer the ship, sail her into New York and reap valuable rewards for their piracy.

Placing a prize crew on board the *Ocmulgee* and hoisting a lantern at her peak the *Alabama* lay to until morning. At daylight her boarding crew had their first lesson in the art of firing a ship. It was the *Sumter's* routine over again. As Lieutenant Sinclair described it, "First, you cut up with your broadaxe the cabin and forecastle bunks, generally of white pine lumber. You will find, doubtless, the mattresses stuffed with straw, and in the cabin pantry, at least a keg of butter and lard. Make a foundation of the splinters and straw, pour on top the lard and butter. One pile in the cabin, the other in the forecastle. Get your men in the boats, all but the incendiaries, and at the given word, 'Fire!' shove off, and take it as truth, that before you have reached your own ship, the blaze is licking the topsails of the doomed ship."

Such were the lurid obsequies of the *Ocmulgee*. First Lieutenant Kell, the *Alabama's* chief appraiser, estimated ship and cargo at 50,000 dollars though the forecastle statisticians, wondering where their prize money would come from if they burned her, rated her oil alone at twenty thousand pounds. Whatever its value it was going up in flames. The oil-soaked deck fairly snatched at the torch. Out of her hatchways gushed dense black smoke that spread in vast involutions to the leeward. Up her masts ran red forked serpents that glided out on her spars. Her stout sides burst open, revealing an inferno within. What once was a stately ship was soon a blackened hull that surged and wallowed until the sea sucked it under. Saddest of those who watched the spectacle was the ship's master who shed honest tears. For him it was tragedy pure and simple. No honor to him was it to be the first of the *Alabama's* victims.

At four bells, Sunday morning, September 6, 1862, off the fragrant island of Flores, the *Alabama's* crew was mustered. Semmes and his officers, in full dress, assembled on the quarterdeck; the "former vagabonds" (as dubbed by Lieutenant Sinclair) would hardly be recognized. Drawn up smartly on deck, neatly arrayed in nobby white and blue ducks, shoes polished, sailor straw hats a-tilt, they looked anything like the unpromising "ruffians" the crimps had "scraped up from the streets of Liverpool." Soap and discipline had already achieved marvels.

The Confederate Articles of War—copied almost exactly from the code "for the better government of the Navy of the United States"—were read to the crew. Two thirds of the offenses enumerated "shall be punished by death." The word, death, had an ominous ring. It brought visions of bodies dangling from yardarms. Jack eyed his mates significantly. He was up against serious business, and he knew it. Already Jack had foretasted the discipline that was to mark the cruise of the *Alabama*. Now, said Semmes:

> He began more distinctly to perceive that he had gotten on board a ship-of-war, instead of the privateer he had supposed the *Alabama* to be, and that he would have to toe a pretty straight mark. It is with a disorderly crew, as with other things, the first blows are the most effective. I have around me a large staff of excellent officers, who always wore their side arms, and pistols, when on duty, and from this time onward we never had any trouble about keeping the most desperate and turbulent characters in subjection.
>
> My code was like that of the Medes and Persians—it was never relaxed. The moment a man offended he was seized and confined in irons, and, if the offense was a grave one, a court-martial was sitting on his case in less than twenty-four hours. The willing and obedient were treated with humanity and kindness; the turbulent were jerked down with a strong hand and made submissive to discipline. I was as rigid with the officers as with the crew, though, of course, in a different way, and both officers and men soon learning what was required of them, everything went on, on board the *Alabama*, after the first few weeks, as smoothly, and with as little jarring as if she had been a well-constructed and well-oiled machine.

Muster over, the *Alabama* slid close to the island where Semmes paroled the *Ocmulgee's* captain and his crew of thirty-six, sending them ashore in their own whaleboats packed with as many supplies as they could save from their own ship. It was a precedent.

Scarcely had the whaleboats shoved off before the lookout spotted a sail, with every stitch of canvas set, racing for the shelter of the charmed marine league. The build and the cut of her cried out "American whaler" across the five intervening miles. Raising English colors, the *Alabama* took off her wraps, but the stranger declined to identify herself. Quickly, Semmes changed flags, breaking out his own. The newcomer was making a gallant try, but the *Alabama* was simply too fast for her. The marine league beckoned, but she was soon under the raider's guns. Semmes humored her for a little "just to show her that I could beat her in a fair trial of speed." For good measure he sent a 32-pounder whistling through her rigging, and the *Starlight* of Boston luffed up into the wind, a captive.

The master of the *Starlight* was truculent. He came aboard unwillingly, to face Semmes and Lieutenant Kell to whom he avowed he was trying to run the gauntlet of the *Alabama's* guns. It was suicidal, he admitted, but these New England skippers were a hardy breed. They would face the de'il himself, if need be, and harpoon him, too, if given half a chance. "He was the cleverest specimen of Yankee skipper I have met; about 27 or 28," said Semmes.

To the angry protests of the *Starlight's* master against the capture of his ship Semmes replied calmly, "Every whale you strike will put money into the Federal treasury, and strengthen the hands of your people to carry on the war. I am afraid I must burn your ship."

The *Starlight* handed Semmes a brief distaff problem. Among her passengers were three ladies en route to Fayal. Instructing his prize master to quiet their fears with assurances of safe landing in the morning, Semmes then ordered the *Starlight's* master and crew put in irons. Distasteful it was, but Semmes' breast rankled at the indignities meted out to the *Sumter's* Paymaster Myers, who was trapped by the American Consul at Tangier. Myers' head was shaved like a felon's. Shackled hand and foot with irons, he was held incommunicado, transported across the Atlantic to Fort Warren, Boston, where he was imprisoned until France's protest reached Washington. Semmes was merely retaliating, justly, as he thought. At that, he did only what gallant Stephen Decatur had done before him to the Barbary pirates he captured after learning of the cruelties visited on Commodore Bainbridge and the crew of the luckless *Philadelphia* that ran aground on the Tripoli coast.

That night the *Alabama* lay to on a calm sea. Next morning Semmes paroled the *Starlight's* master, crew, and passengers and sent them shorewards in their own boats. Hauling off from Flores the *Alabama* loafed along—"still hunting," Sinclair called it— and soon ran down a Portuguese whaling brig, the only foreign whaler he ever overhauled. Semmes knew he was nearing the choicest of the whaling grounds where Down Easters clustered like bees. Near sunset the lookout sighted a large ship that loomed up in the distance like a frigate. Flying United States colors the *Alabama* closed in on the stranger, who, like the *Ocmulgee*, made the mistake of assuming the Confederate ship was a flashy Federal gunboat cruising hereabouts to protect his oil and whalebone. She sailed blithely into the raider's open arms.

Prize Number Three was the *Ocean Rover*, nigh four years out of New Bedford. Stacked in her hold were 1,100 barrels of oil, worth a fortune. Homeward bound, her master was trying for just one more "strike" before breezing off to see his wife and dangle on his knee "babies that were no longer babies."

"I really felt for the honest fellow," confessed Semmes, who seldom allowed himself the luxury of too much sympathy for his victims. "But when I came to reflect for a moment upon the diabolical acts of his countrymen of New England, who were out-heroding Herod, in carrying on against us a vindictive war, I had no longer any spare sympathies to dispose of."

Semmes ironed the crew and master of the *Ocean Rover* overnight. Next morning the skipper came to Semmes' cabin and asked the same indulgence granted the *Ocmulgee's* crew: to depart in their own whaleboats.

"But we're four or five miles from land," parried Semmes, who was really not at all averse to releasing his prisoners. "It's a long way to pull."

"Oh! That's nothing," replied the master. "We whalers sometimes chase a whale, on the broad sea, until our ships are hull-down, and think nothing of it. It will relieve you of us sooner, and be of some service to us besides."

Seeing that the sea was smooth and getting ashore not too risky, Semmes easily yielded to the skipper's plea. Back to his doomed ship hurried the mariner to pack his whaleboats with provisions, whaling gear, and personal effects. It was jolly business —as Semmes later told it—stripping the *Ocean Rover* for her funeral pyre.

"He worked like a beaver, for not more than a couple of hours had elapsed before he was again alongside of the *Alabama*, with all his six boats, with six men in each, ready to start for the shore. I could not but be amused when I looked over the side into these boats, at the amount of plunder that the rapacious fellows had packed into them. They were literally loaded down, with all sorts of traps, from the seamen's chests and bedding, to the tabby cat and parrot. Nor had the "main chance" been overlooked, for all the cabin stores had been secured and sundry barrels of beef and pork, besides. I said to him, 'Captain, your boats appear to me, to be rather deeply laden; are you not afraid to trust them?' 'Oh! no,' he replied; 'they are as buoyant as ducks, and we shall not ship a drop of water.'"

The master evidently wished to leave a good taste in the mouth of his captor. Up the gangway he bore an immense fruitcake, put up in tin, the last of four, cooked for him by his good wife "to hum" to celebrate the wedding day, after an old whaler custom.

"Well," he said, "the wedding day is not at hand yet, but you had as well enjoy the cake, gentlemen."

Night came on. The moon rose out of the sea, but no more would the *Ocean Rover* go a-roving by the light of the moon. Putting her crew under parole, Semmes gave them a hearty good-bye. There was poetry and tenderness in Semmes' description of the flight of the *Ocean Rover's* master and men:

> The boats, shoving off from the side, one by one, and falling into line, struck out for the shore. That night-landing of this whaler's crew was a beautiful spectacle. I stood on the horse-block, watching it, my mind busy with many thoughts. The moon was shining brightly, though there were some passing clouds sailing lazily in the

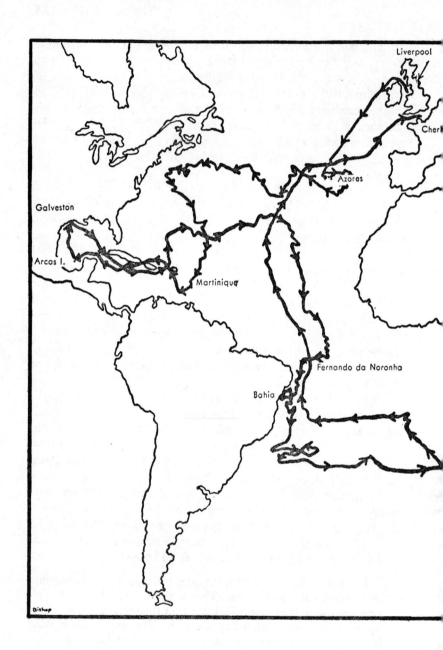

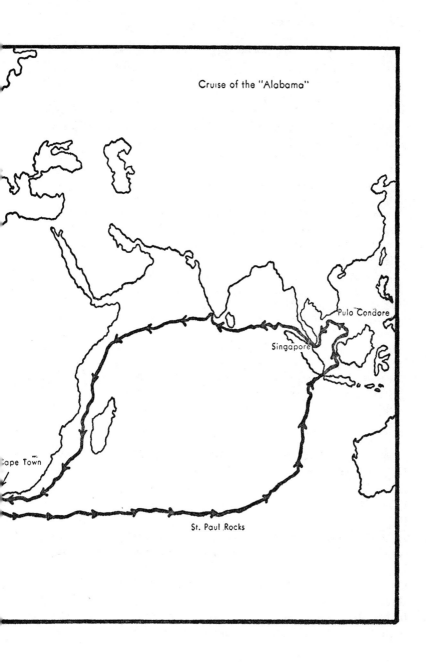

Cruise of the "Alabama"

Pulo Condore

Singapore

Cape Town

St. Paul Rocks

upper air, that fleckered the sea. Flores, which was sending off to us, even at this distance, her perfumes of shrub and flower, lay sleeping in the moonlight, with a few fleecy, white clouds wound around the mountaintop like a turban.

The rocky islets that rise like so many shafts out of the sea, devoid of all vegetation, and at different distances from the shore, looked weird and unearthly, like sheeted ghosts. The boats moving swiftly and mysteriously toward the shore, might have been mistaken when they had gotten a little distance from us, for Venetian gondolas, with their peaked bows and sterns, especially when we heard coming over the sea, a song, sung by a powerful and musical voice, and chorused by all the boats. Those merry fellows were thus making light of misfortune, and proving that the sailor, after all, is the true philosopher.

The echo of that night-song lingered long in my memory, but I little dreamed, as I stood on the deck of the *Alabama*, and witnessed the scene I have described, that four years afterward, it would be quoted against me as a violation of the laws of war! And yet so it was. It was alleged that miles away at sea, in rough and inclement weather, I compelled my prisoners to depart for the shore, in leaky and unsound boats, at the hazard of their lives, designing and desiring to drown them! And this was all the thanks I received for setting some of these fellows up as nabobs, among the islanders. Why, the master of the *Ocean Rover*, with his six boats and their cargoes, was richer than the Governor, when he landed in Flores; where the simple islanders are content with a few head of cattle, a cast-net, and a canoe.

With two prizes near her the *Alabama* lay off Flores overnight. Luck was running, and so was the *Alert* of New London, a large, newly-built bark, which, unlike the *Vigilant*, lived up to her name though too late. Semmes was sleeping soundly when aroused by the officer of the deck. Dressing he came on deck. Apparently realizing she was pursued, the stranger raised every rag of sail she could spread. At daybreak, after a chase of four hours, Semmes broke out English colors. Still the bark refused to answer. Obstinate she was and dashing desperately for sanctuary within the three-mile orbit. So Semmes splashed a warning round shot close to her stern, giving her captain a shower bath. "These shower-baths," mused Semmes, "are very efficacious." So was this with the master of the *Alert*, who broke out the Stars and Stripes and hauled up at once.

Prize Number Four, the *Alert*, was sixteen days out of New London, bound for a whaling station in the South Indian Ocean. A timely catch indeed, with bales of underclothing the *Alabama's* crew could use, choice beef and pork, but best of all, tobacco, "Good choice Virginia twist," that was already on short ration. Jack's eyes brightened at the bare sight of the boxes packed with the fragrant weed. That night pipes glowed afresh and as the inspiring fumes curled up chanties, Limehouse songs and jest rolled up from the forecastle.

Semmes now had three prizes on his hands. Too good a showman to raise the curtain on three acts at once he fired them at different hours, torching off the *Starlight* at 9 A.M., the *Ocean Rover* at 11, and the *Alert* at 4 P.M. The smoke from these three blazes was still rising when a large schooner, Yankee build and rig, hove in sight, hurrying towards the *Alabama*. It was too easy. The newcomer whipped along unsuspiciously until near enough to see that the three mysterious cones of smoke that bewildered her, billowed up from three ships on fire. All at once she smelled a rat and wheeled suddenly in flight. But the jig was already up. The *Alabama's* bow-chaser had her in range, and a blank cartridge did the trick.

Prize Number Five, was another whaler, the *Weathergauge* of Provincetown, six weeks from the land of the Puritan. Semmes was perusing her papers when another still sail broke cover. Hunting was too good, and Semmes wondered just how long he could continue to play high jinks unmolested among the whalers.

Directing his prize master to hold close to the island of Corvo, the *Alabama* streaked off through the falling dusk after the fresh sail. A long chase it proved. Semmes stated it more aptly, "Chasing a sail is very much like pursuing a coy maiden, the very coyness sharpening the pursuit." In this case the maiden led him a beautiful night dance over the merry waters. The moon shone like polished silver, gleaming on the canvas of the fleeing vessel and lighting it up like a snowbank. The very whiteness of her sails, made no doubt from "the fiber of our cotton fields," had an

American cleanness. Huntsman and hunted ran neck and neck for two hours. Gradually, the *Alabama* cut down the intervening water. Just before dawn he overhauled her. She was a Dane! A neutral bark, the *Overman*, bound for Hamburg.

Glumly, the *Alabama* retraced her steps "pretty much as Music or Rover may be supposed to feel, as he is limping back to his kennel, after a run in pursuit of a fox that has escaped him." That day Semmes fired the *Weathergauge*, paroled her crew of fifteen and hustled them ashore in their own whaleboats.

Two days later the whaling brig *Altamaha*, of New Bedford, fell for a ruse and dropped into the *Alabama's* maw. Landing her crew of twenty-three Semmes waited till dark to fire her. A disappointing bonfire she made, "not so beautiful as the other whalers had done." In the *Alabama's* log she was entered as Prize Number Six, and her flag stowed away in the quartermaster's bulging bag.

It was exciting business—chasing prizes—for officers, for men, and for their skipper, who watched with the keenness of sportsmen pursuing a hare. A long, lean racer was the *Alabama*. With her best helmsman at the wheel, every sail set and trimmed to a nicety, few could outrun her. Add to this Semmes' masterly seamanship, and the combination was all but unbeatable. He confessed chasing the Danish bark all night because it "would never do for the *Alabama* to be beaten in the beginning of her cruise." It was good for the crew to know what manner of ship they had under them. (He had already forgotten the American brig which escaped him the first day.) And the whalers, saturated in whale fat made grand pyrotechnic displays, pleasing to the crew, and not wholly displeasing to the islanders, who watched them from afar.

Two nights later—September 13—Semmes retired early, fagged out. But there was "no game up." He was sound asleep when a quartermaster came below, shook his cot and said, "There is a large ship just passed to the windward of us, on the opposite tack, sir." Throwing on a few clothes, Semmes hurried on deck. Off to the windward about three miles, clearly outlined in the moonlight, was a whaler, a fine, big one. Semmes had no need for his powerful night glasses. Nature's own searchlight lit up the scene. Scenting trouble afar, the stranger made a break for the open sea, setting her royals and flying jib, which had been furled. Spreading her own great sails, the *Alabama* put on her seven league boots. Semmes had already made it a practice not to disturb the regular repose of his officers and men during the night except in emergencies. This was no emergency, and the watch on deck executed the necessary orders.

An unshotted gun thundered a summons to halt, but the whaler laughed it off. It took hours to fetch the prey within good range. Time now "to cut short the drama an act or two, and bring it to a close." Firing a second gun the *Alabama* ranged up under the stern of her quarry, who hauled up her courses and lay to. Like a tiger circling and measuring her prey the *Alabama* stole around her captive at about three ship's lengths distance. The ship was American. Every line of her advertised it. To be on the safe side Semmes cautioned his boarding master to run up a light to the peak if his surmise was correct, as it was. Daylight was tinging the edge of the sea when Semmes went below to recoup his lost sleep.

Coming on deck that morning, there lying under the lee was the *Benjamin Tucker* of New Bedford, eight months out, with 340 barrels of oil below decks. A true Old Man of the Sea was her skipper, gnarled and grizzled from years of harpooning, stripping blubber and fighting the watery element. Gamely, he blinked not an eye when told his ship would be burned. He merely thanked God it was no worse. The formalities were soon over. At ten o'clock flames were ravaging the *Benjamin Tucker.*

Lord of the waters, ruler of the ocean for leagues upon leagues, was Raphael Semmes this morning of September 14, 1862. In all the vast westward sweep of the deep, even as far away as the Sargasso Sea, there was no such thing as an American man-of-war to dispute his sway. Two thousand miles away an old commodore, with a fleet of fourteen, was browsing aimlessly up and down the Gulf and Caribbean searching for Semmes.

Out of the early mists next morning a large Yankee schooner came bowling along merrily, unsuspectingly, to her doom. The *Courser* of Provincetown she was, and as Semmes gazed on her handsome young Captain Tilton, he wished he could have lured the gallant fellow away from the "Universal Yankee Nation," but "I steeled my heart and executed the laws of war." He gave the *Courser* the compliment, if it may be called that, of being the first target for the *Alabama's* guns. After "a little practice at her" he burned her and wrote the figure "8" beside her name in the logbook.

Seventy prisoners—the personnel of his last three prizes—now crowded his decks. Running back to Flores, Semmes landed his captives as before, loading them down with gear and trinkets from their own ships. Making sail northward, Semmes took a ninth large prize in his stride, the *Virginia*. A proud name she bore, dear to Southern hearts, but not dear enough to spare her the inexorable torch. Twenty days out of New Bedford, she was fitted for a long cruise. For three hours she tried running away, but, said Semmes, it was like a rabbit trying to outfleet a greyhound. After despoiling her of whatever the *Alabama* could use, the *Virginia* went up in smoke. To vary the routine he waited till nightfall and the freshening wind whirled the flames high in the darkness.

Now it was September 18 and a great storm was threatening. Now the *Alabama* could show off her rough-weather virtues if she had them. Many a smooth-water ship had lost both speed and reputation when seas began buffeting her. The cruiser stepped out confidently, with all the animation of a living thing. Her sticks bent like reeds in the wind, but she "seemed, like a trained racer, to enjoy the sport and though she would tremble, now and then, as she leaped from sea to sea, it was the tremor of excitement, not of weakness." John Laird had selected good timber for the craft he had pronounced the finest cruiser of her class in the world. Her tough English framing held everything in place below. Aloft, not a mast snapped, not a rope-yarn parted, so perfect, so staunch, was every detail of the ship.

At midafternoon, across the rolling sea, the masthead lookout espied a bark easily twice the size of the *Alabama*. The cruiser raced off in pursuit. Desperately, the stranger parried the inevitable. Plunging through the great waves, she hoped for the one chance that the Confederate ship would lose a spar or two in the wind. Stubbornly, she refused to show her colors until the

Alabama's gun sent a loud-mouthed command across the turbulent sea.

Short shrift Semmes made of the *Elisha Dunbar* of New Bedford, a big whaler, bulging with three years' gear and supplies. So raging was the wind, so infuriated the sea, Semmes hesitated about boarding his prize. Darkness was setting in, but there was light enough for what he had to do. Deftly maneuvering the *Alabama* to windward of the prize, Semmes launched his cutter, with orders to fetch only her chronometer and flag, crew and master, and to fire her at once. Her papers were not even examined before sentencing her to the torch. She was Yankee, plainly enough, "the only ship I ever burned before examining her papers."

Outwardly unmoved, but with his heart in his mouth, Semmes stood on the quarterdeck. Concerned chiefly for the safety of his boarding party, Semmes worked the *Alabama* to leeward of the prize so that his cutter need only pull before wind and wave to regain their ship. The "lady," his occasional pet name for her, trod the high-piling seas as lightly as if skipping rope. He breathed a prayer of thanks as his returning boarders drew up under the lee of the cruiser. Semmes now knew he commanded a vessel he could depend on in any weather, any emergency.

Never was the crew of the *Alabama* treated to a more awesome spectacle than the burning of the *Elisha Dunbar*. Hanging to the rail with both hands, salt spray blown from the tops of the waves stinging their faces like small shot, the *Alabama's* tars stood transfixed.

With fine, bold strokes Semmes painted the scene:

> This burning ship was a beautiful spectacle, the scene being wild and picturesque beyond description. The black clouds were mustering their forces in fearful array. Already the entire heavens had been overcast. The thunder began to roll, and crash, and the lightning to leap from cloud to cloud in a thousand eccentric lines. The sea was in a tumult of rage; the winds howled, and floods of rain descended. Amid this turmoil of the elements, the *Dunbar*, all in flames, and with disordered gear and unfurled canvas, lay rolling and tossing upon the sea. Now an ignited sail would fly away from a

yard, and scud off before the gale; and now the yard itself, released from the control of its braces, would swing about wildly, as in the madness of despair, and then drop into the sea. Finally, the masts went by the board, and then the hull rocked to and fro for a while, until it was filled with water, and the fire nearly quenched, when it settled to the bottom of the great deep, a victim to the passions of man, and the fury of the elements.

Now for the score. Semmes' fierce, eleven-day sweep around the Azores had exterminated Northern shipping worth 230,000 dollars, a figure later hiked considerably in the write-off of the Americans' bill against Great Britain. The *Alabama* had already returned nigh her entire cost in enemy ships destroyed! Now, like Alexander, Semmes was to sigh for other worlds to conquer. For the crew of the *Alabama* it was an adventure many an old salt would some day tell in the forecastle to admiring shipmates.

⚓

⚓

18   Sequel at Washington

At four-ten on the afternoon of October 10, 1862, Secretary Welles received a telegram that sent him scurrying over the gravel walk from the Navy Building to the White House as fast as he could go. He bore disturbing news. The "notorious pirate Semmes" was again at large on the Atlantic! It boded ill for Northern shipping. The evidence fairly singed the wire "Old Neptune" laid on President Lincoln's desk:

The rebel steamer 290 has seized and burned five of our whaleships off the Western Islands about the 5th of September. There is a large fleet of whalers requiring protection of the government; an armed steamer or steamers should be sent at once. Answer. J. C. Delano, In behalf of six shipowners of New Bedford.

Two days later came even worse tidings from the U.S.S. *Kearsarge*, at Fayal, Captain Pickering, commanding: "Ten whalers have been destroyed by the *Alabama* (290), commanded by Captain R. Semmes, and one other is missing, reported to have been sunk with all on board. . . ."

Up to this moment, all was serene in the navy's war. The blockade was tightening. Soon the South would be gagging for breath. The navy was daily getting more efficient in chasing blockade-runners. A despatch from Rear Admiral Charles Wilkes at Bermuda—he who had nearly involved the United States in war with Britain—said he was momentarily expecting the "No. 290, or the *Eureka*" (he meant *Enrica*, of course) and confidently promised her a warm reception. Earlier, Rear Admiral David Glasgow Farragut, commanding the Western Gulf Blockading Squadron, had reported the 290 running the gauntlet into Mobile Bay. His sentinels had riddled her to no avail. Actually, it was the *Florida*. She was to be another source of humiliation for the Northern navy. But these days every unidentified ship was the dread, mysterious 290. Until the arrival of Captain Pickering's report no one on this side of the Atlantic even dreamed the ship had been re-named *Alabama*.

It looked as if James Bulloch's prophecy to the Confederate Secretary of the Navy, "You will not be long in hearing of his [Semmes'] movements," was coming true with a vengeance, and at a bad time for the North. Lee's invasion of Maryland had been halted bloodily at Sharpsburg, though the long lists of dead and shattered robbed a dubious victory of its thrill. Nor could the President's advance-notice Emancipation Proclamation—which freed not a single slave—wipe away the tears of thousands whose loved ones lay rotting under fresh graves on Maryland hillsides.

Too often has it been proclaimed that the Federal Navy, irrevocably dedicated to strangling the Confederacy with its gargantuan ship-cordon, could not, and did not, spare war craft enough to run down and destroy the *Alabama*. The Official Records dispute this. Much of this loose talk was nothing but Federal war propaganda—propaganda which has not yet been run to earth. All told, some forty-odd Federal ships engaged in the needle-in-the-hay-stack search for Semmes. It was not that the Navy was too deeply occupied with the blockade. It was that the Union's search was not intelligently handled, and more important, that Semmes was too fast and too foxy for everything sent after him.

Within four weeks after the Confederate cruiser made her fiery debut on the Atlantic scene the Navy Department had despatched fifteen ships after her. The Official Records speak for themselves. Let them name names: *Kearsarge, Wachusett, Tuscarora, Dacotah, St. Lawrence, St. Louis, San Jacinto, Santiago de Cuba, Cimarron, Octorara, Tioga, Vanderbilt,* and *Sonoma.* Admiral Wilkes' "Flying Squadron" alone had seven ships prowling about the West Indies and along the Atlantic seaboard. The fact is, Secretary Gideon Welles ordered a relentless pursuit for Semmes. The "pirate" must be trapped at all costs. This did not mean depleting the blockade, for that was largely made up of second-rate ships. Strange, almost panicky, orders and counterorders fleck the Official Records. Welles even trotted out the old-fashioned ship-of-the-line, U.S.S. *Alabama,* as if there was magic in sharing the name of the Southern "piratical wolf." Never before has the U.S.S. *Alabama* been mentioned. Welles' orders to her were short, sweet and unbelievable. Read them: "Commander Nichols will sail in pursuit of the 290 in such direction as he may probably fall in with her." Little wonder the Federal Navy couldn't catch Semmes.

⚓

⚓

19 Terror on the Grand Banks

The fame of the *Alabama* began with her sweep of the whaling fleet off the Azores. Yet, it was her epic, prodigious assault on

Northern merchantmen off the Grand Banks and down the American seaboard that shot her prestige sky-high and gave her a lustre that was undimmed until the waters of the English Channel sucked her under. By then she was legend.

By the same token Raphael Semmes became one of the two most hated men of the Confederacy, the other being Jefferson Davis. So savage was the animosity against the naval officer that it refused to die with the Lost Cause, but was regurgitated, after Appomattox, in his arrest, imprisonment, and threat of the gallows.

As ship after ship burned to the water's edge, the Northern press whipped up a hate-Semmes hysteria. Frightful pictures were painted of Semmes as a brutal, vindictive Captain Bligh, who drove his banditti crew like dogs, as imaginative as were tales of his torturing prisoners, or of Semmes the arsonist, obsessed with a mania for setting ships afire.

Editorials bristled anew with demands that he be strung up at his own yardarm, if and when caught. Aye, there was the rub: if and when! Semmes had one inviolate, inexorable law: never stay in the same place too long. Strike and be gone! Because of this ubiquitousness, this darting in here and out there, for two years afloat his movements were incalculable to his enemies.

On the *Alabama,* as on the *Sumter,* Semmes was his own intelligence officer, making singlehanded decisions, apparently consulting only Lieutenant Kell, and often not even him. Lieutenant Sinclair vouched for this. Never once, related Sinclair, did "any one on board to my knowledge receive information respecting her destination, present or future. As sailing master, directing and picking off the position of the ship from the chart from day to day, I could often make a reasonably close guess as to our objective point. But in answer to the questions of my brother officers as to where we were bound, my answer had always to be that I could only guess. If a still tongue makes a wise head, our skipper was a Solomon or two."

As with the *Sumter,* Semmes' orders explicitly forbade his engaging enemy warships and confined his operations to cutting down the size of America's merchant marine. He was confident the Washington government would act fast once the news of his mop-up of the whalers became known. Powerful vessels would be sent to intercept him. The American coasts and sealanes to Europe would be patrolled. He failed to reckon on the ineptitude of the Federal Navy Department, though he knew a single commerce raider could not forever defy and elude the growing power of the United States. Soon or late, somewhere, he would be brought to bay and must fight it out.

Cut off from his own ports, alone on the ocean, unable to contact a friendly ship or shore, Semmes still found means to penetrate his enemy's secrets. It was laughably simple. Late newspapers, gleaned eagerly from prizes, and from neutral ships, gave away many a plan to scotch him. Northern scribes apparently were more deeply interested in preserving freedom of the press than in cloaking Northern naval operations.

From the New York *Herald* of October 5, 1862—eight days after its publication—Semmes extracted vital information as to the number and size of the "enemy's gunboats": "One gun, 10 (vessels); two guns, 29; three guns, 32; four guns, 36; five guns, 34; six guns, 28; seven guns, 21; eight guns, 2; nine guns, 13; total 192. Of this whole number there are only 13 superior to myself The first set of propeller gunboats, built after the war began, are said to be indifferent. The second set, very fine and heavily armed. The sidewheel boats not very vast and only tolerable."

This meant the *Alabama* need avoid only thirteen of them. Consider what printing such revealing statistics meant to the Southern raider. To the New York editors Semmes was heartily grateful. They helped him escape many a trap, dodge many a danger, by naming the ships sent after him, their size, their gun batteries, and their cruising grounds. "This, of course," said Semmes, "enabled me to take better care of the *Alabama* than I should otherwise have been enabled to do. This was the only war in which the newspapers ever explained, beforehand, all the movements of the armies, and fleets, to the enemy."

The American Consul at Fayal, in the Azores, one Charles W. Dabney, had quickly rounded up the crews of the burned whalers, chartered a ship and sent them home. Landing at Boston the refugees were welcomed by swarms of reporters, who milked them of many a fairy-tale "atrocity" committed by Semmes. Not only were their homeward expenses paid by the Federal government, but they sold to the islanders, at burglary prices, the boats and bulging cargoes Semmes had let them ferry ashore. They reached home with their pockets stuffed.

Few of the whaler masters and mates ever told the whole truth. They failed to mention, observed Semmes (take it with a grain of salt, if you will), how they implored him to spare their ships, swearing they were the best of Democrats and deprecating the war on the South. Particularly vengeful were they because Semmes had clapped them in irons for a day or two and bunked them on deck under a canopy of spare sail. Captain Tilton, of the *Virginia,* and Captain Gifford of the *Elisha Dunbar,* the last two whalers burned by Semmes, lashed out wrathfully. Yet their complaints boiled down to the single discomfort of being drenched by water splashing over the freeboard in rough weather. This was unavoidable. Semmes saw no reason to oust his men from their hammocks to make room for prisoners. A tent on deck was the best he could do. The menu served his prisoners was precisely that dished out to his own crew, plentiful and nourishing. Captain Tilton admitted a bill of fare of "beef and pork, rice, beans, tea and coffee and bread."

Yet though the tall tales spun by these repatriates made Northern eyes bulge, all agreed on one point: the *Alabama* was the fastest ship they had ever seen, "sliding through the water like a swordfish." She was not to be caught by lackadaisical methods.

At the height of the popular indignation over the destruction of the whalers a further preposterous "crime" was chalked up against Semmes. He "hated the flag." True enough, but for that matter the whole South hated it. Confederate bards reveled in reviling the banner they had once revered. From one of them came lines that were bywords in the South:

Tear down that flaunting lie,
Half-mast the starry flag,
Insult no sunny sky
With hate's polluted rag.

One accusation, at least, was never raised against Semmes. He was not suspected of keeping a beautiful maiden captive in his cabin, as pirates were traditionally supposed to do.

Piracy was, of course, the theme-song of the outcry. Yet, to brand the men before the *Alabama's* mast as an unruly gang of cutthroats, who hated Semmes and watched eternally for an off-moment to murder him and his officers and seize the ship, was subversion of the truth. The *Alabama's* tars were no angels, to be sure. Pretty hard characters, some of them, but said Sinclair, "all the same, a bronzed, stalwart, well-seasoned set of fellows, as promising as any set of men that ever went to sea."

They got gloriously drunk on shore. Getting drunk was a frailty of man-of-war's men for centuries. The Federal and Confederate navies were no exceptions. Their alcoholic leaning was inherited from generations of sailors before them. On the *Alabama* they were well-grogged twice a day with fiery "Old Jamaica," the naval *sine qua non* of that era. It was part of the signing-on deal. In port shore patrols, even as today, often made the rounds of the brothels and rum dens for delinquents and late comers. Occasionally, they smuggled rum aboard, got riproaring drunk in the forecastle, back-talked to their officers, fought with each other only to be subdued forcibly and thrown into the brig. Tipsy with bad liquor a score of them fomented a quick mutiny at Martinique that Semmes drowned out with his dynamic "water treatment."

Sinclair tells how occasionally jugs of "Oh-to-be-joyful" were bootlegged into the forecastle and how "the main brace is spliced so often that soon our lads forget who commands the *Alabama*. Matters getting serious, the beat to quarters is given; they recognize the sound and know they must go there come what will or whatever their state, and Jack drunk or Jack sober, to answer to their names. Such are the effects of discipline. The more mutinous ones are put in irons, the rest are sent to their hammocks to sleep their drunk off."

Lest it be forgotten: the *Alabama's* Jack cussed blue streaks. (So did Semmes on occasion.) Jack expected to be punished for his lapses, and yet, taking him at his worst, the Liverpool crimps had done a pretty good job on short notice. "They were all sailors," said one of their number, "but they were mostly of that class, found in seaport towns all over the world, that ship for the run from port to port, and not for the voyage, and are always a rough mutinous set." The New York *Herald* downgraded the *Ala-*

bama's crew as the "scum of England," a stigma they bitterly resented and were to fire back off Galveston.

It took a strong arm to discipline them, but Lieutenant John McIntosh Kell had just that. He brooked little monkey business. Semmes admitted, "One has all sorts of characters to deal with in a ship's crew, and a vigorous arm is necessary." Yet Kell himself testified, "a braver or more willing crew never floated." Morale on the *Alabama* for the most part was good and it was good because Raphael Semmes made it so.

One hard fact was unanswerable: had Semmes' crew been cat-o'-nine-tailed like dumb slaves the *Alabama* could never have hung up her record of achievement. It had to be teamwork, and so it was.

Semmes' best-known nickname, Old Beeswax, was conferred on him by a forecastle wit. Yet it stuck. Semmes liked it. It gave him many a chuckle. It may be remembered the skipper of the *Brilliant* related at New York how Semmes' steward waxed the ends of the raider's prodigious moustache daily, sharpening the upturned ends like rapier points. The *Alabama's* tars rather fancied Semmes' severe mien, his Mephistophelian air, that so incensed the Northern public. The "limey" forecastle ran off many a jibe at Semmes' adornment, yet one thing they recognized from the start—Semmes was a bold, resourceful leader, equal to any emergency.

Leaving the *Alabama's* crew, Porter's "descendants of the Norsemen," we will step now into the wardroom and meet her officers, ranged about the long mess-table. What better First Lieutenant and Executive Officer could Semmes have desired than true and tried John McIntosh Kell, who had served so ably on the *Sumter?* He sits, as before, at the end of the mess-table facing his captain, who said of him, "He was my right hand, and I knew he would be ready when I called him."

Missing was gay, debonair Lieutenant Richard Chapman, great lover, ready always "to tread one measure, take one cup of wine," or sing madrigals beneath a lady's latticed window. Semmes longed for him, but in his place as Second Lieutenant sat a capable successor, Richard F. Armstrong, a Georgian, and a graduate of Annapolis and the *Sumter.* Next came the Third Lieutenant, Joseph Wilson of Florida, another élève from Annapolis, who had also made the *Sumter* cruise. The Fourth Lieutenant was Arthur Sinclair, a Virginian, with a long naval background and a facile pen.

"A capital seaman and an excellent officer" (Semmes' own estimate) was the English-born Fifth Lieutenant, John Low, an adopted son of Georgia.

Commanding the *Alabama's* non-existent Marines was Lieutenant Beckett Howell, brother of Mrs. Jefferson Davis. Midshipman Irvine D. Bulloch, brother of the man who fathered the *Alabama*, was appointed Acting Master. Presiding over the two handsome, powerful engines that purred like deep-throated music in the heart of the ship, was hearty Miles J. Freeman, former Chief Engineer of the *Sumter*. The Chief Surgeon was another veteran of the *Sumter*, kindly, gentlemanly Dr. Francis Galt. "Pills" they called him. His assistant was a Briton, Dr. David Llewellyn.

Perhaps it was inevitable that a blacksheep should have crept into the wardroom fold. He was Paymaster Clarence R. Yonge, who was to incite a mutiny, turn "Yankee" and earn Semmes' eternal hatred. In his memoirs Semmes left him nameless.

Now take a sampling of the *Alabama's* steerage and warrant officers. You'll meet them as you read along. Boatswain Benjamin Mecaskey had helped Semmes rig out the *Sumter* at New Orleans. He was born, so 'twas said, "with web feet and barnacles on his back." His shrill boatswain's pipe could be heard from deck to main truck.

Master's Mate James Evans was the Argus of the *Alabama's* odyssey. What Jeb Stuart was to Robert E. Lee, Evans was to Semmes: his sharp, military eyes. When uncertain of a faraway ship's nationality Semmes sent for Evans, who possessed an uncanny faculty for identifying Yankee sails. Handing his glasses to Evans, Semmes would order him aloft, "Look at that ship and tell me what nation she belongs to." After gazing a minute or two at the distant stranger Evans would reply, "She's Yankee, sir" or "She's not Yankee, sir. I think she's English" or French or Dutch or whatever he believed she was. Declared Semmes, "When he pronounced a ship Yankee I was always sure of her. I never knew him to fail but once." Semmes simply declined to chase a sail Evans certified as neutral. It saved time and fuel overhauling foreigners to no avail.

Nor should Master's Mate George T. Fullam, diarist, an Englishman by birth, be slighted. As Prize Master, relieving the watch officers, he boarded more vessels than any other officer. Arduous and dangerous it was, boarding prizes in heavy seas with the cutter tossed about like a cockleshell, never knowing what he would face with when he stepped over the side.

Filling out the cruiser's picture were the "powder monkeys," five of them, runaways from the "stews and haunts" of Liverpool, who, caught by the excitement of shipping on the mysterious 290, had smuggled themselves aboard. They, too, were signed on. Pranksters they were. "A tougher case Liverpool could not produce" than Powder Monkey Frank Egan whose idea of fun was to hide the *Alabama's* pet cat in the muzzle of the bow gun. Shortly she was missed and the whole ship was ransacked for the missing tabby. Suspected and spread-eagled in the mizzen rigging, Egan denied all knowledge of the vanished puss. Meantime a sail was sighted. On removing the bow gun's tompion to fire a warning shot at the hoped-for prize, out jumped kitty. Egan confessed putting her there "to see what effect the firing would have on the cat."

Semmes avowed they "were as great a set of scamps as any disciplinarian could desire to 'lick into shape,' but it is astonishing what a reformation soap and water and the master-at-arms (who had charge of them) effected in them in a short time."

Of the humbler ones on the *Alabama*, who also served though they only stood and waited, there were two on whom Semmes laid verbal wreaths: A. Bartelli, his devoted Italian steward, and a Negro slave boy, "Dave" White. Both were to give up their lives in the English Channel.

Bartelli was steward on the *Bahama* that brought Semmes to the Azores. Forlorn, browbeaten by the captain of that ship, and of gentle blood, he asked to serve Semmes in the same capacity on the *Alabama*. Bartelli's besetting weakness was liquor. Semmes made him promise never to touch a drop on ship, on duty. "When you go ashore on liberty, if you choose to have a little frolic, that is your affair, provided, always, you come off sober. Is it a bargain?" "It is, Captain," said Bartelli. "I promise you I will behave myself like a man, if you will take me with you."

Bartelli kept his word. His attachment to Semmes was deep. "He took care of my linen like a woman . . . my table was always well supplied and when guests were expected I could safely leave arrangements to Bartelli; and then it was a pleasure to observe the air and grace of manner and speech, with which he would receive my visitors and conduct them into my cabin. Poor Bartelli!"

"Dave" was a likely negro lad of seventeen, a slave from Delaware, traveling with his master on the prize *Tonawanda*. Semmes seized the youth under the laws of war and accredited him as a wardroom messboy at full pay for his grade, making no distinction between him and the white waiters of the mess. Technically, Semmes freed the boy, who conceived an affection for Dr. Galt, the *Alabama's* surgeon, which "ruder people of the North find it so impossible to comprehend." On liberty, in ports the *Alabama* touched, sundry Yankee consuls sought vainly to lure Dave away from his new-found friends. His loyalty to his ship and what she represented never flagged—even to the end.

Come forward for a quick look-in on the *Alabama's* hearties on a quiet evening. The sea is smooth. Overhead the lookout scans the dark horizon ceaselessly. The crew is lounging on the forecastle. Smoke wreathes from scores of pipes glowing in the dark. The *Alabama's* raconteurs are spinning endless yarns. Leaning against the bow gun, the forecastle fiddler is scraping off a tune. Chanties are rolling out over the shiny waters. A high tenor voice rises above the rest with a pathetic ditty, "Loss of the Lady Sherbrooke," bringing moisture to many a hardened eye. Next, a basso, with a voice like the creaking of a capstan, makes the deck beams shiver with "My Helen is the Fairest Flower," touching off memories of the girls they left behind them at Liverpool.

Suddenly, from the quarterdeck the trumpet sings out, "Strike the bell eight! Call the watch!" The play is over! Merriment ends. The violin saws a bar of the South's national air, "Dixie," plunging the whole ship into an uproar of enthusiasm, "sometimes as many as a hundred voices joining in the chorus; the unenthusiastic Englishman, the stolid Dutchman, the mercurial Frenchman, the grave Spaniard, and even the serious Malayan, all joining in the inspiring refrain, 'We'll live and die in Dixie,' and astonishing old Neptune by the fervor and novelty of their music."

Then, profound stillness. "Dixie" dies on the lips of the singers. The boatswain's pipe shrills, the crew tumbles below to their hammocks, a midshipman comes forward from the quarterdeck with a lantern to muster the night watch. Silence reigns through the night, "broken only by the necessary orders and movements, in making or taking in sail, or it may be, by the whistling of the gale, and the surging of the sea, or cry of the lookouts at their posts, every half hour."

The Azores whaling season was over; the surviving whalers had taken alarm and fled. The September gales had set in. Even the hulking monsters of the deep themselves had bundled off to other waters.

Eager for bigger game and fresh hunting grounds, Raphael Semmes turned the *Alabama's* prow northwest and stretched towards the Grand Banks of Newfoundland, main highway of trade between the United States and Europe.

His target was the great American "junk fleet" lumbering eastward, crammed with the harvests of the vast grain fields west of the Mississippi. Translated into gold in Europe these rich cargoes bought arms and munitions now pouring by the shiploads into New York and Boston.

Semmes' plan was a bold gamble, loaded with risk. It meant straddling the very avenue along which Federal cruisers logically would speed to intercept him. He had no reason to believe the North would leave this vital ocean route unguarded, unpatrolled, or that the fat argosies would travel without escort. He would sweep down the North American coast, strike and vanish before news of his fiery business off the Azores reached Washington. He figured it out carefully, to the day. It gave him a time lag in which to move. By the day it ran out he would be off for the vast elsewhere. For the moment, at least, no one knew where the *Alabama* was. He had spoken only two French barks, both headed east. Mystery would shroud his ship as he moved in for the kill, and the waves told no tales.

Semmes weighed all the odds. Not only would he strike hard and fast, but, if luck favored him, he would dash into New York harbor, flaunt the Stars and Bars before the very eyes of his enemy and leave its shipping a burning shambles. The moral effect of this raid would of itself justify the risk. From this venture—though he did not realize it—the *Alabama* would emerge as the terror of the seas.

Standing northwest, the *Alabama* breezed through gales and heavy weather until she passed into the Gulf Stream, that immense river of the sea, some two hundred miles off the Grand Banks. The overcast was thick, shutting out the sun. The best Semmes could do was guess at his ship's position, within thirty or forty miles. Of a sudden, as if an accomplice in his desperate enterprise, the weather smiled. So did fortune herself at 10 A.M. October 23 when dead ahead, barging straight for the *Alabama* came two freighters, huge three stickers, both American. The cruiser need only laze along and let them drop into her deadfall. They were beauties, big handsome ships, with a profusion of tapering spars and all sails set, from truck to rail. Without bending her course, raising her colors, or make-believe, the *Alabama* sailed on serenely until the two ships were nearly abreast of her and only a few hundred yards distant, off port and starboard. Suddenly she wheeled and fired her bow gun. The Confederate banner fluttered out at her peak. At Semmes' mercy lay two prizes at once! The *Alabama's* boarders raced to their respective captives: the *Emily Farnum* and *Brilliant*, both of New York, bound for England with cargoes of grain and flour. They were the *avant couriers* of the "junk fleet" Semmes had come to despoil.

In Semmes' cabin Captain George Hagar of the *Brilliant* earnestly besought clemency for his ship, as beautiful in her way as any Semmes had seen on the seven seas. The Confederate raider listened quietly. His eyes burned bright. Slowly stroking his piratical moustache, he interjected a word here and there, but closed the case with a positive, "I'm sorry, captain. You've made a fine plea."

Semmes himself declared: "I was much moved by the entreaties of the master of the *Brilliant* to spare his ship. He was a hardworking seaman, who owned a one-third interest in her. He had built her, was attached to her, and she represented all his worldly goods. But I was forced again to steel my heart. He was, like the other masters who had remonstrated with me, in the same boat with the 'political rascals,' who had egged on the war; and I told him he must look to those rascals for redress."

That night Semmes burned the *Brilliant,* and "a brilliant bonfire she made," vindicating her name and illumining the Gulf Stream for miles around.

To his diary Master's Mate Fullam revealed his feelings, "It seemed a fearful thing to burn such a cargo as the *Brilliant* had, when I thought how the Lancashire operatives would have danced for joy had they shared it amongst themselves. I never saw a vessel burn with such brilliancy, the flames completely enveloping the masts, hull and rigging in a few minutes, making a sight as grand as it was appalling."

In dollars, the *Brilliant* was Semmes' biggest blaze so far. The ship alone was reckoned at 93,000 dollars on America's bill against Great Britain for "the depredations of the *Alabama,*" while her cargo ran that high or more. So much had Europe's wheat shortage and America's war inflation skyrocketed the prices of foodstuffs.

For the *Emily Farnum* the verdict was happier. Her cargo of properly-documented British property stayed the torch. Semmes transferred his fifty-odd prisoners to her and freed her as a cartel on ransom bond. Embodied in the release agreement, signed and sworn to by her master, was the stipulation that the ship should continue her voyage to Liverpool. Semmes' object was, of course, to prevent his spreading news of the *Alabama's* operations in the North Atlantic. Yet, hardly had the *Emily Farnum* passed out of sight before her master broke his solemn oath and doubled back for Boston where he sounded the alarm. Overnight news was flashed to the nation that Raphael Semmes was scourging the Atlantic sealanes.

Captain Hagar, hurrying to New York, before a tense audience in the Chamber of Commerce, painted a graphic picture of the scene in "Pirate" Semmes' cabin as he begged for the life of his ship.

From these two prizes the cruiser got the first four of a hundred or more recruits, a development Semmes had not anticipated. The North fulminated at the very thought of it. From here out volunteers from her prizes were to keep the *Alabama's* complement filled. Recruits, said Semmes were "more valuable to us than the prizes." Lieutenant Sinclair explained it, "Jack is a queer fellow, of a roving, restless disposition, fond of excitement and adventure, and loves the new ship and the new sweetheart best. Seeing this natty, trim, and saucy rover of the seas, apparently having a good time of it, he falls head over heels in love with her, and presenting himself at the capstan, desires through the executive officer, a few words with our skipper. The interview proving mutually satisfactory, our hero signs the articles, and presto! from being a prisoner in the lee scuppers, has the privilege and comfort of sampling the *Alabama's* 'Old Jamaica.' This is the way the complement of the cruiser was kept up during the cruise, the places of those left behind in port being supplied from fresh captures."

Late New York and Boston papers, presents from neutrals overhauled or taken from prizes, brought Semmes good news and bad. Lee had crushed braggadocio Pope at Second Manassas; McClellan had halted Lee's advance into Maryland at bloody Antietam. Rare was the morning that Semmes and his officers failed to find a batch of newspapers on the breakfast mess-table. "First, they are carried to the cabin, and the skipper cons them carefully, looking for movements of the enemy's cruisers," related Sinclair. "This accomplished and noted, the lot is sent to the wardroom mess, thence to the steerage, finally reaching the forecastle."

Three days later Semmes struck again. Another grain freighter hove in sight and he snatched her fast, the bark *Wave Crest*, bound for Cardiff. No neutral entanglements shielded her. After clearing her people the *Alabama* riddled her with gunfire. Just before nightfall she was given the torch, another 45,000 dollar ship on the *Alabama's* ledger.

As the cruiser filled away to the northwest the lookout descried a new sail. Putting on her running shoes, the *Alabama* skimmed off in pursuit. The moon rose full in unusual splendor. The fleeing ship had, no doubt, seen the flames of the burning *Wave Crest* and sensed her own doom, if overtaken. Semmes' night glasses revealed her features as distinctly as though the sun were shining. The moon painted the shadows of her masts, yards and sails on the water in sharp outline. Light and graceful she was, an American brigantine; her sails glistened like so many silver wings in the weird moonlight. One could easily imagine her an immense, gleaming waterfowl fleeing through the night.

Read Semmes' own picturesque description of the chase. His crew was sleeping. Only the nightwatch manned the deck. As for Semmes:

> I sat astride of the hammock-cloth on the weather quarter, and watched the beautiful apparition during the whole chase, only taking off my eye, now and then, to give some order to the officer of the deck, or to cast it admiringly upon the buckling and bending masts and spars of my own beautiful ship, as she sped forward, with all the animation of a living thing in pursuit. The poor little, affrighted fawn ahead of us, how its heart must have gone pit-a-pat, as it cast its timid eyes behind it, and saw its terrible pursuer looming up larger and larger, and coming nearer and nearer! Still, there might be some hope. The pursuing vessel might be some peaceful merchant-ship bound on the same errand of commerce with herself, and only trying heels with her, in sport, over these dancing waves, and by this bright moonlight. Alas! the hope was short-lived.

Presently, in the stillness towards midnight, a red flash and the boom of gun, and a "32-pound persuader" went whistling across the gleaming waters. So close on the heels of the "affrighted fawn" was the *Alabama* she had just time to sheer clear by a neat trick of the helmsman. So fell the *Dunkirk* of New York, grain-laden for Lisbon, with no neutral claims to sanctuary.

The hour was late. Semmes was in a high good humor, having won a fair, nip-and-tuck race without steam. Less keyed up with nervous energy than usual, he greeted his prize's skipper at the head of the gangway.

"You made a fine run of it, captain," said Semmes. "But you must have forgotten my little teakettle below. However, I outran you without using it."

"I'm afraid I don't recognize you," said the master.

"I'm Captain Semmes! And my ship, the *Alabama!*" There was

pride in his voice as he made a sweeping gesture towards the shadowy deck.

The skipper gasped. "Semmes! You, Raphael Semmes!"

"None other, captain," smiled Semmes. By lantern light he ran quickly through the ship's papers. "I regret what seems to be indicated."

The *Dunkirk's* condemnation and obsequies were fast. She had been sighted at 9 P.M. In only three hours flames were eating her vitals.

Lining the prisoners on deck Lieutenant Kell inspected them closely, holding a lantern to each face. By the dim light he recognized a worthless "bird of passage," George Forest, who had deserted the *Sumter* at Cadiz only to be cast back at Semmes now as a prisoner. The Confederate Articles of War prescribed death for Forest's offense, but Semmes hesitated. As salutary as a "necktie party" might have been for the rougher element of his crew Semmes compromised by ordering Forest's court martial. Tried before a court of his old officers of the *Sumter,* the culprit was sentenced to serve for the duration of the *Alabama's* cruise, without pay or prize money. "Perhaps," said Lieutenant Sinclair, "recollections of the common dangers and vicissitudes softened the hearts of his shipmates." Yet, Forest was to break cover again, and earn a dubious immortality.

Ennui seldom assailed the crew of the *Alabama.* The Gulf Stream was a sea raider's paradise where Semmes next overhauled the fine packet ship *Tonawanda* of Boston, with passengers for Europe. Anxious-eyed women and children lined the rail, petrified at the very thought of being clutched by the Confederate "pirate." Such was the terror inspired by the very name of the man. When Prize Master Fullam clambered over the side of the *Tonawanda* it was as if Captain Death himself had come aboard. Dire were the lamentations, loud enough, indeed, to be heard on the *Alabama* several hundred yards to leeward.

A cargo of women and children was not too easy to dispose of. Nor could Semmes house them, as he could the men, on the *Alabama's* deck until he found a way out. Nor was it "possible to convert the *Alabama* into a nursery and set the stewards serving pap to the babies," of whom there were a number. Legally, the

Tonawanda offered no neutral impediment to firing her. Yet Semmes released the ship on bond though he kept her cruising in his wake hoping to fall in with another to which he could transfer his prisoners and then burn her.

Once again the foretop sang out the familiar cry, "Sail ho!" and from the quarterdeck, "Where away?" "Off the weather quarter, sir!" Under a cloud of canvas she came striding over the horizon, as if aiming straight for the Confederate raider. To disarm suspicion Semmes hoisted the Stars and Stripes. His prize did likewise. It appeared as if the two ships were "visiting," a custom of the time. As she drew nearer Semmes "invited her, too, to visit me; my card of invitation being a blank cartridge, and a change of flags," and the *Manchester*, of New York, submitted gracefully to her fate. She carried a heavy cargo of corn.

From her master Semmes received a late New York *Herald* that apprised him "where all the enemy's gunboats were, and what they were doing." He fired the ship at ten that night. A vessel ablaze on the ocean in the darkness was a fearsome sight even to hardened sailors, yet even more frightening to the women and children on the *Tonawanda* that still trailed the cruiser. They had little faith in stern-visaged Semmes. Any moment they expected to walk the plank. While the *Manchester* went up in flames Semmes released the *Tonawanda* whose master signed a stiff ransom bond of 80,000 dollars.

The wind was freshening, the barometer fluctuating. Out of the mid-October, squally weather Semmes next seized the American bark *Lamplighter* of Boston, pointing for Gibraltar, her hold stuffed with the weed so dear to Jack's heart and pipe. Packing off as much tobacco as could safely be ferried over the heavy combers, Semmes consigned the *Lamplighter* to her fiery fate, adding 117,000 dollars to his score of destruction.

Semmes had now taken eight ships in twelve days. Behind him lay a track of flames that left his crew breathless, spellbound. He had promised them adventure and excitement. He had supplied an abundance of both. Visions of big prize money began dancing before their eyes.

Only one of the lads on the berthdeck of the *Alabama* ever put his reminiscences on paper, yet this salty little book, that appeared in 1886, has been challenged as a clever literary fraud. Indeed, the presumed author, P. D. Haywood, does not appear on Lieutenant Sinclair's roster of the officers and men of the *Alabama*. Nevertheless this sailor's yarn is packed with action, horseplay, sentiment, and the stuff that made up the life of the man before the mast. Haywood, whoever he was, spun a racy yarn of backstage life with Semmes' lusty brood. Lieutenant Kell, however, arraigned it as a flight of sailor's fancy.

Overlooked, apparently, was this composition of another seaman, a letter to his sweetheart at Liverpool, written from "Lat. 41:30 Long. 45," near the scene of the *Lamplighter*'s demise. Given some circulation on reaching Liverpool, it has lain untouched these ninety-four years.

I know your feelings were not in favour of my embarking in this enterprise, yet I assure you that I am taking well with both the ship, captain, and cause . . . No crew could be more comfortable than ours is, though, from the always watchful nature of the duties which devolve upon us, more discipline and active duty are enforced than we shall, perhaps, get credit for. Plenty to eat, plenty to drink, and plenty of work to do, is the order of the day, and of every day.

It would be an endless task for me to attempt to give you even an outline of the fearful havoc we have committed among the Yankee vessels since we left the shores of the Mersey, or of the destruction of the many splendid ships, of which not one plank was left fastened to another. We have already taken about twenty vessels, laden with every article which it is possible almost for the countries of the world to produce, and they have all been destroyed with the exception of one or two whose commanders have given bonds for various amounts of ransom to Captain Semmes, payable to the President of the Confederate States when peace is proclaimed. The last one which we let off was the *Tonawanda*, which lay beside us several days, and had a good deal of British property, with some doubtful, aboard—the captain and crew being aboard our vessel. They were all glad to get away, but the only reason why such a course was pursued was that they had a large number of females on board as passengers, which the skipper said could not be stowed in our 'fixins' nohow. The historical chivalry of the South would not permit of our disturbing or molesting the females, so we took his bond, put the prisoners we had on board, and sent her away, Semmes declaring that it was

enough to break a man's heart to see that he was compelled to part
in such a way with so splendid a ship.

It is next to a play to hear the prisoners themselves tell how they
were taken, and what they thought of us when first sighted. The
mate of the *Manchester* stated that all on board his ship was in
good order, going with a stiff breeze from S.S.W., when the lookout reported a sail on the beam. The red cross of St. George was flying, and the day being clear, our guns were made out quite visible.
The man at the wheel remarked to the captain, 'There's a British
man-of-war bearing down on us; we had better show our colours.'
The captain shortly after ordered them to be hoisted. Away went
the stars and stripes, and, almost at the same moment, down went
the British ensign, and in its place appeared the full flag of the Confederates. A 10 lb. shot right across the bows astonished the captain, who, after a rapid survey through his glass, exclaimed, "It's
that pirate Semmes; the ship is lost!" I may only add that a few
hours more and they were all prisoners on board the *Alabama*, and
the last we saw of the *Manchester* the succeeding night was a
bright sheet of fire in the horizon line as the darkness fell. The
prisoners we take are treated as well as possible, though our having so
many hands on board prevents them all from receiving what might
be considered proper accommodations. Some are made comfortable
enough, but there are impudent and insulting Yankees who are not
thankful even for their lives being spared, and they must take the
consequences.

Since we have come into these waters we have got some splendid
guns additional, all mounted; and, what with our own crew and brave
volunteers who have since joined us, we are now able to fight as well
as run, and both at the same time if need be so. We have also plenty
of news about ourselves on board in the New York *Times, Herald,*
the *Shipping Gazette,* Liverpool *Mercury,* and *Gore's Advertiser,* &c.
Some of the New York papers, illustrated, give frightful pictures of
the engagements their vessels have had with us, making them all
surrounded with smoke and firing into us, all of which we heartily
enjoy. One thing is certain,—they never will take the *Alabama* nor a
man of us alive. Captain, officers, and men know their duty, and are
quite aware of the doom which would befall them if taken, for there
are no croakers or skulkers here; but if so unlikely a thing should
take place, and the hair of one of our heads be injured, our commander assures us that the Government of Richmond will hang a
regiment of Yankee officers in retaliation.

Captain Semmes (or the admiral, as we call him among ourselves both fore and aft) is of opinion that the war will be settled in the beginning of the year, and in that case we shall all be provided for for life. No more sea for me after that. Previous to the 20th of this month our prize-money alone was worth from 400 to 500 pounds a man. So I am looking forward to the day when I shall return to Liverpool, and, relieved from the drudgery of a sea life, spend my remaining years in peace and contentment. . . .

The *Alabama's* Jack was already counting his prize money. Semmes had assured him the Confederate Congress would vote a whopping bonus, one-half the value of the ships burned and bonded. Good reason, indeed, for his enthusiastic cheers as he spread flames across the ocean. Had the Confederacy won out, each Jack who served the entire cruise would have taken home the tidy figure of 50,000 dollars!

The "uncovered" cargoes of his recent prizes told Semmes his enemy's merchants were still careless, not yet aware of disaster lurking off the Grand Banks. But these same merchants would soon be clamoring at British consulates for certificates "vouching for the neutrality of good American cargoes." Secrecy still veiled the *Alabama*. The New York *Herald*, of October 5, brought by the *Manchester*, had not a word of his Azores sweep. Up to the sailings of these ships the raider was unknown to American ship-owners.

It was claimed Semmes had burned British property on the *Manchester*, yet there was no document to prove it. News of her destruction prompted the Liverpool Chamber of Commerce to protest to Foreign Minister Lord Russell. That august cabinet official, still inclined to the Confederacy, replied that British owners of property shipped in enemy bottoms during a war, must look for redress to the country of the captor, that was, seek compensation in Confederate Prize Courts. Most British and American shippers did a more practical thing. They withdrew their goods from Northern ships, shifting them to British and other neutral bottoms while American vessels, in droves, rushed to the safety of registry under the English flag.

At Washington, statesman William H. Seward went into action. To American Minister Adams at London he wrote a voluminous despatch about what Semmes was doing in American waters. The "British pirate" was burning everything, even British property. Asked Seward: how long will the Lion stand it?

Apparently, the Lion was little ruffled. Every American ship Semmes burned meant more freight for British bottoms.

Since biblical times mariners have described storms at sea, yet it is to be wondered if any have surpassed Semmes' graphic, dramatic portrayal of the hurricane that now bore down on the *Alabama.* For days foul weather had heralded a massive atmospheric disturbance. On October 16 the *Alabama's* barometer, "that faithful sentinel of the seamen," began sinking rapidly. The cyclone had no doubt traveled several thousand miles before it reached the cruiser. Four and a half hours it took for this storm to blow by, howling "like ten thousand demons out of Hades."

As the cyclone enveloped the *Alabama* she reeled drunkenly. Hatches were battened down, lifelines strung fore and aft, sails close-reefed. Officers and men crowded under the weather bulwarks. The wheel was double-manned and the helmsmen lashed to it. Once the *Alabama* lay over on her side until her lee guns were buried under ramparts of green water threatening to bury her a hundred fathoms deep.

With the eye of a scientist Semmes watched this terrible phenomenon of nature. Never before had he sailed straight through a hurricane, from rim to rim, through the vortex, the dead-center, the awesome calm of this vast whirling dervish of the ocean. Semmes timed the three phases of the hurricane. Passage of the circular vortex took thirty minutes by his watch.

Let Semmes give his graphic description of this experience:

> The storm raged violently for two hours. It then fell suddenly calm. Landsmen have heard of an 'ominous calm', but this calm seemed to us almost like the fiat of death. We knew, at once, that we were in the terrible vortex of a cyclone, from which so few mariners have ever escaped to tell the tale! We knew that when the vortex should pass the gale would be renewed as suddenly as it had ceased.
>
> The scene was the most remarkable I had ever witnessed. The ship, which had been pressed over, only a moment before, by the fury of the gale, had now righted, and the heavy storm stay-sail,

which, notwithstanding its diminutive size, had required two stout tackles to confine it to the deck, was now, for want of wind to keep it steady, jerking those tackles about as though it would snap them in pieces, as the ship rolled to and fro. The aspect of the heavens was appalling. The clouds were writhing and twisting, like so many huge serpents engaged in combat, and hung so low, in the thin air of the vortex, as almost to touch our mastheads.

The best description I can give of the sea, is that of a number of huge watery cones—for the waves now seemed in the diminished pressure of the atmosphere in the vortex to jut up into the sky, and assume a conical shape—that were dancing an infernal reel played by some necromancer. They were not running in any given direction, there being no longer any wind to drive them, but were jostling each other, like drunken men in a crowd and threatening, every moment, to topple, one upon the other.

With watch in hand I noticed the passage of the vortex. It was just thirty minutes in passing. The ship, the moment she emerged from the vortex, took the wind from the northwest. We could see it coming over the waters. The disorderly seas were now no longer jostling each other; the infernal reel had ended; the cones had lowered their late rebellious heads, as they felt the renewed pressure of the atmosphere, and were being driven, like so many obedient slaves, before the raging blast. The tops of the waves were literally cut off by the force of the wind, and dashed hundreds of yards, in blinding spray. The wind now struck us 'butt and foremost', throwing the ship over in an instant, as before, and threatening to jerk the little storm-sail from its bolt-ropes. It was impossible to raise one's head above the rail, and difficult to breathe for a few seconds. We could do nothing but cower under the weather bulwarks, and hold on to the belaying pins, or whatever other objects presented themselves, to prevent being dashed to leeward, or swept overboard.

The gale raged, now, precisely as long as it had done before we entered the vortex—two hours—showing how accurately Nature had drawn her circle.

The *Alabama* had behaved nobly yet the hurricane took its toll, leaving scars, wreckage and confusion on deck. Lucky she was that she lost only her main yard and the small sail attached to it and a cutter stove in. All hands pitched in to right the damages. Even the old quartermaster, whose lockers were invaded by sea-water, brought out his Yankee flags, seventeen of them, and hung them to dry on the signal halliards. He was infinitely proud of the display—and so was Raphael Semmes.

The hurricane that struck the *Alabama* on October 16 was, relatively, no fiercer than the furore swirling about Secretary of the Navy Welles at Washington that same day.

Reaching New York, Captain George Hagar of the destroyed *Brilliant*, had given the alarm; and the cat, or rather, the *Alabama*, was out of the bag. A telegram broke the news to the not easily perturbed naval secretary. On its heels came a panicky message from a New York insurance official, "We earnestly request that vessels may be sent in search of the rebel steamer *Alabama* forthwith. Her depredations upon American commerce are very heavy. She is in the track of European bound vessels."

Bad news was coming too fast. Welles had not yet recovered from the shock of the burning whalers in the Azores. Now Semmes had struck the North Atlantic, capturing and ravaging the grain fleet. The idea of convoying these valuable cargoes had not even been considered. The suggestion was to come, not from the Navy Department, but from a shipowner whose vessel Semmes had burned.

It is not easy to imagine the consternation created by the *Alabama*'s flaming raid down the American coast. At Washington the scene was reminiscent of the hectic Sunday when the nation's capital momentarily expected the dread *Virginia*, having destroyed the *Cumberland* and the *Congress*, to steam up the Potomac and shell the Capitol. Into the Navy Department poured a wave of resolutions, petitions, demands for protection from insurance underwriters, marine societies, chambers of commerce, coastal cities and towns, and big-time businessmen and politicos.

Obviously, something must be done, and done fast. Countermanding orders already issued, fresh instructions went flying to this ship and that one to steam at forced draft to the scene of Semmes' latest depredations. Yet, as bluff, seadog Admiral Porter pointed out, Welles' pursuit ships invariably went to the wrong places or got there too late, as if they expected Semmes to wait around for them, "when it must have been known that she (the *Alabama*) would seek the highways of trade as naturally as a blue-fish would seek the feeding-grounds of the menhaden."

Gideon Welles' orders to Captain Glisson of the U.S.S. *Mohican*, give a sample of many such: "Sir, proceed immediately with the U.S. steam sloop *Mohican* in search of the rebel steamer 290 or *Alabama*. This piratical vessel when last heard from was in Latitude 40° N. Longitude 50° 30' W where, on the 3d instant, she destroyed the *Brilliant*. . . ." Hopefully, the secretary added a postscript, "Communicate with our consuls at ports you may visit, and on learning of the destruction of the 290, return with the *Mohican* to Philadelphia."

To help his captains identify the Confederate marauder, Welles sent them photographs of the 290, taken, supposedly and secretly, at Liverpool before James Bulloch staged the 290's two-in-one trial trip and vanishing act.

The psychological effect of the *Alabama*'s coup was instant and profound. Jittery shipping interests went into a tailspin. The lull that followed the *Sumter*'s impounding at Gibraltar broke out in a rising furore of fear. Overnight, insurance rates on Northern bottoms shot up. British consulates at Boston and New York were besieged by shipowners seeking foreign registry. Sailing orders for hundreds of vessels stacked up in Atlantic ports were cancelled. Their owners simply refused to take a chance with this fire-breathing dragon edging down the seaboard. The counterfeiting of foreign ownership certificates suddenly became a big business.

Semmes could have asked no more glowing accolade than that accorded by a despatch from the New York Chamber of Commerce to Secretary Welles, "The American flag, pride of the nation, and once the emblem of its power to protect cargo and passenger on every sea, is dishonored and in disrepute, or is withdrawn from the seas."

⚓

⚓

20   *Southward Ho!*

New York beckoned. Cracking along close-reefed, through blustery weather and high seas, the *Alabama* thrust her prow towards the huge Northern metropolis. She was still in America's sea, the Gulf Stream. Suspense had gripped the raider. Wardroom, steerage, forecastle, powder monkeys, one and all, buzzed with excitement. Great adventure waited just beyond the horizon. The Confederate jack-o'-lantern stood on the enemy's very threshold but there was not a glimmer of a Federal warship. A small armada of neutral vessels was passing east. In four days the *Alabama* overhauled and boarded nine.

Over the rim of the sea, October 23, swept a perfect picture of a ship—"the almost living symbol of a nation's greatness"—rolling gracefully, her masts yielding and swaying to a cloud of sail, her tapering poles shooting skyward, her broad flaring bows slicing the seas as if scornful of their attempt to impede her progress.

Semmes feinted with the British blue ensign. The oncomer fluttered out the Stars and Stripes. Repeating the fly-and-spider routine, on she sailed straight into the *Alabama*'s web. The bow gun spat out a puff of smoke and a warning that broke her trance. Instantly, it seemed, the ship rounded to; her cloud of canvas shriveled as if rolled up by an invisible hand. Captured at 4 P.M., the *Lafayette* of Boston and her goodly cargo of wheat were committed to the flames at ten that night—and the scourge of the ocean filled away towards New York.

Next it was the *Crenshaw*'s turn. She was plowing northeast, three days out of New York and bulging with golden grain. Fat she was, yet she skittered away over the sea like a gazelle running for life. Semmes was averse to using steam; his fires were banked; his boilers barely warm. Twilight was falling. At four miles he let fly a bolt from his rifled pivot gun that threw up a geyser of water just astern of his prey. It was an overpowering come-hither. She came into the wind and waited for the *Alabama* to join her.

Late New York papers carried by the *Crenshaw* bannered news of the Federal gunboat rodeo gathering off the Grand Banks to waylay the "sea wolf." Even the *Vanderbilt*, the million dollar luxury sidewheeler President Lincoln had wheedled out of Commodore Vanderbilt, and named for her donor, had joined the hue and cry. Much-amused, Semmes offered the comment, "While they are running from New York I am running toward it."

The *Alabama*'s prize court settled the *Crenshaw*'s fate in ten minutes, and the flames, whipped by the wind, licked her sides like red-tongued, ravening wolves.

The Confederate flame-thrower moved on, edging nearer the New England coast. Two days later, over the main, bounded the fine bark *Lauretta*. She literally ran into Semmes' arms. Her newspapers were seized as greedily as the ship herself. Apprehension for the safety of shipping at New York and Boston was rising. From the keeper of Boston's Minot's Light came a false alarm of the *Alabama* sneaking by in the night to pillage the Hub City's harbor. Secretary Welles was working the telegraph system overtime rushing gunboats to meet the "sheer mad" invader of the sea. No one knew where Semmes would strike, where he was. Coastal batteries were watching round the clock.

A floating cornucopia was the *Lauretta*, jammed with surprises for Semmes' "pirates," including kegs of nails for "subjects of the King of Italy." Yet Semmes burned her. A stupendous flambeau she made to light up his pathway to the vast city. If smoke of the pyre told tales, well and good. The *Alabama* might have to fight it out and her hearties were spoiling for just that. Down went the nails for the King of Italy's subjects, sizzling to the bottom of the sea.

Wrote Lieutenant Sinclair, "The New York newspapers two days previous are before us. All is excitement in Yankee-land over the depredations of the 'pirate,' and if threats are to annihilate us, we are doomed. But we have (thanks to our enemy who always posts us) the number and destination of our pursuers."

It was now October 29, 1862. The *Alabama* was poised two hundred miles off Sandy Hook. It was the nearest she would ever come to the enemy coast. Semmes was confident, his nerves calm as cold steel. Letting down his propeller he put the ship under steam. It was to be a fast in-and-out. In the wardroom he briefed his officers. He would snatch a prize, burn her under the very eyes of his enemy, strike terror to the Long Island coast and Jersey beaches, and head for the open sea. Round the wardroom table went the toast: New York or Davy Jones' Locker!

Out of the early haze, that October 29, lumbered the brigantine *Baron de Castine*, loaded with planking for Cuba, little dreaming she had a dawn rendezvous with the long arm of the Southern marauder. Semmes grabbed her as if snatching a leaping salmon out of the air, only to release her and pack her off to New York as a cartel, with some forty-five prisoners, including the masters and mates of his last three prizes. Semmes must have his bit of whimsy. ("Piratical impudence," the New York papers called it.) To "Mr. Low," leading spirit of the New York Chamber of Commerce whose blood and thunder resolutions damned Semmes as "pirate," "robber," "plunderer," the Confederate captain, who had just burned one of Mr. Low's ships, sent his deepest appreciation. Semmes instructed the master of the *Baron de Castine* to inform "Mr. Low" that by the time the message was delivered he, Semmes, would be off the port of New York with the *Alabama*. That night the *Alabama* was tense. At supper an extra tot of rum went down the throats of her tars. Tomorrow would bring the great adventure. Tension piled up.

October 30, New York Day, was wild, with half a gale blowing. Hardly was breakfast over before Chief Engineer Freeman entered Semmes' cabin. He had disappointing news. Coal was running out. The *Alabama's* bunkers were down to four days' steaming. Semmes made a quick decision. His raid on New York must be abandoned. Disappointment swept the ship.

"We had nursed the fond hope of overhauling a troopship bound south, but it was not to be," moaned Lieutenant Sinclair. To his diary Master's Mate Fullam repined, "We were startled and annoyed to find that only four days coals were on board. To astonish the enemy in his own waters had been the darling wish of all on board."

Sheering off into the Atlantic, Semmes shaped a southward course for Martinique. Uncertain of his reception in neutral ports and fearing obstacles to buying coal in the market, he had arranged with Captain Bulloch, before parting at Terceira, to despatch the tender *Agrippina* to the French island to re-stock the *Alabama*'s bunkers. Once more sinews were relaxed as the ship made sail for the West Indies. Officers and crew had a few days of *dolce far niente*. On his journal Semmes totted up the *Alabama*'s score: "Total captures to date, 21; burned, 18; released as cartels 3."

An impressive record to friend and foe alike! Incomprehensible it seemed that the *Alabama* should have skirted the coast unchallenged, burned at will, and vanished unscratched. Yet Admiral Porter, surely no friend of the Confederate sea raider, ungrudgingly attributed Semmes' prowess to "good management and forethought." Lieutenant Sinclair offered the comment, "It was a strange thing that the enemy's plan of pursuit was to look for us where last reported instead of studying future possibilities."

Northern newspapers were bitter. They hurled a crescendo of scorn at the Navy Department. In an editorial jeremiad Horace Greeley's New York *Tribune* needled the navy unmercifully, listing eighteen Federal vessels vainly tracking after the *Alabama*, "every vessel a match for the *Alabama*, save in speed, and several well able to overhaul her. . . . It seems strange that the energy and resources of the country cannot result in ridding the ocean of a pestering pirate." He seems not to have recognized his own part in the *Alabama*'s success.

The "pestering pirate's" three last captures—*Lafayette, Crenshaw,* and *Lauretta*—opened another phase of the *Alabama*'s career and again brought into play Semmes' keen mastery of international law. Hereafter claims of cargo immunity were adjudicated by the high-sounding "Confederate States Admiralty Court, held on the C.S.S. *Alabama* on the High Seas." Semmes' cabin was the courtroom, though often the quarterdeck was ample enough. "Chief Justice" of this august tribunal was Semmes himself. To those masters of prizes who faced this one-man star-chamber, Semmes was judge, prosecutor, and executioner rolled into one—a sharp-toothed, pitiless terrorist—though two "Associate Justices," Lieutenants Kell and Low, sat beside him, heard the pleas, examined the ship's papers and concurred in his inevitable decrees.

News of Semmes' captures in the North Atlantic had sent American shippers scurrying to "cover" their cargoes with certificates of neutral ownership, most of them fraudulent, clumsy attempts at deception. Semmes' sharp judicial scalpel dissected the falsities of these claims with the skill of a surgeon. For him it was an enjoyable avocation. He delighted in citing precedents and authorities to buttress his decisions. He spread his decrees condemning vessels to the flames in full on his journal, peppering them with citations from legal tomes packed on shelves in his cabin.

The *Alabama*'s prize court wasted little time on technicalities. It rendered immediate verdicts and executed them with equal alacrity. It is doubtful if Semmes' *ex parte* rulings would have been reversed had they been heard before an unprejudiced tribunal. He based every decree on a precedent or statute of international law.

The attempts to thwart Semmes' torch were often ridiculously ill-contrived. The grain on the *Lafayette*, for instance, was "protected" by a certificate signed and sworn to before the British consul at New York, stating it was neutral property consigned to British firms in Belfast. The New York shippers were merely an American branch of the Belfast firms. That is, they were shipping the wheat to themselves. Semmes caught the flaw at once. International law catalogued neutral merchants domiciled in the enemy's country as enemy merchants.

"Chief Justice" Semmes pointed out shrewdly that possession of the property at the time of the sailing of the ship must be divested out of the enemy-shipper, bolstering his conclusions thus:

See Phillimore on International Law, 610, 612, to the effect, that if the goods are going on account of the shipper, or subject to his order or control, they are good prize. They cannot even be sold, and transferred to a neutral, *in transitu*. They must abide by their condition, at the time of the sailing of the ship.

He then rendered judgment. "The *Lafayette*—ship and cargo condemned."

Actual neutral ownership meant the goods must have been bought and paid for by residents of a neutral country to whom they were being shipped. The case of the flour, pipe staves, and 225 kegs of nails, "property of subjects of the King of Italy," gave the court a laugh. Semmes hacked away at this specious claim of immunity like a skilled legal axeman. Who were the subjects to whom the nails were being shipped? No one could claim the property because no one was named. In support of his decree, "Case of the *Lauretta*—ship and cargo condemned," Semmes went on record, "This certificate (bill of lading) is void for uncertainty. It does not separate the property, and say which of it belongs to the "subjects of the King of Italy" and which to the enemy. For aught that appears, the subjects alluded to may own no more than a single pipe-staff apiece. Indeed, they can own nothing, as it does not appear what they own. Further: If the property was identified in the certificate, the 'subjects of the King of Italy' are not. No man—for there is none named—could claim the property under this certificate. It is, therefore, void, for this reason. See 3 Phillimore, 596."

New York editors charged Semmes with purpling the air of his "court" with salty, unparliamentary oaths. From Captain Wells of the *Lauretta* came an amusing description of the acrid *entr'acte* when he appeared at the bar of the *Alabama*'s prize court to plead exemption for his ship. He claimed—as reported by the New York *Commercial Advertiser*—that Semmes washed up the *Lauretta* case in this fashion:

" 'I'll tell you what' exclaimed the pirate. 'This is a damned pretty business—it's a damned Yankee hash, and I'll settle it,' whereupon he proceeded to rob the vessel of whatever he wanted, including Captain Wells' property to a considerable amount; put the crew in irons; removed them to the *Alabama*; and concluded by burning the vessel."

Semmes no doubt used the damns. He kept a supply handy at

all times. Attempts to deceive enraged him and seldom paid off. It is to be wondered if American shippers did not really consign their goods to the flames themselves by "covering" them with palpable fakes.

Passing out of the Gulf Stream, the *Alabama* slanted off the beaten route of commerce as she headed for Martinique and a rendezvous with the *Agrippina.* Yet, on November 2, Semmes overhauled the New Bedford whaler *Levi Starbuck,* a fabulous marine warehouse flying before the wind and packed with stores for a thirty months' cruise in the Pacific. Semmes was treated to New Bedford and Boston newspapers just four days old. The "Yankee fleet" was romping all over the ocean looking for him.

The *Levi Starbuck* disgorged valuable "plunder," heaps of green goods, cabbages and turnips, "very necessary antiscorbutics," for scurvy was threatening the *Alabama's* crew, now seventy days on a salt diet. Taking her crew of twenty-nine prisoners, Semmes burned the *Levi Starbuck* and Prize Number 22 vanished from the world of ships and men.

Bermuda slid past off to starboard, out of sight. The *Alabama* entered the track of ships homebound from the East Indies and Semmes had hope of gaffing one of these well-filled arks of the sea. On November 8 a splendid Indian trader swam into the lookout's sharp gaze. Indeed, the foretop flushed two ships at once. One, eight miles off, stood out like a frigate. Semmes sent for argus-eyed Master's Mate Evans. "Yankee is written all over, sir," pronounced Evans after a long squint through the glasses. The other was a beautiful schooner, but, sighed Semmes, "We were like a maiden choosing between lovers—we could not have both—and so we took the biggest prize, as maidens often do in a similar conjuncture."

"Terribly astonished" was the *T. B. Wales,* nearing the end of her five months' journey from Calcutta to Boston. Her master had mistaken the Confederate ship for a jaunty Federal gunboat and had eyed her with deep admiration until suddenly she hauled down the Stars and Stripes and waved the Southland's banner. Indeed, the captain of the *T. B. Wales* signalled a greeting of welcome to his unsuspected trapper, the first ship he had spoken since leaving

Calcutta. He was a likable sort. In Semmes' cabin he confessed never having heard of the *Alabama*.

The *Alabama*'s prize court held no session over the *T. B. Wales*. Her cargo was "uncovered." Stowed in her hold were seventeen hundred bags of iniquitous saltpeter, contraband of war, consigned to Baring Brothers' Boston branch. Semmes' memory flashed back to his supreme moment on the *Sumter* when, in the Strait of Gibraltar, he burned the *Neapolitan*, also bulging with sulphur accredited to the same "obnoxious house of Barings," who were as busy as bees importing arms and munitions for the Federal armies. Semmes reveled in the *T. B. Wales* bonfire. "I took especial pleasure in applying the torch."

Before firing this floating dockyard, for such he made of her, Semmes seized her anchors, chains, and, joyfully, her main yard, precise in style and size, to the one snatched from the *Alabama* by the hurricane. "The *Wales*," said Semmes, "was the most useful of my captures." Doubly welcome were nine volunteers from her crew—"a prize more valuable than the prize itself."

Yet, useful as was the *Wales*, she injected an unlooked-for complication, though a rather pleasant one, into the raider's grim business: the patter of little feet on the Confederate's deck.

On his wearisome roundtrip to India the master of the *T. B. Wales* had taken his wife and three small daughters "to bear him company." Returning from India as passengers were a former United States Consul, George H. Fairchild, and his wife, who likewise had three daughters of pigtail age.

Courteously, Semmes brought the ladies and children aboard. Two of his young lieutenants vacated their staterooms to accommodate the visitors. Semmes bestowed the ladies, with their husbands, on the wardroom mess, consigning them to the "care of my gallant friend Kell."

Semmes permitted the ladies to salvage their entire wardrobes though, to the distress of the consul's good wife, he was forced to feed to the flames a number of highly-prized, elegantly-carved ebony chairs. "Her ladylike resignation to the inevitable was very sweet," averred Lieutenant Sinclair. "It has already dwelt in the memory of the writer; but such is cruel war, no respecter of persons. I trust she bears us no ill will."

Next day, Sunday, November 9, Semmes' journal bore witness to the stirrings of his heart at this pleasing interlude, "My menage has become quite homelike with the presence of women and the merry voices of children." For the young ladies, aged four to eleven, being captured by the Confederate "pirate" was quite a lark. They prattled ceaselessly, romped all over the ship, played tag on deck, hide and seek behind the big guns, and made friends with every Jack aboard, including even the powder monkeys.

Capture of the six little folk brought dreams of domesticity and longings for home to Raphael Semmes:

> When I would turn over in my cot, in the morning, for another nap, in that dim consciousness which precedes awakening, I would listen, in dreamy mood, to the pattering of the tiny feet of the children and their gleeful voices over my head. . . . 'Home Sweet Home,' with all its charms, would cluster around my imagination, and as my slumber deepened, putting reason to rest, and giving free wing to fancy, I would be clasping again the long-absent dear ones to my heart.

Yet Semmes little knew what rigors of war his "dear ones" were enduring. His wife and three youngest children were, at this juncture, virtually prisoners of war at Cincinnati. Dutifully, he had written her. Barely a baker's dozen of his letters ever arrived. While Semmes blazed his track across the ocean Northern animosity flared out against his wife. At Cincinnati newsboys paraded under her windows, yelling fake headlines, "Pirate Semmes captured! Read all about it!" In 1863 she was suddenly and peremptorily deported South. Brought east under guard she was conveyed to Fortress Monroe and carried, with her daughters, by boat up the James River to City Point where she was released to the Confederate Commissioner of Prisoners. Mrs. Semmes reached Richmond while the dead Stonewall Jackson lay in honored state in the Virginia Capitol.

Yet of these things Semmes knew nothing. Perhaps well he did not. The discourtesy to his wife embittered him for life. So it had been with Thomas Jefferson, who, never, to his dying day, forgave the British for ill use of his *enceinte* wife.

Semmes found much in common with his New England prisoner, George H. Fairchild, who spent many hours of his ten-day incarceration in Semmes' cabin, as if there were no war between North and South. In 1866 while Semmes lay imprisoned at Washington in the shadow of the gallows Fairchild came forward to testify in his behalf. Semmes had accorded him, his wife and children, said Fairchild, every courtesy within the power of a gentleman sea raider. For this act of kindness Semmes was grateful, and so he recorded in his memoirs, "With all the passions, and especially those of malignity, and hate, running riot through the land, it required moral courage to do this; and I take this opportunity of thanking a New England man, for obeying the instincts of a Christian and a gentleman."

Meanwhile, the *Alabama* flew along southwards, riding trade winds and paced by fleecy trade clouds on high. On November 17 she doubled the east end of Dominica—"the same Dominica that lay so fast asleep in the gentle moonlight on the night that the little *Sumter* ran so close along it, like a startled deer, after her escape from the *Iroquois*." Little now did Semmes fret about meeting the *Iroquois*. He had returned with a far finer, faster ship, armed with metal enough to give the Federal cruiser an equal fight. Yet the *Alabama* came in warily. Enemy cruisers even more powerful than she might be lurking hereabouts.

Cautiously, Semmes eased down the picturesque Martinique coast. Running past St. Pierre where the *Sumter* was blockaded just a year since, Semmes reconnoitred carefully. His telescope revealed no suspicious craft. He then steamed on to anchor at Fort de France, the *Alabama's* first harbor since she was commissioned off the Azores three months agone. There, under the protecting guns of the fort, lay the *Agrippina*, her consort, laden with coal and a batch of mail from home.

"Le pirate" had come again! Back to his old stamping ground! All at once Martinique was agog. Yes, here he was, not with the limping, patched up *Sumter*, but commanding a stylish-looking, rakish man-of-war, with smartly garbed, polite young officers to receive visitors at the gangway and show off the fine points of the ship. The quay soon swarmed. As Semmes stepped out of the captain's gig the throng stared as if they beheld a Captain Kidd or a Blue Beard, "only to find a common mortal, in no wise distinguished from his officers by whom he was surrounded, except that, perhaps, his gray coat was a little more faded, and his moustache a little more the color of his coat."

Briskly, even pridefully, Semmes betook himself to pay his respects to His Excellency, Governor Moussion de Condé, who was still doing business at the old stand. What a change had come over him! The Frenchman was hospitality itself. Forgotten was the verbal jousting he and Semmes had engaged in the year before on the *Sumter's* visit. With Gallic fervor Condé bowed a jolly welcome to the sea raider. Paris may have twitted him for his earlier hostility toward the Southerner. Semmes' exploits had electrified the French capital, and Parisian newspapers likened him unto John Paul Jones, once the darling of the salons and the lovely ladies of that gay metropolis. Ecstatically, they acclaimed Semmes' growing roster of captures. Napoleon III was even at this moment baiting the British with a scheme for plunging into the fray beside the gray legions.

And such exuberant generosity! "Le Capitaine" could have whatever he needed, barring, of course, though reluctantly, shot, shell, and powder. Perhaps, though, whispered Governor Condé, it would be wiser and safer to coal elsewhere, or, if he wished to remain, to anchor his ship closer under the cannon of the fort. Federal cruisers were snooping around.

Condé confided something else that disturbed Semmes considerably. The *Agrippina's* skipper, old Alexander McQueen, had been in port eight days, spending most of his time in the coffee houses half seas over, boasting of his secret services for the Confederacy and of the expected arrival of the fabulous *Alabama*.

News traveled fast and far in the Caribbean. Union warships may already have picked up McQueen's loose-tongued gossip. They could gang up on the *Alabama* and destroy her in a twinkle. Warned in time, Semmes knew that coaling at Martinique was out of the question. In an hour by his watch Semmes bundled the *Agrippina* and grog-happy Captain McQueen off to a new rendezvous, the barren coral islet of Blanquilla, off the coast of Venezuela. It was a well-taken, well-timed precaution.

⚓

⚓

21 *Mutiny and Mr. Vanderbilt's Gold Ship*

In the Sixties, West Indian rum was a far more potent concoction than its delicate, modernized replica. It had a fireball effect that often inspired its imbibers to do and dare almost anything—even mutiny.

It was November 18, 1862. Tropical dusk was falling fast. Having packed the *Agrippina* and her loquacious Scotch skipper off to Blanquilla, though giving it out the tender was heading for Trinidad, Semmes went to his cabin for supper. Only two days before had he boasted to his journal, "Thus far I have never seen a better disposed or more orderly crew."

Since the *Alabama's* arrival that morning bumboats had ringed the cruiser, trading briskly with Jack in tobacco, fruits, orange water, and sundries. All day the master-at-arms and a quartermaster had policed the gangway to foil smuggling liquor aboard. Shore leave and a boisterous spree were in prospect tomorrow. But in the meantime the *Alabama's* crew, sea-weary and yearning for a howling big run on shore, faced a dull, spirits-less evening.

What transpired next originated apparently in the fertile, untamed mind of George Forest, the *Sumter* deserter recently recaptured on the prize *Dunkirk*. Such, at least, was the tale told by P. D. Haywood in his "misrepresentation" of life on the *Alabama* published in 1886. Lieutenant Kell denounced Haywood's unflattering portrayal, yet through it ran an unquestionable vein of truth. Semmes' own findings verified this.

Forest—if we accept Haywood's version—was a born mutineer, though not as dangerous as his buddy in the port watch, a powerful Scotchman, who had enlisted on the *Alabama* under the alias of Gill. "A daring, dangerous ruffian" was he, a trouble-maker, always in hot water with the petty officers. With the men of his watch Gill had promoted mutiny, arguing ingeniously that since the *Alabama* had never touched a Southern port, she was illegally commissioned and taking her over would not be mutiny. It would be easy, he said. He and several others—so he claimed—had mutinied on a Spanish ship, killed their officers and plundered the vessel. "This man's influence was bad," asserted author Haywood, who was tainted, it would seem, with a pre-knowledge of Forest's rebellious plan.

After talking with Gill and other recalcitrants, Forest decided to do something to enliven the dry evening. Whether Forest was lowered out of a berthdeck porthole, or slid down the cable, matters little. Eluding lookouts on deck and sharks in the water, he swam to a nearby bumboat and returned with five gallons of Martinique rum, enough to set the whole watch on fire. Haywood labelled it "the worst liquor I ever drank." Forest passed out the fiery stuff wholesale though the host himself seems not to have touched a drop. Master's Mate Fullam declared flatly, "His aim was to cause a mutiny on board." Whatever it was, Forest knew exactly what it took to get things started.

As the hot rum began working, the uproar on the berthdeck grew louder and more boisterous, with Forest and Gill setting the pace. Lights were lit, against orders. Presently, incandescent with rum, the whole watch rushed for the main deck, led by Forest shouting, "Mutiny! mutiny! Come on! Let's take the ship!" A boatswain, who tried to block the way, was laid low with a belaying-pin. Then, pandemonium swept the deck.

Officers and petty officers, headed by Lieutenant Kell, rushed to the forecastle. "A sailor threw a belaying-pin at me," said Kell, "that but for the drunken aim might have been serious." Ordering the sober crewmen to seize their drunken comrades, Kell met flat refusal. Swinging his fists like bludgeons, huge Gill knocked a gunner's mate's jaw out of place only to be promptly laid low by a capstan bar. Sheath knives appeared. The drunken melee was getting out of hand. Blood speckled the deck. The rioters were swinging crude, deadly sling shots. Sailors are brothers in fights, and the ranks of the rioters were swelled by others who had not even smelled a drop of rum. "Come on and get us!" they taunted, with a volley of oaths. Haywood, fearing gunplay, admitted he got behind the mainmast. Fortunately, the cutlasses and pistols were locked up in the arms chests.

At this juncture Semmes, hearing the confusion, dashed onto the scene. A momentary standoff ensued as he appeared, but Semmes acted swiftly. His gray eyes flashed lightning. At his waist dangled a huge navy pistol. Sharply, he called out, "Mr. Kell, give the order to beat to quarters!"

Somehow the fife and drum were gotten up. So ingrained was discipline, the moment the rum-crazed men heard the familiar drumbeat and fife-shrill they staggered to their guns, some of them so muddled they scarcely knew what they were doing. It was precisely what Semmes had counted on.

"I now had it all my own way," related Semmes. "Thirty armed officers being more than a match for 110 men armed with nothing but sheath-knives and belaying-pins."

Semmes now proceeded to weed out the insurgents. With Kell and a dozen stalwart petty officers, he passed along each gun crew, ordering the obviously drunken ones seized and ironed on the spot. Those who showed fight were beaten to their knees and overpowered. It took five men to clap Forest in irons. Three times eagle-eyed Semmes made the rounds, routing out the chief offenders and others crazed by the burning liquor.

This done, the mutineers, one by one, were hauled to the gangway. Fetching draw buckets, the quartermasters started dousing the noisiest, drunkenest malefactors. It was novel punishment to his foreign-born crew. The culprits greeted it with derision and oaths.

"Come on, you bloody quartermasters! Come on with your water! We're not afraid of water!"

Semmes gratified them freely. Faster and faster the water deluged their faces until they were gasping for breath. The more they struggled the more they were splashed. Soon they were choking, shivering, strangling. The effect was electric. Semmes knew the efficacy of his briny bastinado. It had worked like a charm in the old navy. One by one the maudlin rebels piped down. Their oaths came in sputters between drenchings. The moment they opened their mouths in rushed a stifling flood. It was all they could do to breathe. Their frames shook with cold, they became alarmed. Determined to teach them a lasting lesson, Semmes plied his water-cure inexorably until they began pleading, entreating, begging for mercy.

"Captain, are you trying to drown us? For God's sake, captain, spare us! We'll never do it again!"

The ceremony (as Kell called it) took about two hours. All the while the rest of the crew stood at quarters, tittering as the rioters one by one caved in under the prolonged showerbaths. Presently, Semmes relented. "Mr. Kell, give the order to beat the retreat." The fifes and drums sent the crew below. Taking the irons off the half-sobered, half-drowned mutineers Semmes ordered them to their hammocks to sleep off what was left of their bout with Martinique rum and salt water.

"This was the way," said Semmes, "in which I quelled my first, and only, mutiny on board the *Alabama*. It became a saying afterward, among the sailors, that, 'Old Beeswax' was hell upon watering a fellow's grog.'"

Ringleader George Forest, sober as a judge, defiant as ever, was double-ironed and thrown into the brig until next day when he was triced up in the mizzen rigging, two hours on and two off.

Bright and early next morning, in steamed a greater menace than Martinique rum—the *San Jacinto*, with the "old flag" at her peak and her gunports open. The *Alabama* had the speed of this "old wagon of a ship," but she was no match for her fourteen 11-inch guns, that fired two pounds of metal to the Southerner's one. Hesitating to anchor lest she be interned under the twenty-four hour rule, the *San Jacinto* lay to off the wide mouth of the harbor in easy sight of her quarry. Semmes was penned in once again at Martinique! Through his telescope he calmly watched the Federal ship clearing for action. On her bridge stood Commander William Ronckendorff, a capable, conscientious officer, who sensed glory just around the corner. What the *Iroquois* had failed to do he would do: wind up Semmes' career. He had run the old fox to earth, just as had Captain Palmer and the *Iroquois*. Now to bag him.

The big Yankee ship still basked in the uncertain fame of

waylaying the British packet *Trent*, seizing Confederate Commissioners Mason and Slidell and bringing England and America to
the brink of war. The moment she appeared there was a rush to
the *Alabama*'s rail. A fight, at last! Just what every Jack wanted!
Even the rebels of the night before, fresh as babies after sleeping
off their revelry, shook their fists at the new-comer making elabo-
rate preparations to send the *Alabama* to the bottom. Tradition
avers the berthdeck pleaded with Semmes to steam out and fight.
His speedier ship could run rings around the Yankee, but he had
no intention of tangling with her, if he could avoid it. Nor did he
contemplate waiting nine days, as with the *Sumter*, to escape, but
to do it that very night.

As a precaution Semmes sent his bullion ashore for deposit with
local bankers. The *Alabama* seldom had less than 10,000 dollars
in her strongbox. If disaster overtook her, the gold, at least,
would be saved. To the banker's usurious charge of five percent
for safekeeping his funds, Semmes replied by hustling it back to
take its chances with the ship.

In the afternoon an officer from a French corvette berthed
nearby came aboard to bring Semmes a chart of the harbor,
"from which it appeared that I could run out in almost any direction I might choose." Semmes decided on the southerly route.
Meantime, Governor Condé despatched a billet, inviting the
San Jacinto either to anchor in the roads or to "leave the waters
of France without delay and keep at a distance of three miles outside the bay."

Industriously, Commander Ronckendorff drove nails into what
he thought was the *Alabama*'s coffin. Taking his cue from the
unfortunate *Iroquois*, he arranged with the captain of a Maine
merchantman unloading in the harbor, to fire rocket signals, if
and when the *Alabama* got under way. Should this miscarry, he
stationed two of his cutters, one on each side of the wide harbor,
with red and blue signal lights "to communicate the movements
of the rebel vessel in the event of her going out."

Utterly confident, Semmes paid almost no attention to the elab-
orate, ostentatious battle preparations of the *San Jacinto*. Meanwhile the *Alabama* idled quietly at her anchors and her officers

went ashore as if unaware of the threat of destruction lurking three miles out. Semmes found time to write to Bulloch:

> In a great hurry, & in the midst of preparations to run another blockade, I have hardly time to acknowledge the receipt of your long & interesting letter by the *Agrippina*. I was so much delayed on my way hither, by the burning of vessels (20 of them) that I was a little behind time, & I found that the old bark had been waiting for me some eight days. In this time, her secret had leaked out, & as the enemy, if any, in the neighboring islands, had probably been warned, I concluded to send the bark to another rendezvous, & proceed thither & coal.
>
> So I despatched her, on the very evening of my arrival, intending to follow her the next day, myself, when lo & behold! in the morning of that next day (that is, this morning) the *San Jacinto* appeared off the harbor. She is, as you know, rather too heavy for me to encounter, & so, as soon as the 'shades of evening set in,' I shall run out by her. I shall then join the *Agrippina* in a couple of days, coal up and despatch her. I was obliged to forego my 'raid' off New York harbor, as I found when I had approached it within two hundred & fifty miles, I had but four days coal on board; & as coal was both fuel and water for me, I could not afford to run it quite so close.
>
> I have written to Fraser, Trenholm & Co, by this same mail, enclosing to them for you the sum of three hundred pounds, on acct of coal &c. Please credit me with this sum, & give those gentlemen a receipt in my name for me. Best regards to Mrs. B. & the little ones. . . .*

The fates were more propitious to the *Alabama* than ever to the *Sumter*. Night came on murky, drizzly, and moonless. Mount Pelée need not throw out her sable, protecting shadow this time. Without fanfare as darkness settled the raider got up steam, slipped her cable and stole cautiously over the tranquil waters for the southerly exit. Semmes stood on the bridge, watching, tense. Guns were loaded and cast loose. Stripped to the waist, guncrews stood at quarters, lockstrings in hand, hoping for the magic word, "Fire!" Not a sound was heard save the *Ala-*

* This letter is at the Confederate Museum at Richmond. To the best of my knowledge it has never before been published.—E.B.

bama's cutwater slicing the surface and the low throb of her engines. Any moment might bring the flash and crash of the *San Jacinto's* broadside.

Suddenly, three rockets jetted up through the night. The Yankee merchantman had tattled! The *Alabama* was heading for the south passage! Off dashed the valiant *San Jacinto* but the *Alabama* had dematerialized in the darkness. Semmes had vanished, and the Navy's face was red again. Said Semmes, "We passed out without so much as getting a glimpse of the *San Jacinto*."

Just what happened never did become clear. All night the *San Jacinto's* crew stood at battle stations. Refusing to believe his quarry had eluded him, convinced she was secreted in some cunning nook, or inlet, Ronckendorff sent a cutter on a fruitless reconnaissance up and down the bay. For three days he watched the stable door after the horse had fled. On November 21, bowing to the inevitable, crestfallen, he unburdened the humiliating news in his official report to the Secretary of the Navy, "I have the honor to submit the following statement: the enemy escaped notwithstanding our vigilance."

But Secretary Wells saw little "honor" in Semmes wriggling off the Navy's hook twice at the same place. He riposted with a stinging reprimand that Ronckendorff never lived down.

At the same hour when that Federal officer penned his dismal report the *Alabama* was dropping anchor, seventeen fathoms down, off the beautiful coral island of Blanquilla. Tagging behind her came the tender *Agrippina*, which she had overtaken that morning. Along the gleaming white beach paraded pink and scarlet flamingos, looking, at a distance, not unlike an honor-guard of red-coated soldiers. In the lagoon Semmes found a surprise package, the Yankee whaling schooner, *Clara L. Sparks*, whose crew was rendering blubber on the beach, defiling the clean, pure air with the noxious odor of the crude process.

Seeing the *Alabama* run in under United States colors the whaler's master came aboard, delighted with the arrival, as he supposed, of a powerful Northern gunboat, declaring she was the very ship "to give the pirate Semmes fits, and I hope you find him." Semmes toyed with the old fellow, only presently to inform him he was standing on the deck of the dread *Alabama* herself. The Yankee mariner was aghast, having just denounced the fearsome Semmes to his face as a freebooter. "But I played the magnanimous," avowed Semmes. "I told him not to be alarmed; that he was perfectly safe on board the *Alabama*." Out of respect for Venezuela's territorial waters Semmes agreed not to burn the schooner. However, she and her crew would be held as prisoners until the cruiser put to sea.

For five days the *Alabama* coaled ship, taking half the *Agrippina*'s cargo before despatching her to another rendezvous, Arcas Island, a lonely cay low in the Gulf of Mexico. While the crew fished and swam in the crystal-clear waters George Forest, mutineer, was found guilty of inciting mutiny. Let off easily, he was drummed off the ship and bundled onto the beach with his bag and hammock. Crewman-reporter Haywood claimed his mates chipped in eighty dollars for the incorrigible, defiant Forest who shook his fist and swore to get even as he went shorewards. "I thought it was a good riddance," said Haywood, "but kept my opinion to myself."

Just before the *Alabama* upped anchor Semmes released the Yankee skipper, warning him to make a free sheet of it and "not let me catch him on the high seas, as it might not be so well with him a second time. I question whether he stopped this side of Nantucket." With him went George Forest, off into anonymity.

Crowding on sail the *Alabama* ran north from Blanquilla on a roundabout course for the famed Windward Passage, between Cuba and Haiti. It was the first lap of a bold, imaginative, two-barbed operation, bearing the unmistakable trademark "Semmes." His prime target was a Federal transport fleet he expected soon to rendezvous off Galveston for the invasion of Texas. Union troops had recently won a beachhead at this important Confederate city. Fitting out in the grand manner at Boston was a 30,000-man force commanded by Nathaniel Banks, a political general whom Stonewall Jackson had recently chased helter-skelter out of the Valley of Virginia. The convoy of transports was scheduled to reach the Texas port about January 10, 1863. Boston papers, taken from prizes, dilated on the splendors, the mighty power of the landing forces, even depicting Banks mounted on a "stud-horse" on Boston Common, cocked hat, feathers and all, parading before the populace, breathing fire and brimstone for the Texans. The idea of censoring news concerning the movements of transports carrying 30,000 lives seems never to have occurred to the military or civil authorities.

Knowing the twelve feet of water over Galveston's bar would compel the transports to anchor in the outer roadstead Semmes planned to cripple the fleet by a surprise, dead-of-night raid. Northern newspapers had blabbed the whole operation, enabling him to time his attack to a nicety—he would strike while Banks' army was preparing to debark. If there were escorting gunboats—which he doubted—they would be sleeping in comparative security, with no Southern navy to harry them. Boston newsmongers reported the *Alabama* heading for the coast of Brazil and the East Indies. Catching the escort offguard he would blast his way through the troop convoy, sinking and firing as many transports as he could, scattering the rest to be devoured piecemeal. He calculated that in half an hour he could make his assault, terrorize the transports, set fire to dozens of them and make his getaway before the gunboats could get up steam to pursue him. But first he must slip into the Gulf of Mexico.

Whatever the odds, Semmes knew now he had the ship and the men to cope with them. His steady, strong-handed discipline was paying off. Testified Master's Mate Fullam, "The state of efficiency the men have arrived at reflects the highest credit on both officers and men. Everybody is in the best possible spirits and eager for a fray." The five-day run on shore at Blanquilla—air, sunlight, no rum, no dance halls—had blown away the petty ills and grievances of three months at sea. The mutiny at Martinique was already forgotten. "I regard my crew as in fair fighting trim," Semmes told his journal.

The Gulf of Mexico was a trap, with only two escape routes, the Florida Straits and the Yucatan Passage. A girdle of Federal cruisers stretched across these exits could fence in the *Alabama* like a lone wolf in a big corral to be tracked down, cornered and slain. This Southern sea was fairly alive with enemy warships. Deliberately steaming into the Gulf was mockery of fate herself. Yet Semmes invariably did what his enemies least expected him to do. He may even have entertained hope of dashing into a Confederate port, if for no other reason than to show off his ship and his men, of whom he was infinitely proud. Certainly his heart, if not his judgment, must have considered it.

The six-week interval before the Banks expedition was scheduled to reach Galveston gave Semmes time to try for a jackpot that had long teased his gambler's imagination: a California gold steamer carrying bars of the yellow metal from the fabulous eldorado on the Pacific. Shipped down the coast to the Isthmus of Panama, the bullion then crossed by rail to Aspinwall (now called Colón). Thence, it was transported to the coffers of Wall Street by regular passenger packet steamers. Owned by Cornelius Vanderbilt, these huge liners often bore a million or more dollars of gold in their strong chests. Semmes let himself dream on. With a million dollars the Confederacy could "purchase several more *Alabamas* to assist me to scourge the enemy's commerce."

New York papers provided accurate timetables of the gold ships' sailings. Normally, they passed through the Windward Passage, between Cuba and Haiti. Here Semmes planned to ambush the northbound packet leaving Aspinwall December 1. She would pass his ambuscade three days later.

Like an irresistible mirage, gold fever suddenly dazzled officers and men. For once, Semmes revealed his purpose—and the *Alabama's* gold rush was on! Not since Francis Drake hijacked Spanish treasure galleons on these same waters was a crew so beset by visions of fabulous wealth. Eagerly, every Jack kept his eye on the horizon. Semmes admitted, "Everyone is on tiptoe of excitement, and we have a good many volunteer lookouts." Lieutenant Sinclair gave a more practical view, "We are on watch for the California mail steamer with its millions of gold. Everybody is sure of being rich . . . not on paper, in promises to pay of the Confederate Congress, which may only be redeemed at best in shinplasters, but in hard, shining, substantial gold."

Detouring widely, the *Alabama* fanned along the south coast of Puerto Rico. At nightfall, she threaded her way into Mona Passage, separating that island and Santo Domingo. For miles across the moonlit waterway all was clear. It was inconceivable! On the *Alabama* it was a certainty that at least one Federal cruiser would be stationed there. Semmes still sailed under a lucky star. "Where," asked he of his journal, "can all the enemy's cruisers be, that the important passages are all left unguarded?" Facetiously, he answered his own question, "They are off, I suppose, in chase of the *Alabama.*"

Dawn saw the *Alabama* running with a flowing sheet along the Dominican coast over the same blue waters where Columbus and his caravels blazed their immemorial trail. To the south, blue, hazy hills ran down to indigo seas breaking on the shore in long, pearl-like strands of whitest foam. On past the ruins of Isabella where Columbus planted Spain's first New World colony, sped the Confederate sea-rover.

Now it was Sunday, November 30, and another lucky day. Over the shiny waters came the sizable windjammer *Parker Cooke* of Boston, as if dancing into her lover's arms. Handsome was her dowry. The cruiser's commissariat was running low, but "our Boston friends"—as Semmes had found out on the *Sumter*—were excellent providers. The *Parker Cooke* disgorged enough butter, cheese, beef, pork, and fancy edibles to sustain Semmes' boast of having the best fed crew on the seas. At sunset he torched her off. The flames lighted up the bold hills to the south and vied with the phosphorescence that painted the soft, quiet seas for leagues on end.

Under easy sail the *Alabama* coasted westward. Tortuga Island, one-time haunt of the buccaneers, slid by off the starboard. Cautiously, she edged into the Windward Passage. On the broad expanse of this key artery not a glimmer of a Federal war vessel could be seen. Off Cape Maysi, eastern tip of Cuba, she took up her station to watch and wait. To spice the monotony, a Baltimore schooner, the *Union*, skimmed past Semmes' hideout. He grabbed her joyfully, but soon released her on bond, entrusting his prisoners to her care.

Another Sunday, December 7. Balmy and gentle was the air, the sea like velvet. Off, barely beyond sight in the blue distances, three islands lifted their fronded shores: Cuba, Haiti, and Jamaica. Never from an artist's palette came a seascape of such variegated mood or beauty. The *Alabama* herself was arrayed like a dandy waiting for his best girl. Her polished guns shone like patent leather; decks holystoned, clean as a new pin; brasswork gleaming golden in the sunlight. The boatswain's pipe, "All hands clean yourselves in white frocks and pants," was obeyed with alacrity. Ill-subdued excitement infected officers in gray and gold, men in white ducks and sennit hats.

The treasure-trove was overdue. Where was she? Semmes wondered if he had erred in his timing. Muster passed, forenoon wore away. At five bells, suddenly, the masthead sang out the welcome "Sail ho!" It was music to every ear on the ship.

"Where away?" shouted the deck officer.

"Broad on the port beam, sir!"

"What does she look like?"

"A large steamer, brig-rigged, sir."

The galleon at last! Instantly, the deck was in a ferment, the port rail lined with expectant, eager faces. Still arrayed in the finery of his Sunday uniform, Semmes hurried to the bridge. His glasses verified his hopes. A California steamer! Yonder she was, many miles off, a packet ship moving fast, showing too much top hamper for a man-of-war, mounting no guns. Raising his trumpet, Lieutenant Kell summoned "All hands work ship!" Fires were stoked; sails furled; propeller lowered. In twenty minutes the *Alabama* was ready for the chase, with everything snug "alow and aloft," steam hissing from the gauge cocks.

Old Beeswax appraised his quarry gleefully. She was a luscious sight for those eyes that flickered with fiery zeal. Slowly, he twisted the tips of his spiked mustachios. A strange light played across his countenance. Below the surface, his emotions were fanned to a flame. This was the prize of all prizes. His gaze narrowed as the distance between the two ships lessened. He could see the steamer's great paddle-wheels revolving like mad, her huge walking-beam seesawing up and down, smoke swirling from her prodigious funnel.

Hoisting the Stars and Stripes, Semmes tempted the stranger into breaking out her own flag. Now the *Alabama* moved swiftly, running for the steamer as if to cross her path and speak her. Yet so fast was the newcomer she outsped the cruiser. The latter glided past, in the steamer's wake, hardly a biscuit's throw separating the two vessels. The packet's rainbow awnings were spread; her deck a gay, festive spectacle; her rails alive with passengers.

Ladies in profusion bespangled the scene with bright, summery dresses and ribbons and veils that flirted with the tropical airs. Scores of opera glasses were trained on the *Alabama*, admiring her trim lines, her overall comeliness. On her bridge, unrecognized at the moment, stood the feared, damned, and praised gray ghost of the Confederacy, whom the "nation with a navy of half a thousand vessels has failed to capture."

As the *Alabama* swept astern of the steamer, she whipped about, fired her lee gun and tossed the ensign of the Confederacy to the breeze. Had the old buccaneer, Blue Beard himself, suddenly risen out of the sea no greater panic could have ensued. Ladies screamed—"one of those delightful, dramatic screams," confided Semmes, "half-fear, half-acting, which can ascend only from female voices"—and scampered off the deck. Excited gentlemen dashed hither and yon. A file of military appeared on the hurricane deck. Bayonets glittered. The charming, beautiful spectacle, so much like a grandiose yachting party, had melted as if at the snap of a magician's finger.

The effect of the *Alabama's* gun and her shift of flags was electric on the steamer herself. Instead of slackening at Semmes' command to halt, the packet's captain opened her engine throttle wide. Plunging forward, the great ship pulled away, determined to escape. Like a racer trying to overtake the leader in the stretch, the *Alabama* sprang after her. At the end of a mile or two Semmes saw that unless he cut short the contest with a peremptory summons, he would lose his massive prize. Ordering his "persuader," the rifled bow gun, shotted, Semmes instructed his guncrew to fire at the fugitive's foremast, aiming high enough not to take life. Semmes yawed the ship a little to enable the gunners to take better aim. Then, all at once, a flash, a curl of smoke, and pine splinters showered down on the steamer's deck and awnings. "A gallant shot," said Lieutenant Sinclair. "The mast is nearly cut in two, but holds on by the rigging."

Semmes' "hint" was sufficient. The ponderous paddle wheels slowed down, the walking beam poised motionless in midair. The steamer rounded to, a captive. Ranging up alongside her, Semmes despatched boarders to fetch her captain and papers.

"But," grieved Semmes, "Fortune, after all, had played us a scurvy trick." She was a California gold ship, sure enough, not homebound, however, with a million dollars in gold in her safe, but outbound, empty, from New York. Semmes had bought an elephant, and an embarrassing one at that. She was the mail packet *Ariel*, bound for Aspinwall on the Isthmus of Panama, with five hundred-odd passengers, mostly women and children, a marine battalion of one hundred and forty, and crew enough to bring Semmes' prisoners to over seven hundred.

Meanwhile, the boarding officer had hurried back to the *Alabama* to report that hysterics and alarm had seized the *Ariel's* passengers. Women bathed in tears, even fainting after the manner of the day; everyone expected the worst at the hands of the "pirate Semmes" who now had them in his clutches.

Semmes was disturbed, though not inexperienced in quieting women's fears. Before examining the ship's papers or discussing her fate with her captain, A. G. Jones, the raider decided to allay the plight of the ladies. "I had very little sympathy for the terrors of the males, but the tear of a woman has always unmanned me. And as I knew something of the weakness of the sex, as well as its fears, I resorted to the following stratagem to calm the dear creatures."

He summoned his handsomest lieutenant, the persuasive young Georgian, Richard F. Armstrong.

"Mr. Armstrong," said Semmes, "go below, put on your newest, dressiest uniform. Buckle on the best sword in the wardroom. Tell Bartelli to lend you my brightest sword-knot. Then, report to me for orders."

In a jiffy Armstrong was back, looking as bewitching as a "pirate" could be in a uniform slightly tarnished by sea air. Yet, he was a sea-dandy every inch.

"Now," said Semmes, with a smile, "go over there and coax those ladies out of their hysterics."

"Oh, I'll be sure to do that, sir," replied the Georgian, with a charming bit of vanity. "I never knew a fair creature who could resist me more than fifteen minutes."

Semmes laughed. "All right. Let's see what you can do to convince those ladies we're not pirates. I'm sending Mr. Sinclair along. You may need reinforcements."

To sharpen its effect, Semmes despatched his "charm expedition" in his own graceful captain's gig, newly-painted, stunning with scarlet cushions and fancy rope work. Manning the oars were eight hearties, lithe, bronzed, athletic, spick and span in white ducks. At the tiller, proud as a peacock himself, was Coxswain Freemantle. A few strokes of the ashen blades placed the gig alongside the steamer. Mounting the gangway the young Confederate asked to be shown the ladies' cabin. Entering, he was greeted with dismay and tears. The very sight of his gray uniform provoked a fresh outburst. For a moment ladies-man Armstrong and his aide, Lieutenant Sinclair, were abashed. Gallant they were, but hardly a match for scores of wailing females. Summoning his courage, however, Armstrong mounted a chair.

"Ladies!" There was a momentary hush. The soft Georgian voice had a soothing sound. Never did he look handsomer than at this moment. "The Captain of the *Alabama* has heard of your distress, and sent me over to calm your fears. He asked me to assure you that you have fallen into the hands of Southern gentlemen, under whose protection you are entirely safe."

The sobs died away to sniffles, but the ladies still eyed him askance.

"We are by no means ruffians and outlaws as we have been represented by your people. You have nothing whatever to fear from us."

Stepping down from his perch, he began weaving through the packed cabin, with heartening smiles and words. Semmes jocularly charged the young dandy with "picking out the youngest and prettiest, as the rogue admitted." Armstrong radiated charm; nor was Sinclair devoid of it. Soon tearful faces brightened. Eyes lately dimmed with tears shone confidently. The ice, or rather the panic, melted, and the two young Confederates found themselves taken "prisoners" by bevies of loveliness. Forgotten by the ladies, momentarily, at least, were war, politics, "pirate Semmes," everything except two handsome "enemies" in gray uniforms.

Presently, a young lady, bolder than the rest and pretty to boot, gingerly touched a button that glittered on Armstrong's breast.

Could she have it as a memento of her adventure with the *Alabama?* Her eyes peered deep into his. What else could a gallant sailor-man, even a Confederate "pirate," do than say yes? which is what he did. Magically, a pair of scissors appeared, and away went the shiny button. Another emboldened girl craved the same boon. Another button snipped off! The fair petitioners crowded round their captors, one and all demanding buttons, until—as Semmes told it—"when I got my handsome lieutenant back he was like a plucked peacock—he had scarcely a button to his coat! There were no more Hebes drowned in tears on the *Ariel."*

The male passengers took a dimmer, more practical view. Watches vanished from vest pockets. Trunks were overhauled, money and jewelry secreted. "I verily believe," reported Semmes' buttonless envoy, "these fellows think we are no better than the Northern thieves, who are burning dwelling houses, and robbing our women and children in the South."

Semmes may not have realized it, but his young officer was so intoxicated with the beauty around him he would have given away his coat, cap, sword, and boots had he been asked to do so.

That evening the packet's gorgeous saloon was festive with a gay dinner party. Guests of honor, lionized and adored, were the two chivalrous "pirates" from the *Alabama.* Champagne, beauty and wit enlivened this merry, strangest of scenes amid a bitter, internecine war. To Lieutenant Armstrong's audacious toast, "Jefferson Davis, President of the Confederate States of America!" up came every glass with huzzahs. In response, a pair of lovely lips offered, "Abraham Lincoln, President of the United States of Amercia!" and the toast was downed, all standing and cheering.

The *Ariel's* iron safe held about 10,000 dollars. Semmes seized the cash. He longed to make a bonfire of the packet. Valued at near a million, "she belonged to a Mr. Vanderbilt, of New York, an old steamboat captain, who had amassed a large fortune, in trade, and was a bitter enemy of the South. Lucrative contracts during the war had greatly enhanced his gains, and he had ambitiously made a present of one of his steamers to the Federal government, to be called after him, to pursue 'rebel pirates.'"

Semmes referred, of course, to the U.S.S. *Vanderbilt* that had, in fact, just three days before, limped back from a fruitless 3,570-

mile search for the *Alabama* through the watery mazes of the West Indies.

Semmes estimated each passenger carried a purse of three to five hundred dollars. This money was legitimate prize. "But," he boasted, "not one dollar of it was touched, or indeed so much as a passenger's baggage examined."

The one hundred and forty marines fared less happily. If the tales told when the *Ariel* finally docked at New York are to be believed, their deportment was comparable to Falstaff's army. On sighting the *Alabama* they ran for their guns. Priming, loading, and fixing bayonets, they made ready to repel boarders. When the futility of this gesture became apparent they decided to steal a march on the "pirates" by raiding the steward's wineroom and consuming the potables themselves. Only by tossing his liquors overboard did the steward forestall a saturnalia.

To the humiliation of the soldiers of the sea, Semmes ordered them disarmed and paroled. Reluctantly, with deep chagrin, they stacked rifles on deck only to see them triumphantly snatched off to the *Alabama*.

Now to dispose of his white elephant. Semmes was baffled. He could not squeeze seven hundred prisoners onto his own deck. Nor could he burn the *Ariel* with passengers aboard. Bitterly disappointed, he had either to release her or capture a ship to which he could transfer her living cargo to make a nearby port as best she could. He had not abandoned hope of trapping the homebound California steamer. Nor had he any way of knowing that that vessel had eluded him and was at the moment steaming through Florida Straits with a man-of-war escort and a million dollars in gold in her safe—the very million the *Alabama's* hearties had thought they heard jingling in their pockets.

Even sadder than Semmes was his crew. The excitement of capturing the *Ariel* had buoyed them up, but now the forecastle was wrapped in gloom. For weeks Jack's favorite amusement was keeping a little memorandum of his mounting prize money. The gold ship would top it off. Now his gilded castles had crumbled.

Committing the *Ariel* to Lieutenant Low and a prize crew of twenty, Semmes ordered her to trail along as the *Alabama* tacked down Windward Passage towards Cape Maysi, still on the alert for the *Ariel's* gold-laden sister. Overnight the two vessels lay to. At daybreak, Semmes took the precaution of disabling the steamer by removing an essential steam valve. If her still-hoped-for mate came bounding along, Semmes could give chase without danger of his prize crew being overpowered and the *Ariel* escaping during his absence. Toward evening he restored the steam valve and stood in for Kingston, Jamaica, where he hoped to induce the British governor to permit landing his prisoners and stretch a neutral point by letting him take the *Ariel* to sea for a holocaust.

From a German brig overhauled after dark Semmes learned that yellow fever was raging at Kingston. Reluctantly, he decided to liberate the *Ariel*. "It would have been inhuman to put ashore, even if permitted, (and I greatly doubted this point) so large a number of persons, many of whom were women and children, to become victims perhaps of the pestilence." Sadly, as if to condone his action, he added, "Indeed, where could I take her with hope of being permitted to enter and discharge her live freight?"

Yellow fever was a dread scourge in the Caribbean. Its toll ran high. The very name bore frightening import. Semmes knew well its horrible virulence. Had he invented the yellow fever story— as has been claimed—to foil the *Ariel's* sailing into Kingston after her release and revealing his presence to a nomad Federal cruiser, he would undoubtedly have related it in his memoirs, or to his journal. He invariably disclosed his deceptions.

Off Morant Point, Jamaica, in Semmes' cabin that night, Captain Jones signed a ransom bond pledging Cornelius Vanderbilt of New York, owner of the steamer, to pay 261,000 dollars to the President of the Confederate States, "within thirty days after the conclusion of the present war between the said Confederate States and the United States." Civilities were exchanged. Captain Jones, held hostage up to now aboard the *Alabama,* was profuse in appreciation of the courtesies extended him by his enemies.

As the two ships parted company the twice-balked Semmes stood on the bridge, watching his splendid prize vanish in the night. It was 11 P.M. Perhaps, he envisioned imaginary flames bursting from her portholes, chasing each other in red glee up the rigging. Who knows? Overhead, stars winked down. The moon was near her full. The Windward Passage was a silver sheet without a ripple. From stem to stern the packet was ablaze with joyous lights. War was taking a holiday. There was romance in the air. Across the waters the ladies waved perfumed handkerchiefs and blew kisses to their departing captors. Nor could Semmes repress a smile as he heard them calling, "Three cheers for Captain Semmes and the *Alabama!*" He could hardly believe it.

Yet, he consoled himself. The sea swarmed with prizes. There would be other *Ariels*. As the packet picked up speed a somewhat smitten young lady stood at the rail wondering if she would ever again see the attractive Confederate lieutenant. She never did, yet the button she snipped off his uniform came to light years later at an auction sale in New York. To it was attached a brief, faded note in a feminine hand, "Given me by the lieutenant from the *Alabama*, November 18, 1862."

Semmes' personal booty from his *Ariel* coup was limited to several cases of Drake's Plantation Bitters for which he sent (by the Captain of the *Ariel*) a letter of thanks to the makers. With a heavy base of Santa Cruz rum, the Drake concoction enjoyed high patent-medicine popularity. So Semmes bestowed the bitters on the *Alabama's* sickbay where it performed immediate miracles on his indisposed hearties, who probably detected the enticing flavor of its eighty percent rum and called for more.

Continuing her journey to Aspinwall, the *Ariel* then sped back to New York with a fabulous tale that stirred public imagination far beyond its impact on the course of the war.

Commander L. C. Sartori, a passenger on the *Ariel* en route to a Pacific naval station, left a grim picture of the *Alabama's* sudden swoop. On reaching Aspinwall, he was ordered back to New York to report in person to Secretary of the Navy Welles on "every particular of this lawless piracy."

The Commander said he was dining when the *Alabama* closed in. "I immediately jumped to the deck and beheld a steamer not over 500 yards distant, rebel flag flying and having just fired a lee gun. Major Garland, commanding the detachment of marines (passengers on board bound to California), had them immediately formed in the waist and gangway. I, at once, saw that nothing could be done. She was upon the *Ariel* with a heavy broadside, fully presented, and almost immediately two heavy broadside guns were fired [Semmes, Kell, and Sinclair all say only one shot was fired], and a 68-pound shell struck the foremast just over the pilot house, cutting the mast more than half off. Captain Jones, seeing the utter impossibility of defending the vessel or injuring the enemy in any manner, with my advice and the advice of Major Garland and the voice of all the passengers, surrendered the ship.

"The *Alabama* was then not over 300 yards on the quarter and was training her guns for a full broadside, which if fired must have done terrific slaughter among the 700 passengers, nearly half of whom were women and children."

Commander Sartori also reported of Semmes that, "His whole course while in possession of this vessel was most considerate to all the passengers on board."

⚓

⚓

22   *Battle and Blood on the Gulf*

Well it was that James Bulloch had equipped the *Alabama* with a workshop to make repairs at sea. Hardly had the *Ariel* vanished in the night before a steam valve collapsed, leaving the cruiser a cripple. It was her first mechanical mishap, a warning, perhaps, that her charmed life could not last forever. *Hors de combat*, she was forced to lay low. Semmes picked the secluded, protecting waters of Jamaica's north shore where he could lie as quietly as possible.

For two anxious days up from the engine room clanged a chorus of anvil, bellows, and sledge while Engineer Miles Freeman and his resourceful staff replaced the damaged valve. At nightfall, December 12, the *Alabama*, restored to mechanical vigor, stood westward for the Gulf of Mexico. Rounding Negril Point, the western tip of Jamaica, she stole on like a phantom, heading a bit south of west. Security was vital. "Nothing in sight, and I intend to see nothing," he informed his journal though he added the fading hope, "unless it be a homebound California steamer. It is important I should make the run I contemplate without being traced. God willing, I hope to strike a blow of some importance, and make my retreat safely out of the Gulf."

At this very moment, the night of December 12, 1862, far to the north, General Ambrose Burnside was moving the Army of the Potomac into battle line for its tragic assault on Lee's fortified lines at Fredericksburg.

An old-fashioned norther that whistled through the rigging and gave him the blues, blew the cruiser well down into the Gulf of Honduras, but five days before Christmas she doubled Cape Catoche at the tip of the Yucatan Peninsula and groped into the Gulf of Mexico, "by night, unseen of any human eye, on the land or the sea."

Semmes sighted a large steamer, hull down, headed no doubt for Havana, but scrupulously avoided her. She may have been a Federal huntsman, or, more probably, a French transport from Vera Cruz, port of entry for Maximilian's ill-starred empire. The *Alabama* was on soundings now, the water averaging only twenty fathoms. Two days before Christmas, off his Arcas rendezvous, he overhauled his bluff-bowed, stumpy-masted tender, *Agrippina*. After gently admonishing her incorrigible old skipper, Alex McQueen, for his tardiness, the two ships ran into the triangular basin created by three low-lying cays and anchored in the clear waters. A snug harbor it was, handiwork of the tiny stonemasons of the sea. The trio of lonely cays were desolate, as devoid of alcohol as the Sahara. Shedding his sea-rover role, Semmes, the naturalist, revelled in the wonders of the world beneath the iridescent waters of the lagoon. Seven fathoms down, many-hued fish darted, like animated jewels, among the trees of coral, glinting in the shafts of sunlight that slanted down to the very floor.

As at Blanquilla, the men were refreshed with byplay on shore, swimming, fishing, sporting with the man-of-war birds who resented the rude intrusion of their rookery. For her dash at Galveston, the *Alabama* needed clean heels. She was careened and her befouled copper scraped. Coal bunkers were replenished from the *Agrippina;* decks re-caulked. Her powder was tested and found fast-firing.

"As to the rest," said Semmes, "I trusted to luck, and to the 'creek's not being too high.'"

Another factor tipped the scales in his favor. Jack was proud of his ship. He boasted she could be made to do everything but talk. On December 25 jollity rang through the wardroom. In the forecastle there was an extra allowance of good-cheering Old Jamaica. For Semmes, "My thoughts, naturally, turn on this quiet Christmas day, in this lonely island, to my dear family. I can only hope and trust them to the protection of a merciful Providence."

He opened the New Year, 1863, with a maxim, "Success, as a general rule, attends him who is vigilant and active, and who is careful to obey all the laws of nature." He pursued it implicitly. His secret was still secure. A single sail had passed his hideout at a great distance off. Only now did he reveal to his men the flaming purpose of his intrusion into the Gulf. Forecastle prognosticators had already announced their destination, New Orleans or Mobile. Semmes let it out that, if the fates were propitious, he would give them some "sport" off Galveston. A fight! "A bold and feasible plan," said Admiral Porter of this thrust at Galveston, "and no one can deny that Semmes displayed great daring in thus bearding the lion in his den, and entering waters he knew to be full of his enemy's gunboats."

On January 5, after ordering the *Agrippina* back to Liverpool for another cargo, Semmes laid the head of his ship north to Galveston, allowing five days for the run. He warned himself, "The Banks expedition must be assembling off Galveston, and time is of importance to us, if we would strike a blow at it before it is all landed. If we have good fortune, we shall take the enemy completely by surprise."

Serene and lovely was the day, Sunday, January 11. To the captain of the *Alabama* it seemed that "providence was smiling upon our approach to Galveston." Earnestly had he poured out his paternosters before the shrine in his cabin. His supplications were granted, thus far, at least.

Whether providential or not, at noon that day the *Alabama* stood thirty miles off Galveston. Semmes' timing was exact. Instructing the masthead to keep a bright lookout for an immense fleet, Semmes steered for the Galvestown lighthouse, intending just to sight the flotilla of transports without himself being seen and then to haul off until the moon rose that night, about 11:30, before darting in for his assault.

In the light wind the *Alabama* crept along. On the quarterdeck Semmes and Lieutenant Kell eagerly scanned the distances with their glasses. The afternoon wore away until at 3:30 two staccato calls from the lookout—"Sail ho! Land ho!"—jerked the ship alive.

"How many ships do you see?" trumpeted Kell.

"Five steamers, sir. They look like ships-of-war."

"Do you see a fleet of transports?" shouted Semmes up to the masthead.

"No, sir."

While they peered eagerly towards Galveston a shell, thrown by one of the steamers, soared shorewards to burst over the city with a red blossom. Had his intelligence gone awry? Where was Banks' great expedition? Why was a squadron of five warships outside the bar firing at the city?

Divining it quickly, he turned to Kell. "They wouldn't be bombarding their own people!" he exclaimed. "Galveston's been recaptured. Maybe we'll see our flag soon." He had solved it correctly, as he was to learn later. General "Prince John" Magruder had retrieved the port on New Year's Day. Banks' vaunted armada had shied off to New Orleans. From there the general began his ill-fated invasion of the Red River valley.

Other unspoken emotions smote Semmes. His heart leaped up at the thought that yonder, twenty-odd miles off, just beyond his vision, lay his beloved Southland, warm and smiling in the January sunshine. It was the nearest he would come to the Confederacy he loved so fiercely until long after the deck he now stood on was forty fathoms below the waters of the English Channel.

But this was no time for sentiment. Semmes had to think hard and fast. Caught napping, the lookout had permitted the cruiser to approach near enough to be sighted before sounding his warning. Semmes had certainly not relinquished his lucrative ocean-scorching business in order to tackle five enemy ships-of-war at once. But neither could he run away after promising his crew some sport. He had one recourse, only one, and he knew it: to offer a fight. His decision was immediate, timed to the second with welcome news from aloft, "A steamer is coming out in chase of us, sir!"

Semmes breathed easier. "It was just the thing I wanted, . . . for I at once conceived the design of drawing this single ship of the enemy far enough from the remainder of her fleet, to enable me to decide a battle with her before her consorts could come to her relief."

He must let the enemy chase him—a new role for the *Alabama!*

"We've done a good deal of chasing," smiled Semmes, "but this is the first time we've ever been chased. What does our friend look like?"

Kell squinted hard. "She's not one of the new sloops. Nor an old steam frigate, either."

"Then, I'll match guns with her, *if* we can draw her away from the fleet. We'll have to work fast though, or the other four'll be at our throats."

Cunningly, Semmes began flirting. To carry out his decoying evolution he wore ship, as if to flee from his pursuer. The Federal captain immediately signalled his commodore that the stranger was behaving suspiciously and he would investigate. Still under sail, Semmes lowered his propeller and ordered his engine room to turn the screw ever so slowly, pausing entirely at intervals. Under wraps, the cruiser moved seaward.

Twilight faded into dark. Mile by mile Semmes teased his foe off base until twenty miles separated her from the fleet, distance enough for Semmes' purpose. Now to pounce on her before her sister ships could help her. Furling his sails, he wheeled, pointed for his pursuer and ordered the *Alabama* cleared for action. Gun crews ran to their stations. Tompions were drawn. Powder monkeys tripped over each other gleefully. Shot and shell were stacked at the guns. This was the real thing. The whole crew was ready in an instant.

Each moment the enemy ship loomed larger until Semmes

distinctly identified her as a big, bulky sidewheeler. A converted merchantman, she was probably built of thin, brittle iron, a vulnerable target, with her machinery above the waterline. Sparks flickered from her stack as she rushed through the night. The chips were down and Semmes knew he held aces. He could fight on his own terms. This was his good luck. He would coax her as near as he could and then blow her to smithereens with a fast, unexpected broadside.

Like tigers about to grapple in the dark, the ships closed, slowly now, and stealthily. At hailing distance, one hundred yards or less, both shut off their engines. The *Alabama's* headway lugged her along imperceptibly though the offshore swell swung her head seaward. There was no moon; the night clear. Starlight etched out the dim shapes of both ships. Only the water lapping at the cruiser's sides fretted the deep, ominous hush. Tension gripped the *Alabama's* deck. Gunners had the Federal ship in their sights. Lockstrings were taut awaiting the word; gun muzzles depressed to hit her at the waterline.

The Union ship hailed first, at seventy-five yards. "What ship is that?" Every word came across clear and distinct.

With a twinkle Kell trumpeted back the subterfuge, "This is Her Britannic Majesty's steamer *Petrel!*"

An age loitered by. No sounds. Apparently, the stranger had doubts. Kell's make-believe had fallen on unbelieving ears.

Now the *Alabama* hailed, "What ship are you?" No reply! Kell repeated his query.

Ten seconds, then, out of the night, "This is the United States ship. . . ." The name blanked out. No one caught it, no one cared. It mattered little now. Semmes knew she was enemy. Again, a deadly, awkward pause. Semmes could hear low conversation on his foe's bridge. She spoke again, "If you please, I will send a boat on board of you." Such politeness! Two duellists in the dark presenting arms before shooting to kill. They were coming to verify Kell's words.

"Certainly," replied Kell. "We shall be happy to receive your boat."

They could hear the boatswain's call, the whining of tackles as the cutter dropped to the water, the creak of oarlocks, the splatter of the sweeps. The boat was halfway to the *Alabama* when Semmes spoke quietly, "Mr. Kell, I suppose you are all ready for action."

Kell replied smartly, "Never more so, sir. The men are eager to begin, and are only waiting for the word."

Tense whispers ran along the starboard battery of 32-pounders: "Why don't we fire? What's the matter? We'll blast her to hell with this one!"

Semmes had yearned for this moment when he could lay the *Alabama* alongside and pour her broadside into a Federal ship at such close range he couldn't miss. Now it was here.

"Mr. Kell"—his voice trembled slightly—"don't strike them in disguise. Tell them who we are and give the broadside at the name."

Kell raised the speaking trumpet. In a rising, clarion voice he sang out, "This is the Confederate States steamer ALABAMA! FIRE!"

With a roar, away went the broadside as the 32-pounders stabbed the darkness with a sheet of flame. The *Alabama* rocked and rolled with the recoil. The 8-inch smoothbore and the Blakeley rifle joined the mighty refrain. Instantly, the foe returned the broadside. But it swept high. Pungent, stinging powder smoke billowed across the deck. The first Confederate broadside had staggered the Union ship, crippling two of her guns, wounding her mortally. In the vivid flare that lit up sea and sky Semmes could discern the sidewheeler from stem to stern, heard the ringing of his shot as they crashed through her iron sides.

Now steaming slowly, the two ships began a running fight, barely thirty yards apart. The combat might soon become hand to hand. A turn of the helm, and the two vessels would have locked yardarms. From the *Alabama's* quarterdeck, rifles and pistols poured out a hot, raking fire. Semmes made a mental note—his powder still had strength and force. His shells were exploding with quick, sharp reports.

Semmes' whole fibre tingled. Standing there, bathed in the glare of battle, he was a figure reminiscent of John Paul Jones that night in the North Sea when he fought the British *Serapis* off Flamborough Head. His "Liverpool scrapings" were fighting in fine style, handling their pieces adeptly, like old veterans, calm and determined. He hallooed encouragement to them.

"Give it to the rascals! Aim low, men! Don't be all night sinking that fellow!"

Yells of approval and curses greeted his words. His gunners were even more pungent than he. They had waited long to avenge the slurs cast at them by Northern newspapers and politicians. Resentful at being tagged with "scum," "wharf-rats," and other indelicate appellations, each man fought as if settling a personal grudge. A boatswain's mate went fairly berserk. Savagely, the men behind the guns seasoned their doses with:

"Damn you! That kills your pig!"

"That's from the scum of England!"

"That's a British pill for you to swallow!"

"This one's from the Liverpool wharf-rats!"

Six times the *Alabama* emptied devastating broadsides into the *Hatteras,* for such was the enemy's name. Reply from the Union ship was spirited, but aimed at the *Alabama's* upper works. Had she fired lower the cruiser's light scantling would have crumpled like paper. Fierce, unrelenting, was the Confederate onslaught. A shell from the great pivot gun gouged a hole at the waterline big as a hogshead, ripping off entire sheets of iron. A second lunged into the *Hatteras'* sickbay, setting the ship afire. Another hurtled against a cylinder and the engine room hissed with steam. Men rushed out with the scalding vapor curling behind them like searing serpents. Deep in the hold exploded another, and the ship was afire in two places. Flame and smoke lapped up through the deck.

The captain of the *Hatteras* himself described his ship as "beyond human power, a hopeless wreck upon the waters, with her walking beam shot away, and her engines rendered useless." He kept firing as long as he could, hoping the fleet would come to his succor. He then ordered his magazine flooded. Had he not done so it would have exploded with a blast that would have sent both ships, men and all, to the bottom.

Working closer, the *Alabama's* gunners measured the stricken *Hatteras* for her blazing *coup de grace*. At that instant—exactly thirteen minutes after the first flash of battle—the *Hatteras* fired her lee gun and hoisted a lantern, tokens of defeat.

"Have you struck?" bellowed Kell through the din.

"I have" came the quick reply.

A wild cheer—

"Such a cheer went up from the brazen throats of my fellows, as must have astonished even a Texan, if he had heard it."

"Cease fire! Cease fire!" Kell's resounding voice had a note of triumph.

Thus ended one of the fastest naval duels in history, "the first yardarm engagement between steamers at sea."

Cries for help came fast. The *Hatteras* was settling rapidly, her moments were numbered, and few.

"We're sinking! Can you help us!"

The *Alabama* launched her boats. In six minutes, with smart handling, she picked up every survivor, taking special care of the wounded, and landed them on her deck—a total of seventeen officers and one hundred and one men. Up the gangway came the captain of the *Hatteras*, Commander Homer C. Blake, to tender his sword. Semmes greeted him with a salute and a bow, but Blake displayed not too much of the chivalry of others who wore the blue. Plainly, he felt he had lost a battle to a pirate. He was to intimate as much in his official report.

"I do this with deep regret," said Blake, tendering the blade to Semmes.

The Confederate captain smiled. "I am glad to see you safe on the *Alabama*, sir. We will endeavor to make your stay as comfortable as we can."

There was no exultation, no gloating. Ranged about Semmes were the powder-smeared men who had won the battle.

Blake's sword was to grace the *Alabama's* wardroom, with other trophies, until one day it dived below the chill waters of the English Channel, not far from Semmes' own brand.

In just nineteen minutes from the opening broadside the Gulf had swallowed up the *Hatteras*, her crew and wounded were prisoners, and her conqueror speeding off in the darkness.

Semmes paused long enough to watch the *Hatteras'* gurgling obsequies. Her last agonies were brief. Down she went by the bow. Twinkling lights on the horizon warned him the *Hatteras'* consorts had heard the gunfire, seen the flash of battle and were rushing at forced draft to avenge her. Spreading out like a pack of hounds they scoured across the darkened waters, led by Semmes' old foe, the *Brooklyn*. Dousing all lights, the *Alabama* obliterated herself, leaving no address. At daylight, the tops of the *Hatteras'* masts sticking out of the water told the sad tale to the breathless *Brooklyn* and Commodore Bell. At this moment the *Alabama* was one hundred miles away, heading for the Yucatan Channel.

Escorting his beaten opponent to his cabin Semmes offered wine and the comfort, such as it was, of his own domicile. He made it clear that Blake and his officers would be treated as guests, not as prisoners. The *Hatteras'* seamen were bunked on the berthdeck. The *Alabama's* hearties slept wherever they could find a spot, but they made no complaint. They had won a battle, and the forecastle little cared whether it slept or not. The captured officers shared the wardroom and cabins with their victors. One and all were paroled on the spot.

The morning after the fight Commander Blake came on deck to meet Lieutenant Kell. They had been friends in the old navy.

"How do you do, Mr. Kell? Fortune favors the brave, sir."

Replied Kell, "We take advantage of all fortune's favors, sir."

Blake's official report of the "sad disaster" had an ungracious touch, as we shall see, though Semmes admitted it was "a pretty fair report of the engagement." Had Blake omitted his unchivalrous jabs at his unwelcome, but courteous host, the report would have sounded more sportsmanlike. It was written most likely while he was being accorded the hospitality of a guest of Semmes' own cabin.

Of Commander Blake himself, Semmes said, "he behaved like a man of courage and made the best fight he could" yet, Semmes resented Blake's "discourteous stuff and nonsense" about a "rebel steamer" and "piratical craft."

Nothing was more lamentable to me, during the whole war, than to observe how readily the officers of the old Navy, many of whom belonged to the gentle families of the land, and all of whom had been bred in a school of honor, took to the slang expressions of the day, and fell, pell-mell, into the ranks of the vulgar and fanatical rabble that was hounding the war.

The officers of the Confederate States Navy, to say the least, were as much entitled to be regarded as fighting for a principle as themselves, and one would have thought that there would have been a chivalrous rivalry between the two services, as to which should show the other the most courtesy.

Must the howling Demos devour everything gentle in the land, and reduce us all to the common level of the pot-house politician, and compel us to use his slang?

Comparisons and postmortems of the battle were inevitable. Northern editors depicted the *Alabama* as a monster of speed, a powerhouse of gunfire; the *Hatteras*, as a poor, old, made-over tug or river steamer, with two or three small guns at most. Playing down Semmes' success was in line with an old custom. Semmes readily admitted he had the advantage in weight of metal. The *Alabama's* battery consisted of six 32-pounders, one 8-inch shell gun; one Blakeley 100-pounder rifle; eight guns in all, firing 360 pounds. The sidewheeler, larger than the *Alabama* by one hundred tons, carried four 32-pounders; two Parrot 30-pounder rifles; one 20-pounder rifle and one 12-pounder howitzer, a total of eight guns, firing 220 pounds.

Semmes said frankly there was "a considerable disparity between the two ships in the weight of their pivot guns. The *Alabama* ought to have won the fight; and she did win it, in thirteen minutes—taking care, too, though she sank her enemy at night, to see that none of his men were drowned."

One factor has been neglected, however. Semmes actually fought five ships, or, rather, he fought one knowing four others were sweeping down on him. Had he not succeeded in winning a fast, slashing fight the *Alabama* would have shortly decorated the bottom of the Gulf beside the *Hatteras*.

Casualties were light on both sides. Mortality on the *Hatteras*, though devastated by exploding shells, was limited to two killed and five wounded. A single casualty marred the *Alabama's* slate, a carpenter's mate with a cheek wound.

The Confederate ship had come through her battle almost unscathed. Bullet holes riddled her bulwarks yet there was not a one that needed plugging; nor was there a line to splice. In a day a bit of paint had obliterated the scars of battle.

Missing was the boarding crew despatched by the *Hatteras* to investigate Kell's "*Petrel*" come-on. Caught under the broadsides, this boat had pulled for the shore, to be picked up at dawn by the *Brooklyn*.

With prisoners equal in number to his crew, Semmes shaped his course across the Gulf for Jamaica. Though he had paroled his prisoners, he and his officers slept on their arms. He had to rid himself of this menace as fast as feasible. The situation was loaded with danger. Besides, the Gulf swarmed with Federal ships. Had one crossed his trail he might be caught between two fires.

Battered by a succession of gales, the *Alabama* emerged from the Gulf and slid along towards Kingston. The fifty-three-year-old Semmes was tired, whipped down by the gruelling rack and strain of sea-raiding. His overtaxed nervous system yearned for a letdown, a friendly shelter where he could simply forget. Never was there a moment since he took command at the Azores when he could shuffle off care and responsibility.

His explanation was simple, "On the high seas, with the enemy all the time in full chase of me, constant vigilance was required to guard against surprise; and my battle with the elements was almost as constant, as that with the enemy." Later he was to muse sadly to his journal, "I am getting too old to relish the rough usage of the sea. Youth sometimes loves to be rocked by a gale, but when we have passed the middle stage of life we love quiet and repose."

To his disgust, and amusement as well, he sighted his tender, the *Agrippina*, battling adverse winds as she poked along for Liverpool. Failing to recognize her, he chased her for hours. He did not realize it was the last time he would see her.

On January 21 the *Alabama*, flying French colors, made Plum Point lighthouse off Port Royal, the naval station for Kingston. Evening was deepening into twilight. The *Alabama's* signal for a pilot brought a shrewd young fellow, who eyed Semmes up and down sharply, as if unable to reconcile his gray naval uniform with the French flag. After he had adroitly guided the cruiser through the tortuous channel Semmes informed him the Gallic colors were merely a disguise to which the pilot replied coolly, "I knew all the while that you were no Frenchman."

At dusk the *Alabama* came to rest in the anchorage where once the black flag of Sir Henry Morgan, knighted buccaneer, had floated in the soft, tepid airs.

⚓

⚓

23 *Byplay at Jamaica*

At Jamaica, Raphael Semmes found his Shangri-La, if only for three brief, sun-flecked days. He used the word "empyrean" to describe his magic translation from the cramped cabin and other *desagremens* of shipboard to the ample halls and elegant leisure of an English home perched on the mountainside, overlooking the sea that glistened far below like an endless blue mirror.

Here, too, Semmes found something else: adulation beyond his dreams. Had Horatio Nelson himself stepped ashore he could have received no more spontaneous outpouring of acclaim and affection from the people of this British crown colony. It was the apotheosis of this man, who, enrobed in the glamour of his exploits, had suddenly appeared out of the blue. Nowhere else were emotions stirred so deeply by his coming. On the streets children and grown-ups, freedmen and planters, welcomed him as if he were a hero returning home to his own people. Unheralded, without fanfare, he had slipped into port—and Jamaica went wild over him. Until now Semmes was unaware that the deeds of the *Alabama* had captured the imagination of the world. Nor could he know that Southern bards were already strumming their lyres in rapturous praise of the raider's commander and crew.

Jamaica's sympathy for the Confederate States ran deep. A generation had passed since the island's slaves were freed, yet the planter class still ruled her economic and social systems. These hold-overs of an outworn institution, discerned in the would-be Southern Republic what they had lost but still admired, an economy built on human bondage. It was a tie that bound their emotions to the South, as if they were of the same blood and the same land. Nor did they dream that the struggle now convulsing the American Union, and of which the *Alabama* was the far-ranging Southern knight-errant, was but a mighty step in the extinction of slavery the world over. The news of Lincoln's proclamation of freedom had just reached the island. It fared coolly. With it came more cheering news of the Northern debacle at Fredericksburg.

Semmes had known Jamaica in her palmiest days, when he was a midshipman in the old service. Then, it was a thriving mart of commerce. Port Royal's placid harbor was alive with ships floating the flags of all nations, come to bear away her great staples of coffee, sugar, cocoa, and ginger. Now, thirty years after the extinction of thralldom, Kingston's magnificence had vanished; poverty and dilapidation hung over the island like a pall. Not yet had Jamaica regained her place in the sun, or the negro found a voice of his own.

Close by the *Alabama's* anchorage lay a squadron of three British men-of-war. The flagship immediately despatched a lieutenant to convey a hearty welcome. Night though it was, news of the Southerner's arrival spread fast. Nor was excitement lessened by her unusual passenger list, the rank and file of a Federal warship she had just demolished in a standup fight. Officers of the fleet and garrison flocked aboard to congratulate the doughty, steel-nerved captain whom nobody could catch, who had triumphantly swept Northern commerce from the seas or run it to port, and to inspect the celebrated raider with an interest sharpened by the fact she was built in a British shipyard, armed with British ordnance and manned by a largely British crew.

It was the first English port the *Alabama* had touched since her escape from the Mersey at Liverpool yet no eyebrows were raised, no questions levelled at her antecedents, no doubts cast on her nationality. Nor was the stigma of piracy even hinted at. She was accorded due honors as a Confederate States ship-of-war of which she bore ample credentials: the 120-odd officers and men of the sunken Union warship. Secretary of State Seward had frantically appealed to Britain to seize the *Alabama* on sight as a violator of international law. At Jamaica, as elsewhere, his supplication fell on ears that would not hear.

Next morning, donning his sparkling best, Semmes stepped into his red-upholstered captain's gig to be whisked across the harbor by six brawny seamen in spotless whites to the flagship *Jason*, where he called on Commodore Dunlap, senior naval officer in port. Guns boomed a salute and drums ruffled as he climbed the gangway to be received with unbounded courtesy and friendliness. Semmes' requests were granted. His ship could be re-coaled; needed repairs made; prisoners landed at the discretion of the United States Consul.

Nor could the pro-Confederate reporter of the *Jamaica Tribune and Daily Advertiser* restrain his fervor as he dashed off the news for his avid readers:

> Great excitement has been created here by the arrival of the Confederate States steamer, *Alabama*. Late on Tuesday evening a steamer supposed to be a French man of war anchored at Port Royal. Early in the morning, however, we learned it was not other than the gallant *Alabama*. The news travelled like wildfire. Soon after, some of the officers arrived in Kingston and were greeted at every turn with enthusiasm. A large number of visitors, including, we believe, ladies, went to Port Royal and were received with the courtesy expected from her brave commander and his officers. It is impossible to describe the enthusiasm which prevails and the attentions paid generally to Captain Semmes, his officers and men.

At an early hour the cruiser was overrun with visitors. Among the first to appear was a planter-friend, James Fyfe, whom Semmes had known in England. The Fyfe estate, Flamstead, was a showplace of the island. To the weary Semmes, he extended an invitation to visit his delightful eyrie in the blue Jamaican hills where rest and comfort could restore his wasted energies.

Entrusting the *Alabama*'s coaling and refurbishing to the effi-

cient Lieutenant Kell, Semmes and his host, James Fyfe, rode out
of Kingston and up through tiers of steeps until, at last, he descried Flamstead, beckoning in the distance like a corner of
paradise. That night, in the quiet comfort of this English country
household, Semmes found surcease, "far away from war's alarms,
fanned by the gentlest of seabreezes, in the sweetest of sheets,
and lullabied by the distant breaker, as it stranded itself at regular
intervals on the beach."

> I was awakened the next morning by the merry songs of a hundred
> birds, that came appropriately blended with the perfume of the flow-
> ers that clustered around my windows; and I have seldom looked
> upon a more beautiful picture, than when I threw back the blinds
> and caught a view of the landscape, rejoicing in the morning's sun,
> with all its wealth of tropical fruits and flowers, and the sea—the
> glorious sea—glittering in the distance.

From the piazza, with the aid of a telescope, he could see the
Alabama far below, nestling in the harbor like a gull. For Semmes
it was a new, carefree world, far from the roll and toss and eternal
on-guard of his mission. Time flew by: romantic rides in the hills,
rounds of entertainment. Evening brought music and beauty, the
rustle of silken petticoats and melodious words of adoration.
Semmes had an irresistible charm for women that was enhanced
by his unswaggering mien, his Mephistophelian manner. Beguiled
by bright eyes, and red, red lips, war receded in the distance until
Lieutenant Kell sent word the *Alabama* was ready for sea.

In his journal Semmes dismissed briefly the public reception in
his honor and the volleys of applause climaxed by "Three cheers
for Captain Semmes and the *Alabama!*" At sunset, he crossed the
harbor and went aboard to find that an unpleasantness had occurred in his absence. Kell gave Semmes a fast briefing of what had
transpired.

Semmes' first task was to close accounts with Paymaster Clarence B. Yonge, Southerner born and bred, who had committed
the unpardonable. Kell himself had found it necessary to go
ashore with an armed patrol, drag Yonge out of a brothel and
confine him to his cabin, under arrest, to await Semmes' discipline. Fortified by Jamaica rum, Yonge had consorted too freely

with seamen of the *Hatteras* and apparently gone over to the enemy by arranging a traitorous pact with the Federal Consul. For good measure of infamy, he had used for his own pleasure gold taken from the *Alabama's* sea chest.

Semmes dealt out drumhead justice. In half an hour the recreant was packed off, bag and baggage. The *Alabama* was never to see him again. Semmes scrupulously deleted this man's name from his memoirs though he reported that Yonge later "married a negro wife, went over to England with her, swindled her out of all her property, and turned Yankee, going over to Minister Adams, and becoming one of his right-hand men, when there was any hard swearing wanted in the British courts against the Confederates."

To the paymaster's post Semmes appointed the lovable Dr. Francis L. Galt. His duties as surgeon were assumed by his English assistant, Dr. D. H. Llewellyn. Of Yonge's defection Lieutenant Sinclair commented, "This is the only case of discipline we have to record as regards the officers of the *Alabama*, but one dose of this sort was surely enough. Through this man's influence with our crew, backed by the persuasions of the United States Consul, we lost several valuable seamen. He was afterwards a secret agent of the enemy's diplomatic corps in London."

Yet, Sinclair softened his charges against the rank and file, "our missing men are described on the ship's books as deserters. This, however, is a misnomer. Jack has been kept drunk, and hid away in some den until the sailing of the ship. He will wake up, poor deluded child of Poseidon, to find his home swept from him, his accumulation of pay sacrificed and his *quasi*-friends knowing him no more."

Semmes had expected Jack to celebrate his victory over the *Hatteras*. Nor was he disappointed. Arm in arm with liberty men from the British ships and his late enemies on the *Hatteras*, Jack made Water Street ring with his warwhoops. Of the adventures of his crew Semmes observed good-naturedly:

> It was quite remarkable that in these merry-makings and debaucheries, the Confederate sailors, and the Yankee sailors, harmonized capitally together. They might frequently be seen arm in arm in the streets, or hobnobbing together—the Confederate sailors generally paying the score, as the Yankee's sailor's strongbox had gone down

with his ship, and his paymaster was rather short of cash. They sailed as amicably together, up and down the contradance, and hailed each other to 'heave to,' when it was time to 'freshen the nip,' as though the *Alabama* and the *Hatteras* had never been yard-arm to yard-arm, throwing broadsides into each other.

To Lieutenant Sinclair and a trio of quartermasters fell the duty of corralling the over-timers as the *Alabama's* departure drew near. Knocking at a gay, glittering *maison de joie*, Sinclair was barred at the threshold by a solid line of British seamen, reinforced by a second wave of determined business ladies, who denied him entrance. His visit, they averred, was quite inappropriate.

"Say, Middy, come some other time," volunteered a persuasive maiden. "The tickets to this ball are limited, and the company is select."

"Tell Old Beeswax to go to sea," chimed in another, "burn some more Yankee ships and come back. We'll give up the boys, then, and you'll have your turn."

Diplomatically obdurate, Sinclair slowly infiltrated the ramparts, buying drinks all around and paying special court to the hostesses. In this wise he wheedled the drunk and the sober to bid fond farewell and return with him to the *Alabama*.

Yet hardly had they reached the deck before two agile truants suddenly clambered over the rail, commandeered a dugout canoe alongside from two negroes, seized the paddles and shoved off for shore at a fast gait. Semmes despatched a cutter in pursuit of the fugitives. "A more beautiful, exciting moonlight race has not often been seen," he observed with amusement.

The two sailors had gotten a good start, but the cutter, with her long sweeping oars, was too fast for a canoe with only two paddles. Seeing the cutter gaining on them, one of the sailors called out to his mate, "I'll tell you what it is, Bill. There's too much cargo in this here damned craft, and I'm going to lighten ship a little."

Without ado, he seized a squealing negro and tossed him overboard. The water swarmed with sharks. Grabbing their paddles again, they darted away with renewed speed. Fortunately, the cutter was close behind and rescued the unlucky black. Encouraged at thus gaining on their pursuers, the maneuver was repeated. Into the water went the second negro. Again, the cutter outsped the sharks. But the escapees had run out of ballast. Caught up with, they were ironed and hauled back aboard the cruiser.

When Semmes later brought these two heroes of the moonlight regatta—"Tom Bowse and Bill Bower"—as he dubbed them, before the mast, charged with attempted desertion, they vigorously pleaded not guilty. Concealing his amusement, he listened to their penitential excuses and then said, "You're a pretty pair of fellows. You not only tried to desert your ship and flag, but commit murder, attempting to escape!"

"Murder!" blurted "Bowse," with a start of horror, "We never thought of such a thing, sir. Them Jamaica black boys, they take to water like South Sea islanders. You can't drown 'em, sir."

"That was it, your honor," put in "Bower." "It was only a bit of a joke, you see, sir, played on the officer in the cutter. We knew he'd stop to pick 'em up, and so give us the weathergauge of him."

"But what about the sharks? The harbor was full of them. They might have eaten the boys up."

"Sharks don't eat them black boys, your honor."

"That may do very well for the murder," rejoined Semmes. "What about the desertion?"

"No idea of deserting, your honor," insisted Bowse. "We only meant to have another bit of a frolic, and come back in good time, before the ship sailed."

"That was it, your honor. We had a small drop aboard, and the moon was bright, and Moll Riggs, she had sent us such a kind message! We only wanted to say good-bye to the girls."

The moonlight and Moll clinched their case. Directing the master-at-arms to release them, he turned aside to hide a broad smile. The case was closed.

Semmes released his *Hatteras* prisoners soon after reaching Jamaica though not before Commander Blake had provided a comic relief by engaging in an absurd war of words with the commodore of the British squadron in the harbor. On the evening after the *Alabama* arrived and while Blake was still a prisoner the band of H.M.S. *Greyhound* assembled on her quarterdeck and serenaded her Southern guests by playing "Dixie." Construing the performance of the Confederate national air as an insult to the Stars and

Stripes, Blake sent a hot, formal protest to Commodore Dunlap. That salty British officer decided to finesse his way out of the "grave international" breach of protocol. He ordered the band of the offending *Greyhound*, next evening, first to play "Dixie," and then "Yankee Doodle."

Semmes described this musical passage of arms delightfully:

> When the evening, which was to salve the Yankee honor, arrived, great was the expectation of everyone in the squadron. The band on the *Jason*, flagship, led off by playing 'God Save the Queen,' that glorious anthem which electrifies the Englishman. The *Challenger's* band followed and played a fine opera air. The evening was still and fine and the poops of all the ships filled with officers. It then came the *Greyhound's* turn.
>
> She first played something unusually solemn, then 'Dixie,' with slowness, sweetness and pathos and when the chorus
>
> > *'In Dixie's land, I'll take my stand*
> > *I'll live and die in Dixie!'*
>
> had died away on the soft evening air, such an infernal din, of drums and fifes and cymbals and wind instruments, each after its fashion, going it strong upon
>
> > *'Yankee Doodle Dandy!,'*
>
> arose, as to defy all description! The effect was electric; the officers had to hold their sides to preserve their dignity, and—Commander Blake was avenged!

On January 25, at half past eight in the evening, the *Alabama* bade adieu to Jamaica and its delights. With a touch of nostalgia Semmes stood on his bridge and watched the harbor lights recede. Across the waters the good-byes fainted away in the distance. Never again would he see Jamaica or sip its enchanting nectar. Many were the heart-beatings and teary eyes as the *Alabama* bore away her gallant young Lochinvars, who had wreaked considerable "damage" among the fair islanders. Many were the touching little missives found in the last mailbag handed up to the *Alabama* as she moved off to sea.

With her engine at half speed, the raider steamed past Point Morant and breasted a moderate sea rolling under a stiff northeast breeze. Overhead the clear night sky stretched out like a vast jewel, with a tropical moon mounted in a dark, star-studded setting. Semmes was off again on the long hunt, his longest, indeed. Now he would blaze a trail of bonfires that would light up the Atlantic from Brazil to the shores of Africa.

⚓

⚓

24   *Fire Dance to Cape Town*

News of the sinking of the *Hatteras* reached Washington while the *Alabama* lay at Jamaica. It found Secretary Welles feuding with Admiral Charles Wilkes whose seven-ship squadron was supposedly tracking down the *Alabama* in the West Indies.

Where on earth—blazoned a New York newspaper—was this flying squadron that Semmes could have wriggled into the Gulf (which has only two outlets), demolished the *Hatteras*, and slipped away, leaving no track or trace? Partially, the blame rested with the Union cruisers. Zealously, they pursued blockade runners, which promised prize money, instead of searching the West Indian hiding places for the Southern raider.

The correspondent of a London newspaper reported four Federal warships idling at St. Thomas while Semmes prowled the Leeward Islands nearby, snatching prizes under their very prows. Indeed, while Semmes dallied at Jamaica, Admiral Wilkes himself, on his flagship *Wachusett*, was loitering along the south coast of Cuba, a stone's throw, so to speak, from the raider's anchorage at Kingston.

At all events, the *Hatteras* must be avenged! The Navy howled for the *Alabama*'s blood. Moreover, the hold-up of the *Ariel* presented threatening implications. Cornelius Vanderbilt's gold fleet must be made safe for democracy! Improvising on Cato, a Boston editor sounded off, "*Alabama delenda est!*" Yet, improvising Latin catch-phrases would never trap the wily raider, who, before leaving Jamaica, had mapped out a blazing, zigzag sweep that would strew bonfires from the West Indies, southward to the Equator and the South Atlantic and across to the Cape of Good Hope. Over this track of thousands of leagues he would pluck, burn and scatter the commerce of a nation like spume before a gale.

His major objective was the Atlantic Narrows, between Cape St. Roque, Brazil, and Cape Palmas, Africa. Through this vast watery arch marched untold argosies from India, China, the Pacific, and South America. Semmes had fared scantily on these waters with the *Sumter*. He might do better with the *Alabama*.

Semmes really was nearing the height of his career. So, indeed, was the Confederacy. Southern hopes were running high. The North still staggered under the bloody impact of Fredericksburg. Britain's Parliament echoed with demands for intervention on the side of the South. In the Virginia wilderness at Chancellorsville Lee and Jackson would soon deal out a master blow that would thrill two continents. The *Alabama* was a triviality beside this gigantic struggle yet, in the exploits of this lone raider and her commander the whole Confederate naval effort was dramatized.

Semmes believed the Confederacy was invincible, her triumph ordained by the God of Hosts Himself. In his heart, he saw the South fighting the battle of the oppressed against the oppressor. For him, at least, the Stars and Bars was the banner of the Crusaders of the nineteenth century.

Semmes probably wondered how long his dazzling luck would last. Seemingly, the ocean was his to roam as he pleased. Federal ships hounded after him, always too late, to find only empty, silent wastes, with perhaps a charred spar to mark where he had lit another spectacular bonfire. Admiral Porter spoke knowingly when he asked:

Was there ever such a lucky man as the Captain of the *Alabama?* If he wanted a cargo of provisions, it fell into his hands. If he required to visit a dockyard to fit out his ship, a vessel came along filled with cordage, canvas, and anchors. If he wanted lumber, a lumber vessel from Maine came right into his path; and if he needed to reinforce his crew, renegades from captured vessels would put their names to the shipping articles, after listening to the thrilling tales of the Norsemen, of burning ships and abundant prize-money.

Northern merchantmen were fast leaving the seas or deserting their flag. The great American hegira had set in. Semmes was driving the nation's carrying trade into the arms of Britain, wielding a weapon far more deadly than his torch, fear. Insurance officials, who footed the bill for his depredations, besieged the Navy Department, even offering to equip cruisers at their own expense to run down the man who was threatening to bankrupt them. But American shipowners could not wait. They were simply taking the shortest cut to safety, in placing their ships under British registry. Daily, dozens transferred their flags. Semmes knew this. Captured enemy newspapers carried impressive figures of the American rush to protection under the Union Jack.

Five days at Kingston had advertised Semmes' whereabouts. Now he must put the West Indies behind him. It fitted in nicely with his farflung plans. If he tarried too long in the idleness of the blue island, Federal cruisers could stretch a dragnet across these seagirt stepping stones and fence him in the Carribean. One way or another, sooner or later, vengeance would be exacted for the death of the *Hatteras*.

Morning, January 26, 1863, found the *Alabama*, flying United States colors, coasting along the shining sheet between Jamaica and Haiti. Columbus and his caravels had once crept along this same opalescent track. Bright was the day, but unlucky for the *Golden Rule*, a pretty, freshly-painted bark, from New York, that Kell valued at 112,000 dollars. Semmes ran her down, though, as he put it, "the cat did not long torture the mouse." From the *Golden Rule*, he salvaged a single, much-relished item: a complete set of rigging, masts and all, for the Federal brig *Bainbridge* that had been stripped bare by a gale off Panama. The pleasantest feature was that he had tied up an enemy gun-brig for want of an outfit. It would be months before the *Bainbridge* put to sea.

Remorselessly, he burned the *Golden Rule* and gave the nearby islanders a magnificent fireworks display they would long remember. He said as much, with an added touch of bitterness:

> A looker-on upon that conflagration would have seen a beautiful picture, for besides the burning ship, there were the two islands, sleeping in the dreamy moonlight, on the calm bosom of a tropical sea, and the rakish-looking 'British Pirate' steaming in for the land, with every spar, and line of cordage brought out in bold relief, by the bright flame—nay, with the very 'pirates' themselves visible, handling the boxes and bales of merchandise, which they had 'robbed' from this innocent Yankee, whose countrymen at home were engaged in the Christian occupation of burning our houses and desolating our fields.

Semmes' luck was soaring again. Next evening, out of a stiff northeaster, he skewered a beautiful, taut brig, the *Chastelaine*, headed for Cienfuegos to take on rum and sugar for the "Boston folks." She was skimming along in the moonlight like a great nightbird, silhouetted against a remarkable, perpendicular island of rock which the Spanish adorned with the mellifluous name, Alta Vela, or Tall Sail, because seen from afar it resembled a ship under sail. Semmes' fiat was immediate: apply the torch. At midnight the rocky walls of Alta Vela were bathed in the glare of the burning *Chastelaine*. Removing her crew and setting her ablaze, Semmes sent her floating off into the night, with all sails set, one of the strangest sights of his whole career. The doomed vessel bounded away, over the water, like a sea-dragon breathing fire. "An unusual spectacle," said Semmes, that disturbed the slumbers of the seagulls and cormorants roosting on the stony face of Alta Vela.

Steaming eastward along the coast of Hispaniola, Semmes ran into the historic town of Santo Domingo to disencumber himself of the prisoners from his latest victims. Going ashore, he strolled through the classical old city that had flourished a century before, as he put it, "the *Mayflower* brought over the cockatrice's egg that hatched out the Puritan." Semmes' contempt for the Puritans was absolute. It gurgled out with the least incentive.

Now, with reverent tread, he entered the decaying cathedral to utter devotions before the altar of the Holy Eucharist where burned "a lamp that was lighted in the days of Columbus and has been burning continuously ever since." The Admiral of the Ocean Sea had lived briefly at Santo Domingo, once chief seat of Spain's New World empire. Hither his remains were brought from Spain and here, legend had it, they still reposed.

Antiquity had charm for this man of fire. Standing in the ruined cathedral he let himself dream of those who had gone and whose names were inscribed on the marble slabs over which he walked. Footsteps of generations of the faithful had worn bare the names of those who slept below. Out of the past came surging "the choir of ancient days, music from the lips of many generations of beauties that had faded like the butterfly of the field." He gazed on the silent organ "whose last note sounded a century or more ago, with its gilding all tarnished, its stately carving tumbled down and lying in debris at its feet."

Climbing to the crumbling fortress above the city he gazed, in shame for those who did it, on the iron rings in the wall to which Don Cristobal himself was chained! Yonder, far below on the blue expanse of the roadstead, lay the *Alabama*, with "a strange flag flying from her peak, not only strange to the dead generations of whom we have been speaking, but new even to our own times and history. It is the flag of a nation which has just risen above the horizon, and is but repeating the history of the world. The oppressed has struggled against the oppressor since time began."

Back through the debris of centuries, past mouldering houses and battlements, the Captain of the *Alabama* meandered to his ship, with the text of a sermon running through his mind, "What is man, O Lord! that thou shouldst be mindful of him?"

Next morning, the *Alabama* raised her anchor and headed eastward along the picturesque coast. That evening, keeping a sharp lookout for omnipresent danger, she gingerly threaded Mona Passage, heading north. It was still unguarded! Again, he asked, where were Mr. Welles' men-of-war? Yet, if pursuit vessels had picked up his trail, now he could easily shake them off. The whole Atlantic spread out before him. Hardly had he emerged from the strait before he fell on the *Palmetto* of New York, bound for Puerto Rico with a "neutral" cargo, and covered by a bogus certificate. Semmes enshrined her condemnation in fine legal phraseology that spelled out a single word: fire. In an hour she was only a name on a record.

Filling away from his burning prize, the *Alabama* began running up into the "variables," working her way along the 30th Parallel to gain sufficient easting to turn directly south for Cape St. Roque and the coast of Brazil. Baffled by wind and weather, the going was slow. Mid-February found Semmes philosophizing to his journal. He gave this entry a Vergilian flourish:

> This boisterous Sabbath is the second anniversary of my resignation from the U. S. Navy, and, of course, it has called up many reminiscences. I have more and more reason, as time rolls on, to be gratified at my prompt determination to quit the service of a corrupt and fanatical majority, which even then had overridden the Constitution and shown itself in so aggressive and unscrupulous a form as to alarm us. But what shall we say of its course since? Simply that it has followed the broad way described by the poet; and we might add *facillissime fuit descessus ejus avernus.*

Semmes still couldn't miss. Fate shortly dumped a bonanza into his lap: two prizes at once, "fine, tall ships, under a cloud of canvas, steering, one to the eastward and the other to the westward." Evans pronounced both American. Semmes snatched his eastbound prey first, though not until he had sent a shot spinning over the quarterdeck just missing the master's head. Giving her over to experienced, talented Prize Master Fullam, Semmes dashed after the second fugitive, now hull down, fifteen miles distant, running before the wind with studding sails alow and aloft.

A banner day it was for the *Alabama,* but not for the *Olive Jane.* She crumpled in two hours, less obstinate than her consort, hauling up at the first gun. She was easily Semmes' finest gastronomic prize. Bound from Bordeaux to New York, her manifest read like a gourmet's paradise. Not without smacking his lips did his eye run down the invoices: champagne of rare vintages, cognac, burgundies, clarets, sauternes, delicacies ("knicknack-eries," he called them), a dozen cheeses of immortal fame and tang.

Semmes' orders were strict. "I did not permit so much as a

bottle of brandy, or a basket of champagne to be brought on board the *Alabama*, though, I doubt not, the throats of some of my vagabonds, who had so recently cooled off from the big frolic they had had in Jamaica, were as dry as powderhorns."

Lieutenant Sinclair commanded the boarding crew that broke out the *Olive Jane*'s hold. He, realizing the practical impossibility of keeping his men from sampling the wines, resorted to finesse. On reaching the *Olive Jane*, he promptly ordered the cabin table spread with "sardines, olives, cheese, flanked by bottles of brandy, burgundy, and claret" so that Jack might quench his thirst in an orderly manner rather than breaking open casks and cases and swallowing the liquids wholesale. Jack had no incentive to disobey or get his officer in hot water, particularly if permitted to visit the cabin for a bit and a nip as often as he pleased.

It worked like a charm, said Sinclair, whose pen told about it nimbly:

> And now observe the self-constituted guests at the cabin table of the *Olive Jane*, luxuriating in the comfort of a chair, a snow-white cloth, and, verily, a four-prong fork—the table groaning under the weight of luxuries! Surely Jack could be in no better luck, even as the guest of a Friar Tuck. And you have only to watch narrowly these waifs of the world, and draw for yourself a moral of life. One fellow, but yesterday you had noted at his forecastle deck dinner, a hardtack for his plate, a slab of salt pork on it cut with his sheath knife, handled with greasy fingers to the mouth; the old boyhood training asserts itself, and as he wipes his mustache with his napkin he has given his heart's secret away. A broken-down gentleman with a story! What a storeroom of tragedy, comedy, and heartache the forecastle of a man-of-war frequently is! Material for an army of novelists.
>
> Not a bottle of liquor reached our ship; and the boat's crew under my command returned in a *good humor* only, no more.

Semmes himself chuckled with delight at the disappointment the loss of the *Olive Jane* would bring "the New York shoddyites and other *nouveau riche* plebeians," robbed as they were of rare wines and other delicacies that might have tickled their palates. However, he heaved a sigh that he had not permitted Bartelli and the wardroom stewards to "inspect" these same delicacies.

Now "amid the crackling of flames, the bursting of brandy casks, the shrivelling of sails, as they were touched off by the fire, and the tumbling of the lighter spars of the *Olive Jane* from aloft," Semmes veered eastward to rejoin his second prize, the *Golden Eagle,* bound with a cargo of guano from the Pacific to Cork. Northern-owned were both cargo and vessel. The great bird himself—her figurehead—was seated on the ship's cutwater, wings a-spread, as if he owned all the ocean, unaware of his approaching fate. Semmes had momentary regrets at destroying so fine a ship that "had buffeted the gales of the frozen latitudes of Cape Horn, threaded her pathway among its icebergs, been parched by the heat of the tropics and drenched with the rains of the Equator, to fall into the hands of her enemy only a few hundred miles from her port. But such is the fortune of war." A pity it seemed—but fleeting pity—to destroy so vast a cargo of fertilizer that would have made enemy fields stagger under a wealth of grain, or, if it did not enrich his fields, would pour a stream of gold into his coffers. Said Semmes, "It was my business upon the high seas, to cut off, or dry up this stream of gold." Without compunction he fired her, and hurried away in the night—"on one beam is the *Olive Jane,* on the other, the *Golden Eagle,* both wrapped in flames from the spar-deck to mast-head, the sea and the heavens glowing in the red glare, the flames varying in brilliancy, suggesting the phenomenon of the aurora borealis." Packing the deck were the *Alabama's* people and the crews of the burning ships, struck speechless by the blazing two-ringed circus. It was awesome even to those hardened to such sights.

Thus, Semmes added a third "Golden" to his list of victims: *Golden Rocket, Golden Rule* and now, *Golden Eagle.* It inspired him to observe "how fond the Yankees had become of the qualifying adjective 'golden,' as a prefix to the names of their ships."

The *Alabama* now stood at the "charmed crossing" of the North Atlantic, Latitude 30, Longitude 40, where she turned south for Cape St. Roque along Maury's blazed road. As if to oblige him to the utmost, luck threw the bark *Washington* across his path, but it was not her finely-carved figurehead of the stately Virginia patriot that wooed Semmes' mercy. Neutral cargo and the need to rid himself of prisoners alone stayed his torch. He released her on bond to bear away his captives, rejoicing.

Shortening sail, the insatiate destroyer jogged along leisurely, like a roving sentinel, demanding that each traveler show his passport. By day, by night, always awake, always alert, the *Alabama* sauntered along this busy pathway of commerce, a beast of prey. From the masthead on clear days the lookout had a range of vision of nearly thirty miles. Neutrals crowded the highway, dozens of them, doubtless wondering at the lengthening ribbon of charred wreckage they encountered. Many were American-built, but now they were flying foreign flags. Where were the Stars and Stripes? "Gradually," averred Lieutenant Sinclair, "sinks the proud carrying-trade of the North American Republic."

There was no let up for the boarding crews. Boarding ships in fair weather and foul, theirs was a risky, treacherous business. Often, with a gale blowing, the boarding cutter alongside a prize would be tossed high, poised on the crest of a mountainous wave, high above the prize's spardeck, the next moment she was catapulted into the bottomless trough of the sea, far below her captive's waterline. Miraculous it was how these men escaped being crushed against the side of a restlessly plunging prize or spilled into the raging waters. Prize Master Fullam became as adept as an acrobat in leaping to the deck of a prize as his cutter rode up the wave.

It was an unfortunate wind that led the *John A. Parks*, of Maine, "whose masts tapered like a lady's fingers arrayed in the whitest of petticoats," to engage in a flirtation with the saucy-looking gunboat. She little guessed her chance acquaintance was none other than the Confederate terror of the seas, but she soon learned the awful truth. Below her decks were countless cords of fine pine lumber that sent the *Alabama's* carpenter into ecstasies. Semmes was taken in at first by what appeared a duly-authenticated certificate of neutral ownership. But in prying into the master's letter bag, which the gentleman from Maine had neglected to toss overboard, Semmes ferreted out an epistle revealing the bogus nature of the ship's papers.

Semmes' court, in session on the bridge, was weighing the fate of the *John A. Parks* when Bartelli came on deck to announce breakfast. Inviting the prize's master to his cabin to share a cup of coffee with him, Semmes at the same time broke the bad news— his ship would be burned. "As well as I recollect," recalled Semmes, "he declined the coffee, but I am quite certain that the ship was burned."

Just before the *Parks,* Semmes had nailed the *Bethiah Thayer,* of Rockland, Maine. She came along on a Sunday, "dressed in a new suit of cotton canvas and looked quite demure and saint-like." Then, nearing the Equator, he nabbed three more. The *Punjaub,* of Boston, glided up in the night, like a goblin ship, almost within harpooning distance. English-owned goods won her release on ransom-bond. The *Morning Star* was taken two degrees above the Line, but she, too, had a neutral cargo, which saved her. The *Kingfisher,* an oil-soaked New England whaler, was not so lucky. The hot brand was put to her "just at nightfall, and the conflagration presented a weird-like spectacle on the Line, amid the rumbling of thunder, the shifting, but ever-black scenery, of the nimbi, or rain clouds, and the pouring and dashing of torrents of rain. Sometimes, the flames would cower beneath a drenching shower, as though they had been subdued, but in a moment afterward, they would shoot up, mast-head high, as brightly and ravenously as before."

A harrowing four-day March gale was a sore trial. Not from Semmes' lips, but from his pen came the first intimation he was wearying of perilous days and nights, of lonely vigils in his cabin, that his nerves of steel were fraying a bit. Resolute he was, but frail in body, never a cast-iron man. Yearnings for home and fireside assailed him often. Yet, his confidence in the ultimate triumph of the Confederacy was still unimpaired. Only to the silent companion of his thoughts did he impart his inner feelings.

> For four days now we have been rolling and tumbling about, with the wind roaring day and night through the rigging. Sea-life is becoming more and more distasteful to me. The fact is, I am reaching an age when men long for quiet and repose. During the war my services belong to my country, and ease must not be thought of; but I trust the end is not afar off. The enemy, from many signs, is on the point of final discomfiture. Nay, a just Providence will doubtless punish the wicked fanatics who have waged this cruel and unjust war upon us, in a way to warn and astonish the nations upon earth.

One degree above the Equator the *Alabama*'s lookout sighted two large ships ambling along "lovingly, arm in arm, as it were, as though they had been having a friendly chat, or one of the masters had been dining on board of the other. They were evidently American ships, and had most likely been having a cosy talk about the war, and, perchance, congratulating themselves upon having escaped the *Alabama*."

Semmes roped them both in with the same gun, two heavy-laden salt freighters, the *Charles Hill* of Boston and the *Nora* "of the same pious city." He fired them. Down went their cargoes, and from their crews, he got nine recruits. Service on the far-ranging, far-famed raider was seductive, and Semmes was having to weed out his volunteers, taking the pick of them. Zealously, the *Alabama*'s seamen circulated among the captives to help win recruits. Holding aloof, Semmes and his officers watched the process out of the corners of their eyes. Dignity forbade their taking the initiative in such matters. From the afterdeck he and Kell would watch the crew making the pitch.

"Those lads of ours are steering it OK, captain," Kell would say with a significant smile and look.

"No one could do it better," Semmes would reply with a wink and a twirl of his mustache as he went below to his cabin to await the sequel that came later, as reported by Lieutenant Sinclair:

> It is easy to guess the line of persuasion and seduction that is employed to secure the services of these picked sailor lads. The items most alluring—double pay, *in* gold; generous rations; tobacco *ad libitum*; grog twice a day and in generous quantity; prospective prize money; and last, but not least, kind and sympathetic officers over them. The bid has been made. Our worthies of the lee scuppers are lost in revery. They are thinking of the character attached to this lone rover by her enemy (pirate), what might be their fate if captured, and of other consequences of casting off home protection by the act of enlistment.
>
> There is an ominous silence on the group for awhile. Our men have thoughtfully and judiciously retired to their several tasks, leaving them untrammelled. All at once a concerted move is made for the mainmast; the captain and the first "luff" sent for; and shortly the interview is over, and we have secured half a dozen splendid speci-

mens of old Neptune's bantlings. The very danger of the venture has appealed to their instincts; and the romance of the situation, fully as much as other considerations, has captured them, hearts and hands. Jack's very soul loves daring and adventure.

The *Alabama* crossed the Equator March 29, 1863. Now, again, her bunkers were running low. It was high time to keep a rendezvous with the *Agrippina*. On parting company at the Arcas in the Gulf of Mexico, Semmes had ordered old Alex McQueen to load coal at Cardiff and meet him at the island of Fernando de Noronha off the coast of Brazil. Since then, the bibulous old master had become frightened at the role he was playing in Semmes' high stakes game. Possessing a sparing allowance of loyalty—and precious little of temperance—he had, as Semmes suspected, left the *Alabama* in the lurch, sold his cargo in some port or other and pocketed the proceeds. He later turned up in England and regaled Captain Bulloch with a cock and bull story to account for his knavery. Both Semmes and Sinclair later accused him of peddling his coal to Federal cruisers.

Admiral Porter was so right! Semmes was the luckiest man in the world. Speeding to him on the wings of the winds came the *Louisa Hatch*, bulging with 1,300 tons of the best Cardiff smokeless coal, exactly what Semmes needed. It was fuel made to order by nature for Semmes' operations. Yet, he wavered over her fate, longing to burn the *Louisa Hatch*. With towering masts, and an immense spread of sail, she was fine fare for flames. It grieved him, though, to think of consigning so much coal to Davy Jones' Locker. If the *Agrippina* failed to keep her tryst, he might have to buy coal at 17 dollars a ton or more. He might not even be able to buy it at all. Dismissing the idea of coaling at sea as "interminable," he resolved to take the *Louisa Hatch* with him to Fernando de Noronha. Perhaps, he could wheedle the Brazilian officials on the island to shut an eye while he violated that nation's neutrality. Semmes always hoped for the best—and frequently found it.

He had carefully selected this lonely, isolated post, two hundred miles from the mainland, where Brazil maintained a free-and-easy yet escape-proof penal station. No mariner ever knew the out-of-the-way pinpoints on the oceans better than he, and this one was admirably suited to his purpose. International law would probably cut little figure in this sequestrated penal outpost, peopled by a thousand long-term, incorrigible felons. They roamed at large, for no "resident" had ever escaped this island's rugged confines. Brazil's important "guests" resided here in a rather delightful, democratic community. The Governor, a battalion of soldiers who served as wardens, and the prisoners hobnobbed on the best of terms. So alluring was life on the island that often malefactors who had discharged their debt to society stayed on as residents. Lieutenant Sinclair told of meeting a man, who had to be banished to civilization to get rid of him on completion of his sentence. He straightway committed another crime and thereby won a further sojourn at the delightful resort.

Fernando de Noronha itself is a volcanic island of solid granite that lunged up from the bottom of the sea a million years ago. Its rocky, symmetrical peak rises over a thousand feet, like the spire of a massive cathedral, steeples and all, almost perpendicularly from the waters. A prodigious marker standing on one of the principal commercial thoroughfares of the world, it was a milepost from which passing mariners took new departure and sailed on. It was sighted by more ships, yet visited by fewer, perhaps, than any other spot on the civilized globe. Today the United States is establishing a tracking station for long range guided missiles on this lonely rock.

The island had no harbor, only an open roadstead. Four days of steaming brought the *Alabama* in sight of this cathedral-like landmark. Sliding into the open anchorage under the lee of the precipitous peak, the cruiser and her captive came to rest.

Semmes' surmise proved correct. With persuasive words and finely-shaded, one-sided interpretations of international law, he addressed himself to the Governor, Sebastião José Basilio Pyrrho. That whole-souled official promptly despatched two emissaries to open diplomatic relations with the newcomer. High-powered celebrities seldom came a-knocking. Monarch of all he surveyed, the Governor made decisions to please himself. Delicate, fussy interpretations of neutrality were of no interest to him. If Semmes' tender did not arrive, the captain must, of course, loot his prize of her precious cargo. Flouting his country's neutrality gave **no** pangs to the Governor's conscience, captivated as he was by the suave, fiery naval officer whose fame had penetrated even the rocky bastions of Fernando de Noronha.

Inviting the plenipotentiaries into his cabin Semmes broke out a bottle of champagne. To the popping of corks and bubbling of wine, they generously arranged a diplomatic entente to Semmes' complete satisfaction. Whatever suited the Confederate captain, was entirely agreeable to His Excellency! Semmes bowed and smiled and clinked glasses with the two. A toast to His Excellency! And a toast to the gallant Captain! Lighting fragrant Havanas, this feast ran on until one of the envoys, a German who spoke precise English, let it be known, in the most offhand manner, that he was a convict! Semmes' steward, Bartelli, just uncorking a fresh bottle of champagne, almost collapsed. The raider himself was nearly daunted for the moment. But accustomed to the unexpected, he took it in his stride, though the shocked Bartelli promptly replaced the uncorked bottle in the champagne basket and made his exit. Thus began an entertaining two-weeks *entre acte* at Fernando de Noronha.

Next morning Semmes donned his finery, sword, gold braid, all the trimmings of a Captain of the Confederate States Navy. Bartelli had waxed and twirled his mustachios to rapier points. Accompanied by Paymaster Galt, Semmes hurried off, in an equipage sent by the hospitable Governor, to pay his official respects to that dignitary. Reaching the palace he found a sumptuous levee in full swing. Festivities were halted to pay due honors to the visiting Captain. The Governor's guests, the gentry of the island, the cream of Brazil's criminal crop, were chatting and toasting with the social graces of lords of the manor.

Semmes was slightly taken aback, on being introduced to her Ladyship, the Governess, to discover a sprightly, not uncomely mulatto whose kinkyheaded offspring were brought to him to have their heads patted, which he did with apparent gusto.

> But I was a man of the world, and was not at all dismayed by this discovery; especially when I observed that my *vis à vis*, one of the guests, was a beautiful blonde, of sweet seventeen, with a complexion like a lily, tinted with the least bit of rose, and with eyes so melting and lovely, that they looked as though they might have belonged

to one of the *houris* of whom that old reprobate Mohammet used to dream. To set off her charms still further, she was arrayed in a robe of purest white, with a wreath of flowers in her flaxen hair. She was a German, and was seated next to her father, a man of about sixty, who, as the Governor afterward informed me, was one of his chief criminals.

Noting Semmes' amazement, the Governor hastily explained that the father was no common rogue, but a gentleman, who, in a moment of weakness, had signed another gentleman's name to a check for a considerable amount.

"He's only a forger, then!" exclaimed Semmes.

"That's all," replied the Governor. "He's really a very clever old gentleman and, as you see, he has a very pretty daughter."

Semmes was intrigued—as who would not be?—by the company that overflowed the salon. The guests were stellar attractions of whom His Excellency was exuberantly proud, homicides, forgers, accomplished individuals, who had attained fame in their professions. One dashing young fellow, on whose embroidered shirt bosom glittered a fine diamond brooch, was such a master of the pen that he could cheat a man out of his signature after having seen him write it but once.

"He is an artist," assured the host. "A very talented young man."

"I am sure he must be," agreed the amused sailor, who later reported, "This charming young gentleman had 'done' the Bank of Rio de Janeiro out of a very large sum, which was the cause of his being the guest of the governor."

Only the elements conspired against Semmes here. A heavy swell made it impossible to bring the *Louisa Hatch* alongside. Five days of arduous work it took to coal by small boat. Yet hardly had the last boatload of fuel slid into the *Alabama's* bunkers before two ships appeared in the offing, bearing the unmistakable cut of American whalers. Inspecting the newcomers through his glasses, Semmes saw two whaleboats shove off unsuspiciously for the *Louisa Hatch*, lying at her anchors some distance from the *Alabama*. Prize Master Fullam, wearing no uniform to betray him, received them cordially. They wanted to barter a little whale oil for staples. Fullam invited them aboard, but the two skippers hesitated.

"Have you seen anything of the *Alabama*?" asked one of them.

"Yes," replied Fullam, playing Yankee as best he could, though an Englishman. "She was at Jamaica the last we heard of her."

"What steamer is that?" asked a skipper, pointing to the *Alabama*.

"Oh, that's a Brazilian packet ship. She came in yesterday with a load of convicts."

"What are you doing here?"

Again, Fullman lied. "We sprang a pretty bad leak in a gale. Came in to see if we could get repaired."

Suddenly, the two visitors espied a small Confederate flag flying at the gaff. A stray puff of wind had blown out the drooping telltale piece of bunting.

"Give way, men, give way for your lives!" bawled out the steersman of one of the whaleboats. Pulling vigorously on their oars, they retreated for their ships lying about four miles off.

The "Brazilian packet ship," meanwhile, steam up, was moving quietly out to investigate the newcomers. There was no occasion for guile or coquetry. Not too far beyond the marine league the *Alabama* sealed the fate of the *Lafayette* of New Bedford and the *Kate Cory* of Westport. The mate of the *Lafayette* excitedly tossed her papers overboard, thus enabling Semmes to burn her on the spot. It was a poor show. The Governor and his guests, crowded the shores to watch but the *Lafayette* was obstinate. Much smoke, little flame, no drama.

Foraying out from a neutral, friendly port to capture prizes was flagrantly unneutral. Semmes knew this. He surely had not forgotten his own comment to Governor Codrington at Gibraltar, that, "No belligerent has the right to make this use of the territory of a neutral."

Leaving these clubby environs without making return for sundry kindnesses was, of course, unthinkable. Deeply grateful was Semmes to the jovial dignitary for his twisted concept of neutrality. He and several of his talented guests had expressed longings to watch Semmes stage a rattling good performance of his fire-act. Luck, as always, dashed to aid the intrepid impresario.

A Brazilian schooner just happened into the anchorage. For a few barrels of pork and flour Semmes engaged her to transport his prisoners, "who were now quite as numerous as my crew, there being 110 of them," to Pernambuco, thus enabling him to cast the *Kate Cory*, which he had expected to convert into a cartel, in a leading role of the double bill he now planned for the pleasure of his audience. To display his fire-making technique without offending any lingering sensibilities possessed by his host, he escorted the *Louisa Hatch* and the *Kate Cory* beyond the three-mile limit and waited till nightfall to raise his curtain. Darkness would enhance the grandeur of his show, give his spectators a greater thrill. Never before was the rock so gloriously illuminated. Semmes & Company's act was a smash hit.

On the last day of the *Alabama's* jolly outing at Fernando de Noronha, Governor Pyrrho came aboard for a gala send-off. The raider's cabin flowed with champagne and toasts—to Emperor Dom Pedro!—To President Jefferson Davis!—To Brazil!—To the Confederate States, Queen of the South! Semmes was as adept at partying as at burning ships. But this time the Brazilian official, apparently, had something on his mind. First, however, would the Captain accept this fine, fat turkey, this basket of tropical fruits, this magnificent bouquet of roses from His Excellency's lady? Related Semmes, "The roses were very sweet and made me homesick for a while."

Presently, the Governor unburdened himself. Would the Captain be good enough to write him an official despatch, stating he had captured the *Kate Cory* and the *Lafayette beyond* the marine league. It might come in handy. Overwhelmed at so naive a request, Semmes was charmed to comply on the spot. No one could whitewash his violation of neutral rights so artistically as he. Pocketing Semmes' glowing exoneration of himself, His Excellency said goodbye profusely and clanked down the gangway. Everything was in order, officially, at least. Semmes himself had said so. That was sufficient for genial Pyrrho.

Bunkers full, crew refreshed, the *Alabama* tacked away for Semmes' cherished design of cruising off the coast of Brazil. Boasted Sinclair, "We have had a glorious outing, are fat and saucy, and ready for spoils."

Spoils came fast. In apple-pie order Semmes added four ships to his prize list. He burned them pitilessly. Five degrees below the Equator, he caught the *Nye*, of New Bedford, a bluff old whaler returning from a cruise of thirty-one months in the far-off Pacific, with 425 barrels of whale oil in her hold. "What a pity to break in upon the menage of these old salts, who had weathered so many gales, and chased the whale through so many latitudes!"

But the sea-rover's commiseration was short-lived. Greased to saturation with the fat of her trade, the *Nye* made a splendid conflagration.

The *Dorcas Prince*, forty-four days out of New York, "a fine, taut ship," bound for Shanghai, went into history as Semmes' thirty-seventh bonfire. Coy and shy, she refused to haul up until commanded to do so by the boom of a gun. Hunting was good and getting better.

Next to succumb to Semmes' blandishments were two clipper ships whose masts seemed to stroke the very sky, *Union Jack* and *Sea Lark*. From the former the *Alabama* obtained ten barrels of butter and five cases of crackers intended for "subjects of Her British Majesty." Kell valued the *Sea Lark* at 550,000 dollars, a stupendous figure for that era. Both of the stately clipper ships made impressive fires.

On May 2, 1863, amid his holocausts, Semmes paused to remind his journal, "This is an anniversary with me—my marriage day. Alas! this is the third anniversary since I was separated from my family by this Yankee war. And the destruction of fifty ships has been but small revenge for this great privation."

An anniversary it was for the Confederacy, too—and a disastrous one. That same evening in the scrub oak and pine near Chancellorsville valiant Stonewall Jackson was shot down in error by his own men. The wail of the stricken South resounded through the land. It was a high price, even for the Confederacy's finest feat of arms.

Prisoners again encumbered the *Alabama*, including three women and three infants in arms, "too numerous a colony of the weaker sex," as Semmes put it.

Among the unfortunates taken from the *Union Jack* was a New England ex-dominie, who had forsaken his chosen profession to assume the duties of American Consul at Foo Chow, China. Semmes' scorn of him stung like acid, "He had Puritan written all over his lugubrious countenance, and looked so solemn, that one wondered how he came to exchange the clergyman's garb for the garb of Belial."

An Irish stewardess on the *Sea Lark* provided a bit of amusement for the raiders. Refusing to budge from her cabin, she took fast recourse to the bottle. Soon amply fortified, she played havoc with the boarding crew. Semmes' torch-bearers were nonplussed for once. They could not very well fire the ship and cremate the lady. Nor could they put her in the brig. Exasperated, Prize Master Fullam ordered three hearties to seize and rope her. Landed on the *Alabama's* deck, she marched up to Semmes and dressed him down with a volley of unprintable abuse.

"You're a damned pirate and a damned rebel as well!" she screeched for good measure.

Semmes bowed with great dignity, stroked his mustache quietly for several seconds and then, summarily, ordered the lady ducked— which was done, to the delight of his crew and the discomfort of the abusive lady.

Many have wondered—and still do—why Semmes' blazing junket down the Brazilian coast was permitted to go unchallenged by the Federal navy. On this well-traveled route Semmes and his officers expected any moment to sight an enemy cruiser spanking along on the hunt. Sinclair vowed a schoolboy could have arranged a plan of pursuit.

Semmes' opinion of Gideon Welles, never high, fell to a new low. Geared precisely to his fancy was a limerick that appeared in London's *Punch* about this time:

There was an old fogy named Welles,
Quite worthy of cap and of bells,
For he thot that a pirate,
Who steamed at a great rate,
Would wait to be riddled with shells.

How Semmes belabored the dilatory tactics of the "slow old gentleman for his culpable neglect and want of sagacity in pursuit of me!"

Ever since I left the island of Jamaica, early in January, my ship had been constantly reported, and any one of his clerks could have plotted my track. If Mr. Welles had stationed a heavier and faster ship than the *Alabama*—and he had a number of both heavier and faster ships—at the crossing of the 30th parallel; another at or near the Equator, a little to the eastward of Fernando de Noronha, and a third off Bahia, he must have driven me off, or greatly crippled me in my movements. A few more ships in the other chief highways, and his commerce would have been pretty well protected. But the old gentleman does not seem once to have thought of so simple a policy as stationing a ship anywhere.

His plan seemed to be, first, to wait until he heard of the *Alabama* being somewhere, and then to send off a number of cruisers, post-haste, in pursuit of her, as though he expected her to stand still, and wait for her pursuers! This method left the game entirely in my own hands. My safety depended upon a simple calculation of times and distances.

Burdened with prisoners, the *Alabama* steered for Bahia, Brazil's second most important port. On May 11 she anchored in the harbor to learn that no Northern man-of-war had looked in since the North and South began their fight. It was unbelievable. Bahia was the only port ever touched by the *Alabama* on South America's mainland. To Semmes' discomfiture, he was greeted by a proclamation, issued by the President of the Department of Bahia, and addressed to the "Captain of the *Alabama* at Fernando de Noronha," inveighing against his unneutral rodeo off the festive prison island and demanding prompt apology. Semmes snorted. His scorn of petty officialdom was devastating. This "paper bullet," as he castigated it, reminded him of the "stinkpots" the Chinese tossed at their enemies. Calling on Bartelli for writing materials, Semmes launched a verbal rocket, denouncing the proclamation as a budget of lies. Knowledge that he mounted the heaviest guns in the harbor induced him—so he said—to be a trifle careless in the choice of his phraseology. His veiled threat of calling down on Brazil the vengeance of the Southern Confederacy after it had disposed of its Northern adversary, was most persuasive. The President caved in at once. Local dignitaries hurried aboard with apologies and freedom of the port. Thus, was Brazil's violated honor appeased. Goodwill flowed like the champagne in which the subsequent revelries were immersed.

A British resident merchant, one Mr. Ogilvie, topped off the merry-making by a splendid ball honoring the Confederate visitors. Long was this brilliant fete to gleam in the memory of the *Alabama's* gallant young squires. Bahia's beauty and chivalry assembled en masse. Mr. Ogilvie's lamps "shone o'er fair women and brave men." The Confederacy was toasted to the starlit skies. Life and lion of the party, was her fire-bearer, Raphael Semmes, who walked in glory through the brilliant assemblage like a sea-going Lancelot. Nor were his fetching knights in gray and gold lace far behind. As usual, they made off with many a heart that evening, not forgetting—recorded Semmes—"several tiny kid gloves and scarfs, as mementoes to accompany them on their cruise, every villain of them swearing to return at some future day. So it is always with the sailor. His very life is a poem, and his heart is capacious enough to take in the whole sex."

Next morning Bartelli shook Semmes' cot earlier than usual. A strange ship-of-war had anchored during the night several boat-lengths from the *Alabama*. Semmes sprang up. Ordering Confederate colors raised, he hurried on deck. "Judge of our delight," he enthused, "when we saw the Confederate States colors thrown to the breeze in reply by the newcomer." She was the C.S.S. *Georgia,* another of James Bulloch's offspring, which, like the *Alabama*, had escaped from England to be armed on the high seas. After burning a ship or two she had dashed into Bahia to replenish her fuel. She was the only Confederate warship the *Alabama* ever encountered on her long journey of 75,000 miles. On her bridge was Commander Lewis F. Maury, who had been Semmes' shipmate in the old service. Joyous was Semmes' reunion with two of *Sumter* veterans, Lieutenants Chapman and Evans, now serving on the *Georgia*. To make the occasion even more perfect, a telegram from Pernambuco announced that the *Florida* had reached that port. "Now we can straighten up and put on airs," glowed Lieutenant Sinclair, "and boast of the 'Confederate Squadron of the South American station.' "

Four days of camaraderie at Bahia ended too quickly. Torch in hand, the *Alabama* was on the loose again. But while his ship took him farther and farther away, Semmes' thoughts went winging homeward:

I am quite homesick this quiet Sunday morning. I am now two long, long years and more absent from my family, and there are no signs of an abatement of the war. On the contrary, the Yankee devils seem to become more and more infuriated, and nothing short of a war of invasion is likely to bring them to terms, unless, indeed, it be the destruction of their commerce, and for this I fear we are as yet too weak. Well, we must sacrifice our natural yearnings on the altar of our country; for without a country, we can have no home.

Next day he wrote, "chased and captured American ship *Gildersleeve* and American bark *Justina*. Destroyed the former, and ransomed the latter."

"Borne over the blue waters by the glorious trades," the *Jabez Snow* of Buckport, Maine, was sprinting for Montevideo. She was a clipper, a gallant craft, "as graceful as a swan on the water, and with her snow-white canvas and long, taut skysail masts, a thing of beauty." But for the *Alabama* she might have reached her destination. Taken prisoner on the *Jabez Snow* was a woman, listed euphemistically as a "Chambermaid." Semmes vented his wrath at "These shameless Yankee skippers who made a common practice of converting their ships into brothels, and taking their mistresses to sea with them." For decency's sake, he dispossessed a junior lieutenant to provide a cabin for her.

Jubilantly, Semmes blazed off the *Jabez Snow*. Among the skipper's papers was a letter urging prudence and economy in managing his ship so that her owners could buy Federal gold bonds to crush "this terrible rebellion." Semmes saw red. "Hence our diligence," he proclaimed, "in scouring the seas and applying the torch. Whenever we heard a Yankee howl go up over a burned ship, we knew that there were fewer dollars left, with which to hire the *canaille* of Europe to throttle liberty on the American continent."

Two days later the clipper-bark *Amazonian* of Boston made a run for her life and lost. She never had a ghost of a chance, but she tried it. Said Semmes, "I fired a gun, and hoisted Confederate colors, to intimate to the stranger that I would like him to be polite and save me the trouble of catching him, by heaving to." Refusing "to be polite," the *Amazonian's* master threw on a mass of sail alow and aloft. Old Beeswax worked himself into a temper. The

Northern ship raced off on an eight-hour game of catch-me, forcing Semmes to his inevitable last resort. At four miles he unleashed his pivot rifle and let fly a bolt that screeched off to fall just astern of the fugitive. "These rifle bolts make such an ugly hissing and humming as they pass along, that their commands are not often disobeyed."

With blazing eyes Semmes met the *Amazonian's* master as he came aboard.

"Well, captain!" he flared. "You wanted to be unsociable! Didn't want to call on me!"

The old salt was resolute. He knew he faced the one, incomparable Raphael Semmes. "I did what I thought was best for my ship. You'd do the same thing."

A thin smile crept along Semmes' lips. "Perhaps I would, captain. But there was no use running. You probably forgot I had a little teakettle below where I get hot water. Steam will fetch you when canvas fails."

In half an hour South Atlantic winds were whipping the flames of the once-beautiful *Amazonian.*

Semmes' luck was fantastic. Over the sea, as if sent by the gods, came an English brig pointing for Rio. Semmes struck a bargain with her master to land his forty-one prisoners at Brazil's capital. His first inducement was twice as many provisions as the captives would eat. The virtuous Briton demurred lest he "offend Lord Russell." Semmes quickly removed his scruples by raising his bid with a chronometer. The *Alabama* was glutted with these instruments. Semmes' passion for seizing them had filled a cabin with them. Fifty-odd were industriously ticking away and under strict orders were wound daily. Nothing tempted a skipper's cupidity like a chronometer—and the bargain with the Britisher was soon sealed.

Out of the mist-shrouded dawn next morning, swam the clipper-ship *Talisman.* She carried trinkets for the Chinese at Shanghai and two rifled 12-pounder brass cannon and ammunition for a gunboat the mandarins could use against the cutthroat Taipings. Semmes seized the cannon. The *Talisman* and her trinkets burned brightly.

It was time for Semmes now to stretch over to the Cape of Good Hope for fresh fields and new pastures. He had been three months near the Equator and off the coast of Brazil. Federal ships of war would soon be making their appearance. Semmes had calculated it accurately. He ran southwards for the Tropic of Capricorn to reach the forks of the great Brazilian highway where the stream of commerce branches, one round Cape Horn and the other, over to the Cape of Good Hope. Along this thoroughfare neutrals were again passing by scores, many of them American vessels that had sought refuge under the British flag. It was even more apparent than before that ocean-borne trade was slipping away from the United States and onto the willing shoulders of John Bull. The papers of the vessels were so scrupulously made out that Semmes' Admiralty Court dared not tamper with them. It was irksome, though, to see so many possible prizes slipping through his judicial fingers.

Hurrying along towards the "forks of the road" the *Alabama* picked off a tidy brig, the *Conrad* of Philadelphia, new, well-found and fast, "a more beautiful specimen of an American clipper could not be produced." She was just what Semmes had been looking for. He had toyed with the idea of broadening his operations with an auxiliary cruiser to pattern after the *Alabama*. He armed her with the two 12-pounders he had captured on the *Talisman*, twenty rifles, and half a dozen revolvers, and lo! a new Confederate commerce raider was champing to be off. No vessel was ever converted to war uses with more celerity than the *Conrad*. He adorned her with the name of a pretty little town in Alabama, Tuscaloosa, it being "meet that a child of the *Alabama* should be named after one of the towns of the State." He gave command of her to Lieutenant John Low, the *Alabama's* only English-born watch officer. Semmes himself handpicked her crew of twelve.

The *Tuscaloosa's* christening was short and sweet. Semmes penned her commission, a brief document of grave import that empowered her to rove the sea "and destroy all the enemy's ships that fall into your power." It was a retake of Secretary Mallory's original orders to the raider. In the late afternoon, in the South Atlantic, the *Conrad* ran up the Confederate colors and immediately she was the *Tuscaloosa*. The crew of the *Alabama* manned the rigging, took off their hats and gave three cheers for their fledgling. Back came three answering cheers from the *Tuscaloosa*.

"Thus," said Semmes, "my bantling was born upon the high seas, in the South Atlantic Ocean, and no power could gainsay the legitimacy of her birth. Even England was compelled to acknowledge it. May the *Tuscaloosa* prove a scourge to Yankee commerce."

In twelve short hours he had captured, commissioned, armed, officered and provisioned another Confederate man-of-war and thrust her out on the deep to raid American commerce. With orders to rejoin the *Alabama* at the Cape of Good Hope, the *Tuscaloosa's* sails bellied out as she stood away over the sunset sea. Her long, tapering masts and flaring bow proclaimed how truly American she was. Certainly, on looks, she should prove beguiling to her intended victims.

Lieutenant Sinclair voiced different feelings: "Gloom pervades the ship somewhat akin to that experienced when death has strode into your midst. It is by no means an exultant feeling that catches hold of our messmates as they gather tonight about the messtable. We appreciate that we have sent abroad a most insignificant representative on the ocean—one that, with a prize crew on an enemy's deck, has left the bantam cruiser quite helpless. Our grave fears seem almost a forecast of facts to be. We can only record the *Tuscaloosa's* cruise barren of results, our own ship crippled in numbers, and her officers and crew denied the opportunity of participation in the *Alabama's* future glorious career—a disappointment none but a naval man can fully appreciate."

Creeping into Semmes' confidences to his journal were shadows of the futility of it all. On June 30, 1863, he poured out his heart. One cannot escape the feeling that disillusionment was setting in.

It is two years since we ran the blockade of the Mississippi in the *Sumter.* Two years of almost constant excitement and anxiety, the usual excitement of battling with the sea and the weather and avoiding dangerous shoals and coasts, added to the excitement of the chase, the capture, the escape from the enemy, and the battle.

And then there has been the government of my officers and crew, not always a pleasant task, for I have had some senseless and unruly spirits to deal with; and last, though not least, the bother and vexation of being hurried out of port when I have gone into one by scrupulous and timid officials, to say nothing of offensive espionage. All these things have produced a constant tension of the nervous system, and the wear and tear of body in these two years would, no doubt, be quite obvious to my friends at home, could they see me on this 30th of June 1863. *Sic transit vita hominis, usque ad finum!*

Crossing the Tropic of Capricorn, the *Alabama* slanted east for her stretch over to the Cape of Good Hope. 825 miles east of Rio de Janeiro an amazing enemy struck her: weevils!

Hordes of these minute destroyers invaded the breadroom, infesting the ship's entire supply of the staff of life. It was enough to dismay even the stoutest-hearted. Bread the *Alabama* must have, even if it meant backtracking to Rio, nigh one thousand miles. Some distance to travel to the nearest bakeshop! "Unless I could capture it by the way." In his memoirs Semmes italicized that possibility. Sadly he veered about, never dreaming that luck was still his faithful lady. This time she literally kissed him on the cheek.

It was July 2, 1863. On the hills around the little town of Gettysburg, Pennsylvania, blue and gray were slugging it out. On the morrow twenty thousand gray-backs, flying nineteen red battle flags, would move up Cemetery Hill through storms of shot and shell, to spill in bloody futility at the highwater mark of the Confederacy.

That same day the *Alabama* overhauled eleven ships, all neutrals. Near midnight the twelfth bulked out of the darkness. The *Anna F. Schmidt* of Boston, bound round the Horn, had, unbeknownst to herself, come to his rescue. Examining her hold the *Alabama's* boarding crew stood entranced by what they saw: a profusion of airtight casks packed with bread enough to feed the raider's mouths for thirty days. Incredible! Emptying the *Anna F. Schmidt* was a day's work. Setting her on fire took ten minutes. She flared like tinder, and Semmes turned his ship's head back towards the Cape.

"Miss Schmidt's" fiery petticoats were still flaring when out of the night lunged a huge ship, her billowing sails reflecting the red light of the burning prize. She slithered past the *Alabama* in the moonlight like a phantom. The raider fired a gun to halt her. The stranger boomed back, lit a blue light, and sped on. Stirring her fires, the *Alabama* gave chase. The crew, drawn by the sudden mystery, crowded the deck. Positive were the more superstitious they had scared up the Flying Dutchman. At midnight Semmes overhauled the stranger. His glasses revealed a towering, black-painted vessel, a white streak around her waist, guns frowning through her ports. She was a massive ship of war.

"What ship is that?" thundered Lieutenant Kell's trumpet.

Over the waters came the brisk reply, "This is Her Britannic Majesty's ship *Diomede*. What ship are you?"

"The Confederate States Steamer *Alabama!*" answered Kell.

"We suspected as much when we saw you making sail by the light of the burning ship. We suppose that is some of your work."

"It certainly is," echoed Kell.

Semmes could not insist on scrutinizing the papers of one of Her Majesty's ships, so he sheered off for Africa, as before. One by one his men slunk below to their hammocks, disappointed that they had neither caught the Flying Dutchman, nor a California clipper, nor a fight.

Semmes' torch still flared brightly. On July 6 he captured his last prize in the South Atlantic—the *Express*, of Boston. Weather-beaten and defaced, she had had a long, boisterous journey round the Horn from Peru with a cargo of guano when the *Alabama* suddenly intruded on her. The master's wife was aboard, with a traveling companion. To Semmes, it seemed unkind that two females, who had braved the dangers of Cape Horn, should now be carried off to brave other perils off the Cape of Good Hope. But his sympathies went no further. The ladies were cabined on the *Alabama*, and the *Express* given the torch.

The North Star had long since faded below the horizon. Nightly, new constellations had risen. Overhead, four scintillating stars twinkled down—the Southern Cross—always a bright omen for Semmes. It glittered like a piece of diamond-studded jewelry in the dark purple heavens. On bright nights the stationary Magellanic Clouds hovered towards the nether pole, bringing dreams of far-off worlds. It was cold in the South Atlantic now, for it was midwinter.

On July 4, Semmes went on record again, "This is Independence Day in the old concern; a holiday, which I feel half inclined to throw overboard because it was established in such bad company, and because we have to fight the battle of independence over again, against a greater tyranny than before. Still, old feelings are strong, and it will not hurt Jack to give him an extra glass of grog."

As if to welcome the *Alabama* to Africa and to warn her to beware of the "stormy cape," a cape pigeon, harbinger of tempest like the petrel, wheeled out of the sky, uttered its cheerful scream and skimmed away over the tips of the waves. Then, out of a gale, swept a wide-winged albatross for a landing on deck. Jack eyed the legendary bird fearfully lest someone harm this strange feathered denizen of the southern seas and cast the spell of ill luck and bad weather over the ship.

On July 29, the *Alabama* made the Cape of Good Hope. Prudently, Semmes edged his ship into Saldanha Bay, a spacious, landlocked harbor on the west coast sixty miles north of Capetown. In a cozy, sheltered nook of the bay the *Alabama* found a place to rest her weary hull. She had been almost four weeks under canvas.

That night, with the deck quiet, no strange sails, no storm, to disturb his repose, Semmes "felt like a weary traveller, who had laid down, for a time, a heavy burden." Long minutes he spent on his knees before lights out. Gratitude surged out of his heart. Next morning, for the first time in his life, he set foot on the Dark Continent to find that, even in this distant land, the trumpet of fame was blowing for the "British Pirate."

The Saldanha settlement, though owned by England, was peopled by Boers, Dutch colonists, who flocked to welcome the storm-beaten *Alabama*. The sons of these same Boers would, a generation hence, write imperishable records of gallantry in a futile struggle, like that of the Southern Confederacy, to create a republic of their own.

From Saldanha Bay, Semmes could reconnoitre for Northern men-of-war hovering about the Cape. To his welcome surprise, he soon learned not an enemy ship had been seen off the Cape for months. "Mr. Welles was asleep, the coast was all clear, and I could renew my 'depredations' upon the enemy's commerce whenever I pleased."

Half-done was the *Alabama's* career. She had, unknown to Semmes, already wreaked two-thirds of her destruction of commerce. Since that bright Sunday, off the Azores, when Semmes first hoisted the Stars and Bars over the *Alabama*, she had run up a staggering record. The ship had become legend. Friend and foe alike marvelled at her as something that could not be, but was. Fifty-four prizes had she taken, strewing the ocean floor with the ashes of forty-five of them, bonding the rest for ransoms approaching a million dollars. Northern traders idled in ports all over the world, not daring to venture out lest the ubiquitous, wraithlike Semmes appear out of the nowhere and set them afire. The American flag was all but swept from the sea. To rub it in, Semmes had defied and eluded every ship the United States Navy had despatched to run him down.

Until now, it seemed as if the very stars in their courses had looked down with favor on his mission of fire. Yet, time and triumph run out for every man. One stands at the summit but briefly.

⚓

⚓

25 *Flames over the Orient*

In short order the weary *Alabama* was rejuvenated. Five days of painting, re-caulking, and overhauling obliterated most visible traces of her grinding, unrelenting pace since leaving Jamaica. Once again she was a thing of beauty, "looking like a bride."

The sudden shadow of death darkened the *Alabama's* deck at Saldanha. Third Engineer Simeon Cummings was killed while hunting in the hills. News of his death was brought to Semmes by Lieutenant Sinclair, who reported him "deeply affected, trembling with emotion, brushing away a tear." Overnight, the dead officer lay on the quarterdeck, wrapped in the Stars and Bars, with a guard of honor under the stars.

Next morning, with flags at halfmast, muffled oars and the full ship's company as an escort, the funeral cortege bore their ship-mate's body ashore. Young Cummings, Northern-born, but a staunch Confederate, was laid to rest in the family graveyard of a Boer farmer. Lieutenant Kell read the solemn burial service. Three volleys, and this adopted son of the South was committed to the soil of Africa. A timeworn slab still marks the grave of the only Confederate entombed on the Dark Continent.

By pony courier, Semmes had informed the British Governor, Sir Philip Wodehouse, of his arrival at Saldanha Bay and his impending visit to Britain's Cape Colony where "Mr. Seward and Mr. Adams, Earl Russell and the London *Times* had made the 'British Pirate' famous." Federal cruisers were conspicuous by their absence.

At dawn, August 5, the *Alabama* steamed out of Saldanha Bay and veered southwards for Cape Town, sixty miles away. Idling along in the light wind, she fell in with her fledgling, the *Tuscaloosa*, punctual to the hour for the rendezvous with her parent. Coming aboard, Lieutenant Low reported a lone capture, the East Indiaman *Santee*. She had British property in her cargo, and that had obliged him to free her on bond. The *Tuscaloosa* was not proving a fruitful chapter in Semmes' adventures. Ordering Low to put into Simon's Bay, eastward of the Cape, Semmes voyaged on.

Towards noon, out of the distance, rose the grim old cape, over-draped by its famous table-cloth of fleecy, white cloud. Could Semmes have written the stage directions for his entry into Cape Town to suit himself, he could not have arranged it better. Standing in for Table Bay, the lookout sighted prey on the very threshold of the port, a jaunty, fresh-faced American bark, her sails gleaming like snowbanks, making slowly for the same port. Crowding on steam, the *Alabama* sprinted after her. Six miles from land her long arm reached out and embraced the *Sea Bride* of Boston, a splendid ship, bound with a cargo of muslins, prints, and trinkets for the lucrative native markets of the east African coast. The *Sea Bride's* master might have saved his ship had he been a bit more nimble, though the decoying Union Jack at the *Alabama's* peak betokened no peril. Semmes condemned her instantly, but to prove she was on the high seas, he took immediate compass bearings of headlands and lighthouses. It was inevitable that the American Consul would assail him for violation of British territorial waters.

Leaving Master's Mate Fullam and a prize crew aboard the *Sea Bride*, Semmes ordered her to lay on and off the port until further instructions. Then the *Alabama* swished into Table Bay, her Confederate colors snapping gaily in the breeze. Lining her rails, hats smartly a-tilt, were a handsome, jaunty, and prideful a set of seamen. On her bridge stood the nonpareil Raphael Semmes and his officers, trimly uniformed for the occasion.

At one o'clock the signal station on Lion's Hill had reported "Confederate Steamer *Alabama*, from the N.W., and Federal Barque from the S.E." The news spread fast as light. Thousands dropped what they were doing and scrambled for vantage points on Lion's Hill and Kloof Road. The roofs of houses overlooking Table Bay were soon jammed with standees.

With the capture of the *Sea Bride* under the eyes of the city Semmes sailed in in a golden haze of glory. Almost in the very roadstead he had given the people of this faraway British colony a sample of his wares, a repeat performance, though lacking its fiery setting, of his spectacular entrance at Gibraltar on the *Sumter*.

Jamaica had gone wild over Semmes. Cape Town now gave him and his men an even more tumultuous welcome. What could it mean? Semmes himself marvelled at it. In the *Alabama*, these transplanted Englishmen envisioned a ship of their own creation whose valor and deeds had excited the admiration of the world. For them, Semmes was the dauntless Confederate chevalier, a sort of naval St. George, whose terrible swift torch was scorching their rival, the American commercial dragon, from the seas. The flag he flew was that of a republic that would humble this airy American upstart. Here, in person, was Semmes, the phantom raider, and his phantom ship.

Hardly had the *Alabama's* anchor chain ceased rattling before she was enveloped by an armada of boats, yachts, tugs, passenger boats, skiffs, and even dugouts—anything that could float and take people alongside the renowned visitor.

One of the first to climb the *Alabama's* gangway was the enterprising reporter of the *Cape Argus,* who dashed off to interview the Confederate captain. His eye-witness, front-page account still echoes the sensation of the hour. Hopping into a cab upon word of the raider's approach, he had joined the mad rush to watch the great sight:

Here was to be a capture by the celebrated Confederate craft, close to the entrance to Table Bay. The inhabitants rushed off to get a sight. Crowds of people ran up the Lion's hill and to the Kloof Road. All cabs were chartered, every one of them; there was no cavilling about fares; the cabs were taken and no questions asked, but orders were given to drive as hard as possible. We did the first mile in a short time; but the Kloof Hill for the next two and a half miles is uphill work. The horse jibbed, so we pushed on, on foot, as fast as possible, and left the cab to come on.

As soon as our cab reached the crown of the hill we set out at breakneck pace down the hill, till we came near Brighton, and as we reached the corner, there lay the *Alabama* within fifty yards of the unfortunate Yankee. As the Yankee came round from the southeast and about five miles from the bay, the steamer came down upon her. The Yankee was evidently taken by surprise. The *Alabama* fired a gun, and brought her to. When we first got sight of the *Alabama* it was difficult to make out what she was doing; the bark's head had been put about, and the *Alabama* lay off quite immovable, as if she were taking a sight at the 'varmint.'

Like a cat watching and playing with a victimized mouse, Captain Semmes permitted his prize to draw off a few yards and he then up steam again and pounced upon her. She first sailed round the Yankee from stem to stern, and from stern to stem again. The way that fine, saucy, rakish craft was handled was worth riding a hundred miles to see. She went round the bark like a toy, making a complete circle, and leaving an even margin of water between herself and her prize of not more than twenty yards. This done, she sent a boat with the prize crew off, took possession in the name of the Confederate States and sent the bark off to sea. The *Alabama* then made for port.

We came round the Kloof to visit Captain Semmes on board. We found the heights overlooking Table Bay covered with people. The windows of the villas at the bottom of the hill were all thrown up, and ladies waved their handkerchiefs. There were masses of people as far as the eye could reach.

On getting alongside the *Alabama* we found about a dozen boats before us, and we had not been on board five minutes before she was surrounded by nearly every boat in Table Bay, and as boat after boat arrived, three cheers were given for Captain Semmes and his gallant privateer. This, upon the part of a neutral people, is, perchance, wrong; but we are not arguing a case—we are recording facts. They did cheer, and cheer with a will, too. It was not, perhaps, taking the view of either side, Federal or Confederate, but in admiration of the skill, pluck, and daring of the *Alabama*, her captain and her crew, who now afford a general theme of admiration for the world all over.

Visitors were received by the officers of the ship most courteously, and without distinction, and the officers conversed freely and unreservedly of their exploits. They are as fine and gentlemanly a set of fellows as ever we saw; most of them young men. The ship had been so frequently described, that most people know what she is like, as we do who have seen her. We should have known her to be the *Alabama* if we had boarded her in the midst of the ocean, with no one to introduce us to each other. Her guns alone are worth going off to see, and everything about her speaks highly for the seamanship and discipline of the commander and his officers. She has a very large crew, fine, lithe-looking fellows, the very picture of English men of war's men.

Deeply impressed was the inquiring reporter, who squeezed his way into Semmes' cabin to find the raider affability itself, a willing target for the admiring gentleman of the press.

"Captain Semmes," asked the scribe, "would you mind giving us the names of the ships you've captured?"

"Not at all," smiled Semmes. "We have no secrets."

Patiently, he reeled off the list, winding up with "the *Sea Bride* you saw us take today." Yet Semmes seized the opportunity to play his own game.

"I was forced to burn ships," he explained, "because you English people won't be neighborly enough to let me bring my prizes into your ports, and get them condemned. It obliged me to set up my own prize court on the *Alabama*, try the case of every prize, and condemn the ships I captured, or free them, as the evidence warranted. Certain European powers complain of my burning ships. If they insist on preserving such strict neutrality as to exclude me from their ports, what can I do with my prizes but burn them?"

The reporter did not record his own answer to this, though he apparently hinted the American Consul would protest the capture of the *Sea Bride* in supposedly British waters.

"I presume he will," laughed Semmes. "I'll brush him off like a gadfly."

By night, Semmes' cabin was garlanded with flowers. Ladies tripped up the gangway to lay their offerings at the feet of the flash-and-fire Confederate captain. Tucked in the heart of each bouquet was a delicately scented billet-doux. Nor was he ungrateful for these attentions. Often had he expatiated on the "capacity of the heart of a sailor." Apparently, his own was no exception. He admitted being "carried by storm" and surrendering "at discretion" to the ladies of the Cape though he meticulously explained, "I have always found the instincts of women to be right, and I felt more gratified at this spontaneous outpourings of the sympathies of the sex, for our cause, than if all the male creatures of the earth had approved it, in cold, formal words." He failed to mention the glamour that clustered about him like a halo. Or, was there a bit of flirtation he was too circumspect to mention?

So impassioned and fervid was the obeisance of the ladies, Lieutenant Sinclair feared "that at least one lady in Dixie's far off land might have felt some jealousy at the enthusiasm of this female inundation of the *Alabama's* cabin."

In a frenzy of adulation, autograph hunters, "gentlemen and ladies of distinction," dignitaries in gold lace, and just plain hero-worshippers, besieged Semmes' cabin door where his faithful steward, Bartelli, stood guard with the air of a chamberlain to a king. Versed in all grades of grandeeism, Bartelli put on his finest Chesterfieldian manners as he screened the visitors, who sought to elbow their way into the august presence.

Even the gay ladies of the East End flew into a dither of excitement. They knew *Alabama's* Jack would soon be storming their doors with money in his hand. Sailors were all alike. New ports, new loves.

Yet, even for lucky Raphael Semmes, every rose had its thorns. To Cape Town's Governor, the American Consul sent a sharp protest against Semmes' seizure of the *Sea Bride,* bedaubing it as "clearly in British waters," and "a grievous injury to a friendly power." Semmes' wrath boiled over at the "half demagogue, half diplomat" Consul. He rebutted with a barrage of irrefutable proof, based on bearings taken at the time of the capture in Table Bay and testimony of lighthouse keepers who had watched it. He proved hands down the *Sea Bride* was outside the three-mile shelter. The Governor could do nothing more than declare the *Sea Bride* a legal prize. Thus, Semmes foiled the Consul.

Five days of ovation flashed by like a rainbow. Weighing anchor, the *Alabama* doubled the Cape and steamed round to Britain's naval station on Simon's Bay. Off the roadstead the lookout spotted the *Martha Wenzel* of Boston, poking along for England. This bark was christened under a lucky star. Bearings taken from the headlands showed she was probably within the marine league when the *Alabama* overhauled her. Semmes decided to take no chance of jeopardizing the sympathies of his English friends by opening a new controversy in international law, though he hardly expected to find another awaiting him at Simon's Bay. Dumfounded was the *Martha's* skipper when Semmes announced his verdict: no fire. To the master's profuse thanks for sparing his ship Semmes replied coldly, "You need not thank me. I'm only sorry I'm not able to burn your ship."

Anchored in the bay was the *Alabama's* child, the *Tuscaloosa.* Mr. Seward's "gadfly" was buzzing about her with charges that Britain had no right to recognize this makeshift cruiser as a Confederate man-of-war. So Semmes once more unlimbered his legal cannon. So logical were his arguments that the Governor, with whom the Consul had lodged his second protest, promptly decided: no nation had a right to inquire into the antecedents of the ships of war of another nation. The *Tuscaloosa* was a Confederate warship, and that was that. Unction it was to Semmes' soul. Twice in a week had he brushed off the obnoxious "gadfly."

Yet, Semmes turned aside from the feasting by the naval colony at Simon's Bay to try his hand at a piece of business. While he lay at Cape Town a gentleman representing a syndicate of English speculators had made overtures to purchase the *Sea Bride.* Selling off his prizes had never occurred to Semmes, though the idea had an enticing ring. It was better than burning them, though a trifle irregular. Still, there was no port in the civilized world where he could hand over the ship, if purchased. Good gamblers, the gentlemen were willing to take the risk. So Semmes agreed to sell, for he could well use the gold they proffered. The *Alabama's* sea-chest needed replenishing. Nor was there any barrier to making delivery, argued his customers. Semmes need only take the ship to Angra Pequena on the West African coast, in territory unclaimed by any civilized power on the globe, and ruled by a few Hottentot chiefs, who knew nothing and cared less about the fine points of international law.

Moreover, this sporting crowd agreed to purchase the wool Semmes had captured on the *Conrad*, ship it to London and credit the Confederate States with two-thirds of the proceeds. Building their airy castles even higher, they proposed purchasing every prize Semmes captured on the nearby seas.

Ordering the *Tuscaloosa* to proceed to Cape Town and then escort the *Sea Bride* to the secret rendezvous, Semmes cruised off the Cape a few days hoping to lead a string of prizes to the Bay of Angra Pequena. Bagging no game, he stood in for the bay. Basking in the hot sun was the little flotilla—*Tuscaloosa*, *Sea Bride*, and a schoonerload of Cape Town's leading merchants with bags of gold sovereigns ready to seal the deal. At last, Semmes had found a haven where he could herd in a prize without creating an international dispute, or being nagged by an American Consul. Angra Pequena was not even marked on the map, just a gouged-out dent in Africa's coastal wasteland. The only visible sign of human habitation in this land were a few naked, half-starved Hottentots straggling along the beach, begging for food.

Semmes was strangely reticent about this clandestine transaction, other than to say his chief mission was to destroy enemy commerce, not to waste time selling prizes to speculators. He never repeated it.

Lieutenant Sinclair, on the other hand, drew an intriguing picture of this scene that suggested the old days of piracy and pieces of eight. Surreptitiously, he peered down, through the skylight of Semmes' cabin, on the closing of the sale of the *Sea Bride*. Thus he recorded what he saw:

Our customers were certainly dipping into the adventurous, since they proposed to purchase and trade from port to port in a ship that had no nationality, no responsibility, and no protection but what she could give herself. The affair seemed to us romantic, anyway. Perhaps for the moment the lust of gain was upon us sufficiently to give us a touch of the feeling that inspired the buccaneers of old.

But now, in the cabin of the *Alabama,* as we look down through the skylight from the deck, may be seen a serious and businesslike group. On one side Semmes, and paymaster Galt with the invoices and other papers necessary to an estimate of values. On the other, the gentlemen who were making the venture, with their clerks and bags of gold.

The subject matter has been discussed and satisfactorily arranged, and now may be seen the opening of the bags of gold and telling them out on the cabin table. For hours, in the quiet of our safe and close retreat, may be heard the clink, clink of British sovereigns, as they are verified by our careful paymaster. It was interesting to observe our Jack, one by one, cast a sidelong glance down the cabin skylight, and take in the counting of the gold, and with a wink and remark of satisfaction to his shipmate, saunter leisurely forward. Jack is taking in the practical demonstration, and no doubt mentally indorsing the (at the time taken with a grain of salt) persuasive words of 'Old Beeswax' at Terceira some months since, when in a speech of honeyed phrase he was bidding for a crew.

No better proof of the judicious methods of discipline outlined by Semmes could be submitted, than that under them, though engaged in acts somewhat suggesting the pranks of the buccaneers, our crew were as well held in hand as though serving on an English man of war in times of profound peace, and at the same time in a state of perfect contentment.

The entire cargo of the *Sea Bride* has been sold with the vessel. The wool is to be shipped to England and sold on joint account, for the benefit of both parties to the contract. The transfer is completed, and the *Sea Bride,* a wanderer like ourselves, starts out on her trading venture. She has no papers, no nationality; at the same time, she cannot be regarded as a pirate or outlaw . . . However, the embryo entanglement that might have occupied the attention of an admiralty court, was settled in a summary manner by the loss, later on, of the vessel. She was wrecked on the African coast, and became a total loss.

However, the visible handling of gold in exchange for something we had heretofore been offering up as a sacrifice to the ocean gods, helped our crew realize that not only glory is theirs, but substantial prize money.

Richer by 16,940 dollars in gold sovereigns in her strongbox— not too great a sum when we consider the value of her other prizes —the *Alabama* moved back towards the Cape and coaled at Simon's Town while the *Tuscaloosa* was bundled off to the coast of Brazil.

Never was it given to Raphael Semmes to know a single hour when peril, man-made or elemental, was not lurking to destroy him and his ship. While dining the raider's captain on the British flagship *Narcissus* at Simon's Town, Admiral Walker imparted disturbing news. The Northern bloodhound *Vanderbilt* was baying on the *Alabama's* trail. She had coaled there in Semmes' absence and hurriedly put to sea hoping to fall in with the raider off the Cape and end her dramatic career forthwith. Between mouthfuls of a delightful dinner, the Admiral disclosed, "The *Vanderbilt's* captain said he did not intend to fire a gun at you, but to run you down and sink you." Semmes knew that if the much-heavier *Vanderbilt* struck the *Alabama*, she would slice her open like a watermelon. He took the news without blinking, sipping his wine thoughtfully. He had no desire, or intention, of engaging the *Vanderbilt*. She had the speed of the *Alabama* and threw twice her weight of metal. This converted ocean liner packed, besides lesser weapons, two eleven-inch guns, each firing a 135-pound shot. But she had serious drawbacks. Her boilers were ravenous, burning eighty tons of coal a day. She had, in fact, exhausted the coal pile at Simon's Bay, forcing Semmes to steam around to Cape Town for fuel. And a shot into either of her great paddle wheels would cut her down to a one-wing duck.

While at Simon's Bay the *Vanderbilt's* officers had expatiated on the pirate's fate that awaited Semmes when they caught him. Britain's officers were duly impressed. They regaled Semmes with frightening tales of the *Vanderbilt's* battery and speed. Unconsciously, Semmes added considerably to his prestige by his calm in the face of the *Vanderbilt's* threats.

It is astonishing that of the many Union warships that whipped after the *Alabama* only three ever sighted her: the *San Jacinto*, eluded at Martinique; the *Hatteras*, sunk off Galveston; and the *Kearsarge*, whose part is still in the future. Yet, the *Vanderbilt* turned in the best chase of all.

In January, 1863, Secretary Welles gave the speedy *Vanderbilt* a roving commission to search for the *Alabama*. With keen foresight Commander Charles H. Baldwin mapped out Semmes' probable course in the South Atlantic. His orders from Welles read:

> You will first visit Havana where you may obtain information to govern your further movements. You can then visit any of the islands of the West Indies, or any part of the Gulf, at which you think you would be most likely to overtake the *Alabama*, or procure information of her. When you are perfectly satisfied that the *Alabama* has left the Gulf or the West Indies, and has gone to some other locality, you will proceed along the coast of Brazil to Fernando de Noronha, and Rio de Janeiro, making inquiry at such places as you may deem advisable. From Rio continue your course to the Cape of Good Hope, thence back to St. Helena, Cape de Verde, the Canaries, Madeira, Lisbon, Western Islands, and New York. If at any point word is obtained of the *Alabama* or any other rebel craft, you will pursue her without regard to these instructions.

Yet, this judicious plan was scuttled off St. Thomas by Admiral Wilkes the moment he caught sight of the *Vanderbilt*. Transferring his flag from the *Wachusett* to the much grander *Vanderbilt*, nothing could induce him to part with her until June 13, when finally the Navy Department itself ordered him to free the ship and permit her to proceed southwards after the *Alabama*.

Demoted for his highhandedness (and for a certain lack of candor in some other matters), Wilkes engaged in a long, bitter wrangle with Secretary Welles, emerging with his popularity and prestige considerably dimmed. From first to last, Wilkes, as commander of the West Indies Flying Squadron, had a total of sixteen ships with which to pursue the *Alabama*.

Meanwhile, unflaggingly and with unerring judgment, Commander Baldwin picked up Semmes' trail again. Never once did he lose the scent. Zigzagging down the Atlantic, the *Vanderbilt* touched at Bahia and Fernando de Noronha. Too late, to be sure;

the bird had flown. Surmising that Semmes had veered towards the Cape of Good Hope, Baldwin tracked after him. Yet, he finally located Semmes only to be outmatched by fortune. Ducking in and out of Cape Town and Simon's Town, a day or two apart, the *Vanderbilt* and *Alabama* played hide and seek. One thick, dark night Semmes' glasses revealed a huge vessel, unquestionably a warship and a big one, flitting by like a spectre. So close was she he could hear the splash of her paddle wheels. It was the *Vanderbilt!* Nor did Semmes try to overhaul her as he had H.M.S. *Diomede.* Twice off the Cape these ships passed close enough to sight each other's smoke. Semmes had no desire to clash with her though he would not decline battle if they met.

Crew trouble was inevitable at Cape Town. Vexed by his wayward, riotous "heroes of the hour" Semmes let fly his sharpest word-lashing to his journal, "I have a precious set of rascals on board—faithless in the matter of abiding by their contracts, liars, thieves and drunkards. There are some few good men who are exceptions to this rule."

Fourteen of his "rascals" had vanished into thin air. Of these, at least eight were quartered in the compound of the American Legation, seduced by the gold and promises of the American Consul. Semmes' appeal to the Cape police proved barren. Neutrality forbade invasion of the extra-territoriality of the consulate. Dissipation and debauchery accounted for the other six. These fourteen were enough to cripple his ship. A lesser man might have crumpled, but Semmes was still adept at surmounting obstacles.

Men the *Alabama* must have. Five thousand miles across the Indian Ocean, the Orient was beckoning to his torch. Throughout the East Indies, American ships were plying their lucrative trade, unmolested, little dreaming, perhaps, that Semmes' firebrand would ever reach those distant seas. In his letter accepting command of the *Alabama*, Semmes had promised Secretary Mallory to carry fire and destruction to Northern commerce in the Far East where he would "lay rich burnt offerings upon the altar of our country's liberties." Now he was ready, his ship was ready, but his crew was not. Fourteen men he must have and he was determined to have them come hell or high water or both. It was no time to tinker with delicate interpretations of neutrality or highminded diplomacy.

In his dilemma Semmes turned to a local crimp, a "sailor landlord, one of those shylocks who coin Jack's flesh and blood into gold." Charmingly and convincingly, he reasoned out his plan to bypass the Queen's neutrality. He would not be so ungallant to her Majesty as to violate her laws. Not at all. Said he to himself, "My sailors have gone ashore in her Majesty's dominions, and refuse to come back to me. When I apply to her Majesty's police, they tell me that so sacred is the soil of England, no man must be coerced to do what he doesn't want to do. Good! I reply, a ship of war is part of the territory to which she belongs, and that if some of the subjects of the Queen should think proper to come into my territory, and refuse to go back, I may surely apply the same principle and refuse to compel them."

The crimp, at this moment, had entered Semmes' cabin to announce he had eleven "boarders," who had "volunteered" to fill the places of the deserters.

"So you have some gentlemen boarding at your house who desire to take passage with me?" queried Semmes, with a laugh to himself.

The landlord smiled and nodded.

"You know I cannot ship seamen in her Majesty's ports, but I see no reason why I should not take passengers to sea with me, if they desire to go."

"Certainly, your honor. They can work for their passage, you know," suggested the crimp, shutting one eye significantly.

"I suppose you'll charge something for bringing these *gentlemen* on board?" asked Semmes.

"Somewhat, your honor," said the landlord. Fetching out a greasy memorandum, he began reading, "Bill Bunting, board and lodging, ten shillings, drinks one pound ten. Tom Bowline, board and lodging, six shillings. Tom only landed yesterday from a Dutch ship—drinks twelve shillings."

"Hold on!" said Semmes. "Never mind the board, lodging, and drinks. Lieutenant Kell, will you take the gentleman to the paymaster and see that he is paid his fares for bringing these passengers aboard."

The "passengers" were already alongside. Up the gangway straggled eleven whisky-filled ragamuffins. It wasn't fourteen, but it would do. "If the reader recollects Falstaff's description of his ragged battalion," said Semmes, "he will have a pretty good idea of the personnel I had before me." However, at his wink, Dr. Llewellyn gave them a fast "physical," pronounced them sound and able-bodied and prescribed oceans of soap and water.

On September 24, 1863, the raider stood out for Java Head, Sumatra, Singapore, and the Orient where the great China clippers rolled along like floating tinder boxes.

Towards midnight, in the teeth of a stiff gale that shrieked through the rigging and pitched her about like a plaything, the *Alabama* turned her prow southwards to run her easting down into the Roaring Forties and stand across the Indian Ocean for Sunda Strait and the fabulous entrepôt of the Far East.

The sea was wild that night as the *Alabama*, under steam, fought her way along the rockbound coast of the Cape of Good Hope. Vividly, Semmes described the start of his odyssey to the Orient:

> The struggle of this little ship with the elements was a thing to be remembered. The moon was near her full, shedding a flood of light upon the scene. The Bay was whitened with foam, as the waters were lashed into fury by the storm. Around the curve of the 'horse-shoe' arose broken, bald, rocky mountains, on the crests of which were piled fleecy, white clouds, blinking in the moonlight, like banks of snow. These clouds were perfectly motionless. It appeared as if the Devil had spread a great many 'table cloths' around False Bay that night, or rather, a more appropriate figure would be, that he had touched the mountains with the stillness of death, and wreathed them with winding sheets. The scene was wild and weird beyond description. It was a picture for the eye of a poet or painter to dwell upon.
>
> Nor was the imagination less touched, when, from time to time, the revolving light upon the grim old Cape—that Cape which had so long divided the Eastern from the Western world—threw its full blaze upon the deck of the struggling ship. Overhead, the sky was perfectly clear, there being not so much as a speck of cloud to be seen—and this in the midst of a howling gale of wind! At three A.M. we cleared the Cape, and keeping the ship off a few points,

gave her the trysails, with the bonnets off. She bounded over the seas like a stag hound unleashed. I had been up all night, and now went below to snatch some brief repose before the toils of another day should begin.

Not for six months would Semmes again see the stormy Cape. Dipping down to the fortieth parallel, the *Alabama* bore east, ploughing through unceasing gales. On his birthday, September 27, facing a falling barometer and a confused, angry sea, Semmes soliloquized darkly to his journal,

> Today is the fifty-fourth anniversary of the birth of the unworthy writer. How time flies as we advance towards old age! May God in His mercy protect and preserve us and restore us, before another anniversary shall roll around, in peace to our families. How strange seems the drama of human life when we look back upon it; how transient, how unsatisfying!

Sails set, fires banked, propeller hoisted, the *Alabama* was swept along by the brave west winds. Through gloom and rain she sped past the two barren rocky islets, St. Peter and St. Paul, halfway between the Cape of Good Hope and Sunda Strait. He had hopes of picking off a whaler or two around these granite mountaintops that jut up from the great deeps of the sea, but evil weather drove him on. Amid these dreary wastes of waters the storm gods were holding high carnival—"The scene was sublime to look upon. The seas were literally running mountains high, the wind howling with more than usual fury, and a dense snowstorm was pelting us from the blackest and most angry looking of clouds."

On October 17, Semmes sighed, thinking of his home in Alabama. Depressingly, he calculated he was diametrically opposite, on the other side of the world, to his own hearth and fireside, yet he found "one comfort: I cannot very well get any further away from home. Each day's run from this point, whether east or west, must carry me nearer to it. When will the Almighty, in His providence, permit me to return to it? The merciful veil that hides from us the future keeps this secret likewise."

Twenty-four days from the Cape of Good Hope the raider crossed the Tropic of Capricorn and entered the hot belt. October was on the wane. Gentler winds, softer weather, greeted the Confederate stranger. Behind her lay 4,410 miles of waters. She had averaged 178 miles per day, or about seven and a half knots—not an impressive speed. Not in nineteen days had they sighted another ship. Butter and coffee were running low, and so was tobacco.

Now that they were in milder seas the ship was put to rights. Gun and cutlass drills began again. Drooping spirits revived. Brasswork was polished until it shone like mirrors in the tropical sunlight. Fresh paint gave the deck a touch of newness. Soon the *Alabama* sparkled like a diamond. And the ragamuffins taken on at Cape Town were fast shaped into man-of-war's men.

Sunday muster was resumed. As the *Alabama's* tars, hat in hand, doubled the capstan, the eyes of Semmes and Kell proclaimed eloquently their pride in the men's natty appearance.

Staunch and gallant was the *Alabama,* but she was no longer the fleet-footed greyhound of old. Hers was a hard life and she needed rest, but there would be none yet. Some things could be refurbished at sea. There were other things that could not. One was her speed. Her copper, worn thin now, was curling in rolls from her bottom. Now she must pocket her pride and make up what she had lost in speed by maneuver, strategy, and stealth.

Five weeks under canvas, and the *Alabama* stood in for the Sunda Strait, that sea pass between Java and Sumatra. By an English bark bound out of the Strait, Semmes was informed the United States cruiser *Wyoming,* another of the *Iroquois* class, was lying in the narrow channel, ready to dispute the *Alabama's* passage. Startling news, but if fight he must, so be it. "I have resolved to give her battle," Semmes assured his journal. "We will do our best and trust the rest to Providence." Apparently, the *Wyoming* was halting sails right and left in the Strait, resting by night off Krakatoa, an island athwart the waterway. Knowing the waters of the Strait and its uninhabited islands had international status, Semmes even planned to surprise the *Wyoming* in her very lair, if he could. But *Wyoming* or not, there would be no slackening of the business that brought the *Alabama* to these waters.

Moaned Lieutenant Sinclair naively, "We want to burn something. We are like the fire-laddies after a long and tedious interregnum, spoiling for a fire." And burn they did.

Off Java Head, near the mouth of the Strait, the *Alabama*

sighted first game of the new hunting season. "Sail ho!" and she darted off to show what she could do on this side of the world. Her quarry was the *Amanda*, of Boston, bound from Manila to Queenstown, Ireland, with hemp and sugar. The *Alabama's* gun brought up the welcome Stars and Stripes. Burning like tinder, the *Amanda* opened Semmes' Far Eastern cruise. At midnight, flames lighted up Sunda Strait, reddened Sumatra and distant Java Head, advertising far and near that Raphael Semmes, torch in hand, stood in the track of the China clippers.

On November 8, with a double lookout, guns ready, the *Alabama* entered the Strait itself. Coolly, she glided along the waterway to anchor overnight off Krakatoa where the *Wyoming* had held station until just two days before when she steamed off to coal at nearby Batavia. Daylight revealed a landscape as rare as an artist's dream. On the one hand lay Sumatra; on the other, Java. Their shores glistened in the sun like gorgeous tropical tapestries. "Like playhouse scenes the sleepy shores slid past" the wondering eyes of the *Alabama's* argonauts as she loafed along towards the eastern exit of the Strait.

Just where Sunda Strait debouched into the Java Sea, suddenly, dead ahead, out of a blinding rain squall, rose a tall, full clipper. Nor were the friendly guns of the *Wyoming* there to protect her. In ten minutes Semmes cut her short with a gun. She was the *Winged Racer*. Semmes pronounced her doom instantly. And what a windfall! Sugar, coffee! Just what the messes needed. And Manila tobacco! Jack's pipe was running low. He had been skimping for a fortnight.

Anchoring off North island, near his prize, Semmes' boarding crews despoiled the *Winged Racer* eagerly. It took hours. It was well beyond the mid-watch before the ship was given the torch. Malay bumboats, meanwhile, had appeared like magic out of the warm tropic night to trade green-goods and squalling chickens with the *Alabama's* stewards, not realizing the *Winged Racer* would soon be destroyed. The first leap of flame sent these vendors scurrying in terror, like the frightened chickens they were selling. As if by sorcery the intense darkness suddenly flowered with the brilliant red hue of the *Winged Racer's* sacrifice on the "altar of Confederate liberties."

Semmes had now lighted bonfires at both ends of the celebrated roadway. News would travel fast, and it was best to move on. With lights out, the *Alabama* steamed out into the Java Sea. Boasted Lieutenant Sinclair, "We shall accomplish more in the utter consternation and demoralization among the China fleet than in the actual destruction." This was true enough.

But where was the *Wyoming?* Somewhere, perhaps, in the mazes of Sunda Straits, on her way back to Krakatoa. Why, asked many, did not her lookout, peering through the night, sight the distant blaze of the *Winged Racer?* Why, instead of a single cruiser—herself a fair match for the *Alabama*—were not one or two more stationed in these narrow, well-beaten thoroughfares?

Daylight found the raider pointing north over Java Sea for Gaspar Strait. She had left the beautiful blue waters of the Indian Ocean, with its almost unfathomable depths. Now she was slicing through a sea of shallow, whitish-green water. Letting her steam die, the *Alabama* was taking it leisurely, under sail.

Presently the lookout's vigilance paid dividend. Yonder, five or more miles off the port bow, standing towards the *Alabama,* was one of the most beautiful ships Semmes had ever set eyes on. Under a press of sail, she was homebound for America. There was no need to guess her nationality. She bespoke it herself in words that seemed to call out across the waters, "I am an American." An anthem in pine and oak and billowing sail, Semmes confessed being a little premature in his eagerness to clutch so beautiful a prize. But clutching was not to prove so easy. Indeed, it was to prove something else at the same time.

The clipper was wary. Semmes approached cautiously lest he excite suspicion. At four miles he broke out United States colors. The clipper replied in kind. Firing a gun, Semmes hauled down his masquerade and threw to the breeze the Confederacy's handsome new naval ensign, "that splendid white flag, with its cross and stars," not unlike Britain's St. George's cross. Crowding on her studding sails, away darted the clipper like a frightened deer. She was making a run for it. It was to be a gallant one. The *Alabama's* men crowded the deck to watch the "Derby" on this far-off raceway. With a fresh breeze blowing the quarry was knifing through the water, steadily gaining. Yard by yard she pulled away from her pursuer. The *Alabama* had met her match at last!

Fuming, Semmes ordered steam added to sail. He would show her. It took twenty minutes to raise a head of steam, then "we gave the ship all steam, and trimmed sails to the best possible advantage." Still, the fugitive drew away. Something was wrong. Nor could Semmes understand it. For the first time the *Alabama* seemed dull. The touch of the lash brought no response, no surge of speed. Perhaps, she was out of trim by the bow, thought Semmes. He ordered his forward guns shifted aft. He even sent the ship's officers and men aft. It helped a little. Here he was, giving her sail and steam, an unbeatable combination up to now, yet the clipper was running away from him. Worried, he sent for Third Engineer O'Brien on watch in the engine room.

"What's the matter?" he asked. "Can't you give her more steam?"

"We're working our fires for all they're worth, captain," replied the sturdy Irishman. "The teakettle won't stand any more. If we attempt it, we'll scatter the pieces for the chase to pick up."

A cloud, a shadow, touched Semmes' face for a moment. He knew his corroded, weakened boilers were already pushed to the danger point.

"Very well, sir," he said resignedly, "Do the best you can."

Leaning silently against the rail, glasses in hand, his quarry about to beat him at his own game, he must have realized that the *Alabama* was nearing the end of her long tether. Standing near him were Kell, Sinclair, and O'Brien, no doubt thinking the same thoughts.

Yet, steam would have its triumph. The breeze began to die. The *Alabama* closed up. The elements were winning a race for the once swift-footed raider. Had the wind freshened Semmes would have lost this proud and plucky clipper. He knew it well enough.

Coming at last within long range, Semmes sprayed the clipper's quarterdeck with a rifle shot. Convinced, she luffed into the wind and lay to, awaiting her doom. Running up, the *Alabama* circled twice around her magnificent prize, the *Contest*, bound from Yokohama to New York with Japanese curios, teas and silks, the fastest clipper on the run. Regretfully, Semmes sentenced her to die. Never had he captured so beautiful a vessel. A revelation of symmetry, she was the handiwork of the master builder of clippers, Donald McKay. To Sinclair, it seemed a "sacrilege, almost a desecration" to destroy so perfect a specimen of the shipbuilding craft.

When Captain Lucas of the *Contest* came aboard Semmes put out his hand to congratulate him on a skillful, hard-run race. Lucas was cheerful in the face of his ill luck.

"You made a beautiful run, captain," said Semmes. "I thought for a while you'd get away from us."

"I would have," spoke up the skipper, "if the wind hadn't turned against me."

Semmes merely nodded. He knew Captain Lucas spoke the truth and it hurt. That night the clipper *Contest*, swathed in flames, set the waters of the Java Sea aglow for miles around.

The story of the capture of the *Contest* would be incomplete without the testimony of the clipper's Chief Officer, James D. Babcock of New Bedford. Babcock has been quoted Bible-like by Semmes' detractors. This account, prepared for the American Consul at Singapore, suggested, among other sins, cowardice on the part of Semmes and his officers:

> Manned by 23 officers and 130 men; crew much dissatisfied, no prize money, no liberty, and see no prospect of getting any. Discipline very slack, steamer dirty, rigging slovenly. Semmes sometimes punishes, but is afraid to push too hard. Men excited, officers do not report to captain, crew do things for which would be shot on board American man of war; for instance, saw one of crew strike a master's mate; crew insolent to petty officers; was told by at least two thirds of them they will desert on first opportunity. Crew all scum of Liverpool, French, Dutch, etc. *Alabama* is very weak; in any heavy sea her upper works leak badly; she has a list to port that she may fight her starboard guns. Fires kept banked; can get full steam in twenty minutes. Except at muster no uniforms worn. Crew rugged; keep a lookout at fore topgallant yard daytime; at night, two waist lookouts. Officers on duty have cutlass and revolver; never saw Semmes in uniform; puts on sword at muster. Have given up smallarm drill afraid to trust crew with arms. While on board saw drill only once, and that at pivot guns, very badly done; men ill disposed and were forced to it; lots of cursing.

On returning to the United States Babcock amplified his statement. Semmes and his officers were afraid to venture below decks lest they be waylaid and murdered. Morale and discipline on the *Alabama* was bankrupt. The ship seethed with mutiny.

What were the facts? Babcock was a prisoner for only four days. If, in those four days he interviewed eighty-odd (two-thirds, he said) of the *Alabama's* personnel, he must have had a busy time of it as well as complete run of the ship. But Semmes gave no prisoner free rein. On November 13, while Babcock was still aboard, Semmes arrested three of his crew for insubordination. He had ordered a quantity of cigars taken from the *Winged Racer* to be divided among the men. Two seamen and a quartermaster contemptuously threw their shares of the smokes overboard and urged others to do the same. It is probable they were unhappy over the allotments. As at Martinique, Semmes arrested them on the spot. Two days later he courtmartialed them. The seamen were freed, but the quartermaster was broken and consigned to the brig, in double irons, on bread and water, for thirty days. This hardly sounds as if Semmes was intimidated or fearful his crew would murder him. If mutiny it was, he broke it summarily. He was still the captain of his crew and his ship. His crew was unruly, but never out of hand.

Desertion was something else. It plagued him often. But his case was not unique. Seamen have deserted their ships down through the ages. The official war records of the United States Navy are dotted with desertion reports. The *Alabama's* crew were no exceptions to this unhappy rule. But when the *Alabama's* crucial moment came these men, unruly, or not, stood to their guns until the deck sank beneath them.

Having burned the *Contest* near Gaspar Strait, Semmes veered southeastward across the Java Sea for Karimata Strait. His purpose was to shake off the *Wyoming* by playing the old hare-and-hound trick of doubling on her. He knew she would pick up his bonfire trail in the Sunda Strait and follow him to the Gaspar Strait where the *Contest* met her fate. Semmes plotted Commander McDougal's probable movements to a nicety. Arriving at the charred wreckage of the *Contest*, McDougal concluded that the *Alabama* had continued north through the Strait into the China Sea to play havoc with the clippers coming down from Canton and Shanghai. So the *Wyoming* rushed towards these ports. Very calmly, Semmes did just the opposite. In doubling, the *Alabama* passed within twenty-five miles of the speeding *Wyoming*.

Wafted over calm, idyllic seas, the *Alabama* cruised on through Karimata Strait, with Borneo gleaming off the starboard. Gingerly, she picked her way past the coral reefs that fringed the romantic, iridescent archipelagoes of the Strait. Luck still favored him. The monsoon came sweeping out of the northwest. Yet he negotiated Karimata Strait in five days, whereas other vessels often took thirty making the passage. A profusion of British and Dutch sails went by, but no American. "Where is the Yankee," asked Semmes, "that he is permitting all this rich harvest in the East to pass away from him?"

Skirting Sarawak, he was tempted to veer in and visit his old friend, Sir James Brooke, the "White Rajah," an Englishman to whom the natives had taken a fancy and clothed with imperial power. But social amenities must wait. He had other work to do. With Singapore as his objective, he decided first to stretch across the China Sea to the coast of Cochin China, straddle the track of ships coming down from Canton and Shanghai and then work his way down to the Strait of Malacca where Singapore lay. Finding this trade route bare of American vessels, he shaped his course for the solitary islet of Pulo Condore, off the Cochin China coast, to rest and repair before venturing down to Singapore.

On December 2, the *Alabama* picked up Condore's sea-mark, the White Rock, and anchored overnight in the lee of the island. Next morning she ran into the snug and cozy harbor, as smooth as a millpond. Semmes had expected to find this lonely speck of coral and rock garrisoned by a handful of nomad Malay pirates, who infested the China seas. With a broadside or two he planned to blast out the Malays, raise the Confederate flag and proclaim it Confederate territory. The Southern Republic would thus acquire a naval harbor off the coast of Asia from which she could menace American trading in Far Eastern waters.

To his surprise, he found that France had already—two years before—annexed Pulo Condore. In the harbor lay a pint-sized gunboat, wearing French colors, keeping watch and ward. Nor was it long before a personable French ensign, Monsieur Bizot, who doubled as captain of the gunboat and ruler of the island, came aboard to offer the wayfarers such hospitality as Pulo Condore afforded. Inviting the young officer to share a bottle of Rheims champagne, the party was soon jolly enough. Semmes knew the way to French hearts. Belligerent rights and neutrality restrictions were not even mentioned.

It was the *Alabama*'s first haven since leaving the Cape of Good Hope. Here she could rest and relax. From stem to stern she cried out for swarms of mechanics to repair, refit, and resuscitate an ailing, weary ship. And new boilers to replace those that threatened to explode with every head of steam. Only in a drydock could all these things be done, but even so, much could be done here.

At Pulo Condore, Semmes secured himself against intrusion. He took the immediate precaution of attaching springs to his cable by which he could, in a few minutes, present his broadside to the narrow mouth of the harbor and rake the *Wyoming* fore and aft, if she attempted to slide through and get alongside. The *Wyoming*, in fact, must have passed within sight of the wily raider's covert—passed it, indeed, while Semmes was watching the monkey population bury one of their patriarchs on the nearby beach.

To his host, Semmes complained pleasantly, "Monsieur, you have spoiled a pet project of mine. France has stolen a march on me."

"How so?" inquired the officer.

Facetiously, Semmes explained, "I had hoped to find Condore unoccupied. A few Malays, perhaps. I intended to seize it, raise my flag and play Rajah for a few weeks, like my friend Rajah Brooke over in Sarawak."

The young gentleman laughed merrily. "But, Monsieur le Capitaine, you carry more cannon than I, and you *will* be Rajah during your stay."

"Never, never, monsieur," rejoined Semmes, well aware the tiny French man-of-war of less than one hundred tons, carried one small carronade and a crew of twenty.

At least one of Semmes' officers, Lieutenant Sinclair, was thinking along the same lines, "Here is a chance for conquest seldom met with. We can carry the 'fleet' and garrison by storm without the loss of a man."

At Pulo Condore, the *Alabama* was given the best going-over since leaving the Mersey. Masts were scraped, rigging tarred and—best of all—copper patched below the waterline where it was stripping off. Ingeniously, Lieutenant Kell and the ship's carpenter contrived a hydraulic caisson that, fastened to the bottom, enabled the carpenters to work on the hull below the surface of the water.

On December 15 Semmes took leave of his courteous host and weighed anchor. That night, heading for Singapore, melancholy thoughts crept into his journal:

> Well, we are on the seas once more, with our head turned westward, or homeward. Shall we ever reach that dear home, which we left nearly three years ago, and which we have yearned after so frequently since? Will it be battle, or shipwreck, or both, or neither? And when we reach the North Atlantic, will it still be war, or peace? An all-wise Providence has kindly hidden the answer behind the curtain of fate.

The Confederacy's back by this time was to the wall and he knew it. The anaconda's folds were tightening around his beloved South. Northern armies were cutting the heart out of her. It sickened his very soul to think of it.

"And now for Singapore, God willing!" he exclaimed to his journal on December 19. Sliding down the China Sea, he crossed the Gulf of Siam to find the American flag a stranger on the waters. Rounding into the Strait of Malacca, three days before Christmas 1863, the *Alabama* steamed into the roadstead of Brittain's famed entrepôt in the Far East and nuzzled up to the P&O dock, as if seeking a shoulder on which to lean her tired hull. Once again, a conqueror's welcome greeted the Confederate standard bearer.

But it was not the hospitality, nor the courtesies, nor the sumptuous entertainment, nor the adoration of the small Confederate colony, that gave Semmes' heart its much-needed lift. It was the spectacle that greeted his eyes in the Singapore roadstead. There, rotting at their anchors, caged in this neutral harbor, lay twenty-two Northern ships—dismantled and laid up! Balm and recompense for many days and nights of anxiety and peril was the forest of masts of this vast flotilla of idle ships. Semmes' first bonfire in the Sunda Strait had struck terror to American shipping throughout the East Indies. Like chickens before the swoop of a hawk they had thrown on sail and rushed for refuge—to Singapore, Bangkok, Canton, Shanghai, Manila, Yokohama. At this crossroads of the Far East Northern commerce was stagnant, dead, just as if Semmes had destroyed every Northern ship on this side of the globe. It unlocked the mystery of the disappearance of American trade in the China Sea and adjacent waters.

The Singapore *Times* had already commented pungently on the sight of so many American merchantmen cooped in the harbor, afraid to stir: "It is a picture quite unique in its nature; for the nation to which these seventeen [sic] ships belong has a navy second only to that of Great Britain, and the enemy with which she has to cope, is but a schism from herself, possessed of no port that is not blockaded, and owning no more than five or six vessels on the high seas."

Singapore saw Semmes at the supreme moment of his destiny as a commerce raider. Yet, here at his very zenith, Semmes decided to turn homewards—or rather towards Europe—lest the *Alabama* go to pieces before he got there. What had he to gain further in the Far East? The panic was complete. Freights for American ships simply did not exist. Insurance was denied them and shippers refused to take a chance. He knew, of course, that after he had gone, the birds would spread their wings for flight again, but not until the terror of the seas was far, far away.

He made his decision alone, confiding it first to his journal: "I will try my luck around the Cape of Good Hope once more; then to the coast of Brazil; and thence, perhaps to Barbados for coal; and thence . . . ?" He left it a question mark. Old Beeswax himself was showing the wear and tear of months of watching, thinking and anxiety. His eyes that once flashed with fiery zeal were growing misty. A sad sort of weariness had come over him. He probably realized there was only one way out for the *Alabama*, if she survived the long journey back. It was a dismal appraisal. Her boilers were almost burned out. The fire in her furnaces, "like that

of the fire-worshipping Persians," was seldom permitted to die out
—only a rare hour or two for the engineer to clink his bars and
scrape off the destructive salt incrustations that were eating up his
boilers. The copper patchings on her hull were again peeling off.
Her seams were spreading. She was loose at every joint. Was there
no port where a jaded, tired ship of the Confederacy could go for
rest and recuperation? Was the *Alabama*, homeless like the *Sumter*, to be abandoned, denied the chance to make a grand, magnificent exit?

⚓

⚓

26 *Through the Lonely Sea*

On Christmas Eve, 1863, after a forty-eight hour stay, the *Alabama*
cast off from the Singapore dockside to wind and twist through
the vast, silent fleet of clippers she had immobilized. Kell's "bad
boys" were safely aboard; Paymaster Galt had filled the bunkers
and storerooms through the potency of gold sovereigns from the
strongchest. Again, came the goodbyes of admiring crowds, the
flutterings of ladies' handkerchiefs. Hauling out into the Strait of
Malacca, the *Alabama* turned wearily homewards—westward. Or
where was her home?

Yet, she still had work to do. Semmes' torch still must flare.
Four bells—dinner time and three hours out of Singapore—the
lookout cried down "Sail ho!" Semmes quickly hove the stranger
to with a shot. Her English ensign belied her obviously American
build. Across her stern, newly lettered in gold, was her name,
Martaban, of Maulmain. She was bound from India to Singapore,
laden with rice.

Boarding Officer Fullam, himself an Englishman, reported to

Semmes the ship was duly registered as English, yet her crew was mostly American, her mates long, slab-sided Down Easters as was her skipper, Captain Samuel Pike of Maine. A truculent fellow, he flatly refused to come aboard the *Alabama* at Fullam's request, falling back on his rights as an "English subject." Pike admitted the *Martaban* was the former *Texan Star* of Boston, transferred to British registry only ten days before. Unable to reconcile all the facts and appearances, Fullam tried to be diplomatic. The clipper-built vessel, the rawboned skipper who talked through his nose, and the two mates of the same model and rig, were anything except English.

Semmes smelled a rat. Obviously, he could not compel an "English" master to leave his ship. There was no other recourse than to assume the role of boarding officer. It was the only time he ever boarded a prize.

"All right," he agreed, "if the mountain won't come to Mohammed; Mohammed must go to the mountain."

Manning his gig and taking Lieutenant Kell with him, Semmes was soon presiding over the Confederate States Admiralty Court in the cabin of the *Martaban*.

I could but admire the beautiful, 'bran new,' English flag, as I pulled aboard," wrote Semmes, "but every line of the ship was American. In the person of the master, the long, lean, angular-featured, hide-bound, weather-tanned Yankee skipper stood before me. Puritan, May-Flower, Plymouth Rock, were all written upon his well-known features. No amount of English customhouse paper, or sealing wax, could, by any possibility, convert him into that rotund, florid, jocund Briton who personates the English shipmaster. His speech was even more national than his person. When he opened his mouth, a mere novice would have sworn that he was from the State of Maine—there, or thereabouts. When he told me that I 'hadn't-ought-to' burn his ship, he pronounced the shibboleth which condemned her to the flames.

"Judge" Semmes gave the *Martaban* short shrift though not without a stormy scene. There was no serious flaw apparent in her papers. John Bull had every right in the world to buy an American vessel and hoist his flag over her. But there was no bill of sale—the necessary *prima facie* evidence—among the *Martaban*'s papers.

Semmes' cross-examination of Pike was keen and incisive like a surgeon's scalpel. Why, he asked, if the ship was transferred to a British owner, had the ship kept her Northern skipper and mates? Probing deeper into the legality of the transfer, Semmes suspected the papers were forged. Examining the crew list, he became certain of it. The muster-roll was a mute and powerful witness, written throughout, signatures and all, in the same hand—the signatures being as like as two peas in a pod. Added to that, the freshly painted, assumed name, *Martaban*, on her stern was scarcely dry.

The evidence was in. For some seconds Semmes was silent. He gave his mustache a couple of twirls. Completely in character, he suddenly turned to Pike with a cold stare, "I'm going to burn your ship."

The Maine-man flared. Springing from his chair, he thrust his long, bony finger up the companion-way to the English flag flying from his peak and shouted, "You dare not do it, sir; that flag won't stand it!"

Semmes' face never changed. Utterly composed, he riposted, "Keep cool, captain. The weather is warm, and as for the flag, I shall not ask it whether it will stand for it or not. The flag that ought to be at your peak, will have to stand it, though."

In half an hour the *Texan Star*, alias the *Martaban*, was robed in fire. Her beautiful new English ensign was marked with the day, the latitude and longitude of the capture and stowed away by the old signal quartermaster in his bag bulging with Northern flags.

Semmes took a long chance with the *Texan Star*. Yet, Prize Master Fullam had found among the ship's papers a copy of a letter from Captain Pike to the owners in which he gloated at having "taken such precautions as would deceive Semmes and all the Confederates." The ship's cargo was *bona fide* English property all right. But the owners of it had conspired to perpetrate a fraud by shipping it on an American vessel flying false colors. That condemned it along with the ship.

At 7:30 that night the Court met again in Semmes' cabin. Captain Pike was the chief witness, now under oath. Apparently, Semmes was apprehensive. He wanted to extract the truth from Pike's own lips.

"Now, captain," he said, "when you and I had that little conversation in your cabin, you had hopes of saving your ship, and, moreover, what you said to me was not under oath. You were, perhaps, only practising a pardonable *ruse de guerre*. But now the case is altered. Your ship being destroyed, you have no longer any possible interest in misstating the truth. You are, besides, under oath. Be frank; was, or was not, the transfer of your ship a *bona fide* transaction?"

"I will be frank with you, Captain Semmes," said Pike after a moment's reflection. "It was not a *bona fide* transaction. I was alarmed when I heard of your arrival in the East Indies, and I resorted to a sham sale in hopes of saving my ship."

The court adjourned. The case of the *Martaban-Texan Star* was closed.

On Christmas Day, 1863, the *Alabama* paused at the village of Malacca where Semmes paroled and landed his prisoners taken from the *Texan Star*. The day was hot, depressing, "each rather gloomily wrapped in his own thoughts," said Sinclair. Yet, as custom demanded, the main brace was spliced and all hands had a pull at "Chinese ardent."

Nor would the ladies of the English garrison at Malacca forget the Confederate man of fire. They "smiled their sweetest smiles— and no one knows how sweet these can be, better than the sailor who had been a long time upon salt water, looking upon nothing but whiskers and mustachios. They were very pressing."

Next morning, off the western exit of the Strait of Malacca, the lifting mists revealed two "monster ships" that looked "sort o' Yankee." Anchored, in the waterway, they were waiting for a fair wind to whisk them out onto the Bay of Bengal.

Ambling up to her helpless captives, the *Alabama* unfolded her bright, new naval ensign, which, incidentally, the master-at-arms had cut out, pieced and sewed together since reaching the Far East and learning of the change prescribed by the Confederate Congress. The *Sonora* and the *Highlander*, both New Englanders, were quickly added to the roster of her conquests. Safely moored at Singapore, they had been victimized by misinformation. Deceived by reports that the *Alabama* was prowling up into the China Sea, they had innocently ventured out of their refuge, in ballast, for Burma, to take on cargoes of rice.

The *Sonora*'s skipper was a perky, cheerful soul. Coming aboard with his papers, he strode up to Semmes on the quarterdeck, remarking good-humoredly as he offered his hand, "Well, Captain Semmes, I have been expecting for the last three years to fall in with you. Here I am at last."

Semmes smiled broadly. "Well, captain, I'm glad you found me after so long a search."

"Search!" exclaimed the Down Easter. "It is such a search as the Devil may be supposed to make after holy water. The fact is, I have had constant visions of the *Alabama*, by night and by day. She has been chasing me in my sleep, and riding me like a nightmare, and now that it is all over, I feel quite relieved."

A gritty pair, those two Yankee skippers, fine examples of the fearless buoyant spirit in any adversity of the American sailor. Semmes' admiration was outspoken. When they asked permission to provision their own small boats and make for Singapore, four hundred miles distant, he consented at once.

Sinclair pictured the scene appealingly:

> Bidding us goodbye, and with a hearty handshake, they shoved off in the light air under oars. As the boats strung out in line, the crew opened with a familiar seasong. The refrain borne over the still waters, intermingled with the dip of the oars dying away gradually in the distance, emphasized the romance of the situation. We could but admire their never-say-die pluck, and you may be sure our sailor sympathies were with them.

New Year's Day, 1864, greeted the raider crawling across the Bay of Bengal towards India. Despondency gnawed at Semmes' heart. "Alas!" he brooded to his journal. "Another year of war and toil and privation has passed over me, leaving its traces behind." The strain of commerce raiding was telling on him visibly. He was more taciturn than ever, and failing physically—like his ship. His officers probably saw it but from Lieutenant Sinclair comes the only picture of Semmes as he entered the twilight zone:

> On the quarter deck is the leader of us all, Captain Semmes—the man we have followed now for many weary months. Where he has directed we have gone confidently. He has carried us so far without

a disaster; and we would trust him to the utmost, and follow still. He is pacing the deck, his brow contracted, pulling, as is his wont, at his gray moustache. Back and forth he strides, not a word to anyone. He is in deep communion with his own thoughts. What can be so occupying him that he is oblivious to surroundings? Perhaps hatching some deep scheme for future punishment of his enemy. Maybe his thoughts are reverting to our dear land in the last throes of a sinking cause; for he is only human like ourselves and under a haughty bearing carries a touch of sympathy for sorrow, and love for home. He may be in a day-dream now, bringing dear ones close to himself in fancy. Be his thoughts what they may, the silent man before you will never seek your sympathy for himself.

It was well for Sinclair and his shipmates they could not read Semmes' communion with his journal: the slow sinking of his heart as his once-sturdy ship retraced her dejected steps homewards.

Rounding Ceylon, the *Alabama* moved up the Malabar coast where Semmes snatched and burned the *Emma Jane* of Bath, Maine. The freighter was hopping from port to port, searching in vain for a cargo, as were scores of her American consorts. Sailing on, the *Alabama* anchored at Anjenga to find this Indian port stacked with idle Northern bottoms while their skippers lounged about the bazaars, consigning to the ocean deeps this Confederate dragon that had invaded the trading dovecots of the Far East. They little dreamed how soon their yearnings would be gratified.

Under canvas, pushed by northeast trades, the *Alabama* then turned about and began her long southwestwards jaunt across the Arabian Sea for Cape Town. A blessed respite it was for Semmes and his men. Inhaling the soft breezes, flagging spirits revived, depleted energies perked up. The old ocean was a sailor's paradise now. Once again the nature-lover asserted itself as Semmes eloquently painted the glories of the heavens scintillating with stars, the deep blue of the sea that seemed redolent with Araby's spices and with visions of pearly grottoes.

For twelve successive days we did not have occasion to lower a studding sail, day or night! We have had a constant series of clear skies and gentle breezes. The nights were serene and transparent, and the sunsets magnificent beyond description. The tradewind is, par excellence, the wind of beautiful sunsets. Bright, gauzy clouds, float along lazily before it, and sometime the most charming cumuli are piled up on the western horizon while the sun is going down. Stately cathedrals, with their domes and spires complete, may be traced by the eye of fancy, and the most gorgeous of golden, violet, orange, purple, green, and other hues, light up now a colonnade, now a dome and now a spire of the aerial edifice. And then came on the twilight, with its gray and purple blended, and with the twilight, the sounds of merriment on board the *Alabama*—for we had found a successor for Michael Mahoney, the Irish fiddler . . .

Steadily, the trades bore the *Alabama* on to her fate, whatever it was. Jack was a good boy now and as full of fun as ever. The ship's glee club was in full tide of song again. Missed was Michael Mahoney, who had deserted at Cape Town, but the last batch of recruits had brought a fiddler who could really "scratch" the violin. Letting down his dignity, Semmes of evenings seated himself on the bridge, lit a fragrant manila and smoked away the hours listening to the old songs, winding up at eight bells, as always, with "Bonny Blue Flag" and "Dixie." Little did these light-hearted fellows consider the future.

St. Valentine's Day found the *Alabama* anchored at Johanna, chief island of the Comorro Group at the head of Mozambique Channel. Here she spent a week taking on water, fresh meat and vegetables. Coffee and sweet drinks flowed in the local bazaars and cafes, but not a drop of rum or whiskey. Mohammed had reserved these luxuries for the afterlife, as Jack discovered to his disgust. It led Semmes to spin off a bit of humor at Jack's plight:

> I gave my sailors a run on shore, but this sort of liberty was awful hard work for Jack. There was no such thing as a glass of grog to be found in the whole town and as for a fiddle and Sal for a partner—all of which would have been a matter of course in civilized countries—there were no such luxuries to be thought of. They found it a difficult matter to get through with the day and all were down at the beach long before sunset—the hour appointed for their coming off—waiting for the approach of the welcome boat. I told Kell to let them go on shore as often as they pleased, but no one made a second application.

Sliding down Mozambique Channel, between Madagascar and Africa, the *Alabama* cruised on toward Cape Town. On the way Semmes recorded an act of heroism that augured well for the courage of his "vagabonds" when came the trial by fire of the *Alabama* herself.

In a good topgallant breeze the *Alabama* was skipping through a frisky sea when the classic cry of centuries rang out, "Man overboard!" A convalescent Jack sunning on deck, had somehow fallen over the rail to leeward. Farther and farther astern, the invalid was battling for life. Without hesitation, Seaman Michael Mars threw a grating into the water, then mounted the rail to follow it.

Lieutenant Kell dashed on deck at once. Seeing Mars about to dive overboard, Kell ordered him not to try it in such rough water. The lifeboat was already being lowered. One of the crew was enough to lose, if any. Mars replied, "Keep cool, Mr. Kell! I'll save him" and in he dived. Pushing the grating ahead of him, he swam rapidly to his almost exhausted shipmate and shoved the grating under him to await the lifeboat coming up with powerful sweeps. More dead than alive, the invalid was hauled in. Wild cheers greeted Mars' act of heroism.

Order restored, Semmes mustered the ship's company on the quarterdeck. Mounting the horseblock, he paid a ten minute tribute to the gallantry of Michael Mars, Ordinary Seaman—"an indorsement any man might be proud to receive from his commander," added Lieutenant Sinclair. With a hitch of his trousers, blushing like a school girl, the bearded, embarrassed Mars observed, "The captain has made a bloody fuss over nothing."

Nearing the stormy Cape Semmes' spirits again ran low. Day and night gales buffeted the *Alabama*. From sweltering heat she had passed into cooler temperatures.

"My ship is weary," confessed Semmes to his journal, "as well as her commander, and will need a general overhauling by the time I can get her into a dock." Yet, facing a nameless future, his indomitable spirit flashed out, "If my poor services shall be deemed of any importance in harassing and weakening the enemy, and thus contributing to the independence of my beloved South, I shall be amply rewarded."

In a violent equinoctial gale the *Alabama* made Table Bay and let go both anchors. Six months less a day had elapsed since she embarked on her foray to the Orient. The African coast was clear now of enemy cruisers. The *Vanderbilt* had long since vanished. "That huge old coal box," said Semmes, "was now probably doing a more profitable business, by picking up blockade-runners on the American coast. This operation paid—the captain might grow rich upon it. Chasing the *Alabama* did not."

Cape Town's welcome was as hearty as before, but Semmes was not to tarry. He stayed just long enough, indeed, to fight another diplomatic battle. The unfortunate *Tuscaloosa* was again entangled in a web spun by the vigilant American Consul. She had returned to Cape Town in Semmes' absence. Egged on by "Mr. Seward's gadfly" the British had seized her as an uncondemned prize, brought into their waters in violation of the Queen's orders of neutrality. Worse still, they had decided to return her to her owners in Philadelphia. To Governor Wodehouse, Semmes now indited his last official protest.

Basing his chief argument on the Governor's original decision, that one nation cannot inquire into the antecedents of another nation's warships, Semmes stayed the *Tuscaloosa*'s sentence. It was his last legal triumph. In time, London ordered the *Tuscaloosa* restored "to some person who may have authority from Captain Semmes, of the *Alabama*, or from the Government of the Confederate States, to receive her." In the meantime the would-be commerce destroyer basked in the sun at Simon's Bay. She remained there until after the Confederacy fell, when she sailed back to Philadelphia to be greeted by ringing church bells and an outpouring of citizenry.

Three days only did Semmes pause at Cape Town. Not once did he set foot ashore. Hurriedly, he coaled and replenished his larders. While there, a bright gleam shot through the gathering gloom. The cruiser's strongbox was liberally replenished with gold sovereigns, proceeds of the sale of the *Tuscaloosa*'s wool, part of the deal Semmes had arranged with the speculators at Angra Pequena. Bragged Sinclair, "The *Alabama* is now a wealthy as well as a bold buccaneer."

On March 25 the *Alabama* hoisted anchor and steamed out of

the roadstead for journey's end. Semmes really doubted the ability of his ship to keep going until he reached England. "My intention now was, to make the best of my way to England or France." Late Northern newspapers at Cape Town were depressing. Signs of the Confederacy's dissolution were abundant. Were her sacrifices, her sufferings, her glories to come to naught? So it seemed. Her fortunes were fading inexorably. There would be no Southern Republic such as he had dreamed of. He must have realized that the cruise of the *Alabama*, her spectacular destruction of Northern commerce across three quarters of the globe, was to add up to a fine, futile gesture, though fate still veiled her destiny as well as his own. Yet, he clung desperately to hope, "No power on earth can subjugate the Southern States, although some of them, as Maryland and Kentucky, have been guilty of the pusillanimity of making war with the Yankees on their sisters."

Four weeks under canvas brought the *Alabama* to St. Helena where Semmes lingered, hoping to pick off a prize, musing over the fate of the "Great Captive" once immured on this barren rock. Feelingly, he complained of the same vicissitudes of climate that had harassed Napoleon. A vast fleet of merchant ships was passing, and all the vessels were under European flags. He noted with satisfaction this was his handiwork.

Yet Semmes was still the Confederate Captain, terror of the seas to the North, hero of the *Alabama* to the South. His torch still flickered. Off the coast of Brazil he struck again. It was an all-night stern chase, and he stayed on deck to watch it. Like an old rheumatic hound the *Alabama* still had a few good leaps left, but not until steam came to the rescue could she get near enough to round up her prize with a shot. Dawn was coming up over the eastern edge of the sea. "It was the old spectacle," commented Semmes, "of the panting, breathless fawn and the inexorable stag hound." His prize was the sizable American bark, *Rockingham*, bound from Peru to Cork with a cargo of guano. She was condemned at once, as Sinclair put it, "by our prize court of one member." Before ordering her fired, Semmes turned to his First Lieutenant, "Mr. Kell, take off the crew and give your men a little target practice. Up to this time we have carried out the instructions of the Department, destroying the enemy's commerce and driving it from every sea we have visited while avoiding their cruisers. Should we now fall in with a cruiser not too heavy for us, we will give her battle."

It was the first target shooting in months. The gun crews blithely blazed away at the *Rockingham* for two hours. Kell then inspected the damage. The *Alabama*'s gunnery had wrought fine execution. The marksmanship was excellent. The prize's hull was riddled, her cabin and upper works knocked to splinters. But there was a flaw in the picture. Many shells had failed to explode. Those that did were sluggish, giving off no sharp, quick, vigorous reports as in the *Hatteras* fight. Yet, Kell counted fifteen holes where a hundred pound shell had exploded. He was later to say it "justifies me in asserting that had the one hundred pound shell which we placed in the sternpost of the *Kearsarge* exploded, it would have changed the result of the fight." Afterwards every fuse and cap in the magazine was examined. Those that looked defective were thrown overboard, but this was not the answer. It was obvious the powder itself had lost its vigor.

"It is curious," reflected Sinclair, "to compare the fine execution in this target practice with the woeful failure in the *Kearsarge* engagement, which closely followed it."

On April 27, 1864, while still below the Equator, Raphael Semmes captured his last prize, the clipper *Tycoon* bound round the Horn for the Golden Gate. Her obsequies were brief. She was the *Alabama*'s fifty-fourth bonfire, her sixty-ninth prize. Two hundred and ninety-five vessels of every flag afloat had she overhauled on her sweep across the oceans. Sinclair tagged the burning "the last act of retaliation on the part of the *Alabama* for the invasion of the South."

Through thunder, lightning, and rain the *Alabama* pressed on, up through the Atlantic Narrows, over waters she had made a fiery graveyard on her sweep down the Atlantic. On May 2, 1864, she re-crossed the Equator. How nicely fate timed things for her! That same day the Army of the Potomac, under Grant, crossed the Rapidan in Virginia on its deadly final thrust at Richmond. It would take a year, but it would crush the last breath out of the prostrate South.

Gazing back to this same day, Semmes was to sigh:

The poor old *Alabama* was not now what she had been then. She was like the wearied fox hound, limping back after a long chase, footsore, and longing for quiet and repose. Her commander, like herself, was wellnigh worn down. Vigils by night and day, the storm and the drenching rain, the frequent and rapid change of climate, now freezing, now melting or broiling, and the constant excitement of the chase and capture, had laid, in the three years of war he had been afloat, a load of a dozen years on his shoulders.

The shadows of a sorrowful future, too, began to rest upon his spirit. The last batch of newspapers captured were full of disasters. Might it not be, that, after all our trials and sacrifices, the cause for which we were struggling would be lost? The thought was hard to bear.

Boldly, up the middle of the Atlantic, strode the *Alabama*. Nothing but blue sky above and the blue dreary waste of water below. She wore no foreign flag now, no disguise. If a Federal cruiser came along, she would hoist her own beautiful ensign and fight it out then and there, and may God save the right! If down she went, she would go with a resounding Amen! down, down to the bottom where she had sent so many others.

On past the Azores where Semmes had christened her, she moved straight for the English Channel. Off the Lizard, at England's tip, she picked up a Channel pilot. Cold and fever racked her commander. With a southwester brewing, he had spent an anxious night on the bridge. He could hardly stand another. Seeking his cabin, he turned for moments to his journal to let go his pent up feelings, "Wretched, wretched English Channel! I pity the poor mariner who frequents you in wintertime, with awful gales and long, long nights." One final duty before his eyes closed. How often had he performed this same sacred duty! Dropping to his knees he poured out his heart in thanks to God.

At thirty minutes past noon, June 11, 1864, the *Alabama* limped into the harbor of Cherbourg, France. "And thus," said Semmes, "thanks to an all-wise Providence, we have brought our cruise of the *Alabama* to a successful termination."

Seventy-five thousand miles of cruising lay behind her. She had reached her last port. The book was closed on her record of destruction. It was to stand unbeaten even unto this day.

⚓

⚓

27 *Come Out and Fight!*

The *Alabama*'s arrival at Cherbourg created a sensation overnight. The news was flashed far and fast. The telegraph line out of the port fairly shivered with messages to every capital in Europe.

Nobody in Europe had known where Semmes was for more than four months. His last two captures in the Atlantic on the way north were ashes and his thirty-seven prisoners still aboard the *Alabama*. Nor had tidings of his latest visit to Cape Town yet reached the continent. Mystery had shrouded the *Alabama* until she dramatically appeared, ghostlike, out of the Channel mist off the Cherbourg breakwater. All at once the French city was agog, and the citizenry clattered to the waterfront to get a glimpse of the dread raider, now lounging off the naval dock.

Spruced up by a good night's rest, elegantly uniformed, his colorful gig touching off a furore in the harbor, Semmes went ashore to present his compliments to the Port Admiral, but, more importantly, to ask permission to land his prisoners and to run his ship into drydock for much-needed repairs. The French dignitary received Semmes with awed courtesy. The captain of the *Alabama* was a memorable figure in Gallic naval circles. His audacious sweep of the seas had caught the imagination of this glory-loving people. Disembarking his captives presented no neutral obstacle, but repairing and docking a belligerent warship, particularly the worn-out, homeless *Alabama*, posed delicate diplomatic complications that must be unraveled at the summit. Only Emperor Napoleon III could grant such a touchy boon, and that genial gentleman, whose pointed and twirled mustachios rivalled Semmes', was vacationing at Biarritz and not expected at Paris for perhaps a week. The port official regretted Semmes had not entered a harbor equipped with commercial docks. Cherbourg was exclusively a French naval station. However, in the temporary absence of His Majesty, the twenty-four hour rule would be relaxed. The Confederate ship could linger until the Emperor returned to Paris and issued his royal yes or no.

It was Semmes' intention, had his ship promptly been drydocked, to give his officers and crew a two-months' leave of absence while the *Alabama* was being refurbished. In twenty-four hours, he declared, they would have been dispersed, adding, "the combat, therefore, which ensued, may be said to be due to the Emperor's accidental absence from Paris."

Whether Semmes knew Cherbourg was provided only with government docks was never clarified. Well-intentioned biographers have insisted Semmes knew the port's military status, that he could have selected one of a dozen Channel havens, but that he deliberately chose Cherbourg. He was not pursued into Cherbourg, so to what purpose, it might be asked?

At the moment Louis Napoleon was winking at the construction of two ironclad rams for the Confederacy to be used crushing Lincoln's blockade of Southern ports. Semmes, unquestionably, knew the Emperor was openly friendly to the South and intriguing against the North. It was common knowledge he had angled to persuade England to join France in a plot for intervention in the American contest on the side of the South. Knowing definitely Cherbourg offered drydock facilities, Semmes no doubt trusted to his persuasive pen, the Emperor's overweening Southern leanings, and his unfailing luck for the rest.

Punctilious as always, he promptly announced his arrival by telegraph to Confederate Commissioner John Slidell at Paris and to Flag Officer Samuel Barron, ranking Southern naval official in Europe, who was then visiting the French capital.

Nor was Edouard Llais, American Vice Consul at Cherbourg, slothful in assuming his role in the drama fast unfolding. Hardly had the *Alabama* appeared in the roads before he flashed the news to William Dayton, American Minister at Paris. That diplomat—who, incidentally, was soon to die suddenly and embarrassingly in the home of a French lady, a zealous Confederate partisan —promptly importuned Foreign Minister de Lhuys to invoke the twenty-four hour rule against the "rebel corsair"—kick her out, or bottle her up. To seal the doom of the Southern wayfarer, Dayton hastily alerted Captain John Ancrum Winslow whose ship, the *Kearsarge*, was anchored in the Scheldt River, off Flushing, Holland.

Winslow needed no urging. He had for a year followed rumors of Semmes' whereabouts, without success. With the raider plying her trade on far off waters, he had quested in European waters. Firing a gun to recall his men on shore, the chunky, round-cheeked, stubby-whiskered captain mustered his ship's company and broke the welcome news, "Men, I congratulate you in saying that the *Alabama* has arrived at Cherbourg, and the *Kearsarge*, having a good name in France and England, is to have her cruising ground off that port." Within two hours the *Kearsarge* was speeding out of the Scheldt into the North Sea and heading for Cherbourg.

Until now the *Kearsarge* had played an inconspicuous role in the war on the seas. Her search for will-o'-the-wisp Confederate raiders off the coast of Europe had brought no special lustre. She had blockaded the Confederate *Florida* at Brest only to lose her. The *Georgia*, too, had given her the slip. Winslow himself, at this historic juncture, was just another captain whose war service was nothing to write home about. Farragut, Porter, Dahlgren, Du Pont, and Worden, were getting the big naval play-up. Winslow's name meant little outside of navy circles. Actually, he was under the ban of Secretary Welles. Command of the *Kearsarge* was a semi-exile imposed on him by the vindictive, crotchety chief of Lincoln's navy.

Blunt, capable, North Carolina-born, Winslow was a stocky seadog who said what he thought. Disgusted by General Pope's disastrous defeat at Second Manassas, Winslow had (according to a Baltimore newspaper) rubbed salt on the Federal wound by blurting out, "I'm glad of it. I wish they would bag Old Abe." To say the least, it was hardly a tactful commentary on his Commander-in-Chief, though many a Northerner indulged in similar sharp digs. Viewing Winslow's words as semi-treasonable, Welles disciplined the officer by ordering him abroad. Apparently, Winslow was safely parked for the duration where he could hardly speak out of turn again.

Meanwhile, fate wasted no time setting her stage and assembling her cast. Napoleon III, without waiting to return from Biarritz, announced his royal edict on the *Alabama*. With a show of neutral virtue, and no doubt impressed by Grant's slugging offensive towards Richmond, he quietly notified the port officials at Cherbourg that the *Alabama* was unwanted. She must leave or be interned.

At mid-afternoon, Tuesday, June 14, the *Kearsarge* steamed round the Cherbourg breakwater into the roads, with sailors' heads craning for a peek at her famous quarry. Stopping his engines, Winslow lay to near the *Alabama*. Lowering a boat, he sent an officer ashore to ask French permission to ship the prisoners Semmes had just released, a request that was refused. This done, the *Kearsarge* steamed within pointblank range of the *Alabama*, studied her intended victim closely and passed out of the western exit to take up her vigil off the port, where she could intercept any possible dash for the Channel.

Was it a challenge? What else could it have been? Winslow's slow, menacing parade of his ship past the *Alabama* had all the aspects of it. To French naval observers, watching intently, it looked as if Winslow was daring Semmes to "Come out and fight!" Winslow denied it. Yet, Semmes picked up the gage at once. Going to his cabin, he composed his celebrated challenge—addressing it not to Winslow personally, but to Monsieur Ad. Bonfils, Confederate agent at Cherbourg, requesting that gentleman to relay it, through Vice Consul Llais, to the captain of the *Kearsarge*. Wrote Semmes:

Sir: I hear that you were informed by the U. S. Consul that the *Kearsarge* was to come to this port solely for the prisoners landed by me, and that he was to depart in twenty-four hours. I desire to say to the U. S. Consul that my intention is to fight the *Kearsarge* as soon as I can make the necessary arrangements. I hope these will not detain me more than until tomorrow evening, or after the morrow morning at furthest. I beg she will not depart before I am ready to go out.

I have the honor to be, very respectfully, your obedient servant,
R. Semmes, *Captain*

It was as simple as that, couched in far less complicated rhetoric than the circuitous ceremonials demanded by the code of two duellists preparing to shoot each other down at twenty paces on the field of honor. Entrusting his missive to Lieutenant Beckett Howell, it reached Winslow's hands that same evening, and the stage was set for the clash.

Considerable nonsense later emanated from Northern papers, denying Winslow had meant to challenge a "pirate," and denying that he would lower his dignity by accepting one from a "pirate." Yet Winslow had come to destroy the *Alabama*. How could he destroy her unless he tempted her to venture out of her neutral refuge? He had sped to Cherbourg for just one purpose: to sink the *Alabama* as fast as God and his 11-inch guns would permit.

In his report to the Secretary of the Navy, he commented bluntly, "I received a note from Captain Semmes, begging that the *Kearsarge* would not depart, as he intended to fight her." On his part Semmes said his "defiance was understood to have been accepted."

Semmes knew his man pretty well. Two years Winslow's senior, they were once messmates and shipmates. In the schism of the Sixties Southern-born John Winslow had elected to follow the Old Flag.

To the wide-eyed crew of the *Alabama*, the Northern vessel looked enormous. Curiosity vied with excitement as the *Kearsarge* rounded the breakwater. What impressed the *Alabama*'s men most were the yawning black muzzles of the Northerner's two 11-inch guns. The *Alabama* had nothing to match them. Thinking hard, Jack watched the *Kearsarge* slowly circle the harbor and slide out the western pass. It was common knowledge on the berthdeck that the *Kearsarge* yearned to close quarters with the raider. On the long, weary trek back from Singapore many a time had Jack roared out a chantey composed by the forecastle bard:

We're homeward bound, we're homeward bound,
And soon shall stand on English ground.
But 'ere that English land we see,
We first must fight the Kearsargee!

From the bridge, Semmes and Lieutenant Kell focussed their glasses on the Northern ship. She was a fine, modern steam sloop, a sister to the *Tuscarora* and *Wachusett*. They could see her officers making similar appraisals of the *Alabama*. Yet, Semmes apparently did not detect a strange bulge amidships. This was the plank boxing that concealed the chain armor with which Winslow had wisely sheathed his ship. A "shirt of mail," Semmes was to call it when he later claimed it had cheated him out of a fair fight.

Having despatched his challenge, Semmes summoned Kell and closed the cabin door.

"Kell, I'm going out to fight the *Kearsarge*," he announced bluntly. "What do you think?"

Honest as daylight was John McIntosh Kell. He looked his captain straight in the eyes. "I'm not sure it's the thing to do, sir, but . . ."

"Why not?" interrupted Semmes, his eyes flashing their oldtime lightning.

Kell minced no words. "First, our powder's gone foul. Every third shot we fired at the *Rockingham* failed to explode."

Semmes demurred, tapping the cabin table. "I'm aware of that. But one lucky hit could do the trick. Two of our guns are capable of sinking any wooden ship afloat."

"That goes for the *Kearsarge*, too, sir," interposed Kell. "She carries two 11-inch pivots. She's a man-of-war, built to fight. The *Alabama* once had the speed of her, but not now."

"Granted," agreed Semmes. "In a fair fight I can win. At the worst, we have a fifty-fifty chance. I see nothing rash in offering battle to Winslow. Our ships are well-matched. We carry one gun more than the *Kearsarge*, though she throws a little heavier broadside. I've considered everything. I intend to fight her. Notify the men. Clear your ship for action. I'll make formal request for coal and notify the Port Admiral we hope to complete our arrangements by Saturday night, sooner if we can."

In depicting this interview in Semmes' cabin, Kell later wrote, "I saw his mind was fully made up so I simply stated these facts for myself. I had always felt ready for a fight, and I also knew that the brave young officers of the ship would not object, and the men would not only be willing, but anxious, to meet the enemy! To all outward seeming the disparity was not great between the ships, barring the unknown (because concealed) chain armor."

Semmes laid out his plan of battle. He would fight at long range, if possible. He had supreme trust in his rifled gun. He knew the *Kearsarge*'s 11-inch weapons would be devastating at close range. If the two ships came to yard-arm quarters, he would board her, confident the splendid physique of his daredevils would make short work of the *Kearsarge*'s superiority in numbers.

Semmes might have slipped out of Cherbourg under cover of darkness. He had done so twice at Martinique, but this was no time to run away. He never even considered it. Equally distasteful was the thought of being bottled up in the French port.

Should Semmes win a dramatic, cleancut victory in sight of France and England, it would shed fresh lustre on a dying cause, and breathe, momentarily, at least, new life into Southern political hopes in Europe. If he lost, it would be one ship less for the Confederacy, a vessel grievously run down, which only a long period in a shipyard could restore to what she once had been. Her bolt was shot. The outcome, either way, could have little effect on the bloody conflict heaving to its close across the Atlantic.

But something else impelled him at the moment. Nor was it military necessity. The eyes of the world were fixed on him. Here was a heaven-sent chance for glory—a triumph to top off his cruise and crown the *Alabama* with the accolade of victory over a powerful enemy ship—and then, the curtain. If he could slay the *Kearsarge* before the rest of the pack arrived it would raise him and his men to the very heavens of acclaim.

Connected with this, a yet deeper motive urged Semmes on to a finish fight—pride. Lightly-veiled intimations of cowardice had stung him and his men to the quick. They had heard them at Singapore, Cape Town, elsewhere. He was—so ran the taunt—aggressive, bold as a lion in running down and burning defenseless merchantmen, but skulking as a fox in avoiding combat with Union warships. With disdain, he had brushed aside these scoffings, but they hurt, nevertheless.

Semmes loved his ship with a sailor's devotion. She had become a part of him. His faith in her was unshakable. Bodily, he was as tired as she. If, by chance, this was to be her valedictory, she would go out fighting and make her exit lustrous by showing the world how valiantly she could stand and take it on the chin.

Semmes' crew backed him to a man. For all their shortcomings, their lawless, rum-loving hilarity and hell-raising on shore, they were fighting men. Discipline on ship had whipped them into men on whom he could depend when the chips were down. They, too, were sick of execration and reproach heaped on them by Northern newspapers and politicians. They had inflicted tremendous damage on their gigantic foe, but, like Semmes himself, they were tired of commerce raiding. Their fighting blood was up and they wanted to come to blows. So much for the insinuation that they were "disaffected."

Promptly, Semmes began clearing the *Alabama's* deck for the most spectacular sea-duel Europe had witnessed since the days of Horatio Nelson. It was, in fact, the only pre-arranged naval battle since the War of 1812 when Captain Philip Broke, commanding the British *Shannon* on blockade off Boston, invited Captain James Lawrence of the American *Chesapeake*, "to meet and try the fortunes of our respective flags."

"I entreat you, sir," Broke had said, seeking battle with Lawrence. "I beg she [the *Kearsarge*] will not depart before I am ready to go out," implored Semmes.

News that the two ships were to square off spread through France like wildfire. Newspapers whipped up the furore. Little else was talked of in the cafes, on the boulevards. Duelling in any form was an ancient, highly-honored French custom—and a sea-duel between two such distinguished opponents shot France's martial ardor skyhigh.

On his journal, Semmes sentimentalized:

> My crew seem to be in the right spirit, a quiet spirit of determination pervading both officers and men. The combat will no doubt be contested and obstinate, but the two ships are so equally matched that I do not feel at liberty to decline it. God defend the right, and have mercy upon the souls of those who fall, as many of us must.

Dutifully, Semmes notified Confederate Commissioner Slidell at Paris of his intention to engage the *Kearsarge*. Slidell kept hands off because "I have the most entire confidence in his judgement, his skill and his cool courage. I believe he would not proceed to the encounter of the *Kearsarge* unless he thought he had a reasonable chance of capturing her. She may succumb in the contest, but the honor of her flag will be maintained."

From Flag Officer Samuel Barron came a communication giving Semmes complete discretion in the matter. One voice alone protested, that of Monsieur Ad. Bonfils, who besought Slidell to forbid Semmes to fight.

To the care of Monsieur Bonfils, Semmes entrusted four and a half sacks of British gold sovereigns (4,700 in all) for "the issue of combats is always uncertain." The *Alabama* had really come "home" with more gold than she started out with. With the gold went the payrolls, showing, up to the day, the amount due each man and officer. With the same gentleman Semmes deposited the ransom bonds of the ships he had captured and released. Next, he sent ashore the precious chronometers he had so meticulously gleaned from the prizes taken by the *Sumter* and *Alabama*. In whose safekeeping he placed them was never revealed. After the battle, they were shipped to England, sold, and the proceeds divided among the survivors of the fight. His nearly one hundred captured United States flags never left the *Alabama*. Nor did the trophies that graced the walls of the wardroom, including the sword of Captain Blake of the *Hatteras*. Strangely, Semmes kept his journal with him. There is no record that Semmes wrote—as was the custom of duellists—a farewell letter to his family. Nor did he make a will, or urge his officers and men to do so.

Semmes applied at once to the French authorities for coal. His bunkers were empty. After a trifling protocol delay, the *Alabama* was coaled to capacity. This, in itself, in a neutral harbor, was renunciation of any further dispensation. He had to move out, or be interned.

Meanwhile, the *Alabama* hummed like a beehive as she was readied for action. Coolly, every last Jack turned his hand to something, even little Dave, the wardroom negro boy, who had cast his lot with the *Alabama* and was soon to share her fate. Jokingly, he was catechised on the state of his courage and his ivories flashed at the banter. Confident he was that no harm could befall him.

The *Alabama* could not lose. Captain Semmes would not let her lose. Even Bartelli was infected by the excitement of the coming battle. A victory celebration there would be—or so he was convinced—and the captain's cabin must be shipshape. He polished his glasses and arranged them in neat rows on the sideboard. Then, he fetched a dozen bottles of champagne from the Captain's locker. What toasting there would be!

The whole ship was keyed up. Jack went through his pre-battle paces like a racehorse prancing at the barrier. His morale was never higher. He wanted a fight and he didn't want to wait till Sunday for it. Many a jibe and jest he tossed at the *Kearsarge* poised outside the breakwater. Gunner Cuddy and his gang overhauled and cleaned the battery, arranged relays of shot, powder, and shell from the magazines. Gun crews were briefed to the last detail. Boatswain Mecaskey's detail took down the light spars, stoppered the standing rigging and disposed of top hamper. Decks were holystoned, brasswork polished. For her last, climactic scene, the raider bedecked herself like a great tragedienne for the farewell bow of her career.

Pikes and cutlasses were brought out, sharpened and practiced with. Boarding exercises were rehearsed. The *Alabama*'s one hundred and forty-nine officers and men were out to win. Lieutenants, midshipmen, boatswain and boatswain's mates, master's mates, gunner's mates, quartermasters, quarter-gunners, coxswain, foretop and maintop men, cooks, engineers, firemen, ordinary seamen, carpenters—one and all were animated with a single purpose, victory over the *Kearsarge*.

Lieutenant Kell was ubiquitous. It was his task to send the *Alabama* into battle, fit, trim, ready from stem to stern, to shoot it out. Apparently confident of the outcome, he planned to run up to Paris after the combat to celebrate with old friends.

On shore, evenings, Semmes' officers made merry. The cafes rang with "Vive les Confederates!" A gray uniform was passport to the rarest vintages the town afforded. Jack found himself lionized. He grew expansive. He would make short work of the Yankee!

From Paris, Confederate naval officers dashed to Cherbourg, eager to take part in the impending fray, but French officials said flatly no. The Port Admiral, apparently imbued with Southern sympathies, sent an officer to visit the *Kearsarge* in the offing. This embassy reported back that Winslow's ship wore chain armor. According to Lieutenant Sinclair, this vital intelligence was transmitted to Semmes at once. Sinclair added that Semmes could have likewise protected the *Alabama*. Stowed in her lockers was an abundance of anchor chain. Yet, Semmes insisted he knew nothing of it beforehand. Otherwise, he would not have engaged the *Kearsarge*.

But it was no secret. The *Kearsarge* had worn her "shirt of mail" for over a year. She went into the battle with her vital midriff and boilers protected by 120 fathoms of sheet chain, bolted down, boxed and hidden by one-inch planking.

Saturday, June 18. The *Alabama* was at her fighting peak, ready as she would ever be. Semmes notified the Port Admiral he would steam out in the morning to do battle with his enemy. All day crowds lined the docksides to gaze on the Confederate champion and speculate on her chances on the morrow. Towards evening, the men were given five hours' liberty, but cautioned to conduct themselves with propriety and pride in their ship. Tomorrow called for clear heads and steady nerves. They must return on the hour.

Dusk was falling and harbor lights twinkling when Semmes summoned his officers to his cabin for their final get-together. These stalwarts had stood at his right hand, night and day, in storm and stress. They had helped create the legendary *Alabama*, and made her dreaded the world over. They loved this taciturn, aloof man who had led the way for them.

One by one they entered, bearded, bronzed-faced, ranging themselves about him. To each he gave a salute. The scene was reminiscent of the last meeting on the *Sumter*, without its sombreness.

"Gentlemen"—Semmes' voice was quiet, his eyes, such eyes, alight—"tomorrow we fight the *Kearsarge*. Only the good God knows what the outcome will be. Thus far, He has shielded us. I believe He still watches over us. I have taken this responsibility alone. It was the only way out, with honor. If I have done wrong, if I fail, the fault will be mine. The *Alabama*'s record speaks for itself. You can be proud of it. It is my intention, with God's help, and yours, to sink or capture the *Kearsarge*."

That was all. Presently, Semmes went ashore. Alone, with reverent step, he trudged up the hill to the little Catholic church to attend mass and plead his last case before the God of Battles. By ten o'clock he had come aboard the *Alabama*, turned to his cot and said "Goodnight" to Bartelli, who dimmed the cabin lamp.

On the berthdeck the men were already dutifully turning in. In their darkened cabins, officers were chatting in jerky, eve-of-battle whispers. Soon, save for the nightwatch, the *Alabama* was asleep. It was her last night on the surface of the waters.

⚓

⚓

28 *"So Flashed and Fell the Brand Excalibur"*

Sunday was Semmes' lucky day. It was Sunday when the summons came to draw his sword in defense of the South. On a Sunday he had run the Union gauntlet out of the Mississippi and escaped into the Gulf with the *Sumter*. Sunday it was, radiant as a diamond, when he christened the *Alabama* off the Azores twenty-two months before. On another Sunday he had captured the California steamer, *Ariel*. Prize after prize had he taken on the Sabbath Day. And Sunday, too, when he had vanquished the *Hatteras*. Now, another Sunday was smiling down from the heavens as the *Alabama* steamed out to joust for keeps with the *Kearsarge*.

Had the oracle been consulted as in ancient Rome the auguries would have been propitious. Victory would surely spread her wings above the Confederacy's standard!

Mild and balmy, a westerly breeze came dancing over the waters. From a cloudless sky the sun poured down, gilding the sea like a rippling cloth-of-gold. No tournament could have asked a more perfect, exhilarating day. After a good night's rest the men of the *Alabama* rose fresh and ready. Old Beeswax had prescribed a leisurely, comfortable breakfast, with the best the mess could provide. Eat well and plenty! The battle might be long. Beyond stirring the fires under the boilers, there were no early tasks for Jack this morning.

Hardly had Semmes opened his eyes—he was still in his bunk—when a French naval officer appeared alongside with word from the Port Admiral, notifying him that the newly-built ironclad frigate *La Couronne* would escort the *Alabama* to the three-mile limit. There she would anchor to guarantee France's waters against violation during the encounter.

Fine weather had drawn crowds to Cherbourg. Not since knighthood was in flower had so colorful a spectacle been spread before the eyes of France. The heights above Cherbourg were both bleachers and grandstand. The mole, the upper stories of houses commanding views of the sea, the fortifications, and the shore, all were dotted with spectators. Hotels and lodging houses were swamped with guests eager to watch the *Alabama* sail out to make a Roman, or rather, a French holiday, of the *Kearsarge*. Every headland had its crowds. Many brought lunchboxes and campstools. From Paris came a trainload of ladies of fashion, boulevardiers, and sports-fans. It was a bonanza to the cafes of the town. The popular favorite, sympathetically, at least, was the *Alabama*, the Confederate ship without a home. Here and there small Confederate flags gave a flash of color. The duel to the death between these two champions of the rival American States had sparked France's martial ardor. Europe had thrilled over the *Merrimack-Monitor* fight in Hampton Roads, with its vast implications and impact on naval warfare. Now, here on her threshold, the North and South were about to fight a battle that would decide the fate of the most aggressive commerce raider the world had ever known.

At 9:45 the *Alabama* weighed anchor and pointed straight for the western entrance to the harbor. Black smoke ribboned from her funnel, and streamed out over her wake. Her Stars and Bars fluttered defiantly in the breeze. There was something of heartbreak, of pathos, of gallantry, about this lone, hunted-round-the-world Confederate ship sailing out to battle for a dwindling cause. Not more fearlessly did the *Chesapeake* flaunt her colors that bright day off Boston than did the *Alabama* the Southland's banner this tragic Sunday morning.

It was the hour of prayer in London, in Paris. In the little church on the Cherbourg bluff, where Semmes had knelt the night before, mass was being sung. When it was over the dominie would lead his nuns and his flock out to witness the thrilling show. From the heart of many an onlooker rose a prayer for the valiant paladin of the South.

Three thousand miles across the Atlantic, this same Sunday morning, General Robert E. Lee would kneel in St. Paul's Episcopal Church at Petersburg, Virginia, and give thanks that he and his army had come in the nick of time to save this backdoor to Richmond from Grant's plunging blue veterans.

The moment the *Alabama* churned seawards thunderous cheers rolled across the harbor. The tilting was about to begin. All it lacked was a fanfare of bugles and heralds in bright regalia. And how France loved a thrill! The scene from the deck of the *Alabama* as she passed out that morning was never effaced from the memory of those who saw it.

On leaving her moorings, the raider began weaving through the dense shipping in the harbor. At her heels came the ironclad *La Couronne*, grim and silent. She would, in a sense, be the referee of this bout. Next came a fine gesture of goodwill. The crew of the French line-of-battle-ship, *Napoleon*, anchored in the harbor, leaped into the rigging to give three mighty cheers for the *Alabama* as she skimmed past while her band broke out the rousing strains of "Dixie," sending the *Alabama* into combat with the South's national air ringing in her ears.

Bringing up the rear of the cavalcade were three French luggers, pilot boats, that trailed along packed with harbor officials, naval officers, and local Important People, to take up a ringside station outside the breakwater.

Semmes stepped out of his cabin that morning in fine fettle. Saluting the deck officer, he received the usual touch of the hat in return. Then he greeted Lieutenant Sinclair cheerily, "If the bright and beautiful day is shining for our benefit, we should be happy at the omen."

Semmes placed great store by omens. His gaze ran forward and he noted the crew had entered "the spirit of the fight with bright faces." Pointedly, he asked, "Mr. Sinclair, how do you think it will turn out today?"

The young officer was caught offguard. Seldom did Semmes seek opinions of subordinates on weighty matters. The embarrassed lieutenant hedged, "I cannot answer the question, sir. I can assure you the crew will do their full duty and follow you to the death."

"Yes, I know they will," agreed Semmes as he fell to pacing the quarterdeck.

Rounding the western tip of the breakwater, the *Alabama* sighted the *Kearsarge*. Yonder she was, about three miles offshore to the northeast, waiting implacably. Bravely, the *Alabama* headed for the open sea—and for the *Kearsarge* with her 11-inch guns.

The crew, at battle stations, were in their best uniforms, spanking fresh, as if arrayed for Sunday inspection. All except the gun crews, who were stripped to the waist, bare arms and breasts, looking like athletes in the pink. Spirits ran high. There seemed to be little tension. The men looked fit and able enough to slay the devil himself today if need be.

As the *Alabama* cut through the sea towards the *Kearsarge*, batteries were cast loose, decks sanded down, tubs of water placed along the spar deck. Kell made a last-minute inspection of his gun crews, giving a word or two of encouragement to the men, ordering them to lie flat on the deck, at quarters, until they neared the fray. It would rest them.

Semmes himself was at his sartorial finest. On his new, frock-coated gray uniform gleamed three rows of Confederate brass buttons. At his side his sword glistened like a sunbeam. Gold-braided epaulettes adorned his shoulders. He was a vibrant, long-remembered figure as he walked out fresh from the ministrations of Bartelli, who had waxed his mustachios to keen points. Battle-light glowed in his eyes. This was to be his great day. Not that he was contemptuous of his foeman, but, rather, that he was confident. He knew the power of the *Kearsarge's* 11-inch guns, yet he counted on his great rifle gun to win for him. At his chosen distance, a mile and a half, he could blast the heart out of the Northern ship before her big smoothbores got near enough really to damage the *Alabama*.

Not until the morning of the fight was any special notice taken of an English yacht, the *Deerhound*, that had been at Cherbourg for a week. Her owner, John Lancaster, an Englishman of ease and affluence, had reached Cherbourg the evening before the battle and gone aboard. Mr. and Mrs. Lancaster, three sons, a niece and a nine-year-old daughter, Catherine, had been traveling on the continent. The *Deerhound* had steamed over to Cherbourg to pick them up for the last leg of their journey home across the Channel.

Reaching Cherbourg, the Lancasters were thrilled to find they had arrived on the eve of a sea-fight that had all France on pins and needles. Anchored close to the *Alabama*, the *Deerhound's* skipper, Captain Evan Jones, was naturally curious to have a look at the famed raider. While awaiting his employer, Jones had gone alongside and asked to come aboard, only to be politely turned aside at the gangway. No open sesame was his reminder that the *Alabama* and the *Deerhound* had kindred ancestry, that both were built in the Laird shipyards at Birkenhead. The *Alabama* was too busy preparing for her Sunday engagement to entertain visitors.

After the Lancasters came aboard their yacht, the family held a consultation to decide whether to go to church on the morrow or run out and watch the fight. There was little need to ask the young folks their preference. Mr. Lancaster put it to a vote. The three brothers eagerly cast their ballots for seeing the fight. Mr. and Mrs. Lancaster and their niece voted to remain in port and attend divine services. From nine-year-old Catherine, came the casting vote, making it four to three, for watching the combat. Thus did Providence or fate make this little girl the means of saving the lives of Raphael Semmes and forty-one of his officers and crew.

Early this bright Sunday morning the *Deerhound* steamed out of the harbor. On her bridge were the Lancasters and their children. In rapt, awed silence, they passed the Confederate raider, making her final preparations.

The oncoming duel with the *Kearsarge* may have been just a "quixotic joust" to Thomas C. De Leon, a Confederate newspaperman, but not to Raphael Semmes and the men behind his guns. Nor was it such to John Ancrum Winslow and the men of the *Kearsarge*. Since arriving off Cherbourg and receiving Semmes' challenge the Northern ship had cruised to and fro off the break-water, at a respectful distance outside the three-mile limit. Dayton had warned: "If you lose nothing by fighting six or seven miles off the coast instead of three, you had best do so." This was agreeable to Winslow, who had no idea of violating the rules of international law. Nor had he any notion when the *Alabama* would come out. He knew only that he must be ready to accommodate her, any moment, night or day. Semmes was unpredictable. That Winslow knew. Semmes might easily attempt a surprise night attack on the *Kearsarge*. Winslow took every precaution. He would be ready for action on the instant.

Winslow had already decided, even before receiving Dayton's note, to engage the *Alabama* well beyond the marine league, if he could lure her that far offshore. He believed that if the *Alabama* saw she was getting the worst of the fight, she would avail herself of the nearby sanctuary of French territorial waters, with *La Couronne* standing by to see that the neutral line of demarcation was strictly observed. The same escape-door was available to the *Kearsarge*, if fate favored her opponent. But Winslow's idea was to give battle at such distance it would be too late, or too far, for the *Alabama*, if crippled or worsted, to take refuge under French wings. He was, of course, denying himself the same privilege.

On the *Kearsarge* this Sunday the bell was tolling for divine service on deck. Her captain was standing before his officers and crew, prayerbook in hand, preparing to read the scripture, when suddenly the lookout cried down, "The *Alabama's* coming out!" Instantly, Winslow folded the book, picked up his trumpet and ordered the drum to beat to quarters. The hour was 10:20. Fearing, as he said, "the question of jurisdiction might arise," Winslow turned his ship's head about and raced away northeast for the open sea, intent on drawing the *Alabama* well away from the land before commencing action. To the thousands of onlookers it seemed as if the *Kearsarge* was running away from the pursuing *Alabama*.

As the *Alabama* emerged from behind the breakwater and headed seawards Semmes and his officers saw their opponent speeding away. In the raider's wake *La Couronne* moved out approximately to the three mile limit where she anchored. She was a tough-looking war steamer. There was no doubting her ability to protect France's neutral zone. She was never to leave the spot until the curtain fell.

Presently, the pipes of the *Alabama's* boatswain and his mates summoned all hands aft. They came on the run. Semmes mounted a gun carriage. Erect, eyes ablaze, he was a memorable, knightly figure, elegant in his trim, neatly-tailored uniform. The ladies who had all but fallen at his feet at Gibraltar, at Jamaica, at Cape Town, at Singapore, should have seen him at this crowning moment of his career. His face was paler than usual, a bit drawn with excitement, but, within, he was calm. In a clear, tremorless voice he spoke to the men of the *Alabama* for the last time. Not since the day he commissioned the ship off the Azores had he addressed them in this wise:

> Officers and Seamen of the *Alabama!*—You have, at length, another opportunity of meeting the enemy—the first that has been presented to you since you sank the *Hatteras!* In the meantime, you have been all over the world, and it is not too much to say, that you have destroyed, and driven for protection under neutral flags, one half of the enemy's commerce, which, at the beginning of the war, covered every sea. This is an achievement of which you may well be proud; and a grateful country will not be unmindful of it. The name of your ship has become a household word wherever civilization extends. Shall that name be tarnished by defeat? The thing is impossible!

Enthusiastic replies of "Never! Never!" broke the utter silence that had prevailed. The crew roared them out as if in one, protesting voice. "Never!" would they permit their ship's name to be sullied. Semmes spoke on:

> Remember that you are in the English Channel, the theatre of so much of the naval glory of our race, and that the eyes of all Europe are at this moment, upon you. The flag that floats over you is that of a young Republic, who bids defiance to her enemies, whenever, and wherever found. Show the world that you know how to uphold it! Go to your quarters!

On shore the crowds were rooting and cheering vociferously for the *Alabama*, but the odds-makers would have figured it otherwise. The smart money would have been laid on the *Kearsarge* to win at five to four, or slightly better.

Completed in October, 1861, the *Kearsarge* was nine months older than the *Alabama*, but the age disparity meant little. In size, they were fairly matched, the *Alabama* measuring 1,016 tons, the *Kearsarge* 1,031. The 212-foot Southern ship was eleven feet longer than her foe. Though provided with sail, both fought under steam alone. With her bottom cleaned only three months before, the *Kearsarge* enjoyed the edge in both speed and maneuverability.

The hopes of the two captains lay in their great pivot guns, which were on the center line and could fire to either side of the ship. Besides his Blakeley rifle on the forecastle, which fired a 100-pound shell, Semmes had his 8-inch smoothbore amidships, shooting 68 pounds. In addition, three old-style 32-pounders fired to port, and equal number to starboard. The total weight of his broadside, the pivot guns plus three of the 32-pounders, came to 264 pounds. While heading towards the *Kearsarge* another 32-pounder was shifted to a spare port on the engaged side, increasing the broadside to 296 pounds. It also created a list to starboard of about two feet, which, though it exposed much less surface to enemy fire, retarded the *Alabama*'s already reduced speed.

Winslow's two 11-inch smoothbore pivot guns fired 135½ pounds each. Their effective range was about half a mile. Besides these he had a 30-pounder and four old 32-pounders, half on either side, bringing his broadside to 365 pounds. So the Federal cruiser was well up on the Southerner in this respect. But Semmes' faith in his 8-inch smoothbore and his Blakeley rifle was implicit. He was confident he could win in a fair fight.

A factor Semmes chose to ignore was the state of his powder. Not since the *Alabama* sailed away from England had her magazines been replenished. Fast changes in climate had sapped its explosive vigor. Kell and Semmes had already seen ample evidence of it. Firing at the *Rockingham* on the way to Cherbourg they had watched many of their shells fail to explode. Others broke with a dull flash and grayish smoke. In contrast, the *Kearsarge*'s shells were to flare brightly, with a resounding report and faint blue smoke.

With his crew still cheering, Semmes took his battle station on the horseblock abreast the mizzenmast. From this exposed vantage point he directed the fight and the maneuvering of his ship. The officers, like Semmes, were smart-looking, alert, in their dress uniforms. Commanding his gun divisions were Second Lieutenant Armstrong, with the 100-pounder Blakeley rifle; Third Lieutenant Wilson, with the eight-inch pivot gun and two 32-pounders; Fourth Lieutenant Sinclair, with the 32-pounders amidships.

A magnificent fighting figure of heroic proportions, a first officer par excellence, was Lieutenant John McIntosh Kell at this hour of battle. He moved and spoke with authority. Towering head and shoulders over his shipmates, he was everywhere it seemed: now giving a word to this man or that one; now conversing with Semmes; now training his glasses on the approaching enemy. Dependable, unafraid, he was ready to die on the instant for the man on the horseblock.

Forty-five minutes after the *Alabama* passed the breakwater, about seven miles northeast of Cherbourg, the ships were about a mile and a quarter apart. Without warning, the *Kearsarge* wheeled about and steered straight for the *Alabama* head on. Swift as a greyhound she closed, great streamers of smoke whirling from her funnel like the dark wings of an avenging angel. With deadly purpose, Winslow rushed to ram and sink the *Alabama*, if he could; if not, to engage her at close quarters or pass astern and rake her.

At 10:57 Semmes glanced at his watch and turned to Lieutenant Kell.

"Are you ready, Mr. Kell?" he asked.

"Aye, aye, sir. Ready and willing."

"Then, you may open fire at once, sir."

At 1,200 yards, the *Alabama* opened up. Boom! Lieutenant Armstrong's 100-pounder blazed out with a roar and a burst of smoke. Hurtling across the water, the shell fell short with a great splash. Then, with a deafening roar and a curtain of fire-flecked smoke, away went her starboard broadside, shaking the ship to her very keel. The guns strained at their tackles; the *Alabama* trembled under the recoil. Harmlessly, the missiles screamed through the *Kearsarge's* rigging.

Nimble as youngsters, the gunners leaped to swab, tighten the gun tackles, check their sights, lug up fresh shot and shell and drive them home. A second broadside rocked the *Alabama*, and a third. What was the matter with the *Kearsarge?* What was John Winslow waiting for? Finally at nine hundred yards—half a mile—the Union ship broke her impressive silence. Her first broadside roared out. The prodigious blast of the 11-inchers boomed across the water. Their shells, falling short, threw up tall geysers of green water. No hits! On the *Alabama* the hoorays soared to the skies.

Now Semmes had to act fast. Under a full head of steam the *Kearsarge* was still boiling head on for her enemy. Porting his helm sharply, Semmes sheered off. Winslow followed suit instantly. By his quick move Semmes had nullified the possibility of being raked astern. But had failed to keep Winslow from closing the range. Like two horses in a circus ring, the two ships now began pursuing each other, clockwise, in a series of gradually diminishing circles, with a three-knot current bearing them westward as they fought. Round and round they were to go, seven times in all, firing as they passed, each presenting her starboard broadside. Gradually, the two ships neared each other, until, in the last two or three circles, they were hardly five hundred yards apart—the range at which the 11-inch Dahlgren became utterly accurate, inconceivably devastating.

The *Alabama's* gunners were firing fast, two shots for every one of the enemy's. But they were shooting too high, too wildly. From the start Winslow's gunners fired with deliberate precision, without hurry. After the first exploratory broadsides, they began to score hits on the Southern ship. John Winslow's carefully-trained gunners simply couldn't miss. He ordered his 11-inchers to aim for the *Alabama's* waterline, his 32-pounders to sweep her decks.

Yet, for all their poor shooting, fifteen minutes after they opened fire, the crew of Lieutenant Armstrong's Blakeley rifle lodged a 100-pound shell in the stern-post of the *Kearsarge*, near her rudder. The Union ship reeled under the concussion. Through his telescope Semmes watched the projectile drive into the vital spot. The explosion would render her helpless. Brief moments of triumph surged through his heart. He almost danced on the horse-block. "Splendid! Splendid!" Intently, he watched for a blossom of smoke and flame near the *Kearsarge's* stern. One, two, three, four, five—long moments. Too long, the shell had refused to burst!

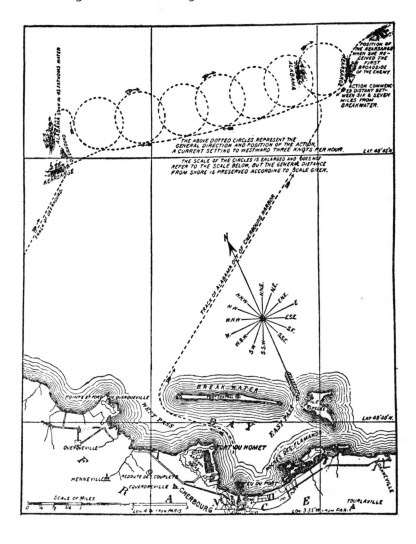

Eighteen minutes had gone by. The *Alabama's* gunners were getting steadier. Not firing so fast, not firing so wildly. A Blakeley shell bashed in the *Kearsarge's* starboard bulwark, exploded on the quarterdeck and wounded three of the crew of the after 11-inch. Two more shots passed through open gun ports, but did no damage. Another exploded in the hammock nettings, setting the ship on fire. The guns kept firing; the flames were quickly doused. A 32-pounder struck the forward 11-inch, almost toppling gun and carriage, but like the 100-pounder in the sternpost, failed to explode.

There would be no boarding in this fight. No grim and bloody boarders charging over the rails brandishing pikes, cutlasses, and pistols. Semmes saw it plain enough; so did Winslow. It would be a stand-up, finish fight, at a constantly lessening distance, until one of the cruisers was shot to pieces. The *Kearsarge's* 11-inch smoothbores were in their glory now. They had the right range. Their burly iron shells detonated like volcanoes, smashing, crashing, breaking into a hail of deadly fragments, spewing out clouds of sulphurous, stifling smoke, showering the deck with killing splinters. They ripped jagged holes in her side, tore off sections of her bulwarks. They crunched their way through wood and metal like paper. They were blasting the heart out of the *Alabama*.

The chips were surely down. Winslow's incessant drill was paying off. His gunners were handling their pieces with admirable precision: Semmes, with no surplus ammunition, had been too sparing in target practice. The *Alabama* was taking a terrific beating. The battle roar was rising. Carnage was piling up. Wounded began to scream. Gunners were cursing, damning. The *Alabama's* smokestack was a sieve; her deck was ripped up by bursts of 32-pounders. Wreckage, pieces of woodwork and rigging, shell boxes, littered her deck.

An 11-inch shell breached through the *Alabama's* 8-inch gun port. The compressor man, Michael Mars, son of Erin, was on his knees to retard the recoil. The gun was loaded; her snout run out to fire. Then, through the port plunged the Yankee shell. Disemboweling the first man on the port side of the gun, it killed and wounded eighteen others like so many ten pins in a row, splashing the deck with a mass of human fragments. A gruelling sight! The planking looked like the floor of a slaughter house. Blood dribbled and blotted in the sand. Seizing a shovel, Mars scooped up the gobs of flesh and bone, tossed them overboard and re-sanded the deck.

The *Alabama's* gaff was shot away and her ensign came fluttering down. It was replaced immediately at the mizzen masthead. The 11-inch monsters shook the *Alabama* like a leaf. A second killed a man and wounded several others; a third struck the 8-inch gun carriage, failed to explode and spun about on the deck until a seaman grabbed it and heaved it overboard. A fourth crashed through at the waterline and smashed into the engine room.

Yet, Armstrong's and Wilson's shots were hitting the *Kearsarge* repeatedly. A 100-pounder sizzled through the Union ship's engine room skylight. For a moment it looked as if it had smashed the *Kearsarge's* boilers. Cheers went up from the *Alabama*. Up to now there had been precious little to cheer about. Repeatedly, the *Alabama's* shells hit the *Kearsarge* only to explode or rebound harmlessly against her sides. Was she another ironsides? Semmes was appalled at the ineffectiveness of his shell. He could see them hit without penetrating, explode without damage. He called to Kell.

"Mr. Kell, use solid shot! Our shell strike the enemy's side and fall into the water!"

Still they smashed harmlessly against the *Kearsarge's* side. Round shots were equally futile. It was baffling, dismaying. Choking, blinding, stinging smoke, eddied along the *Alabama's* deck like a pall. Down below, the engine room was like an inferno. Firemen and enginemen were gasping for breath. Sulphur fumes cut at their throats like knives. There was no breeze to carry it off.

Nor was there any let-up from the *Kearsarge*. Implacably, she poured out her killing breath. She might have won the fight hands down with her 11-inch guns—the weapons Semmes had believed well matched by his Blakeley and the 8-inch pivot. Outgunned, outclassed, outshot, the *Alabama* was a setup, making her last stand—but she couldn't take it much longer, and Semmes knew it. There was no panic. The men were steady. They faced up to it as he had always known they would.

A shell fragment gashed Semmes' right arm. Bleeding profusely, he calmly called the nearest quartermaster and had him bind and sling the wounded arm. Not for a moment did he leave his station

on the horseblock though he knew his ship and his men were fast
being slashed to shreds.

It was no longer a fight. Soon it would be a massacre. There
was no way out this time. Luck had at last left him in the lurch.
It was a crushing realization. Still, the ships circled and circled.
Now they were on the seventh. If he could only get yardarm to
yardarm and board the *Kearsarge*, his blackened, sweaty banditti
would leap over her like tigers and tear her crew to shreds. But it
was too late to come to grips now, too late for anything but the
thing he dreaded, unless he could do what his prizes had so often
tried vainly to do: reach the sanctuary of the three-mile limit.
Often had he laughed at fine ships putting on every inch of sail,
reaching out desperately for the sanctuary of the marine league,
only to snuff out their hopes by a shot across the bow. This time
the shots were not rebel shells across the bow of a Yankee merchantman. These were Yankee shells, plunging into the *Alabama*.

Water was pouring through the rents in the *Alabama's* side. She
began to list, making water fast. She was whipped. Semmes
knew it. He might, unless luck had deserted entirely, stave off capture, if he could reach French waters. How sirenlike they beckoned to him! The two ships were completing their seventh circuit
when Semmes called out:

"Mr. Kell, as soon as our head points to the French coast in
our circuit of action, shift your guns to port and make all sail for
the coast."

The evolution was beautifully performed. But again the *Kearsarge* countered, by speeding to a position where she could rake
the Southern ship. Yet, strangely, she did not fire. Noting how
sluggishly the *Alabama* responded to her helm, Lieutenant Kell ordered John Roberts, a stalwart English sail trimmer, to loose the
jib. Haste was imperative. Neatly, Roberts executed the order and
was returning when a shell incised his groin, opening it wide like
a slit melon. It was, said Lieutenant Sinclair, "the most remarkable case of desperate wounding and after-tenacity of life" he had
ever witnessed. In this pitiful plight, Roberts clung to the jib
boom, worked his way along a footrope to the topgallant deck and
thence climbed to the spar deck where, in a spasm of agony,

shrieking and beating his head with his arms, he expired convulsively. His entrails spewed out in a red mass.

But the *Kearsarge* had already blocked Semmes' hope for escape by placing herself squarely between his ship and the French coast. It was precisely what John Winslow had expected and had determined to prevent. Semmes' groggy, staggering, ship was cornered, sinking.

Engineer Miles Freeman dashed to the horseblock to report, "I can't work my engines any longer. My fires are flooding."

There was no choice, though. Going to the hatchway Kell called down, "Give her more steam, or we'll be whipped."

Young Matt O'Brien, responded valiantly, "Aye, aye, sir. Let her have the steam. We'd better blow her to hell than let the Yankees whip us!"

Deep down in the engine room Engineer Pundt had his say, too, "Well, I suppose Old Beeswax has made up his mind to drown us like a lot of rats!"

With hell roaring on deck above them, these men stuck to their posts, caught between the water that rose insistently and the fires in their furnaces.

Semmes was grasping at straws now. He never thought it would ever come to this.

"Go below, Mr. Kell, and see how long the ship can float."

A sickening sight met Kell's eyes as he entered the wardroom. At his post, his white apron splashed with blood, stood Assistant Surgeon Llewellyn. A Dahlgren 11-incher had just swept through. Roaring like an erupting volcano it had snatched away his operating table and the wounded seaman over whom he was working. Man, table, knives, saws, bandages, vanished in one dread instant. There stood Llewellyn, dazed, bandage in hand, staggering like a drunk.

Kell sped through the ship, made his appraisal quickly, and hurried back to Semmes. No time to mince words now. He spat it out—in the raw.

"We can stay afloat perhaps ten minutes!"

The fires in Semmes' eyes seemed to burn out all at once. He had no choice, no time to wait, no time for anything but surrender. In a last anguished silent protest he raised his eyes appealingly to the flag of the Confederacy floating above the ship he loved with his heart and soul.

"Then, sir," he commanded—and brave words they were— "cease firing, shorten sail, and haul down the colors. It will never do in this nineteenth century for us to go down and the decks covered with our gallant wounded."

A quartermaster seized the halliards. Down came the colors, fast. Lieutenant Sinclair insists that when Semmes gave the order to strike the colors there was a protesting rush to the horseblock. Powder-caked, sweaty, blackened men and officers demanded, "No surrender! no surrender!"—and a quartermaster, so the dramatic story ran—brandished his cutlass, daring any man to touch the halliards until Lieutenant Kell brought him to his senses with a pistol at his head. The flag would never be desecrated! They preferred sinking with the ship than lowering her colors!

But Semmes had surrendered! The unbelievable—to him, at least. Yet, hardly had the ensign touched the hands that lowered it before the *Kearsarge* fired one, two, three, four, five shots—to tarnish her escutcheon and the glory of her victory with having fired on a fallen foe. Four hundred yards off she lay, her guns packed with grape for raking. Seeing the *Alabama's* flag come down, Winslow coolly gave the order, "He's playing a trick on us; give him another broadside."

In his report Winslow condoned his action. He was "uncertain whether Captain Semmes was not using some ruse." Yet, it could hardly condone firing on a lot of beaten, bleeding men, even "pirates."

The *Alabama* was a mass of blood, death and destruction, a sinking wreck. As the *Kearsarge's* blast swept across the deck Kell called out, "Stand to your quarters, men! Don't flinch!" Not a man stirred. They were a gritty lot. To Quartermaster Freemantle, "Show a white flag from the stern!"

Kell was to ask the question, "Was this a time for a ship to use a ruse, a Yankee trick?" Winslow claimed the *Alabama* fired several shots after striking her colors. It was never proved. French officers on *La Couronne*, watching every moment of the battle, stated flatly that they did not see or hear a single shot from the *Alabama* after her flag descended.

Semmes spoke again. "Mr. Kell, despatch an officer to the *Kearsarge* and ask them to send a boat to save our wounded—ours are disabled." Alas! So were the *Kearsarge's* boats.

To Master's Mate Fullam—he who had boarded so many of the *Alabama's* prizes—Kell assigned the task of asking the *Kearsarge* for help and carrying with him as many wounded as could be loaded into the dinghy that had miraculously escaped smashing by enemy fire. Tenderly, the shattered men were passed over the side of the sinking ship. Doctor Galt went with them. The dead were left to go down with the *Alabama*.

Desperately wounded was a young Irishman, James King, nicknamed "Connemara" for the county whence he came. Hot tempered he was, often vexatious to his officers, in and out the brig, yet utterly loyal to his ship and the men who commanded him. As he was lifted gently from the deck to be passed down into the dinghy, he sent for Lieutenant Kell.

Reaching out his feebling hand, he said, "I have sent for you, Mr. Kell, to ask your forgiveness for all the trouble I've made since I enlisted on the *Alabama*. Please forgive poor Connemara. He is going to his long home."

Kell knelt at his side and stroked his forehead. The boy was only twenty-five. "Connemara, there's nothing to forgive. I have nothing against you, brave lad. You'll be in better trim soon."

"No," replied the Irishman, "Connemara is going fast. Goodby, Mr. Kell. God bless you, Mr. Kell!" He died on the *Kearsarge* and was buried in the Channel not far from the *Alabama*.

There was little time now to wait. The ship was sinking fast. Down, down, down, the terror of the seas was hurrying to join the fifty-odd prizes she had buried. Air hissed through the holes in her decks; water roared into the ghastly rents in her side. One opening was big as a barrel. Her beautiful, swanlike clipper bow was slowly rising, her deck slanting. Air bubbles were exploding below as if the ship were in agony. She was still making headway, slowly, leaving a line of wreckage astern on the bright waters, like a broad ribbon of crepe.

Now it was everyone for himself! Semmes stepped down from the horseblock. Seamen and officers gathered about him, anxious to shield him from the inevitable. Affection and respect shone on blackened, battle-stained faces. One tendered this little service, another one, that. One man was as good as another now, with death staring them all in the face. The Channel waters were ruffling—the wind had freshened—as if to take a hand in finishing off what was left by the *Kearsarge*.

Kell stood beside his captain. Kell, who would have died willingly for him and almost did. And little Dave, the former Delaware slave boy, who had chosen the "pirates" for his friends, and, like Bartelli, never dreamed such a fate could overtake him.

The *Kearsarge* held her distance. The *Alabama's* dinghy, overloaded with wounded, was on her way to the victor.

Michael Mars, ordinary seaman and brave as a lion, asked Semmes what service he could perform. Semmes had forgotten until now his diary—so often quoted in this book—and the ship's papers. Mars volunteered to fetch them. With Bartelli, he waded into the captain's cabin and returned with the two small, precious packages. To Michael Mars and Quartermaster Freemantle Semmes entrusted each a package, put up tightly between small slats. Each thrust a package in the bosom of his shirt.

"We're good swimmers, captain," assured Mars with a smile. "We'll take good care of them." They did. Mars swam with one hand, holding Semmes' diary above the water.

With tears in his eyes Bartelli told his captain the cabin had been shattered and a fine painting of the *Alabama* destroyed.

It was time to go. Water was slapping at their feet. Kell thundered out, "All hands overboard and save yourselves! Jump in with a spar, an oar, or a grating and get out of the vortex!"

Two seamen helped Semmes disrobe. Quickly, they pulled off his boots. Off came the splendid, gray coat laden with bright buttons. How these diadems shone in the noonday sun! Kell and the officers and men were already stripping. Kell shucked off to his underclothes. Semmes kept on his trousers and vest. It wouldn't do for the captain to appear in such *deshabille*. Together they would all go into the Channel and perish with the *Alabama* unless help came speedily. Just how a man, with a wounded, bound-up right

arm, could buck the choppy waves was something Semmes did not
—could not—consider. He still had one good arm.

Yet, before he plunged into the sea there was something else he
must do. Unbuckling his sword, he gazed on it reverently. Brightly
it shone in the warm sun. No enemy hand had ever touched it.
Better to commit it to the deep than desecrate it thus. He would
put it beyond reach of his foe. He raised it with his left arm. For
long moments he gazed up at it and then, deliberately, hurled the
blade out over the water, as once Sir Bedivere had tossed Arthur's
mighty brand into the mere. Flashing, wheeling, glistening, it
struck the water and vanished. It was done!

The *Alabama* writhed in her death throes. Guns, gear, spars,
tackle, wreckage were sliding aft, gaining momentum, as her stern
sank deeper and deeper.

Where was little Dave the while? One moment he was standing
with the group, around Semmes, smiling, his white teeth agleam,
confident as always that he was safe with those he had served so
loyally. The next time someone looked, he was gone. And what of
Bartelli! Poor Bartelli! Like Dave, he was no swimmer. His last
service was to fold Semmes' gray coat and smooth it out on the
horseblock. Was there anything else he could do? His fine, blue
Italian eyes were blurred. No, nothing more. He must save himself, said Semmes, not knowing Bartelli couldn't swim a stroke.

The *Alabama's* meteor flag! Where was it! She had lowered it,
yes. Down it would go with the *Alabama*, untouched, untainted,
unsurrendered!

Silently, the *Kearsarge* watched the *Alabama* die!

As the water reached the taffrail, Kell and Semmes threw themselves into the sea. Semmes wore a life preserver; Kell had a grating. As rapidly as one arm would permit Semmes struck out from
the sinking ship to avoid being sucked under by the foaming
whirlpool of her death. The water was doubly cold after the hot
excitement of battle. The sea around him was a mass of bobbing
heads, struggling, battling for life. White caps were breaking over
them, as if to wipe out the last human vestige of the *Alabama*.

What were Semmes' thoughts at this moment when his battle
was lost, his ship shattered, his men dead and dying, and the waters reaching for more? Let him tell:

No one who is not a seaman can realize the blow which falls upon the heart of a commander, upon the sinking of his ship. It is not merely the loss of a battle—it is the overwhelming of his household, as it were, in a great catastrophe. The *Alabama* had not only been my battlefield, but my home, in which I had lived two long years, and in which I had experienced many vicissitudes of pain and pleasure, sickness and health. My officers and crew formed a great military family, every face of which was familiar to me; and when I looked upon my gory deck, toward the close of the action and saw so many manly forms stretched upon it, with the glazed eye of death or agonizing with terrible wounds, I felt as a father feels who has lost his children—his children who had followed him to the uttermost ends of the earth, in sunshine and storm, and been always true to him.

Shattered and blasted, the *Alabama* was fast settling now. Her furnaces were cold and wet, a trickle of steam and smoke still spewed from her funnel. Water splashed hollowly through Semmes' cabin. Churning, choking, chuckling, rollicking it ran through her hull. Vast sobs seemed to shake her once-comely frame as she made ready for her last plunge. Even in death, she held her head high—proudly it seemed to those who watched her die. Up-ending slowly, she raised her beautiful, clean prow higher and higher, as if in a last appeal to heaven against such a fate. Her hulk agonized like a living thing. Forty fathoms down she would be lost to all save love and fame and memory.

Yet, if the *Alabama* must die, this was the way Semmes preferred it. Better to perish in battle than be broken up in a shipyard. Her guns were still hot, her deck anointed with the blood of the men who had fought her battle valiantly, and as yet untouched by enemy foot. What better moment to pass to the Valhalla of brave ships! Nor would her bones be picked, as were the *Merrimack's*, and sold for souvenirs on the streets of Washington.

The water was cold. It pierced Semmes to his marrow. Swimming close beside him was Kell, undaunted, faithful, holding on to a grating. Fifty yards from the sinking wreck Semmes turned for a last, heartbroken look at the once-beautiful ship he had loved so well. Just before she disappeared her main-topmast, almost severed by a shell, went by the board. As she began her downward slide

her foremast gave way with a crash. Swinging wildly were her anchors. Smoke ebbed from her shot-up funnel, which suddenly
shook free from its moorings. Her rent sails bellied out as, if trying to stave off her fate to the last. Suddenly, she shot her bow
high out of the water, poised for brief moments and then descended swiftly, stern first, to her last resting place.

Again, what were Semmes' feelings? What else could they be?

A noble Roman once stabbed his daughter, rather than she should
be polluted by the foul embrace of a tyrant. It was with a similar
feeling that Kell and I saw the *Alabama* go down. We had buried her
as we had christened her, and she was safe from the polluting touch
of the hated Yankee!

It was exactly 12:24. One hour and twenty seven minutes
since the *Alabama* fired her opening shot. Semmes' luck had vanished forever in the smoke and blaze of battle.

One by one heads were vanishing beneath the choppy waves.
Semmes and Kell kept together as best they could, giving a cheery
word to this man and that. A little float of empty shell boxes
drifted by. Kell called to a seaman swimming near at hand to examine it. The seaman did so and called back, "It's the doctor, sir.
He's dead." Poor Llewellyn! Dead in sight of England and home!
He had stood to his task of mercy to the last. The 11-inch bruiser
had swept away his table, everything. Water was licking his knees
when Lieutenant Sinclair rushed in and cried out, "Why, Pills,
you'd better get yourself and your wounded out of this, or you'll be
drowned!" He replied, "I must await orders, you know. I can't
leave these men like this." Seeing his wounded safely transferred to
a boat, unable to swim, he committed himself to an improvised
raft of two empty shell boxes, one under each arm. And thus he
passed.

Young Midshipman Maffitt, noting that Kell's grating was not
too buoyant and the waves breaking over his lieutenant's head,
swam to his side to say, "Mr. Kell, take my life preserver, sir.
You're almost exhausted." He was already disengaging it. Kell refused. The boy's pallid face told him that heroism had risen superior to self.

Long minutes went by. The men battling for life in the icy water were weakening fast. Still, the *Kearsarge* looked on sullenly! Semmes knew he could hardly keep up much longer. Unless help came. . . . The bandaged right arm was blotted red. The salt water had started his wound bleeding afresh.

At 12:30, by her log, the English yacht, *Deerhound*, sped to the rescue. She had stood off at a safe distance to the windward, throughout the contest. The youthful fight-fans on her bridge had viewed the blazing battle from a front row seat. It was the biggest thrill of their lives. Now they saw the water dotted with drowning men and the *Kearsarge* gazing on as if too stunned to make a move. John Lancaster decided to do something about it and do it instantly.

Running up at full steam, the *Deerhound* came under the stern of the victor. Winslow himself, through his trumpet, hailed her, "For God's sake, do what you can to save them!" Yankee carpenters were feverishly patching their shot-ridden boats. In the meantime the vanquished must make the best of it. The *Kearsarge* made no move to close the survivors and toss them lines.

At 12:50 the *Deerhound* reached the scene. Slowing down as she nosed into the wreckage of the *Alabama*, she lowered her boats at once. With powerful sweeps they pulled amid the flotilla of bobbing heads on the water. Tossing ropes to some, hauling others in, they went at it like trained lifesavers. The yacht's chief steward, William Roberts, in one of the boats, recognized the almost exhausted Semmes, who was about to slide under. Roberts had seen the Confederate captain two years before when the *Sumter* steamed into Gibraltar.

Semmes was fished out and laid on the sternsheets, "as if dead." Next, they heaved in the half-drowned Kell. Working fast, they soon had a boatful.

Kell's powerful physique had stood him in good stead. He revived quickly. To prevent recognition by the *Kearsarge* searchers he donned a crew hat, with the word *Deerhound* on it, took an oar and passed himself off as one of the yacht's crew.

By now the *Kearsarge* had lowered several boats that pulled quickly to the scene and began dabbling about the wreckage.

From a *Kearsarge* boat a blue-clad officer inquired sharply, "Have you see Captain Semmes?"

Kell thought fast. The implication was clear. Get Semmes dead or alive!

"Captain Semmes is drowned," replied Kell, and thus he saved Semmes from making a Puritan holiday in the streets of Boston.

They were pulling the survivors in rapidly now. The two French pilot boats had come up and were helping. Forty-two cold, dripping, water-logged men were huddled in the *Deerhound's* boats, which hustled back to the yacht. They had rescued Semmes, Kell, Lieutenants Sinclair and Howell, several petty officers, and twenty-seven crewmen.

Miserable, exhausted, his wound still bleeding, Semmes was led into the *Deerhound's* cabin. Hot coffee and a bit of rum for each man worked miracles. Yet John Lancaster quickly found his errand of mercy had involved him in a question of international law. What should he do with the Confederate sailors he had saved? Deliver them over to the *Kearsarge?* He consulted Semmes.

"I think every man has been picked up, Captain Semmes. Where shall I land you?"

Unhesitatingly and very properly, Semmes replied, "I am now under English colors and the sooner you put me, with my officers and men, on English soil the better."

His position was incontestible. Abruptly, the yacht steamed rapidly away from the scene. As she sped off Winslow's officers urged him to fire a shell and halt the *Deerhound's* "flight." He declined, stating "It was impossible, the yacht was simply coming round." Officer after officer begged him to fire at her. He refused. They pointed out that his "coveted prize," Raphael Semmes, was aboard the yacht and was now "escaping." Winslow actually believed that, after rescuing the drowning Confederates, the *Deerhound* should have come alongside and handed them over to the *Kearsarge* as prisoners. It was preposterous. The "flight" of the *Deerhound* spawned a tornado of Northern howls against her owner, John Lancaster. It meant nothing more than chagrin at not having captured Semmes, who had not tried to escape, but merely to save his life. It was Winslow's own fault that he did not capture the most-wanted "rebel."

The final rescue count ran:

The *Kearsarge's* boats picked up seventy, including six officers.

Of the seamen, seventeen were wounded. Two of them died soon after they were brought aboard. The French pilot boats saved several, including Lieutenant Armstrong. These were landed and freed at Cherbourg. Nor did the French rescuers even think of turning these survivors over to the *Kearsarge*.

Lieutenant Sinclair, incidentally, was first picked up by the *Kearsarge* men. After being lugged out of the water, he slid over the side and swam to a *Deerhound* boat. He had no stomach for being a prisoner.

Casualties on the *Alabama* ran to forty-two. Nine were killed in action; twenty-two wounded; twelve were drowned needlessly after the *Alabama* had gone to the bottom. Among the latter were Bartelli, Semmes' faithful steward; the gallant Englishman, Dr. David Herbert Llewellyn; and the negro slave boy, Dave White.

In reporting the rescue by the *Deerhound*, the *Times* of London bore witness:

> When the men came aboard the *Deerhound*, they had nothing on but their drawers and shirts, having been stripped to fight; and one of them [Michael Mars], with a sailor's devotedness, insisted on seeing his captain, who was then lying in Mr. Lancaster's cabin, in a very exhausted state, as he had been intrusted by Captain Semmes with the ship's papers, and to no one else would he give them up. The men were all very anxious about their Captain, and were rejoiced to find that he had been saved. They appeared to be a set of first-rate fellows, and to act well together, in perfect union, under the most trying circumstances.

Late that Sunday afternoon the *Deerhound* steamed into Southampton to land her passengers. News of the battle had already reached the port and the townspeople flocked to the dock to give the unlucky fighting men a welcome of which the victor would have been proud. The hearts of England went out to these men and their captain. Hospitality and kindness flowed in from all classes. They had fought a good fight, and England admired them for it.

Hurrying down from London, Confederate officials offered Semmes a new ship, when and if he was ready to go to sea again. Just where they would get it no one knew. Wounded, jaded, depressed, his health shattered, Semmes shook his head. He needed rest and quiet.

But other duties came first. With the gold he had sent ashore at Cherbourg before the fight Semmes paid off his surviving officers and men in full, even sending the allotments of those who were killed to their nearest relatives. But there would be no prize money, no living at ease for Jack for the rest of his life on the 50,000 dollars he had dreamed of as the *Alabama* swept prize after prize into her hot maw. For each of the survivors, Semmes had a personal farewell and heartfelt thanks for his valor and his loyalty. This done, he accepted the invitation of his friend, The Reverend Francis W. Tremlett, to rest and recuperate in the "rebel home" at Belsize Park parsonage.

To replace the flag that went down with the *Alabama*, "A noble English lady" wrought, with her own hands, a splendid Confederate banner of purest, richest silk and presented it to the Captain. A sister of the Chancellor of the Exchequer, William E. Gladstone, begged the privilege of aiding Semmes' seamen until a new *Alabama* was ready to put to sea.

To replace the sword Semmes had so gallantly worn, defended and "buried with his sinking ship," officers of the British Navy united in a testimonial that assumed the shape of a magnificent, gold-mounted sword on which was inscribed:

> Presented to Captain Raphel Semmes, C.S.N., by officers of the Royal Navy and other friends in England, as a testimonial of their admiration of the gallantry with which he maintained the *Alabama* in the engagement off Cherbourg, with a chain-plated ship of superior power, armament and crew, June 19th, 1864.

The career and gallant exit of the *Alabama* seemed to have fired the imagination of every youth in England. Half the adventurous young spirits in Britain's schools and colleges claimed the privilege of serving under Semmes on his *new Alabama*.

The London *Times* struck a note that vibrated on the heartstrings of the British people:

> Fathoms deep in Norman waters lies the good ship *Alabama*, the swift sea-rover, just so many tons of broken up iron and wood, and

wearing away in the huge depository of that genuine and original marine store-dealer, Father Neptune!

Should any painter conceive a fantasy of the ocean akin to that of Raffet in "Napoleon's Midnight Review," the famous Confederate cruiser would be one of the first ships his imagination would summon from the depths of the sea, and amongst this spectral fleet of high-beaked Danish galleys, of antique Spanish caravels, of bluff and burly British three-deckers and saucy British frigates, there would be room for this quick and cunning craft that raced so swiftly and roamed the deep so long. She was a good ship, well handled and well fought, and to a nation of sailors that means a great deal. So ends the log of the *Alabama*—a vessel of which it may be said that nothing in her whole career became her like its close!

All was not praise from Semmes' beloved South. Mary Boykin Chestnut, diarist extraordinary of the Confederacy, was not overly generous when she wrote:

> Semmes, of whom we have been so proud, risked the *Alabama* in a sort of duel of ships. He has lowered the flag of the *Alabama* to the *Kearsarge*. Forgive who may! I cannot.

But the Richmond *Enquirer*, a leading journalistic voice of the Confederacy, summed up best the Confederacy's grief at the loss of the *Alabama* and its pride in the manner of her going:

> So the noble *Alabama* sleeps full fathoms five. She has well earned a glorious repose on the bed of the old ocean. How many Yankee clippers full of riches has she sent before her? It is safe to say the *Alabama* has paid for herself five hundred times. She could afford to die. There are those who blame Captain Semmes for going out to fight a heavier vessel. He could have remained in the harbor or skulked away without fighting, but not without some disgrace. It is better as it is. The *Alabama* neither ran away, nor was she taken. She fell by the chance of battle fighting to the last, and not a shadow now dims her glory.
>
> We have lost the gallant *Alabama*, but no Federal flag floats in triumph from her masthead. In the caves of the ocean she lies with all but honor lost. Ships may be replaced, but honor once tarnished requires far heavier sacrifices than the cost of navies.

In his first official report of the battle Semmes laid this simple wreath at the feet of his crew: "My officers and men behaved steadily and gallantly, and though they have lost their ship, they have not lost honor."

John Ancrum Winslow sailed back to the United States a hero. Paeans of praise greeted him. For him, his crew, his ship, there were laurels. But Winslow was no turkey-cock strutter. He had sunk the *Alabama*, and that was that; he did a workmanlike job no one else had been able to do. Yet, when the news arrived home, he ascended to the heavens of fame. He was appointd to the rank of Commodore to date from the hour he shot the *Alabama* to the bottom. Yet, in a surge of bitterness at Winslow because he failed to capture Semmes and had paroled his prisoners, Secretary Welles deliberately held up Winslow's promotion until popular indignation forced him to relent.

From Admiral Farragut, amid the general adulation poured on Winslow, came an odd piece of praise. Writing to his son soon after receiving news of the sea-fight, he said:

> The victory of the *Kearsarge* over the *Alabama* raised me up. I would sooner have fought that fight than any ever fought on the ocean. Only think! It was fought like a tournament, in full view of thousands of French and English, with perfect confidence on the part of all but the Union people that we would be whipped. People from Paris came to witness the fight. Why, my poor little good-for-nothing *Hatteras* would have whipped her (the *Alabama*) in fifteen minutes, but for an unlucky shot in her boiler. She struck the *Alabama* two shots for one while she floated. Winslow had my first-lieutenant of the *Hartford*, Thornton, in the *Kearsarge*. He is as brave as a lion and as cool as a parson. I go for Winslow's promotion.

The admiral was overstating things, to say the least. The facts of history fail to support his enthusiastic backview of the *Hatteras-Alabama* fight. But the "unlucky shot" question that he raised, Semmes himself was later to exploit: the failure of the *Alabama*'s shell to explode in the *Kearsarge*'s sternpost.

This shell in her vitals was the only trophy of the *Alabama* the

Kearsarge brought back to Boston. Of this shot Semmes was to say,

> I should have beaten him in the first thirty minutes of the engagement, but for the defect of my ammunition, which had been two years on board, and become much deteriorated by cruising in a variety of climates. By Captain Winslow's own account, the *Kearsarge* was struck twenty-eight times. The *Alabama* was not mortally wounded until after the *Kearsarge* had been firing at her an hour and ten minutes. In the meantime I had mortally wounded that ship in the first thirty minutes of the engagement. I say, 'mortally wounded,' because the wound would have proved mortal, but for the defect of my ammunition. I lodged a rifled percussion shell near her sternpost—*where there were no chains*—which failed to explode because of the defect of the cap. If the cap had performed its duty, and exploded the shell, I should have been called upon to save Captain Winslow's crew from drowning instead of his being called on to save mine. On so slight an incident—the defect of the percussion cap —did the battle hinge. The enemy was very proud of this shell.

It was quite natural that the "enemy" should be proud of this shell, which, at the personal request of President Lincoln, was sawed out, with a piece of the oaken sternpost, brought to the White House for his inspection and placed on exhibition in Washington. It is the most famous dud in American history. Had it detonated the story of the *Alabama* would have had a different ending. This unexploded missile may today be seen in the Naval Academy Museum, at Annapolis.

In expiation of his defeat Semmes brought up an issue he should have, with better grace, left untouched. He tabbed Winslow as unchivalrous for clothing his vessel in the celebrated "shirt of mail." Not even Semmes' Confederate compatriots agreed with him. James Bulloch, builder of the *Alabama*, was one of these dissenters. He was to write that, "the result of the action was determined by the superior accuracy of the firing from the *Kearsarge*."

There was no reason why Winslow should have informed Semmes that the *Kearsarge* wore a protective covering of chain. If Semmes did not know it, the fault was his own. He should have

known it or suspected it. The *Kearsarge* passed close enough to
the *Alabama* in Cherbourg harbor for all to see the strange bulge
around her side, and, as Sinclair writes, the French told Semmes
of the foe's chain protection. It is to be wondered how this seemingly omniscient captain could have overlooked this matter. As
Bulloch said, "Captain Winslow was quite right in doing whatever
he could to increase the defensive power of his ship, and was not
bound to inform his adversary that he had encased her most vulnerable parts with chain-cables. It has never been considered an
unworthy ruse for a commander, whether afloat or ashore, to disguise his strength and to entice his weaker opponent within his
reach." Two years earlier Farragut had employed the same device to protect the *Hartford's* vitals when she ran the gauntlet of
the forts below New Orleans.

The Federal government's contention that the moment Semmes
lowered his flag and raised a white one, he had given his moral
parole and became Winslow's prisoner, bordered on the absurd.
Semmes, so the charge ran, had even violated his parole by saving
himself from a watery grave. It might have been chivalric and
noble in Raphael Semmes to let himself drown, but he did not see
it that way. He was never called upon to surrender by any officer
of the *Kearsarge*. He was perfectly free the moment his own deck
left him in the water. His white flag was simply a token he desired
to save a further "effusion of blood" and the lives of his men. And
he was ready to surrender himself—if the *Kearsarge* had come to
save him!

It might be added that Winslow, in the still-smoky glow of victory, perhaps was uncertain of himself. He certainly did not rush
to get Semmes. He promptly took his own prisoners to Cherbourg
and paroled them. What he would have done with Semmes he
never said.

From Secretary Welles came the most absurd charge: Semmes
had no right to throw his sword into the sea! It belonged to the
United States government! A biographer even insisted the "traditions of the sea" demanded that a beaten commander hang on
until his foes came to get him.

To the many aspersions Semmes replied unanswerably, citing,
among other precedents, the escape of the officers and men of the

U.S.S. *Congress* after she had struck her flag to the Confederate *Virginia* at Hampton Roads:

> I did not betake myself to a boat, or seek refuge in flight. I waited for him (Winslow) or *his* boat, on the deck of my sinking ship, until the sea was ready to engulf me. I was ready and willing to complete the surrender which had been tendered, but as far as was then apparent, the enemy intended to permit me to drown. Was I, under these circumstances, to plunge into the water with my sword in my hand and endeavor to swim to the *Kearsarge?*
>
> Was it not more natural, that I should hurl it into the depths of the ocean in defiance, and in hatred of the Yankee and his accursed flag? When my ship went down I was a waif upon the waters. Battles and swords, and all other things, except the attempt to save life, were at an end. I ceased from that moment to be the enemy of any brave man. A true sailor, and above all, one who had been bred to arms, when he found that he could not save me, as his prisoner, should have been glad to have me escape from him, with life, whether by my own exertions, or those of a neutral. I believe this was the feeling, which, at that moment, was in the heart of Captain Winslow.

Yet, aside from the "ifs" and the "but-fors," one fact was indisputable: the *Kearsarge's* victory was absolute, the *Alabama's* defeat, utter.

⚓

⚓

Voyage-End

The restless *Alabama* slept at the bottom of the English Channel. Her momentous saga was done. So, in a large sense, was that of Raphael Semmes. The rest of his "cruise" was all anticlimax. It could hardly be otherwise.

"I considered my career upon the high seas closed by the loss of my ship," he declared.

In October, 1864, bettered in health, Semmes embarked on a British steamer for Havana, to make his way via Cuba and Mexico, back to the Confederacy and on to Richmond. A dangerous, tortuous journey it was, but this was no time to take a chance. The Union blockade had been alerted to keep a sharp lookout for him. Secretary Welles' determination to capture him had not slackened; it was even whetted by Semmes' "escape." There was still a price on his head, and a halter waiting for him.

From Matamoras, he crossed the Rio Grande into Brownsville, Texas. As his foot touched Southern soil for the first time in nearly four years, tears surged into his heart and eyes. He could have knelt down and kissed the very earth under his feet.

By this time the blue waves of Mr. Lincoln's army were rolling inexorably over the South. Traveling slowly, circuitously, to avoid capture, he came home at last to Mobile. His own people hailed him and welcomed him to their hearts once more.

After a brief pause, he hurried on to Richmond. Crossing the devastated track of Sherman's march to the sea, he made his way slowly through a land that was gasping for breath. At Richmond, he was welcomed by a government that had only praise for his deeds and admiration for his gallant last fight.

Both Houses of the Confederate Congress paid him honor. At President Davis's request, Semmes was created Rear Admiral, but rear admiral of what? There was nothing to be rear admiral of. In any event not even the Confederate Congress could confer a rank that transcended "Captain of the *Alabama*."

The Confederacy was mortally stricken, sinking like the blasted raider off Cherbourg. A small, penned-up flotilla on the James hardly required an admiral. Certainly, it was no task for a man whose theatre of operations had been the oceans of the world. Yet, he served as best he could. When Richmond fell he blew up his five little vessels and led his tiny naval brigade out of the flaming city southwards—not to Appomattox where Lee, encircled by Grant's legions, was to give up the struggle—but to Danville where President Davis conferred on him another well-meaning, but empty honor. He was appointed Brigadier General, though still retaining his naval rank.

Late in April, 1865, Semmes was paroled at Greensboro, North Carolina, within the terms of General Johnston's surrender to General Sherman. He soon rejoined his family at Mobile to begin life anew. But Raphael Semmes' heart was burned out. His beloved South was ravaged—the heel of a conqueror on her throat—his ship destroyed—the flag he revered, desecrated and blotted from the skies.

At Mobile, on December 15, seven months after he had pledged himself never again to take up arms against the United States, marines, acting under orders from Secretary of Navy Welles, arrested Semmes at his home. The "Old Man of the Sea" would have his pound of flesh. Taken to Washington, Semmes was imprisoned in the shadow of the Capitol and the gallows for four months. Welles would hang Semmes, if he could. His animosity burned like avenging fire.

What were the charges against Raphael Semmes? That he had violated the laws of war in the fight with the *Kearsarge*—he had been perfidious in "escaping" after giving his "moral parole"—he had taken prizes in neutral waters—he had been cruel to his captives—he had burned Northern merchantmen—he had raised deceptive flags to lure Northern ships to their doom.

Fortunately, John A. Bolles, Solicitor of the Navy, was fair-minded. Fearlessly, impartially, he sifted the evidence, refusing to be swept away by the hysteria of revenge. The case collapsed. In April, 1866, President Johnson released Semmes, who, two years later, was "pardoned," as were many others who had fought for the Confederacy, in the President's general amnesty.

Semmes went back to Mobile, where the years ran out fast. A professorship was not to his liking. He was, after all, a man of action. A stint at newspapering came to naught. So he returned to his old love, the law. Honored, respected, venerated, he spent his last years among the good folk of Mobile, who presented him with a home on famed Government Street. Never again was he to set foot on a quarterdeck, or hear the wind shrieking through the rigging of nights or be tossed by the heaving waves. "Home is the sailor, home from sea, And the hunter home from the hill."

In 1869, he finished his *Memoirs of Service Afloat*, perhaps the finest literary production by those who actually played leading roles in the massive strife between North and South.

On August 30, 1877, Raphael Semmes embarked on the unknown sea, firm in the Catholic faith of his fathers. In 1900, Mobile unveiled a bronze statue of Raphael Semmes. It stands at the corner of Government and Royal Streets. Arrayed in the uniform of an Admiral, one hand holds his binoculars, the other rests on the hilt of his sword.

Yet, not as Admiral would history and the world—and, immemorially, the South—remember this prodigious man of valor. He was, and ever will be, *Captain of the Alabama*. As such, he won undying fame.

What spirit stirs 'neath the sunless keel,
And wakes in her silent shrouds,
O, hearts of oak, with the grip of steel?
Or was it the passing clouds?

She has lain so long by a foreign shore,
With never a watch on deck,
With her sunken bells sounding o'er and o'er
To the dead men in her wreck.

Yea, come from your graves, ye tars that have shared
Her glory, her anguish, her pain!
For the mystical moment of time is bared
And she sweeps the ocean again!

Nor port, nor harbor, nor home is hers
As she breaks from her silent lair;
But the mighty heart of the great South stirs,
For the spirit of Semmes is there.

Yea, corsair, or viking, pirate or king?
Let history, answering, speak!
For out of the years shall her record ring
While honor stands at her peak!

—Virginia Frazer Boyle, 1909

Ships Captured, Burned, or Ransomed by the *Sumter*

1861

July 3	bark *Golden Rocket*
July 4	brigantine *Cuba* #
July 4	brigantine *Machias* #
July 5	brigantine *Ben Dunning* #
July 5	brigantine *Albert Adams* #
July 6	bark *West Wind* #
July 6	bark *Louise Kilham* #
July 6	brig *Naiad* #
July 25	schooner *Abby Bradford* #
July 26	bark *Joseph Maxwell* #
Sept. 25	brigantine *Joseph Park*
Oct. 27	schooner *Daniel Trowbridge*
Nov. 24	brig *Montmorenci* *
Nov. 24	brig *Arcade*
Dec. 3	ship *Vigilant*
Dec. 8	whaler *Eben. Dodge*

1862

Jan. 18	bark *Neapolitan*
Jan. 18	bark *Investigator* *

* Ransomed
\# Escaped, recaptured, or returned to owners by Spain

Ships Sunk, Burned, or Ransomed by the Alabama

1862

Sept.	5	whaling schooner *Ocmulgee*
Sept.	7	merchant schooner *Starlight*
Sept.	8	whaling bark *Ocean Rover*
Sept.	9	whaling bark *Alert*
Sept.	9	whaling schooner *Weather Gauge*
Sept.	13	whaling brig *Altamaha*
Sept.	14	whaling ship *Benjamin Tucker*
Sept.	16	whaling schooner *Courser*
Sept.	17	whaling bark *Virginia*
Sept.	18	whaling bark *Elisha Dunbar*
Oct.	3	ship *Brilliant*
Oct.	3	ship *Emily Farnham* *
Oct.	7	bark *Wave Crest*
Oct.	7	brig *Dunkirk*
Oct.	9	ship *Tonawanda* *
Oct.	11	ship *Manchester*
Oct.	15	bark *Lamplighter*
Oct.	23	bark *Lafayette*
Oct.	26	schooner *Crenshaw*
Oct.	28	bark *Lauretta*
Oct.	29	brig *Baron de Castine* *
Nov.	2	whaling ship *Levi Starbuck*
Nov.	8	ship *T. B. Wales*
Nov.	30	bark *Parker Cook*
Dec.	5	schooner *Union* *
Dec.	7	mail steamer *Ariel* *

1863

Jan.	11	steam gunboat U.S.S. *Hatteras*
Jan.	26	bark *Golden Rule*
Jan.	27	brig *Chastelaine*
Feb.	3	schooner *Palmetto*
Feb.	21	bark *Olive Jane*
Feb.	21	ship *Golden Eagle*

Feb. 27   ship *Washington* *
Mar. 1   ship *Bethia Thayer* *
Mar. 2   ship *John A. Parks*
Mar. 15   ship *Punjaub* *
Mar. 23   ship *Morning Star* *
Mar. 23   whaling schooner *Kingfisher*
Mar. 25   ship *Nora*
Mar. 25   ship *Charles Hill*
Apr. 4   ship *Louisa Hatch*
Apr. 15   whaling bark *Lafayette*
Apr. 15   whaling brig *Kate Cory*
Apr. 25   whaling bark *Nye*
Apr. 26   ship *Dorcas Prince*
May 3   ship *Sea Lark*
May 3   bark *Union Jack*
May 25   ship *Gildersleeve*
May 25   bark *Justina* *
May 29   ship *Jabez Snow*
June 2   bark *Amazonian*
June 5   ship *Talisman*
June 20   bark *Conrad*
July 2   ship *Anna F. Schmidt*
July 6   ship *Express*
Aug. 5   bark *Sea Bride*
Aug. 9   bark *Martha Wenzell*
Nov. 6   bark *Amanda*
Nov. 10   ship *Winged Racer*
Nov. 11   ship *Contest*
Dec. 24   bark *Texan Star*
Dec. 26   ship *Sonora*
Dec. 26   ship *Highlander*

1864

Jan. 14   ship *Emma Jane*
Apr. 23   ship *Rockingham*
Apr. 27   bark *Tycoon*

* Ransomed. The *Martha Wenzell*, captured in neutral waters, was released.
Appraised value of ships burned by the *Alabama*: $4,613,914
Ransomed ships: 562,250
                                                     ‾‾‾‾‾‾‾‾‾‾
                                                      $5,176,164

⚓

⚓

Bibliography

Battles and Leaders of the Civil War, 1886

Bell, Herbert C. F., *Lord Palmerston*, 1936

Bigelow, John, *Retrospections of an Active Life*, 1909

Bradford, Gamaliel, *Confederate Portraits*, 1914

Bulloch, James Dunwoody, *Secret Service of the Confederate States in Europe*, 1883

Cable, George W., *Old Creole Days*, 1879

Chestnut, Mary Boykin, *A Diary from Dixie*, 1952 and 1905

Clay, Mrs. Clement C., *A Belle of the Fifties*, 1904

Confederate Imprints, 1955

Confederate Index (a London Weekly), 1862-1865

Congressional Globe, The, 1861-1864

Cruise of the Alabama and the Sumter, 1864

Dalzell, G. W., *Flight from the Flag*, 1940

Davis, Jefferson, *Rise and Fall of the Confederate Government*, 1881

De Leon, Thomas C., *Four Years in Rebel Capitals*, 1890

Douglass, Ephraim, *Great Britain and the American Civil War*, 1925

Durkin, Joseph T., *Stephen Mallory*, 1954

Ford, Worthington C., *A Cycle of Adams Letters*, 1920

Fullam, George T., *Cruise of the Alabama*, 1863

Harper's Weekly, 1861-1864

Haywood, P. D., *Cruise of the Alabama*, 1886

Hendrick, Burton J., *Statesmen of the Lost Cause*, 1939

Hergesheimer, Joseph, *Swords and Roses*, 1928

Illustrated London News, 1861-1864

Kell, Lieutenant John, *Recollections of a Naval Life*, 1900

Meriwether, Colyer, *Raphael Semmes*, 1913

Monaghan, Jay, *Diplomat in Carpet Slippers*, 1945

Official Records of the Union and Confederate Armies

Official Records of the Union and Confederate Navies

Porter, Admiral David Dixon, *Incidents and Anecdotes of the Civil War*, 1885

——————, *Naval History of the Civil War*, 1886

Reid, Stuart J., *Lord John Russell*, 1895

Roberts, W. Adolph, *Semmes of the Alabama*, 1938

Roman, Colonel Alfred, *Military Operations of General Beauregard*, 1884

Schaff, General Morris, *The Spirit of Old West Point*, 1907

Scharf, J. T., *History of the Confederate States Navy*, 1887

Reports of the Secretary of the Navy of the Confederate States, 1862-1864

Reports of the Secretary of the Navy of the United States, 1862-1864

Semmes, Raphael, *Memoirs of Service Afloat During the Mexican War*, 1851

——————, *Memoirs of Service Afloat During the War Between the States*, 1869

Sinclair, Lieutenant Arthur, *Two Years on the Alabama*, 1895

Soley, James Russell, *The Blockade and the Cruisers*, 1883

Strode, Hudson, *Jefferson Davis*, 1955

Tilby, A. Wyatt, *Lord John Russell*, 1931

Villiers and Chesson, *Anglo-American Relations, 1861-1865*, 1919

Welles, Gideon, *Diary*, 1911

West, Richard S., Jr., *Gideon Welles*, 1943

Index